RELIGION AND ART OF
WILLIAM HALE WHITE
("Mark Rutherford")

Religion and Art of
William Hale White

("MARK RUTHERFORD")

BY
WILFRED STONE

Stanford University Press • *Stanford, California*
London: Geoffrey Cumberlege • *Oxford University Press*

STANFORD UNIVERSITY PUBLICATIONS

UNIVERSITY SERIES

LANGUAGE AND LITERATURE

VOLUME XII

STANFORD UNIVERSITY PRESS, STANFORD, CALIFORNIA

Published in Great Britain, India, and Pakistan by Geoffrey Cumberlege,
Oxford University Press, London, Bombay, and Karachi

The Baker and Taylor Company, Hillside, New Jersey
Henry M. Snyder & Company, Inc., 440 Fourth Avenue, New York 16
W. S. Hall & Company, 457 Madison Avenue, New York 22

Library of Congress Catalog Card Number: 54-6171

Preface

Originally, my interest in William Hale White (1831–1913) was roused by a chance reading of *The Autobiography of Mark Rutherford* and *The Revolution in Tanner's Lane*. The strange quality of these books and their superiority to much of the other "minor" fiction of the late Victorian period led me to investigate his other works and, subsequently, to seek out some knowledge of the man himself and some critical evaluations of him. In these last two areas I was, in the early stages of my search, disappointed. Except for reviews and brief critical comment in journals and newspapers, I discovered only four studies of any considerable length or critical acumen. These were William Robertson Nicoll's *Memories of Mark Rutherford* (1924); A. E. Taylor's "The Novels of Mark Rutherford" in *Essays and Studies by Members of the English Association* (Vol. V, 1914); Willard L. Sperry's "Life and Writings of Mark Rutherford" in *The Harvard Theological Review* (Vol. VII, 1914); and the Griefswald University dissertation of Hans Klinke, *William Hale White, Versuch einer Biographie* (1930). As my investigations proceeded, I discovered many other studies, mainly doctoral dissertations, which treated Hale White at greater length and, in general, with more intellectual seriousness; but it became increasingly obvious that a published book, combining both a biographical introduction to and a critical evaluation of Hale White, was seriously wanting and long overdue. I have attempted to satisfy that want.

But indebted as I have been to other critical explorations in this subject, the study would have been impossible without the generous assistance of the Hale-White family, especially Dr. and Mrs. Reginald Hale-White of Regent's Park, London, and Mrs. Dorothy Vernon White of Sherborne, Dorset. My gratitude arises not only from their kindness in allowing me to examine and borrow a wealth of private materials pertaining to Hale White, but from their warm friendship and hospitality. To Hale White's daughter, Miss Mary Theodora Hale-White of Langton Green, I also owe thanks for permission to examine a few letters and for an afternoon of valuable conversation.

The book as it now stands represents a revision and reduction in size of a doctoral dissertation submitted to Harvard University in 1950. For direction and encouragement in my original researches I wish to thank Professors Howard Mumford Jones and Albert Guerard, Jr. I owe a particularly large debt to Professor Douglas Bush, whose characteristic generosity led him into a wise and painstaking criticism of the original manuscript.

Opportunity for research in England was afforded by a Fulbright Grant (1949–50), which permitted the investigation of source materials in private hands, the British Museum, and Dr. Williams' Library, and enabled me to profit from the help and criticism of English scholars, in particular Mr. Simon Nowell-Smith, Professor James R. Sutherland, and Professor Basil Willey. My debt to Professor Willey is not easily described and can never be repaid: he gave generously of time and energy in the early stages of my investigations and in reading drafts of the finished manuscript; above all, he brought to my subject a sympathetic understanding which had much to do with my own confidence in its value and importance.

I wish also to thank the editors and staff members of *The Norfolk News, The Rochdale Observer, The Birmingham Daily Post, The Aberdeen Herald*, and *The British Weekly* for allowing me to rummage their files and copy from Hale White's writings or from critical comments about him. With particular pleasure and appreciation I remember the kindness and assistance of Mrs. Trude Robitschek of *The Norfolk News* and Mr. Peter R. Scott of *The Rochdale Observer*.

The *University of Toronto Quarterly* has been generous in permitting me to employ certain materials from my article on Mark Rutherford appearing in their issue of October 1953.

In revising the original manuscript for publication I have been assisted in many ways by many people, but I wish to acknowledge a special indebtedness to Professors William Irvine and Charles Allen of Stanford University and to Mr. Stephen M. Parrish of Harvard for reading and criticizing the manuscript. In these final stages of preparation, the resources of a Ford Foundation Fellowship and a Stanford Research Grant have also assisted me—the one in permitting me to exploit again the riches of Widener and Houghton libraries at Harvard, the other in partially paying for the cost of typing the manuscript.

Wilfred H. Stone

Cambridge, Massachusetts
April 1954

TABLE OF CONTENTS

PAGE

TABLE OF ABBREVIATIONS viii

Introduction   "Mark Rutherford" and Hale White: The Man
    and the Masks 3

Chapter One   ORTHODOXY 11

Chapter Two   APOSTASY 32

Chapter Three   NEGATION 43

Chapter Four   NEW BIRTH 63

Chapter Five   RENUNCIATION 82

Chapter Six   AFFIRMATION 95

Chapter Seven   SPINOZA 101

Chapter Eight   MASKING AND UNMASKING: THE *Autobiography*
    AND *Deliverance* 122

Chapter Nine   THE NOVELS: FACT AND FICTION 143

Chapter Ten   THEMES IN THE NOVELS: DELIVERANCE 165

Chapter Eleven   THEMES IN THE NOVELS: INCOMPATIBILITY.... 184

Chapter Twelve   STYLE 199

BIBLIOGRAPHY OF W. HALE WHITE 215

INDEX 233

ABBREVIATIONS

Books

A.	*The Autobiography of Mark Rutherford* (Oxford, 1936)
D.	*Mark Rutherford's Deliverance* (Oxford, 1936)
R.T.L.	*The Revolution in Tanner's Lane* (Oxford, 1936)
M.S.	*Miriam's Schooling* (Oxford, 1936)
C.F.	*Catharine Furze* (Oxford, 1936)
C.H.	*Clara Hopgood* (Oxford, 1936)
P.J.	*Pages from a Journal* (Unwin, 1900)
M.P.	*More Pages from a Journal* (Oxford, 1910)
L.P.	*Last Pages from a Journal* (Oxford, 1915)
L.3F.	*Letters to Three Friends* (Oxford, 1924)
G.D.	*The Groombridge Diary* (Oxford, 1924)
Sp.a.	Preface to Spinoza's *Ethic* (1883)
Sp.b.	Preface to Spinoza's *Ethic* (1894)
E.L.	*The Early Life of Mark Rutherford,* by Himself (Oxford, 1913)
B.	*John Bunyan* (Hodder & Stoughton, 1904)
T.	Preface to Spinoza's *Tractatus de Intellectus Emendatione* (1905)

Source Materials and Newspapers

P.N.a.	Private Notes by John Harry White ("Jack"), Hale White's second son. Typescript, in possession of Dr. Reginald Hale-White. (All page references to this and other typed material are to pages in the author's personal copy of this typescript.)
P.N.b.	Private Notes by Sir William Hale-White, Hale White's first son. Typescript, in possession of Dr. R. Hale-White.
P.L.	Extracts from letters written to his second son and second son's wife. Typescript, in possession of Dr. R. Hale-White.
S.B.a.	Scrapbooks kept by Hale White. In possession of Dr. R. Hale-White.
S.B.b.	Scrapbook of clippings, in possession of Mrs. D. V. White, Hale White's second wife.
B.N.B.	*The Black Notebook*, a book of notes kept by Hale White. In possession of Mrs. D. V. White.
D.B.	*The Dorothy Book*, a notebook of jottings and scraps of letters kept by Hale White during his courtship of Mrs. D. V. White. In possession of Mrs. White.
B.D.P.	*The Birmingham Daily Post*
B.J.	*The Birmingham Journal*
B.D.P.J.	*The Birmingham Daily Post and Journal*
A.H.	*The Aberdeen Herald*
R.O.	*The Rochdale Observer*
N.N.	*The Norfolk News*

RELIGION AND ART OF
WILLIAM HALE WHITE

("Mark Rutherford")

"MARK RUTHERFORD" AND HALE WHITE: THE MAN AND THE MASKS

This book is an attempt to do simultaneously many things: to introduce an author of real excellence whose merits have too long gone begging for serious critical recognition; to study the transitions and tensions of the nineteenth-century cultural milieu in which he found himself; and to examine the biographical facts that help to elucidate his writings—fictional, scholarly, and self-confessional. That seems an ambitious task indeed for a study of this length, but actually the treatment intended is intensive rather than extensive, particular rather than general. Our dominant concern is with William Hale White himself, his experience and writings, but the peculiarities of his work and life do not favor any orthodox biographical or historical approach.

The reason is this: nearly every word that William Hale White wrote was the product of a self-confessional impulse, or at least the reflection of a deep intellectual or emotional engagement. That could, perhaps, be said of any serious writer, but with Hale White the emphasis is particularly valid. His first two important books, *The Autobiography of Mark Rutherford* (1881) and *Mark Rutherford's Deliverance* (1885), were, for all their fictional disguises, obvious self-confessions of a man whose aim was not to achieve literary fame but to share a burden of spiritual pain. And the four novels which followed—all under the pseudonym "Mark Rutherford"—widened but little the distance between the author's personal experience and his fictional creations. A study of Hale White's works, therefore, takes us immediately into a study of his biography; and a study of his biography takes us immediately into a phase of Victorian cultural history (roughly from 1840 to 1913) which was an intimate part of Hale White's own history. Actively, his participation in the great issues of Victorian *Sturm und Drang* was minor, but as an observer and critic he was intensely involved. In him we find, therefore, a microcosm of great significance, a sensitive center around which clusters a vital share of the experience defining an age. To call this study a "critical biography" would be to label it somewhat extravagantly, for it cannot claim to chronicle or evaluate *exhaustively* all the events of the man's life. But in so far as it does merit this title, it is a biography emphasizing the drama of an inner struggle rather than battles in public arenas; and it will treat his written work less as the fruit of an artistic impulse than as the product of a peculiar—yet strangely representative—private malaise.

To describe fully the nature of that malaise here would be to anticipate this book, but we need some foreknowledge of its major moods and charac-

3

teristics. Hale White did not begin writing "fiction" until he was past fifty years of age, and when he did so he hid the act, like some guilty thing, from the attention both of the public and his immediate family. Not only did he cloak himself from public gaze in the anonymity of a double pseudonym ("Mark Rutherford" and "Reuben Shapcott," the supposed editor of his books), but his own wife never knew until nearly ten years after the *Autobiography* appeared that her husband was an author. The confessions of "Mark Rutherford" doubtless would have been recognized by her and they would, unquestionably, have given her pain. But his associates in the Civil Service or his neighbors in Carshalton could hardly be expected to see much kinship between Mark Rutherford and Mr. White. For the author of the *Autobiography*, the agonized spiritual exile obsessed with an awareness of his own weakness and failure, shared few obvious qualities with the prosperous, punctilious, businesslike Assistant Director of Contracts at the Admiralty. The man who showed his face to Victorian society appeared as a conventional occupant of suburbia, a rate-paying and public-minded citizen who had been known to break his habitual reticence by an occasional letter to newspapers about such matters as modern architecture or the enclosure of public lands, but who could hardly be suspected of harboring either the capacity or the impulse to expose his bleeding heart to public gaze.

The duality between Hale White and Mark Rutherford can be taken as symbolic of a basic duality which marked nearly all phases of the man's life. He was born in 1831 in Bedford—at that time one of the greatest strongholds of Puritanism to be found in England. As a young man he moved to London to study for the ministry, but shortly after his arrival the school authorities detected an heretical bent in his opinions and he was, in effect, "excommunicated." Bedford was behind him both geographically and spiritually, but it was a joyless exile. And it is no exaggeration to say that Hale White spent the rest of his life trying to find some substitute in the world of men for the community of belief he had known in his provincial birthplace. His intellectual repudiation of the decayed Calvinism at Bunyan Meeting was complete; his emotional dependence upon the security of a fixed faith remained to plague his inner peace throughout a tortured lifetime. Bedford was the home of Mark Rutherford, but London—cold, secular, impersonal—was a place where the needs of Mark Rutherford had to remain well hidden, for there men were joined, if at all, by business interests rather than by affection and in competition instead of bonds of faith. Deprived of any real love as a child and rigorously trained in the virtues of honesty and fortitude, Hale White brought a strange ambivalence to his experiment in apostasy. Abnormally vulnerable to the laughter or criticism of his associates, he built out of the materials of his Puritan upbringing a hard protective armor against both their curiosity and their indifference. More than anything he dreaded emotional and spiritual loneliness, but the means he chose to combat those fears almost assured their presence. In the *Deliverance*, he makes a remarkable confession of the kind of defense he employed:

Nobody [at the Admiralty Office] knew anything about me, whether I was married or single, where I lived, or what I thought upon a single subject of any importance. I cut off my office life in this way from my life at home so completely that I was two selves, and my true self was not stained by contact with my other self.[1]

This quarantine of a "true" self from a contaminating "other" self typified the method he used, on many levels of experience, to bring order and security into his life. It was, to view it most simply, the apostate Puritan's reassertion in an alien and secular context of the same well-defined dualistic patterns he had known as a believer. Clean and unclean, right and wrong, saint and sinner—the "ancient antagonism,"[2] he insists, must be maintained. "No religion . . . ," he writes, "has dwelt like Christianity with such profound earnestness on the bisection of man—on the distinction within him, vital to the very last degree, between the higher and the lower, heaven and hell."[3] Unfortunately, however, Hale White no longer had the aid of an undamaged theology in making such distinctions, and he had neither the intellectual nor the emotional equipment to be a nineteenth-century Calvin. Just where was the dividing knife to fall in separating the higher and the lower, the pure and the impure? The answers to such questions became for Hale White a matter of trial and error, of remorseless experimentation upon himself and the raw materials of his existence as he confronted them. He consulted the old books, but no longer could he accept their recommendations without qualification, without questioning. They seemed to meet but imprecisely the problems facing a sensitive and emancipated man in the nineteenth century. The old dualistic habit prevailed, but it had to exercise itself on strange materials and half-defined moral conditions. Hale White had moved from a sanctuary to a laboratory: in the one place he was at home and an expert; in the other he was a lonely and frightened amateur. But, at great psychological cost, he remained in the latter place, and he brought to the discovery of truth in that cold and alien environment whatever wisdom he could salvage from the wreck of his old convictions.

But he was always an amateur. And the method of bisecting the issues of human life remained always his most trusted intellectual resource. The method had its roots in the old Christian conflict between the higher and lower self (Hale White could never be a true scientist, for he had to make value judgments in the very act of analysis), but it became applied in all phases of his life. The dividing knife dropped between Hale White the citizen and Hale White the resident of a spiritual utopia, between the writer and his public, between the lover and the husband, between the

---

[1] P. 110.

[2] *D.*, p. 95. A list of the abbreviations used in the footnotes may be found on p. viii.

[3] *Ibid.*

skeptic and the believer, between the real man and his dream self. But he never was completely satisfied with these divisions, and frequently he sliced so often and so variously at the problem before him that it was reduced to a pulp.

One result of such methods was that he bisected not only the issues of his ethical thinking and the organization of his personal life, but he bisected his personality.

Amid the hated vulgarities of Victorian life, he felt a desperate need for sanctuary, for some oasis of sanctity where he could, in something like an absolute sense, feel proud of himself, feel a confidence in his own election to spiritual eminence. But in the Victorian market place and council chamber he could find no society of saints, no elect minority in whose heroic rightness he could wholly believe and wholly surrender himself. So he accepted, proudly and defiantly, his status as a lonely outsider and built of his own solitude a spiritual citadel. His was the dream of sanitation, of clean hands, but to make that dream come true required constant washing and resulted in an almost pathological awareness of the dangers of infection. It was only after much suffering that Hale White discovered the isolation of his public from his private life, of an "other" from a "real" self, to be a tragic transliteration of the Christian emphasis upon higher and lower. It brought not wholeness but fragmentation, not heaven but hell. For the two selves were, after all, lodged in the same body, and he was, after all, a member of that very society which, in many of its aspects, he loathed. His books are a record of the growing realization that he needed people, real people, and that he really hated saints; that the inexpert application of the "ancient antagonism" of Calvinism could mean self-mutilation rather than salvation; that good and evil, love and hate were, in reality, not separable but inextricably joined.

This, in briefest outline, is the malaise which the confessions of Mark Rutherford delineate for us, and there are probably no literary documents in the nineteenth century to equal them for intimacy or precision of statement. As we attempt, in ensuing chapters, to relate the character of Mark Rutherford to the man who wore this pseudonym, we shall be moving toward the resolution of a dualism which Hale White never fully resolved. But his life's direction was consistently toward wholeness and away from fragmentation and self-division. And it is this degree of increase that makes his work such a significant record—not only of the psychological travail of one individual but of the metamorphosis of an age of absolutism into one of compromise. The main effort of Hale White's life was how to find happiness without absolutes—how to build an ethic, a political society, a religion out of the raw materials of the world as it exists and not out of some transcendent vision of that world. For him this was a task of prodigious and exhausting difficulty. Not only was he by temperament and training an absolutist who dwelt uneasily in the shadow of suspended judgment, but to the end of his life he showed a tragic persistence in solving his problems by ranging one part of his personality against the other and fighting it out, as in an old morality play. At times he was nearly destroyed in the crossfire. But the drama of that inner conflict—so intimately and lucidly analyzed—is an invaluable chapter in that "wandering between two worlds" which characterized so much of Victorian religious, social, and political experience. For finally, in spite of all their gray sadness, the record of Hale White's novels and stories is not one of sterile frustration but of the traumatic agonies of a world and personality struggling to be born.

The very act of writing books was, for Hale White, part of this process of self-discovery and self-realization. He addressed his confessions not to God but to the public, to that world of sinful men wherein could now be found the only absolution or justification the apostate was entitled to command. In the opening pages of the *Autobiography* he declared as his purpose in writing that "some few whose experience has been like mine may, by my example, be freed from that sense of solitude which they find so depressing."[4] But his aim was not simply to help others escape from the prison of self-absorption; the book—like nearly all his others—was a prayer as well as a lesson. And the prayer was full of ambivalences. He wanted those "few" to judge, but he also wanted them to love and forgive; he wanted to expose his inmost soul, with no veil between himself and the reader, but he also felt the need of that double disguise afforded by the pseudonyms, "Mark Rutherford" and "Reuben Shapcott." By wearing these two masks he could, in a sense, write his own indictment and apologia: as Mark Rutherford he could expose with merciless candor his failures and jealousies and despair, but he could do so knowing that he had a "friend" who would provide an introduction and conclusion setting forth those virtues and achievements omitted in the testimony of his own devil's advocate. The *Autobiography* begins, for example, with these words:

Now that I have completed my autobiography up to the present year, I sometimes doubt whether it is right to publish it. Of what use is it, many persons will say, to present to the world what is mainly a record of weaknesses and failures? If I had any triumphs to tell; if I could show how I had risen superior to poverty and suffering; if, in short, I were a hero of any kind whatever, I might perhaps be justified in communicating my success to mankind, and stimulating them to do as I have done. But mine is the tale of a commonplace life, perplexed by many problems I have never solved; . . . and blotted by ignoble concessions which are a constant regret.

I have decided, however, to let the manuscript remain. I will not destroy it, although I will not take the responsibility of printing it.[5]

But the book ends with these qualifying words from the pen of "Reuben Shapcott":

I am afraid that up to this point he has misrepresented himself, and that those who read his story will think him nothing but a mere egoist, selfish and self-absorbed.

[4] P. 2.   [5] *Ibid.*, p. 1.

Morbid he may have been, but selfish he was not. A more perfect friend I never knew, nor one more capable of complete abandonment to a person for whom he had any real regard, and I can only hope that it may be my good fortune to find the materials which will enable me to represent him autobiographically in a somewhat different light to that in which he appears now.[6]

One of the experiences recounted in the *Autobiography* and in the poem prefacing that volume is Mark Rutherford's frustrating search for a "perfect friend," for some human being embodying absolute capacities for love and understanding. And this effort is but one example of his early attempt to transplant, directly and boldly, values appropriate only to some Celestial City to human society. Not finding such a "perfect" friend, he invented one; the fictitious editor was a wish-fulfillment, a projection of Hale White's own bitter frustration. And this invention of a solace he could not at this time find in real life reveals one of the ways in which Hale White made the writing of books a means of personal therapy. He was both Reuben Shapcott and Mark Rutherford, he both loved and hated himself, he was his own critic and flatterer.

> I once did think there might be mine
> One friendship perfect and divine;
> Alas! that dream dissolved in tears
> Before I'd counted twenty years.[7]

But the creation of Reuben Shapcott at the age of fifty is evidence enough that the dream had never quite dissolved. The love Hale White really desired could only be found in Galateas of his own devising, and it was by slow degrees that he learned to temper his needs more to the capacities of real men and women.

The basic theme of this study is, therefore, one of conflict and resolution, of dualisms slowly moving toward unity, like enemies after a truce. The resolution and the unity are not, in Hale White or the age in which he lived, so striking as the discord and self-division; but in the fact that Hale White found, however partially, some "deliverance" lies the whole point and significance of this study. He does not provide us with a well-formulated philosophy or ethic, nor do we find him at the end of his life a completely healthy or integrated personality; but out of his long contention with inner discord he learned some salutary lessons, not the least of which were that humility is not necessarily inconsistent with manliness and that arming one's self against the contagion of evil is not the way to love or be loved by one's neighbor. He never completely freed himself from the notion that life was a battlefield and that it must be lived in terms of great issues, nobly contested between the forces of good and evil. But as the years passed, he discovered that "fighting the good fight," as a Luther or Cromwell or Bunyan could fight it, was, in the nineteenth century, a tragically anachronistic ambition. The lines of conflict were

6 *Ibid.*, pp. 165–66.
7 *Ibid.*, p. xxxvii.

no longer clearly drawn and no matter how much he longed to be the single champion engaging with Satan and Apollyon in mortal duel, he finally came to realize that the wars of truth were now waged on no such simple terms and that his was, at best, a desk job in a standing army. One of Hale White's persistent temptations was to oversimplify; the degree to which he resisted this temptation is the measure of his greatness. In his novels as in his own life (and the first are a direct reflection of the second) we detect a gradual softening of his insistence upon the "ancient antagonism" and a sad acceptance of the complexities and qualifications which an age of science and enlightenment had imposed upon men's final explanations. He relaxed, in the end, the distinction between Hale White and Mark Rutherford, and strove to join in one person the citizen and the exile, the sinner and the saint, the hero-worshipper and the hero, the man of action and the self-pitying introvert. He would certainly have agreed with John Donne that "by discord things increase," but he doubtless would have added that discord cherished for itself issued in death rather than victory.

Besides the *Autobiography* and the *Deliverance*, the books which record most dramatically these self-discoveries are the four other "Mark Rutherford" novels: *The Revolution in Tanner's Lane* (1887), *Miriam's Schooling, and Other Papers* (1890), *Catharine Furze* (1893), and *Clara Hopgood* (1896). They were books which, in their own day, spoke for a lost generation much as Joyce's *Portrait of the Artist as a Young Man* spoke for a later one, and their merits lay almost as much in their qualities of style as in their message. Only a few critics have told us of their first acquaintance with Mark Rutherford, but they have all, in various ways, recorded a strange excitement, a sense of discovery. William Dean Howells, for example, heralded the first two books as holding promise of "a new era in English fiction,"[8] and William Robertson Nicoll—one of Hale White's most ardent and loyal admirers—declared:

If there are any books of this generation better written than this, I do not know them. There is very little colour and no apparent elaboration, but the words perfectly fit the thought. The author is like the painter who can produce a perfect circle. I had seen no style quite like this—a style translucent in its simplicity, and yet incapable of any amendment.[9]

Hale White's later audience widened to include such men as H. W. Massingham, André Gide, and D. H. Lawrence, plus a host of more parochial readers. Around the turn of the century the *Autobiography* and *Mark Rutherford's Deliverance* became almost best sellers, and—partly owing to the Oxford Press reprint of all six novels in 1936—Hale White's literary achievements have continued to arouse a small but persistent interest among scholars and critics to this day.

Less well known, however, are Hale White's other writings: three

---

[8] "Editor's Study," *Harper's Monthly Magazine*, LXXII (February 1886), 485.
[9] W. R. Nicoll, "Mark Rutherford," *The British Weekly*, XX (July 9, 1896), 185.

volumes of journals, translations of and introductions to Spinoza's *Ethic* (1883) and *Tractatus de Intellectus Emendatione et de Via* (1895), *John Bunyan* (1904), and contributions as both editor and critic to studies of Wordsworth, Coleridge, Dr. Johnson, and Carlyle. In addition, there is the virtually unknown accumulation of nearly twenty years' work as London correspondent for a number of provincial journals, together with over a hundred articles and letters to periodicals and newspapers. A fragmentary collection of his personal correspondence was made by his second wife, Dorothy Vernon White, and appeared under the title, *Letters to Three Friends* (1924). A companion volume to this, *The Groombridge Diary* (1924), is a collection of reminiscences and letters written or compiled by Mrs. White, which offers an invaluable insight into the character and experience of Hale White in his declining years.

All these plus a large body of unpublished and fugitive writings will be drawn upon in the present study. Hale White has been repeatedly referred to as a "neglected genius," but the evidence supporting either part of that title has never been fully examined, and no published study has appeared to join the man as he appears masked in the novels to the man who lived and wrote under his own name. My present effort is to make a contribution, at least, toward such a synthesis. It is an effort not merely to blow the dust off a half-forgotten classic in the Victorian section, but to examine closely a case history in the psychological experience of an age. We shall begin with Bedford, for that was Hale White's birthplace and spiritual home, but Bedford will serve more as a symbol than as a place, more as the starting point of an emotional pilgrimage than as a geographical or historical fact. The place names and events of Hale White's actual history are all, properly considered, important as the data of a private and not a public experience, the mere "objective correlatives" of an inner travail. And as we look back from this mid-point in our own Age of Anxiety at this lonely man in a strangely distant Victorian age, we may perhaps be able to find in the record of his inner turmoil some hint of psychological agonies which are now familiar under other names and which seem increasingly characteristic of our own *mal de siècle*.

Chapter One

ORTHODOXY

In 1852, William Hale White was expelled from New College, London—a Nonconformist theological school—on a charge of heresy. This experience marked the great spiritual watershed of his life. On the one side of this event lay his early life in the Calvinistic Dissenting society of Bedford and Cheshunt College; on the other lay an uncharted country he was to spend the rest of his life exploring. Though our main concern will be to study his wanderings in the wilderness of unbelief, we cannot do so without a knowledge of that older and more carefully charted land of his origin and nurture. For there he had acquired the muscles and learned the habits which conditioned and limited his success in spiritual exploration. And there, at that point of no return, he had known an emotional homeland for which he longed throughout his exile. Though the older land was infected with religious and social decay which had forced him, by degrees, to move further and further toward its borders and finally out of it altogether, he nevertheless had a keen historical memory for what it had once been, and a great love for the ardent affirmations which had once toughened the souls of its people. Naturally ingrown, he found his self-absorption painfully intensified by his sojourn in the wilderness; naturally endowed with a taste for "tremendous problems"[1] and a need for certainty, he discovered that such tastes and needs can in the world of experience become instruments for self-torture. These frustrations impelled him, again and again, to see in Calvinism an explanation of human life closely corresponding to the actual facts and to make of his pilgrimage a closed circle.

It would be a mistake to suppose that the creed in which I had been brought up was or could be forever cast away like an old garment. The beliefs of childhood and youth cannot be thus dismissed. I know that in after years . . . they revived under new forms, and that I sympathized more with the Calvinistic Independency of the sixteenth and seventeenth centuries than with the modern Christianity of church or chapel. At first, after the abandonment of orthodoxy, I naturally thought nothing in the old religion worth retaining, but this temper did not last long. Many mistakes may be pardoned in Puritanism in view of the earnestness with which it insists on the distinction between right and wrong. This is vital. In modern religion the path is flowery. The absence of difficulty is a sure sign that no good is being done. How far we are from the strait gate, from the way that is narrow which leadeth unto life, the way which is found only by few! The great doctrines of Puritanism are also much nearer to the facts of actual experience than we suppose.[2]

The consummation of a full home-coming was, however, forever denied

[1] *D.*, p. 84.
[2] *E.L.*, pp. 77–79.

11

him. The sense of rightness in revolt which had sustained the morale of the old Independents was still necessary to him, even though the dogmatic support for such confidence had given way. And the very honesty he had learned in his native community was partly responsible for his heresy, for he could not blink the hollowness of its existing creed once he had seen it. He was driven to justify his revolt, to work out grimly his own salvation. These compulsions lay behind the self-revelations in all his books, and the agony of unbelief has seldom been studied in such excruciating detail. But though the Separatist habit persisted and the respect, if honesty demanded it, for splendid isolation, Hale White soon learned that all the splendor was gone, all assurance of a reward for the lonely sacrifice. Could it be that this self-humiliation before the truth was only a form of spiritual pride? Because of these and other doubts the pilgrimage of Hale White gave rise to psychological as well as theological problems—in fact, one of the most striking aspects of his writing is the progressive substitution of a psychological for a theological vocabulary. Monomania, hypochondria, melancholia—these three—were the names he found for the chief devils besetting him, but as they had only partly been admitted by his separation from orthodoxy, they could only partly be exorcised by a new creed. What he sought was rather a new strength, the strength of physical and emotional health, which would give him release from the slavery of his own personality and which could express itself in welldoing without such desperate dependence upon the prop of systematic explanation.

These struggles are part of the common trials of a doubting generation. Such men as James Anthony Froude, Arthur Hugh Clough, Matthew Arnold, Francis Newman, and many others shared with Hale White a longing for their own Bedfords, and were equally sobered by the loneliness of apostasy. But Hale White's case is unique. For he is the only one among them whom we can, without qualification, call a Puritan; and he is the only undoubted Puritan of his generation to expose the bare nerve of his suffering in such disciplined and appropriate language. Other men of his age, Leslie Stephen for example, could speak of their loss of faith as a relief from a "cumbrous burden," as a discovery, not that the creed was false, but that they "had never really believed it."[3] Hale White could never know such clean-cut emancipation. His was rather the case of a man who has lost a gangrenous limb but continues to feel pain in the missing foot. And, though there is something universal in all such pain, that which Hale White experienced could be fully realized only by those who had walked his peculiar road to Damascus and had once known the strait and narrow way of Nonconformist Calvinism.

Bedford, of all the provincial towns in England, was the one most richly endowed both by tradition and habit in the ways of Puritanism. It had been the home of John Bunyan, and in the *Pilgrim's Progress* was the celebrated starting point of Christian's journey to the Celestial City. The

3 F. W. Maitland, *The Life and Letters of Leslie Stephen* (London, 1906), p. 145.

meetinghouse where Hale White received his early religious training—Bunyan Meeting—still bore the name of its founder and was still deeply under his influence. But in other ways too—in its social life, its political prejudices, its business—the town bodied forth its Puritanism. All these aspects of its being entered into Hale White's memory and all contributed to making of Bedford a symbol both of his rebellion and love. For though he could paint its life with a harsh, satirical brush, there is always mixed with his scorn an affection he cannot conceal. In the year following the publication of the *Autobiography* Hale White confessed to a friend that Bedford was then closer to him than it had ever been,[4] and after the publication of his *Bunyan* in 1904 he described the joy of the effort by saying that "Elstow and the Ouse and in a measure the temper of the man are in my blood."[5] Above all, Bedford was for Hale White the symbol of a wholeness he would never know again : of a time and place not requiring a man to be vague or contradictory about the religion he professed ; where a man could wear a Puritan hair shirt without fearing that neighbors would see in the act mere egoism or masochism ; where one need never doubt that a God noticed his self-denial ; where monomania, hypochondria, and melancholia could be channeled through one's life in constructive and socially acceptable ways. If we can imagine the Bunyan of *Grace Abounding* without a theology, we shall perhaps have some idea of how rudderless and abandoned Hale White felt without the security and permanence of all that Bedford symbolized. To understand that symbol well is, therefore, essential to this study.

Bedford in the 1840's—the years of Hale White's adolescence—knew nothing of that industrial "progress" which has since changed its character and defaced its beauty. It was then a small market town enjoying the same provincial isolation it had known since Cromwell's time. Once or twice a week a freight "waggon" made the journey from London, and every evening, punctually at eight, the mail coach rattled across the stone bridge spanning the Ouse and stopped at the turnpike gate opposite Hale White's house on the High Street—an event he celebrates again and again in his books. These were Bedford's only contacts with the outside world. The coach—usually the "Peveril of the Peak"—brought an occasional tradesman and a small, unimpressive bundle of printed matter. He writes in his weekly column for *The Birmingham Post* in 1877 :

Into our town of about ten thousand people not a dozen copies of a newspaper came daily, and the only weekly newspaper which I remember seeing, except perhaps a religious newspaper, was *Bell's Weekly Messenger*. A man must have been tolerably well off then to stand the expense of a *Times* or a *Morning Chronicle*, sent down by coach.[6]

This provincial isolation is the most marked characteristic of the pictures of Bedford which Hale White gives us in his books. Cowfold in *The Revo-*

---

[4] Letter to George Mayes dated March 7, 1882. Copy in *S.B.a.*
[5] *L.3F.*, p. 328.   [6] *B.D.P.*, August 18, 1877. See also *A.*, pp. 2–3, 32.

lution in Tanner's Lane and *Miriam's Schooling*, Eastthorpe in *Catharine Furze*, Water Lane in the *Autobiography*, "my native town" in the *Deliverance*, and Langborough in the short story, "Mrs. Fairfax," are all, with remarkably little variation, drawn after the Bedford of his childhood. The picture is by no means idyllic, but it is sketched with loving care.

> The town of Langborough in 1839 had not been much disturbed since the beginning of the preceding century. The new houses were nearly all of them built to replace others which had fallen into decay; there were no drains; the drinking-water came from pumps; the low fever killed thirty or forty people every autumn; the Moot Hall still stood in the middle of the High Street; the newspaper came but once a week; nobody read any books; and the Saturday market and the annual fair were the only events in public local history. Langborough, being seventy miles from London and eight from the main coach-road, had but little communication with the outside world. Its inhabitants intermarried without crossing from other stocks, and men determined their choice mainly by equality of fortune and rank. The shape of the nose and lips and colour of the eyes may have had some influence in masculine selection, but not much: the doctor took the lawyer's daughter, the draper took the grocer's, and the carpenter took the blacksmith's. Husbands and wives, as a rule, lived comfortably with one another; there was no reason why they should quarrel. The air of the place was sleepy; the men attended to their business, and the women were entirely apart, minding their household affairs and taking tea with one another. In Langborough, dozing as it had dozed since the days of Queen Anne, it was almost impossible that any woman should differ so much from another that she could be the cause of passionate preference.[7]

In this sleepy town there was "absolutely no competition," and though nobody but the banker and the brewer got rich, "nearly everybody was tolerably well off."[8] And if the competition for money and women was not intense, the competition for ideas was even less so. Although Hale White had the opportunity, owing to his father's position as bookseller, to make an early acquaintance with Byron, Coleridge, Milton, and Scott, such was not the common lot of Bedford tradesmen. If their reading ever got beyond the Bible, and few of them read even this,[9] it was generally limited, in poetry, to Dr. Watts, Pollok's *Course of Time*, and perhaps a little Cowper,[10] and, in prose, mainly to religious newspapers and, very occasionally, an approved novel. The barrenness of the intellectual life of the place is cruelly drawn—and perhaps somewhat caricatured—in Hale White's picture of a "Dorcas" meeting in the *Autobiography*. The new minister, Mark Rutherford, was expected to preside over this weekly gathering of the elect under the watchful eye of the head deacon, Mr. Snale. In his innocence, the well-meaning Mark had chosen to amuse and instruct the group by reading from *The Vicar of Wakefield*. This was the result:

> . . . Mr. Snale took an opportunity of telling me, after I had got through a chapter or two, that he thought it would be better if it were discontinued. "Because, you

---

7 "Mrs. Fairfax," *P.J.*, pp. 218–19.

8 *A.* p. 3.

9 *M.S.*, p. 65. See *E.L.*, p. 37. *Chambers' Journal* and *Miscellany* and Charles and Mary Lamb's *Tales of Ulysses* were also part of Hale White's early reading.

10 See *R.T.L.*, p. 166, and *A.*, p. 39.

know, Mr. Rutherford," he said, with his smirk, "the company is mixed; there are young leedies present, and *perhaps*, Mr. Rutherford, a book with a more requisite tone might be more suitable on such an occasion."

. . . the next time, in my folly, I tried a selection from *George Fox's Journal*. Mr. Snale objected to this too. It was "hardly of a character adapted for social intercourse," he thought; and furthermore, "although Mr. Fox might be a very good man, and was a converted character, yet he did not, you know, Mr. Rutherford, belong to us." So I was reduced to that class of literature which of all others I most abominated, and which always seemed to me the most profane—religious and sectarian gossip, religious novels designed to make religion attractive, and other slip-slop of this kind. I could not endure it, and was frequently unwell on Dorcas evenings.[11]

Between the intellectual vitality of Hale White's own home and the mental state of the town in general, there was a marked contrast. And throughout his novels, his provincial heroines suffer discontent from the fact that they are better-read than their neighbors and have intellectual ambitions finding no outlet in the cramping atmosphere of a small town. The burden of such snobbery has never been more poignantly depicted. And they are, as we shall later see, drawn from the experience of Hale White himself.

But while such narrowness as Snale's was intolerable to him, Hale White had, nevertheless, a good word for the simplicity of Bedford's intellectual life. These untutored tradesmen may not have known anything about romantic poetry or German philosophy, but they knew themselves. Well wadded though they were in their own bovine contentment, they were yet of one piece; they concerned themselves only with what had a natural growth in their lives;[12] they never had to confess, as Hale White later did, to being "muddled by Shelley, Byron, Carlyle, Emerson, Goethe, Coleridge."[13] With one side of his nature, Hale White was convinced that virtue lay in such simplicity.

Granted that the conversation was personal, trivial, and even scandalous, it was in a measure philosophical. Cowfold, though it knew nothing, or next to nothing, of abstractions, took immense interest in the creatures in which they were embodied. It would have turned a deaf ear to any debate on the nature of ethical obligation; but it was very keen indeed in apportioning blame to its neighbours who had sinned, and in deciding how far they had gone wrong. Cowfold, in other words, believed that flesh and blood, and not ideas, are the school and the religion for most of us, and that we learn a language by the examples rather than by the rules. The young scholar fresh from his study is impatient at what he considers the unprofitable gossip about the people round the corner; but when he gets older he sees that often it is much better than his books, and that distinctions are expressed by a washerwoman, if the objects to be distinguished eat and drink and sleep, which he would find it difficult to make with his symbols.[14]

Hale White himself was that scornful scholar and never learned completely

11 *A.*, pp. 36–37.
12 See *E.L.*, p. 20, and *A.*, p. 120. The second reference probably provides a portrait of Mrs. Elizabeth Street, following whose death Hale White wrote a moving eulogium.
13 *D.B.*, p. 20. Entry, September 1908.   14 *R.T.L.*, p. 162.

how to practice the wise tolerance he preaches here. But in later years, when he, like Matthew Arnold, became baffled and revolted by the "multitudinousness"[15] and moral anarchy of the later nineteenth century, his sympathies returned to these people who could, without shame or self-consciousness, *be themselves.*[16]

Bedford's habit of making nice distinctions in its social levels was also, one suspects, a custom with which Hale White was not entirely unsympathetic. Although the town carried its pride of class to ridiculously subtle extremes, and although Hale White described those distinctions with a sharp pen, his satire never has the ring of strong disapproval. Hale White was himself consciously and proudly middle class, and betrayed in thought, dress, and even handwriting a love of neatness and meticulous order. Bedford's class system had a place for everything and everything kept its place. To be sure, these class pretensions might be fraught with hypocrisy and might bring pain to the unrecognized, but the *principle* of accepting a higher and a lower as the order of things was, as we have already seen, a rooted prejudice. As he later moved on the tide of Nonconformist liberalism into support of democracy, he found himself frequently embarrassed by his love of a class system on the one hand and his support of the people on the other. He always "disliked mankind in the mass,"[17] and in late life came to see the breakdown of the old social forms as ushering in dangerous mob rule. But this was Bedford in the 'forties:

The grades in Eastthorpe were very marked, and no caste distinctions could have been more rigid. The country folk near were by themselves. They associated with none of the townsfolk, save with the rector, and even in that relationship there was a slight tinge of ex-officiosity. Next to the rector were the lawyer and the banker and the two maiden banker ladies in the Abbey Close. Looked at from a distance these might be supposed to stand level, but, on nearer approach, a difference was discernible. The banker and the ladies, although they visited the lawyer, were a shade beyond him. Then came the brewer. The days had not arrived when brewing—at least, on the large scale—is considered to be more respectable than a learned profession, and Mrs. Colston, notwithstanding her wealth, was incessantly forced by the lawyer's wife to confess subordination.[18]

But the forces which in a few decades were to dissolve this pattern of things had already manifested themselves in Bedford. In *Catharine Furze*, Hale White shows Catharine's mother, the wife of an ironmonger, entertaining the idea that if she could purchase a house on "The Terrace" she might be visited by Mrs. Colston, who, as the wife of the brewer, could not do so now.[19] Her ambition provides the plot of the novel—a fact which

---

[15] *The Letters of Matthew Arnold to Arthur Hugh Clough*, ed. H. F. Lowry (London, 1932), p. 97.
[16] See Hale White's essay, "Ourselves," in *M.P.*, p. 176: "It is a common falsehood of these times that all knowledge is good for everybody, the truth being that knowledge is good only if it helps us, and that if it does not help us it is bad." See also *L.P.*, pp. 295–96.
[17] *P.N.b.*, p. 38.
[18] *C.F.*, p. 60.
[19] *Ibid.*, p. 12.

becomes doubly interesting when we know that Mrs. Furze shared many dominant characteristics with Hale White's own mother. According to *The Early Life of Mark Rutherford*, his mother was also "a little weak in her preference for people who did not stand behind counters," and had urged Hale White to study for the ministry because "she desired equality with her sister-in-law,"[20] who had a son in training. At another place in the *Early Life* he writes more specifically :

My mother was by no means democratic. In fact she had a slight weakness in favour of rank. Somehow or other she had managed to know some people who lived in a "park" about five or six miles from Bedford. It was called a "park", but in reality it was a big garden, with a meadow beyond. However, and this was the great point, none of my mother's town friends were callers at the Park.[21]

Hale White's attitude toward such behavior was both approving and disapproving, but there can be little doubt that his mother modeled for some of the more unpleasant female characters in his books. The reasons for this will become clearer later on, but what interests us here is the fact that Mrs. Furze's social pretensions involved an alteration in her religious allegiance. Her courting of Mrs. Colston demanded also a flirting with Anglicanism, for the town's caste system was ordered along religious and sectarian as well as economic lines. And these distinctions carried over to the political sphere : "church" and "chapel" were almost synonyms for "Tory" and "Whig" (later Liberal). Hale White explains these niceties in the *Deliverance*.

In our town we were all formed upon recognised patterns, and those who possessed any one mark of the pattern, had all. The wine-merchant, for example, who went to church, eminently respectable, Tory, by no means associating with the tradesfolk who displayed their goods in the windows, knowing no "experience," and who had never felt the outpouring of the Spirit, was a specimen of a class like him. Another class was represented by the dissenting ironmonger, deacon, presiding at prayer-meetings, strict Sabbatarian, and believer in eternal punishments ; while a third was set forth by "Guffy," whose real name was unknown, who got drunk, unloaded barges, assisted at the municipal elections, and was never once seen inside a place of worship. These patterns had existed amongst us from the dimmest antiquity, and were accepted as part of the eternal order of things ; so much so, that the deacon, although he professed to be sure that nobody who had not been converted would escape the fire—and the wine-merchant certainly had not been converted—was very far from admitting to himself that the wine-merchant ought to be converted, or that it would be proper to try and convert him. . . . Such an event . . . could no more come within the reach of our vision than a reversal of the current of our river. It would have broken up our foundations and party-walls, and would have been considered as ominous, and anything but a subject for thankfulness.[22]

[20] *E.L.*, pp. 55–56.
[21] *Ibid.*, p. 42. Mrs. Furze's nervous temperament also corresponds with what we know of Hale White's mother. Mrs. D. V. White, Hale White's second wife, declared that she was "frightfully high strung," and that Hale White once remembered his mother's begging her husband "not to send her away." Mrs. D. V. White thinks Hale inherited his mother's disposition. (Conversations at Sherborne, October 17, 1949.)
[22] *D.*, pp. 36–37.

The religious life of the town, to which this introduces us, was deeply imbedded in a social and political context and cannot be considered apart from it. In Hale White's youth the idea that religion (at least in the more orthodox Calvinistic sects) could be separated from politics had only just begun to be thought of, and long after he broke with orthodoxy he maintained those political sympathies and social habits which had been part of his early Dissenting heritage.

Bedford was heir to several of the "particularising" free church sects which had grown in strength and influence in the preceding century. Besides the inevitable Anglican Church, there were three Dissenting meeting-houses: the Wesleyan, "new, stuccoed, with grained doors and cast-iron railing"; the Baptist, "ultra-Calvinistic, Antinomian according to the other sects, dark, down an alley, mean, surrounded by a small long-grassed graveyard, and named ZOAR in large letters over the long window in front";[23] and *the* chapel, "Bunyan Meeting," the ugly three-gabled structure which in 1707 had replaced the barn in which Bunyan had preached.[24] This last was the most influential of the chapels and the center of Dissenting activity for the whole district. Hale White's father, William White, was one of its leading members. His position as the town's printer and bookseller (from 1830 until 1848) gave him the opportunity, owing to the semi-intellectual nature of his work, to deal with both church and chapel; but until he left the Meeting in 1851 his Dissenting sympathies were outspoken. He was a generous and warmhearted man, and deeply loved by his son, but his churchgoing habits were strict.

The view which Hale White gives us of a Bedford Sunday merits a place with the most vivid of Victorian pronouncements on this forbidding subject, perhaps outdoing even Gosse or Butler. On weekdays he knew Wordsworthian animal pleasures of swimming, fishing, or skating—depending on the season—but Sunday was "a season of unmixed gloom." No reading "more secular than the Evangelical Magazine was tolerated" and the boy's gustatory instincts were rudely offended.

The meat was cooked beforehand, so that we never had a hot dinner even in the coldest weather; the only thing hot which was permitted was a boiled suet pudding, which cooked itself while we were at chapel, and some potatoes which were prepared after we came home.[25]

Every effort was made to avoid all possible work on the Sabbath, but hardships of other kinds were generously provided in the chapel itself.

There were three services every Sunday, besides intermitting prayer-meetings, but these I did not as yet attend. Each service consisted of a hymn, reading the Bible, another hymn, a prayer, the sermon, a third hymn, and a short final prayer. . . .

The first, or long prayer, as it was called, was a horrible hypocrisy, and it was a sore tax on the preacher to get through it. . . . It generally began with a con-

23 *R.T.L.*, p. 158.
24 A picture of this structure is included in *E.L.*, following p. 16.
25 *A.*, p. 5.

fession that we were all sinners, but no individual sins were ever confessed, and then ensued a kind of dialogue with God, very much resembling the speeches which in later years I have heard in the House of Commons from the movers and seconders of addresses to the Crown at the opening of Parliament.

In all the religion of that day nothing was falser than the long prayer. Direct appeal to God can only be justified when it is passionate. To come maundering into His presence when we have nothing particular to say is an insult, upon which we should never presume if we had a petition to offer to any earthly personage . . . but our minister seemed to consider that the Almighty, who had the universe to govern, had more leisure at His command than the idlest lounger at a club. . . .

The sermon was not much better. It generally consisted of a text, which was a mere peg for a discourse, that was pretty much the same from January to December. The minister invariably began with the fall of man; propounded the scheme of redemption, and ended by depicting in the morning the blessedness of the saints, and in the evening the doom of the lost. There was a tradition that in the morning there should be "experience," that is to say, comfort for the elect, and that the evening should be appropriated to their less fortunate brethren. The evening service was the most trying to me of all these. . . . The atmosphere of the chapel on hot nights was most foul . . . Oftentimes in winter, when no doors or windows were open, I have seen the glass panes streaming with wet inside, and women carried out fainting.[26]

This ritual and the theological assumptions which supported it had remained substantially the same from Bunyan's day onward. But the quality of the creed and the nature of the preaching had, as Henry A. Smith has pointed out, undergone a profound change even since the beginning of the century. This picture shows a dead creed, a mummery enacted without enthusiasm, from which all real meaning had gone. Hale White was throughout his life deeply religious, and the fact that he could satirize his native church so trenchantly in the *Autobiography* and *The Revolution in Tanner's Lane* is more a measure of his religious sincerity than of any taste for iconoclasm. Brother Holderness, the traveling draper, was the very embodiment of the hypocrisy he hated:

He never prayed without telling all of us that there was no health in him, and that his soul was a mass of putrefying sores; but everybody thought the better of him for his self-humiliation. One actual indiscretion, however, brought home to him would have been visited by suspension or expulsion.[27]

The congregation as a whole held together out of "the simple loyalty which prevents a soldier or a sailor from mutinying, although the commanding officer may deserve no respect."[28] The commanding officer in this case was the Reverend Mr. John Jukes, minister of Bunyan Meeting from 1840 until 1867,[29] and the creed which he taught was that mid-century abortion known as "moderate Calvinism." Because this hollow creed and this bone-dry man were important forces hastening both Hale White and his father

26 *Ibid.*, pp. 6–8.

27 *Ibid.*, p. 13.

28 *E.L.*, p. 16.

29 The identification of Jukes with Broad and Harden with Hillyard was first brought to my attention by Henry A. Smith in "The Life and Thought of William Hale White" (Doctoral dissertation, University of Birmingham, 1938).

out of the Dissenting fold, we must view them in more detail and try to understand how they came there.

The condition of the free churches throughout England was, around the mid-century, a troublesome one. Doctrinal differences had become increasingly confusing and were constantly being challenged; heresy and schism were widespread; and the impact of Biblical criticism and scientific discovery made naïve acceptance of traditional Christian belief increasingly difficult for many people. The Tractarian Movement, the Oxford Movement, the Broad Church Movement, the rise of Unitarianism were just a few of the external signs of a deep inner ferment. Bedford, if we may accept Hale White's picture of it, read little and thought less, and, on the surface at least, seemed to sleep contentedly in its provincial detachment from these disturbances. But this is not quite so. Although the town's main lines of social and religious difference remained intact, the *Zeitgeist* had nonetheless moved in like a low fog over the fens. Bedford went to church still, but its motives for doing so had become almost as much social as religious. Baptist and Wesleyan, Anglican and Independent gave voice to their various creeds, but something of the old insistence was gone. We can read a parable in the situation of the minister of Zoar, who was considered a social pariah by the rector and the Independent and Wesleyan ministers. "This was not," writes Hale White, "because of any heresy or difference of doctrine, but because he was a poor man and poor persons sat under him."[30]

How can we account for such softening of theological lines of difference? Henry A. Smith, in a most perceptive and thorough examination of this phase of Hale White's religious life,[31] points to the Evangelical movement as the main cause. This great religious awakening which had blazed across England at the end of the preceding century had left its mark not only on the Church of England but on the Nonconformist churches as well. While the revival's influence on the Nonconformist churches was "more gradual and less revolutionary" than on the Establishment, it had been felt—not as a "sudden outbreak of new life," but as a "warming and quickening of the life that was already there."[32] In Bunyan Meeting this influence had been displayed most prominently in the predecessor of John Jukes: the Reverend Mr. Samuel Hillyard who came to Bedford in 1790 and remained minister at the Meeting until his death in 1839. The Reverend Mr. John Brown, who succeeded Jukes, outdoes himself with enthusiasm when he describes Hillyard's work and personality. He characterizes him as "a veritable 'bishop' among the churches of the county."

Every good cause seemed to awaken the interest and inspire the ardour of this warm-hearted man: the evangelization of the heathen abroad, and the spreading of

[30] *R.T.L.*, p. 159.
[31] "The Life and Thought of William Hale White."
[32] W. B. Selbie, *Nonconformity* (London, 1912), p. 194.

the gospel among the villages of Bedfordshire at home; the emancipation of the slave, and the enfranchisement of his fellow countrymen.[33]

But when Brown describes Jukes, he can say only that he was a contrast to his predecessor, a man of "weight and worth," who performed "good service of a steady sort through the more than twenty-six years he was pastor of the Bedford Church." He was "defective in the quality of humour and in power of imagination," but, writes his apologist, his preaching was "instructive and impressive."[34]

Now there can be little doubt that these are the two men appearing in *The Revolution in Tanner's Lane* as James Harden and John Broad, and that Hale White saw between them an even more severe contrast.

The Reverend John Broad was certainly not of the Revival type. He was a big, gross-feeding, heavy person with heavy ox-face and large mouth, who might have been bad enough if nature had ordained that he should have been born in a hovel at Sheepgate or in the Black Country. As it happened, his father was a woollen draper, and John was brought up to the trade as a youth; got tired of it, thought he might do something more respectable; went to a Dissenting College; took charge of a little chapel in Buckinghamshire; married early; was removed to Tanner's Lane, and became a preacher of the Gospel. He was moderate in all of what he called his "views;" neither ultra-Calvinist nor Arminian; not rigid upon Baptism, and certainly much unlike his lean and fervid predecessor, the Reverend James Harden, M.A., who was educated at Cambridge; threw up all his chances there when he became convinced of sin; cast in his lot with the Independents, and wrestled even unto blood with the world, the flesh, and the devil in Cowfold for thirty years, till he was gathered to his rest. A fiery, ardent, untamable soul was Harden's, bold and uncompromising. He never scrupled to tell anybody what he thought, and would send an arrow sharp and swift through any iniquity, no matter where it might couch. He absolutely ruled Cowfold, hated by many, beloved by many, feared by all—a genuine soldier of the Cross. Mr. Broad very much preferred the indirect mode of doing good, and if he thought a brother had done wrong, contented himself with praying in private for him.[35]

This contrast, according to Smith, was due not just to temperamental differences between the two men, but to the fact that the religious climate of the 'forties did not foster men of Harden's breed. As Hale White writes, Broad "could not doubt, for there was no doubt in the air; and yet he could not believe as Harden believed, for neither was Harden's belief now in the air."[36] The belief in the air was that strange hybrid known as "moderate Calvinism," a phenomenon which we must understand in some detail in order to understand the reasons for Hale White's apostasy.

[33] John Brown, *John Bunyan* (London, 1885), pp. 422–23. Dr. John Brown occupied the pulpit of Bunyan Meeting from 1864 until 1903. In a clipping found in Mrs. D. V. White's *Scrapbook* he is quoted as saying: "I believe that I am the man referred to in the novel, who, after the revolution, was appointed as Mr. Broad's successor." (See *R.T.L.*, p. 260).

[34] *Ibid.*, p. 424.

[35] *R.T.L.*, pp. 169–70. W. Robertson Nicoll in *The Bookman* (July 1896), p. 439, declared that the Whites "cherished a strong feeling of resentment against Mr. Jukes" for his refusal to support Hale White in his dispute with New College. This fact no doubt accounts for some of the vitriol in his characterization of Jukes.

[36] *R.T.L.*, p. 170.

So long as revivalistic enthusiasm remained high, the obvious contradictions between the Calvinist doctrines of predestination and election, and the Evangelistic preaching of free pardon for all and unlimited efficacy of the Atonement, were not much noted. "How I hate," wrote Hannah More in 1802, "the little narrowing names of Arminian and Calvinist. . . . *Bible* Christianity is what I love. . . ."[37] But thirty years later the fires of enthusiasm had begun to burn low, and those "little narrowing names" once more began to demand attention. Under the impact of "broader and more liberal modes of thought" and the stimulation of the Tractarian movement, Evangelicals, about the year 1840, "began to feel the change and to modify their position."[38] In this period a growing desire to reconcile preaching and creed became evident, and a growing awareness that the orthodox line could not be held unless the doctrinal basis of religion was both reasonable and consistent. In support of this point, Mr. Smith quotes from R. W. Dale's *History of English Congregationalism*, which offers the clearest account available of the crisis facing the free churches in this period—precisely the period when Jukes took over for Hillyard at Bunyan Meeting. The conflict which Dale describes had been implicit in the Evangelical movement from the start—for Whitefield had been a Calvinist while Wesley was Arminian—but in the heat of the revivalistic enthusiasm it had largely been ignored. By the 1840's, however, it was insistently demanding attention.

. . . the children of hereditary Independents were still taught the Assembly's Catechism; and the Independent theologians still maintained the great Calvinistic doctrines of Original Sin, Election, and the Final Perseverance of the saints. But the characteristic genius of the Revival was silently working against the Calvinistic creed. The preachers who had caught its true spirit vehemently appealed to men to repent, and to trust for eternal salvation in the mercy of God revealed through Christ. They might hold fast to the creed that only the elect would really repent and appeal to the divine mercy; but they preached as if they thought that every man might repent and trust in Christ. They might be assured that, according to the eternal counsels of God, Christ died only for the elect; but they preached as if they thought that He died for every man in the congregation.

. . . Then it became common to believe that in a sense Christ died for all men, though it was God's eternal purpose that only the elect should be actually redeemed by His death; and Independents began to describe themselves as "Moderate Calvinists." They thought that while preserving the strong foundations of the Calvinistic theology and its method, they could modify some of the Calvinistic doctrines, which in their rigid form had become incredible to them. But they were attempting an impossible task. . . . They had not learnt that theologians who begin with Calvin must end with Calvin. "Moderate Calvinism" was Calvinism in decay.[39]

---

[37] Quoted in Elie Halevy, *England in 1815* (London, 1949), p. 437.

[38] V. F. Storr, *The Development of English Theology in the Nineteenth Century* (London, 1913), p. 73.

[39] R. W. Dale, *History of English Congregationalism* (London, 1907), pp. 587–88. For other studies touching on this phenomenon, see Eugene Stock, *The English Church in the Nineteenth Century* (London, 1910), pp. 66 ff. and Henry W. Clark, *History of English Nonconformity* (London, 1913), II, 385.

According to Henry W. Clark, the abandonment of "high Calvinism" represented, at first, "a systematic and reasoned modification in theological thought," but as time went on Calvinism decayed through a "process of mere drifting—following upon or concurrent with a tendency to emphasize the divineness of man rather than the greatness of God. . . ." The result was that "the earlier Calvinistic doctrine of predestination, whether any sufficient substitute were adopted for it or not, became impossible to practically all."[40]

In *The Revolution in Tanner's Lane*, Hale White celebrates both the beginning and the close of this process. Mr. Bradshaw, a minister of Harden's stamp, held firmly to his "master" Calvin but, while admitting that God may "irradiate" the minds of the reprobate with "some scintillations of His light," he had touched upon this doctrine of election only once in his entire ministry.[41] But Bradshaw had made this emphasis only because he was caught up in the works of the Revival and not because he was afraid of offending his congregation.

It was quite otherwise, however, with John Broad and the "moderate Calvinism" he preached. In his day the creed had become thoroughly adulterated and, although no conscious hypocrisy was involved,[42] motives of expediency came to rule the words which were issued from the pulpit. Writes Hale White:

They were taught what was called a "moderate Calvinism", a phrase not easy to understand. If it had any meaning, it was that predestination, election, and reprobation, were unquestionably true, but they were dogmas about which it was not prudent to say much, for some of the congregation were a little Arminian, and St. James could not be totally neglected.[43]

A creed so altered to pamper the prejudices of its hearers could not long merit the respect of men like Hale White and his father who, above all else, admired forthright honesty and courageous conviction. Though his father declared that "a moderate Calvinism suited him best," it was certainly not the brand delivered by Jukes, for he was as critical of this man as Hale White himself. Jukes may have been "as sincere as his build of soul and body allowed him to be,"[44] but the Whites had little tolerance for such unillumined sincerity. "Neglect to observe the finest distinctions," wrote Hale White in later life, "continually involves damnation";[45] and there can be little doubt that the poetic justice meted out to John Broad in the novel was only what Hale White felt the man deserved for his grossness and stupidity.

If I find a doctrine to be true but unpalatable, and endeavour to reason myself out of it, I fatally injure my capacity for apprehending truth. The next time I encounter a truth it will be easy to evade it or I may even be able to affirm it to be a heresy,

40 Henry W. Clark, *History of English Nonconformity* (London, 1913), II, 385.
41 *R.T.L.*, p. 93.
42 See *R.T.L.*, p. 170.
43 *E.L.*, pp. 16–17.   44 *R.T.L.*, p. 170.   45 *M.P.*, p. 238.

and at last I shall be deprived of the capacity—damned literally, I then am—to recognize truth when I see it.[46]

John Broad was an object lesson in such dissolution.

With the passing of ardent religious conviction in Bedford came the passing of that vigorous political partisanship which had once accompanied it. The Reverend Mr. Jukes is described by John Brown as "erring on the side of caution,"[47] and something of that caution is doubtless reflected in the timid opportunism of John Broad, who decides to remain neutral in a hotly contested Cowfold election. Although he had no sympathy for the Tories, he felt that his first care must be "the ministerial office and the church which Providence has placed in my charge"[48]—a species of pious evasion which Hale White and his father despised. Neutrality was, it would seem, one of the few fixed principles upon which Boad worked, for he wrote to his son, himself a fledgling Dissenting preacher, that he believed a young minister

. . . ought to confine himself to what is generally accepted, and not to particularise. For this reason he should avoid not only all disputed topics, but, as far as possible, all reference to particular offences. I always myself doubted the wisdom, for example, of sermons against covetousness, or worldliness, or hypocrisy. Let us follow our Lord and Master, and warn our hearers against sin, and leave the application to the Holy Spirit.[49]

The same Gantry-like opportunism is served up again in the pious language of the canting Deacon Snale, whom we have already met, and who criticized Mark Rutherford's agitation for a reform in the town's water supply in much the same spirit. Snale wrote, anonymously, in the town newspaper: "How can many of us accept the glorious gospel on the Sabbath from a man who will incur spots during the week by arguing about cesspools like any other man?"[50] These need not be taken, however, simply as the portraits of two gross, venal men. They can equally well be taken as symbols of a creeping paralysis which manifested itself more and more obviously in the Nonconformist churches as the century wore on. The tendency to separate the affairs of the world from religion, so brilliantly advertised in Broad and Snale, was part of the heritage Dissent had received from the Revival. It had worked in subtle ways to render the Protestant Dissenters politically conservative.

As their interest in theological polemics had cooled, they had lost their old taste

---

[46] *L.3F.*, p. 162. Hale White criticized Coleridge for just this failing. In *L.3F.*, p. 163, he writes: "In the recently published letters of Coleridge you will find some whose [*sic*] abject orthodoxy is shocking. He was no hypocrite in the vulgar sense of the word, but in the latter part of his life he brought himself into such a condition that he could not only reason in favour of any theological dogma, but was not aware that he had not the fullest faith in it."

[47] Brown, *Bunyan*, p. 424.   [48] *R.T.L.*, pp. 214–15.

[49] *Ibid.*, p. 232. This son is quite certainly portrayed again in the *Autobiography* as the Dissenting student who is always "dawdling after the sex." One of his indiscretions occupies a prominent place in the *Revolution*.

[50] *A.*, p. 51.

for discussion, their former love of argument. And as their prejudices in favour of ecclesiastical autonomy weakened, their individualism in politics weakened simultaneously.[51]

And the Reverend Mr. Hillyard, for all his ardent humanitarianism and passionate attachment to "the great principles of civil and religious freedom,"[52] had unconsciously contributed to that weakening of "ecclesiastical autonomy" which accompanied the weakening of political Dissent. He was the animating spirit of the Bedfordshire Union of Christians, a nonsectarian evangelical organization which strove to de-emphasize denominational differences in the name of universal Christianity. In such activity, he was, of course, at one with a fundamental aspect of the Revival's program, for in the early years of the nineteenth century literally dozens of similar groups proliferated, having as their general aim the attempt to get men to regard themselves not as members of a denomination but as brothers under Christ. The Religious Freedom Society, the Evangelical Voluntary Church Association,[53] and, in many respects, the Broad Church itself are but three organizational movements sharing the same animus as the Bedfordshire group. Wrote Thomas Arnold:

I groan over the divisions of the Church, of all our evils I think the greatest . . . that men should call themselves Roman Catholics, Church of England men, Baptists, Quakers, all sorts of appellations, forgetting only that glorious name of CHRISTIAN, which is common to all, and a true bond of union.[54]

The general similarity between his words and those of the Reverend Mr. Samuel Greatheed, who opened the Bedfordshire movement on August 24, 1796, is obvious:

We wish to excite your *zeal*, not to alter your opinions; we long to promote your love to *all* fellow-Christians; not to lessen your attachment to those with whom you are immediately connected.[55]

Hillyard could stand on the hustings in support of the liberal Lord John Russell in 1830, and he was active in working for prison reform and the emancipation of the slave, but he had nevertheless been an unconscious contributor to the forces softening political as well as religious lines of difference. He still believed in proclaiming openly from the pulpit his Liberal politics along with his Bible Christianity, but the man who replaced him in that pulpit proved to be perversely conditioned in that very atmosphere of theological compromise which Hillyard had helped to create. To his successor, political timeserving seemed inevitably to follow from theological

---

51 Halevy, *England in 1815*, p. 423.

52 Brown, *Bunyan*, p. 423.

53 Herbert S. Skeats and Charles S. Miall, *History of the Free Churches of England, 1688–1891* (London, 1891), pp. 490–91. See also F. D. Maurice, *The Kingdom of Christ* (London, 1838).

54 Quoted in Lionel Trilling, *Matthew Arnold* (New York, 1949), p. 58.

55 John Brown, *The History of the Bedfordshire Union of Christians* (London, 1946), p. 19.

timeserving, and both could be piously justified as furthering Christian "amity" and "understanding."

This is not to say that the Dissenters were politically inactive or apathetic, but only that a wedge was slowly being driven between the chapel and the world outside it. The same Lord John Russell whom Hillyard had supported could give them credit for most of the reforms before the midcentury:

> I know the Dissenters. They gave us the emancipation of the slave. They gave us the Reform Bill. They gave us Free Trade. And they will give us the abolition of the Church Rates.[56]

Although a man of Jukes's stamp doubtless favored these causes too, we can see in him that impulse to "get on in the world" which by degrees directed the concern of Nonconformists more to mounting profits than to their treasure in heaven. And as congregations increasingly tended to favor Mrs. Gooch's Golden Rule over the old catechism, the preachers had to be on their guard lest the sheep begin to stray to the Church of England. As late as the 1880's, Nonconformity still continued to be the "poor man's church," but this was so largely because many Dissenters, as they grew wealthy, "tended swiftly to gravitate to the respectability and prestige of the Established Church."[57] We have already observed this phenomenon in the behavior of Mrs. Furze, whose social aspirations needed some pious enforcement. And her daughter, Catharine, had been sent to a Calvinistic-Evangelical finishing school expressly designed for the children of Dissenting *nouveaux riches* "who hardly knew the manners and customs of the class to which they aspired,"[58] and yet must somehow acquire them without openly betraying their sectarian allegiance. It is interesting to note that, had it not been for the Test Acts, Hale White himself would have gone to Oxford—a university which, interestingly enough, he lashed severely in letters and printed comment throughout his life.[59] In his *Aberdeen Herald* weekly article for January 28, 1865, he comments that Dissenters are jealous of the Established Church and have become aristocratic now that they are no longer persecuted—a remark that may arise as much from personal experience as from historical knowledge. For although Hale White himself resisted joining any church after his expulsion, all of his children gravitated to the Church of England, and his second wife was a lifelong member. This shifting of the old sectarian and religious alignments represented, of course, a drift away from religion rather than toward it, for the motives behind the shift were mainly worldly and competitive. In the liberal writing of the period we find the matter treated

---

[56] Selbie, *Nonconformity*, p. 201.

[57] H. M. Lynd, *England in the Eighteen-Eighties* (Oxford, 1945), p. 331.

[58] *C.F.*, p. 63. Even dancing was taught there.

[59] See *G.D.*, p. 33, and *L.3F.*, p. 163. In *R.O.*, July 20, 1867, he writes, for example: ". . . there is not a dirty third-rate German University which has not, with all its poverty, served the world better, even in classics, than Oxford. There are two studies they prosecute there to perfection—boat-rowing and cricket . . ."

sometimes satirically, but always with concern. Frederick Foxton, in a book Hale White doubtless knew as a yonng man, wrote:

The modern Dissenter in his relations to the national Church is much in the position of Gil Blas, when he smelt from *outside* the walls of the Palace the savoury odours of the Archbishop's kitchen, and no doubt, like the hero of Le Sage, he will end (if he has the opportunity) of [*sic*] taking service in the Archepiscopal scullery . . . Now your modern Dissenter is certainly not proud of his poverty, of whatever else he may be proud, and he is as fond of a title of distinction as a German postmistress.[60]

Though this remark refers to the 'sixties and not the 'forties, the appetites of which he speaks were being whetted in the Bedford of Hale White's youth.

But there were still men in Bedford who would not compromise their religion or politics for the sake of worldly considerations, who belonged to that older tradition of heroic political Dissent. High among them were William White and his devoted son. Hale White has been called "a belated Jacobin of the school of 1794,"[61] and it is quite true that his sympathies, if not his actions, betrayed such allegiance. His love for the "Calvinistic Independency of the sixteenth and seventeenth centuries," which he declared in the statement quoted at the beginning of this chapter, represented an affection for political as well as religious Puritanism, and something of that same Cromwellian spirit could be found in the heroes of the Revolutionary era. In his column to *The Birmingham Daily Post* for December 23, 1871, he writes in a characteristic strain:

Soldiers who read Plato and Milton are not only likely to handle the musket better than the average French Catholic peasant, or the refuse of Paris, but their courage will probably be of a more enduring kind. If I were a general, I think I would much prefer the temper begotten by Milton to all the *élan* in the world.

To Hale White and his father politics and religion were merely opposite sides of the same coin. Divorcing them, as John Broad did, was a certain indication that the religion was decadent. "What has Christianity to do with politics?" Hale White answers the question in one of his letters:

If it has nothing to do with politics or daily life it is not a religion. A religion is not a tangle of metaphysical subtleties nor a nostrum for preserving eternally the salt that keeps our carcases from putrefaction.[62]

And again, writing in *The Norfolk News*, he deplored the flabby morals of a later day which saw something unnatural in the union of piety with politics:

The "political Dissenter" has for a long time been a favorite dummy to be battered and mauled by political Church people after the fashion of Mr. Quilp with the figurehead. For my own part I must confess that I do not quite know what kind of creature this political Dissenter may be. He is supposed, I believe, to be a creation

[60] Frederick Foxton, *The Priesthood and the People* (London, 1862), p. 26.
[61] *The Morning Post*, March 17, 1913.
[62] *L.3F.*, pp. 211–12. See also *M.P.*, p. 246.

of modern times, and in some way or other his political convictions, which are strong, are understood to interfere with his piety. But as a matter of fact the old Dissenters, whom I remember as a child, were far more political than their descendants, and I was about to say more pious . . . An ancestor of the present writer of this column, a godly elder of his Church, had his windows smashed because of his ardor in the cause of reform before the Reform Act of 1832 was passed, and his father refused to illuminate for the victories over the French because he considered that we ought to let the French people manage their own affairs, and that if we had not interfered with them they would not have interfered with us. Cromwell and Milton were political, and are supposed to have had a few religious convictions. It is surely impossible indeed for a man to have imperious and ardent beliefs on religion without having beliefs equally ardent and imperious on a subject so important as politics.[63]

The "ancestor" referred to here was Hale White's father, and the Dissenter who refused to illuminate for the French victories was his grandfather,[64] both of whom share, we suspect, in the composite portraits of George Allen and Zachariah Coleman of *The Revolution in Tanner's Lane*. The first of these portraits is the more readily identifiable, for Allen broke with the chapel for much the same reasons William White did. The real William White had engaged in nearly all the political battles agitating Bedford throughout the 'thirties and 'forties, some of which can be traced in the novel. In 1832, "he and the Whig Committee were besieged in the Swan Inn by the mob"[65] for his support of the Reform Bill; in 1843 he headed the opposition to a movement begun by the Reverend Isaac E. Lockwood requiring that all masters and assistants in the schools under Bedford's Harpur Charity be members of the Church of England; in 1844, after rousing the town to defeat Lockwood's proposal, he engaged in a public controversy over the matter with the Reverend Edward Swan, answering his criticisms in a forceful pamphlet, *The Bedford Charity Not Sectarian*.[66] In 1847 he is reported as "breaking a lance" with Charles J. F. Russell in the by-election hustings occasioned by the death of Mr. Astell[67]—and it was this political antagonist who later appointed him, in 1854, to the position of doorkeeper of the House of Commons. Besides these activities, he was a trustee of the Bunyan Meeting, superintendent of the Sunday school from 1842 to 1850,[68] and a popular lay preacher. In the obituary notices of him appearing in Bedford papers, he is acclaimed as "beyond comparison the best public speaker Bedford ever had,"[69] and once Sir David Dundas exclaimed, after hearing him speak, "Why, that is old

---

[63] *N.N.*, July 1, 1882.

[64] See *E.L.*, p. 21.

[65] *E.L.*, pp. 28–29. This is doubtless the incident recounted in *R.T.L.*, pp. 235–36.

[66] See John Brown, "The Late Mr. White," *Bedfordshire Mercury*, March 11, 1882; and J. P. Coombs, "Recollections of Fifty Years," *Bedfordshire Mercury*, April 20, 1889. For an interesting contrast between the robust father and the introspective son see S. J. Whitmee, "Mark Rutherford," in the *British Weekly* of April 3, 1913.

[67] C. J. F. Russell, "The Late Mr. W. White," *The Bedfordshire Times and Independent*, March 18, 1882.

[68] Ransome, "Mr. William White," *The Bedfordshire Times and Independent*, March 11, 1882.

[69] *Ibid.*

Cobbett again, *minus* his vulgarity."[70] Unlike Jukes, both William White and his father before him had been of the "radical reformer type," and like his father, William White had suffered for his devotion to high causes. "Mr. White," writes an admirer, "did not find it 'good for trade' to be too independent in his views,"[71] but he did not for this reason compromise with them. Boycotted by the book-buying townspeople of the opposition camp, he was forced out of business in 1846 and became a partner (or a "sleeping partner"[72]) with his brother-in-law in a tannery. The Reverend John Brown writes of him:

He was not a wealthy man—true patriots seldom grow rich . . . I venture to think he was not in the highest sense an intellectual man: if I might discriminate I should say his mind was forcible rather than intellectual. But he was public-spirited in a high degree; he had a clear head, strong common sense, a resolute will, forcible speech, and above all an honest purpose; no one ever doubted his integrity or suspected him of seeking mean and selfish ends.[73]

And in 1851 this same uncompromising integrity forced him to leave the chapel when, as Hale White writes, "he had completed the discovery that the 'simple gospel' which Calvinism preached was by no means simple, but remarkably abstruse." He goes on to say, in a declaration most significant for our study, that

It was the *Heroes and Hero Worship* and the *Sartor Resartus* which drew him away from the meeting-house. There is nothing in these two books directly hostile either to church or dissent, but they laid hold on him as no books had ever held, and the expansion they wrought in him could not possibly tolerate the limitations of orthodoxy.[74]

This then was the man who was Hale White's earliest example and most influential teacher. Though he was admired by the townsfolk, he had not been treated kindly by many of them, and he was in general cast in a political and religious mold quite unlike the average Bedford tradesman of the 1840's. His heroes, and those of his son, were those rebels of an earlier day whose portraits hung in the parlor of Zachariah Coleman, the leading character in *The Revolution in Tanner's Lane*: Major Cartwright, Byron, Scott, Paine, Burns, Rousseau.[75] And like Zachariah he belonged to those

[70] Russell, "The Late Mr. White."   [71] Ransome, "Mr. William White."

[72] See Smith, "The Life and Thought of William Hale White," p. 188. Of the unpublished studies which have come to my attention, this University of Birmingham thesis stands first in terms of thoroughness, accuracy, and readability. When I first had the opportunity to examine Mr. Smith's work, my study was already far advanced; but I discovered that our general plan of organization bore, especially in earlier chapters, a marked similarity. Inasmuch as we both employed, in large degree, identical source materials and were both investigating Hale White's biography, some duplication of effort and plan was almost inevitable. Our interpretations, however, differ widely; and I have been at pains to indicate any specific indebtedness I owe his work.

[73] Brown, "The Late Mr. White." See *A.*, p. 76 for a possible reference to William White's bankruptcy.

[74] *E.L.*, p. 38.

[75] According to Sir William Robertson Nicoll, *Memories of Mark Rutherford* (London, 1924), p. 34, these were among the portraits hanging in Hale White's own study at Ashtead and Hastings.

Independents who were "happily for them, committed to nothing, and . . . not subsidised by their reputations to defend a system."[76] To that collection of poets and reformers could be added contemporaries inheriting something of their temper: Carlyle, Bright, Mill, George Jacob Holyoake, and Sir John Trelawney. As a boy, Hale White visited the Trelawneys in company with his father, and remarked in his *Early Life* that they "will never be forgotten, not so much because I was taught what to think about certain political questions, but because I was supplied with a standard by which all political questions were judged, and this standard was fixed by reason."[77] One wonders whether Hale White is, in any degree, remembering some of these visits in the conversation he gives us between the Allens and the Colemans in the *Revolution*. They are discussing the change in political temper which had become apparent in the late 'forties, and the mildness which had crept into the sermons of one who had once been an insurrectionary preacher:

> "A sad falling off," said Zachariah, "from the days . . . when the Dissenters were the insurrectionary class. Mr. Bradshaw, last Sunday, after his sermon, shut his Bible, and told the people that he did not now interfere much in political matters; but he felt he should not be doing his duty if he did not tell those whom he taught which way they *ought* to vote, and that what he had preached to them for so many years would be poor stuff if it did not compel them into a protest against taxing the poor for the sake of the rich."[78]

But whatever the source of this conversation, we can be certain that such feelings of nostalgia for a more heroic age were definitely part of the mood of William White and his son in this period. While others were getting richer, he was getting poorer, and largely because he was honest, courageous, and outspoken; while others seemed indifferent to the quality of their religion, he was gradually forced to confess that what he heard at the chapel "taught him nothing and satisfied no want."[79] It is inevitable that he would feel isolated and cheated, deserted by those who did not love the old ship as he did. The following statement by Pauline, Zachariah's future wife, must have described very closely the state of mind of William White and his son in those distressing last years of the 'forties:

> "The highest form of martyrdom . . . is not even living for the sake of a cause, but living without one, merely because it is your duty to live. If you are called upon to testify to a great truth, it is easy to sing in flames. Yes, yes, Mr. George, the saints whom I would canonise are not martyrs for a cause, but those who have none."[80]

If this was not the way William White felt, it most certainly was the way Hale White felt as he looked back upon the scene thirty-five years

---

[76] *R.T.L.*, p. 219.

[77] *E.L.*, p. 35.

[78] *R.T.L.*, p. 220. This refers to the Corn Law agitation and doubtless to the time of repeal in 1846.

[79] W. Hale White, "The Late Mr. White," *The Bedfordshire Mercury*, March 18, 1882.

[80] *R.T.L.*, p. 222.

later. And that fact tells us some important things about Hale White.
Unlike his father, he was shy, introverted, silent, but no less than his father
he longed to fight the good fight in the old Puritan way. But though he
brought away from Bedford something of the old fighting spirit and not
a little of the desire for martyrdom, he found himself a would-be hero
without a battlefield and without a clear-cut cause. His father had known
something of the struggle and was a natural warrior who would seek out
new issues. But Hale White, too young to have experienced the battle himself, and of a brooding rather than an active nature, took out his frustrations on himself. His energies turned inward, he exercised his will and
demonstrated his courage by suffering rather than fighting, and found, to
a large degree, a kind of martyrdom in self-pity and a kind of strength in
hero worship.

Chapter Two

APOSTASY

The last important event in Hale White's religious life before he left
Bedford in 1847 was his conversion. It had been decided in that year that
he should prepare for the ministry—his own wishes to become an artist
being overruled by his mother[1]—and Cheshunt College[2] in Hertfordshire
was decided on. But before he could be admitted he had to declare that a
change had taken place in his soul. It will repay us to examine Hale
White's "conversion" somewhat closely, for not only does it provide added
evidence of the hollowness of the creed under which he was expected to
serve, but it was for Hale White an act of hypocrisy for which, one suspects, he never forgave himself.

After a preliminary examination by two deacons, the novice was expected to stand before the whole church and give an account of his spiritual
history. The confession was normally expected to be somewhat dramatic,
but Hale White, painfully reticent before others, could neither put on a
good show nor confess to any "experience" worth the name. He could
only humbly admit that his "experience had not been eventful" and that
he "was young and had enjoyed the privilege of godly parents."[3] The
agony and the shame of this event left their mark deep in his memory,
and in his novels, letters, and *Early Life* he dilates at length on the moral
problem involved.

What was conversion? It meant not only that the novice unhesitatingly avowed
his belief in certain articles of faith, but it meant something much more, and much
more difficult to explain. I was guilty of original sin, and also of sins actually committed. For these two classes of sin I deserved eternal punishment. Christ became
my substitute, and His death was the payment for my transgression. I had to feel
that His life and death were appropriated by me. This word "appropriated" is the
most orthodox I can find, but it is almost unintelligible. I might perhaps say that I
had to feel assured that I, personally, was in God's mind, and was included in the
atonement.

This creed had as evil consequences that it concentrated my thoughts upon my-

1 See *E.L.*, p. 56, and *G.D.*, pp. 28, 33.
2 See *E.L.*, p. 63. Cheshunt belonged to the Countess of Huntington's Connexion,
which was Anglican-Evangelical, but which admitted Dissenters who would sign 36 or
37 of the Thirty-nine Articles. (See Halevy, *England in 1815*, p. 403.) In *B.D.P.*, November 15, 1879, Hale White wrote: "The Countess lived at a time when Whitfield and
Wesley were rousing the land from its religious apathy, and she took great interest in
the movement; but she inclined to Calvinism rather than to Arminianism, and certainly
had not the least faith in a ritual. Like all the religious enthusiasts of the eighteenth
century, she believed in a religion of the emotions, and ceremonies were nothing, or
next to nothing. She was therefore the very polar opposite of the present dominant party
in the Church, which is Arminian and not Calvinistic, and places its main reliance on the
due observance of forms."
3 *E.L.*, pp. 57–58. For a dramatic picture of this episode, see *A.*, p. 11 ff.

self, and made me of great importance. God had been anxious about me from all eternity, and had been scheming to save me. Another bad result was that I was satisfied I understood what I did not in the least understand. This is very near lying. I can see myself now—I was no more than seventeen—stepping out of our pew, standing in the aisle at the pew-door, and protesting to their content before the minister of the church, father and mother protesting also to my own complete content, that the witness of God in me to my own salvation was as clear as noonday. Poor little mortal, a twelvemonth out of round jackets, I did not in the least know who God was, or what was salvation.[4]

Hale White, with his keen eye for hypocrisy and cant, spent himself in later years violently denouncing those who signed the Thirty-nine Articles as a matter of form and not belief and who, by rationalizing, gradually and unconsciously became little better than liars. The Anglican clergy came in for particular abuse in his weekly newspaper articles, but he was no more severe on others than he was on himself. In a letter to Miss Sophia S. Partridge on September 8–11, 1897, he writes:

> There is no theological dogma so important as the duty of veracity. It is the lack of veracity which is the curse of all our institutions, trade, intercourse, which saps our morals and will eventually, if not checked, ruin us. No religion is possible unless veracity lies at its base.[5]

And he ends this same letter with a statement which suggests that he regarded his expulsion from New College—to which he went in 1851 after three years at Cheshunt—as a kind of expiation for his earlier compromise with veracity.

> You will pardon me, perhaps, a self-reference. More than forty years ago the whole course of my life was changed by my refusal to slur over a difference between myself and my teacher on the subject of the inspiration of the Bible. I might easily have told him "You and I mean really the same thing," or used some other current phrase contrived in order to stifle conscience. I might have succeeded in being content with a *mush* of lies and truth, a compound more poisonous than lies unmixed, but I was enabled to resist. I have never regretted the decision then taken. I can see now that if I had yielded I should have been lost for ever.[6]

It is to this crisis in Hale White's life that we must next direct our attention.

After remaining at Cheshunt from September 1848 until June 1851, Hale White removed on October 1, 1851, to New College, London (now a part of the University of London and then affiliated with it), which had been newly opened on that date. The new principal was Dr. John Harris, who had also been president of Cheshunt during Hale White's stay there. On the opening day, Dr. Harris delivered an inaugural lecture on "The Inspiration of Scripture,"[7] and on February 3 of the fol-

---

[4] *E.L.*, pp. 58–59. See also *A.*, pp. 10–13, and *G.D.*, p. 71.

[5] *L.3F.*, pp. 160–61. In *N.N.*, November 30, 1878, he reports on a lecture by Miss Helen Taylor on "Veracity" with complete approval. He writes: ". . . the greatest liars are those in whose minds there is the greatest confusedness . . . the difficulty is intellectual haziness. . . . [O]ne of the best correctives to lying is habitual commerce with facts . . ."

[6] *L.3F.*, p. 164.

[7] Contained in New College, London. *The Introductory Lectures Delivered at the Opening of the College* (London, 1851). Harris' lecture is found on pp. 1–65.

lowing year the theological class was examined on the contents of the lecture. Three of the students—Hale White, Frederic Meriton White,[8] and Robert M. Theobald—were suspected of heretical views. In his opening remarks Dr. Harris had declared that the subject of inspiration was "the topic of the day,"[9] and before we can fully understand the reasons for the expulsion we must remind ourselves why such a topic was so timely and urgent.

Until about the middle of the century the Dissenting churches had remained more or less impervious to the growth of Biblical criticism and the new discoveries in biology and geology. This was partly due to the fact that few of the clergy were scholars and few read German, but it was mainly due—as we have already noted—to that Evangelicalism which had directed their attention almost entirely to spiritual religion and away from speculative theology. The Evangelicals were dedicated to saving souls, not to the "independent pursuit of truth." "Doctrine," writes V. K. Storr, "was utilised for this end; and they showed too often a tendency to wrest the meaning of isolated texts or passages in the Bible, so as to make them fit in with their doctrinal scheme."[10] But when a more rational temper began to prevail, the doctrinal bases of religion could no longer be ignored; and men like Dr. Harris—an earnest theologian with an Evangelical bent—were quick to scent danger and to sound the alarm that "moderate Calvinism" could have validity only if the Bible were accepted as the literal word of God. On this the whole religion stood or fell—and on this depended the one chance, in his conception, of finding a *via media*. His problem was precisely that described by Henry W. Clark:

The ultimate difficulty always came to be this, How could sufficient liberty be given without giving too much? How could full justice be done to the claims of enquiry and to the modern spirit without admitting that *everything* was open, and that therefore the Church might possibly be left suspended in the air, a building with its foundation knocked away, in the end?[11]

And in the year 1851 the forces of doubt were being keenly felt. One no longer had to know German to read Strauss's *Leben Jesu* (George Eliot's translation had appeared in 1846), and books like Hennell's *Inquiry Concerning the Origin of Christianity* (1838) and R. W. Mackay's *Progress of the Intellect* (1850) were turning others besides George Eliot away from orthodoxy.[12] The danger of much of this new criticism lay in the fact that it demonstrated a new kind of religious faith and was not

---

8 No relation to Hale White.

9 "Inspiration of Scripture," p. 4.

10 Storr, *Development of Theology*, p. 70.

11 *History of English Nonconformity* (London, 1913) II, 373.

12 Some of the important books of criticism between 1840 and 1851 were: Coleridge, *Confessions of an Inquiring Spirit* (1840); Charles Bray, *The Philosophy of Necessity* (1841); J. A. Froude, *Shadows of the Clouds* (1847) and *The Nemesis of Faith* (1849); F. D. Maurice, *The Religions of the World* (1847); William Rathbone Greg, *The Creed of Christendom* (1851). Most of these writers were influenced by such German thinkers as Strauss, Feuerbach, and Schleiermacher.

aimed merely at undermining the old. Men like Francis Newman, for example, whose popular book, *The Soul, Its Sorrows and Aspirations* (1849) advertised "Spirit, not form in religion; the free movement of personal intuition, unfettered by creed or definition,"[13] could by their religious sincerity provide a more insidious enemy than the textual critics themselves. Although Harris mentions none of these new rebels by name (probably most of the students had never heard of them), he inveighs heavily against that "self-sufficient spirit" which ignores the Bible as a book "superannuated and outstript" and replaces it with "the religion of human nature."[14] He would have seen in Mackay's statement the very devil he was trying to smoke out:

. . . divine revelation is not contained exclusively or pre-eminently in the facts and inspirations of any one age or nation, but is co-extensive with the history of human development, and is perpetually unfolding itself to our widened experience and investigation.[15]

There were, of course, only two ways of dealing with this religion of "human nature": either make room for it in your theology, or call it false and hold the line firmly against it. Harris, unfortunately, was one of those "subsidised by their reputations to defend a system,"[16] and had no choice. Strict limits must be observed by the orthodox individual in the exercise of his reason:

Reason, not satisfied with interpreting the book, assumes to be its judge; and, with the appearance of Rationalism, revelation disappears. Emotion, inward experience, under various names, assuming to be, not the mere light in which truth is to be studied, but as truth itself, gives birth to a pious mysticism, which modifies revelation at pleasure. In other words, the claims of the Bible itself are now brought in question, and consequently the Divine authority of all texts and doctrines alike.[17]

But Harris did recognize that a new theory of inspiration was needed and made a rather futile attempt to supply it. He allowed that not every word of Scripture need be regarded as inspired, but that wherever the phrase "Thus saith the Lord" appeared, it was a mark of direct inspiration. The truth was always from God, but the *language* was that of the writer, who retained the free use of his "human faculties and characteristics." "The individuality of the man," writes Harris, "—as expressed in his vocabulary, mental associations, range of knowledge, and general dispositions—remained, and moved with conscious freedom under the eye of the Divine Agent."[18] Inconsistencies could, therefore, appear to exist without existing at all, and there was no need to suppose—as some critics had alleged—that because the Bible is all true, one part must be read uniformly with another. All of Harris' proofs were, however, drawn from

---

13 Storr, *Development of Theology*, p. 375.
14 "Inspiration of Scripture," p. 5.
15 Quoted in Basil Willey, *Nineteenth Century Studies* (London, 1949), p. 229.
16 *R.T.L.*, p. 219. See Chap. I, note 76.
17 "Inspiration of Scripture," p. 4.
18 *Ibid.*, p. 35.

the Bible itself as the only valid authority, and his argument is a well-described *petitio principii*: "No theory can be accepted in contravention or limitation of the Biblical idea of inspiration, which does not rest on authority equal to that of the Bible itself."[19] To Dr. Harris, of course, there was no such substitute authority.

While the Principal was forced into defending a reactionary position, there is little reason to suppose that he was, as Hale White draws him, an unlettered, doctrinaire hypocrite. Henry A. Smith accumulated five pages of evidence to prove that he was not only a genial and eloquent man, but, considering his position, broad-minded.[20] Yet the portrait of the "President" in the *Autobiography* is supposed to represent Harris:

I see him now, a gentleman with lightish hair, with a most mellifluous voice and a most pastoral manner, reading his prim little tracts to us directed against the "shallow infidel" who seemed to deny conclusions so obvious that we were certain he could not be sincere, and those of us who had never seen an infidel might well be pardoned for supposing that he must always be wickedly blind.

About a dozen of these tracts settled the infidel and the whole mass of unbelief from the time of Celsus downwards. The President's task was all the easier because he knew nothing of German literature; and, indeed, the word "German" was a term of reproach signifying something very awful, although nobody knew exactly what it was.[21]

Several critics have regarded this portrait as seriously distorted. In a bulletin of the present Cheshunt College at Cambridge, the author protests:

It is curious that White should never have appreciated the real humanity of Harris, and that a man who offended the Church leaders of the time by his plain speaking on the fatal connection between the Church and money should have been described by Mark Rutherford as an "elderly gentleman" (Harris was then only forty-eight) who wrote "prim little tracts".[22]

The "plain speaking" here mentioned undoubtedly refers to Harris' essay, *Mammon, or Covetousness the Sin of the Christian Church* (1836), for which he won the tidy prize of 100 guineas, and the "Church leaders" who were offended were the Reverends James Ellaby and Algernon Sydney Thelwall. An even more bitter criticism was voiced by A. Victor Murray, B.D., the present president of Cheshunt College:

. . . Hale White . . . maligned Harris. Harris seems to have been a very forward-looking progressive person, quite a good German scholar and familiar with continental theology. But White refers to him in "Mark Rutherford" as . . . a reactionary . . . when he had already created some disturbance in the denomination for being, if anything, too much the other way. White seems to me to have been a thoroughly unbalanced fellow altogether.[23]

---

19 *Ibid.*, p. 49.

20 Smith, "Life and Thought of William Hale White," pp. 90–95.

21 *A.*, p. 16.

22 *Cheshunt College, Cambridge, England*, pp. 8–9 (n.d.).

23 Letter dated October 12, 1949. William White, in his pamphlet *To Think or Not to Think* (p.16) points out that Harris, as an editor of *The Biblical Review*, had permitted the expression of very liberal views on the subject of inspiration, and that J. D. Morrell in his *Philosophy of Religion* wrote: "Little as is the progress which the lofty

There is probably some truth on both sides: while Harris was unquestionably defending a reactionary position with a shaky argument, Hale White was willing to alter a few facts in order to caricature his one-time superior.

The reasons for Hale White's hostility toward Harris do not, we suspect, arise solely from the fact of the expulsion. In the *Autobiography*, Hale White gives us an account of his first experience as a student-preacher, and in it we see something both of the honesty and depth of his spiritual cravings and of the truculence and self-pity with which they were accompanied.

Nearly every doctrine in the college creed had once had a natural origin in the necessities of human nature, and might therefore be so interpreted as to become a necessity again. To reach through to that original necessity; to explain the atonement as I believed it appeared to Paul, and the sinfulness of man as it appeared to the prophets, was my object. But it was precisely this reaching after a meaning which constituted heresy. The distinctive essence of our orthodoxy was not this or that dogma, but the acceptance of dogmas as communications from without, and not as born from within.

Heresy began, and in fact was altogether present, when I said to myself that a mere statement of the atonement as taught in class was impossible for me, and that I must go back to Paul and his century, place myself in his position, and connect the atonement through him with something which I felt.[24]

These are the words of an honest and earnest romantic, engaged in the same spiritual adventure that occupied other sensitive rebels of his generation. Dr. Harris heard this sermon and afterward gave him what can be seen as well-meant, kindly, and intelligent advice. But Hale White brought not a little Byronic pride to the effort, and he took Harris' faint praise as a mortal insult:

He said that my sermon was marked by considerable ability, but he should have been better satisfied if I had confined myself to setting forth as plainly as I could the "way of salvation" as revealed in Christ Jesus. What I had urged might perhaps have possessed some interest for cultivated people; in fact, he had himself urged pretty much the same thing many years ago when he was a young man . . .[25] but I must recollect that in all probability my sphere of usefulness would lie amongst humble hearers, perhaps in an agricultural village or a small town, and that he did not think people of this sort would understand me if I talked over their heads as I had done the

spiritual principles of Schleiermacher have openly made in this country, yet there are very significant indications of their gradual development. I would particularly call attention to the *Biblical Review*, as taking an eminently broad and philosophical ground in discussing the nature of religion and the basis of Christian theology." Pages 16 through 21 of this pamphlet contain quotations of heretical opinions appearing in *The Biblical Review*—from Coleridge, Neander, Dr. Arnold, Schleiermacher, and others. The evidence was gathered, of course, to prove Harris a hypocrite, but it can also be used to demonstrate his intellectual breadth and tolerance.

24 *A.*, pp. 24–25.

25 As a matter of fact, after 1851 Harris published works to prove "that there is a theology in nature which is one with the theology of the Bible" (*Dictionary of National Biography*, XXV, 15). Harris seems simply to have been put in an embarrassing position by Hale White and, while his own mind was remarkably open for a man in his position, he felt it his duty to permit no shadow of doubt to cross the minds of his students.

day before. . . . His words fell on me like the hand of a corpse, and I went away much depressed. My sermon had excited me, and the man who of all men ought to have welcomed me, had not a word of warmth or encouragement for me, nothing but the coldest indifference, and even repulse.[26]

This incident took place no doubt in the autumn of 1851 and leads us to suspect that Hale White had prepared himself for rebellion well before the crisis came in February. He had already learned contempt for the creed and for the man who taught it, and though it was a sincere and necessary dissatisfaction, it was at least partly inspired by the fact that this man had not seen in him the makings of a new Messiah.

The details of the expulsion itself are set forth in a 31-page pamphlet by William White (1807–82) entitled, *To Think or Not to Think* (1852),[27] which he wrote in defense of the students and which, though a valuable repository of facts, was at least as angry as it was objective. The facts seem to be these. On February 3, during the examination, the two students later expelled with Hale White asked some questions about the formation of the canon and the authenticity of the separate books. "They were immediately stopped by the Principal in summary style," who declared:

"I must inform you that this is not an open question within these walls. There is a great body of truth received as orthodoxy by the great majority of Christians, the explanation of which is one thing, but to doubt it is another, and the foundation must not be questioned."[28]

Harris, no doubt, recalled his own words from the inaugural address and thought these insubordinate youths perfectly illustrated his fears:

According to this undiscriminating generation, every earnest man is a prophet, every poet is inspired, every brilliant idea is a revelation, every admiring soul is a worshipper, and so much of God is in every living man as only to require development in order to entitle him to the claim of divine messenger.[29]

The three students were summoned on February 13, 1852, before a special meeting of the Council, a body composed of Dissenting ministers and laymen, and were asked the following questions: (1) Will you explain the mode in which you conceive the sacred writers to have been influenced? (2) Do you believe a statement because it is in the Bible, or merely because it is true?[30] (3) You are aware that there are two great parties on this question, one of which maintains that the inspiration of the Scripture differs in kind from that of other books—the other, that the difference is

---

26 *A.*, pp. 26–27. The advice given to Thomas Broad (*R.T.L.*, p. 191) by an "elder student" was precisely of this nature—one indication of the close parallel between the events in Hale White's novels and those in his real life.

27 This is a rare document and exists only, so far as I know, in the hands of Dr. Reginald Hale-White.

28 *E.L.*, p. 64.

29 "Inspiration of Scripture," p. 13.

30 See Harris' inaugural address (p.16): "The Apostles did not say, 'Our communications are true, therefore they must be from God;' but, 'They are from God, therefore they must be true'."

only one of degree. To which of these parties do you attach yourself? (4) Are you conscious of any divergence from the views expounded by the Principal in this introductory lecture? (5) Are you conscious of any divergence from the well-defined standard of Christian truth held by the supporters of this institution?[31]

As a result of this inquisition the Council decided their views to be "incompatible with the retention . . . of their position as students for the Christian ministry."[32] In a further meeting with the fathers of the students on February 23, the fathers remonstrated against the summary nature of the proceedings and demanded: (1) that the students' moral character be placed above suspicion, (2) that the opinions for which they were condemned be explicitly stated, and (3) that they should be furnished with a copy of the creed by which they were judged. None of these requests was complied with, and the Council on March 3 asked the students to withdraw for three months to reconsider their views. Hale White described the answer he gave to this request in a letter to his father.

11 SERLE STREET
6 March 1852

DEAREST FATHER

We were a very short time with the Committee yesterday. We were out by six and had tea there meanwhile—not meeting till past five. Theobald had just time to run into his office in P.N. Row and send a copy of their resolution which I suppose you got this morning—"Retire for three months"—Of course we refused. No surrender. No compromise. I said that if I could change my opinion in so short a time that [*sic*] I would abandon all thoughts of public speaking. They seemed to think that such a change was possible but said very little about it—thought that we should gain in the estimation of my friends and the world, that it would argue modesty etc. They pressed us not to reply definitely but send it in writing. I have seen Coombs this morning . . . to ask when the Council met next and I find it is on Wednesday week—so I shall pack up all my traps next week and be off. I shall save money by so doing, for I am not certain that I shall have to meet the Council any more. They will most probably send a reply to our communication in writing, and even if I have to appear before tham [*sic*] I can come up for the day. I shall I think, come home till the Council meeting is over and the matter definitely settled, *and then off to Portsmouth. . . .*[33]

On March 17, their final dismissal was announced.

The affair caused some stir in Dissenting circles[34] and William White's little *Areopagitica* drew sympathetic letters from Charles Kingsley and F. D. Maurice.[35] A short time later, in another connection, Hale White

[31] Quoted in *E.L.*, pp. 65–66, and in *The Nonconformist*, March 31, 1852. See Appendix A, pp. 549–58 of "Religion and Art of William Hale White ('Mark Rutherford')" (Dissertation, Harvard University, 1950) by the present author.

[32] White, *To Think or Not to Think*, p. 30.

[33] *P.N.b.*, p. 54. This is one of the few copies extant of Hale White's early correspondence.

[34] See letter from Thomas White (father of F. M. White) in *The Morning Advertiser*, March 30, 1852, and Edward Miall in *The Nonconformist*, April 28, 1852.

[35] See Stone, "Religion and Art of William Hale White" (Harvard thesis), Appendix A, pp. 561–63. For a copy of a letter from Hale White to John Harris see *ibid.*, p. 558 or *P.N.b.*, p. 31.

received a letter from James Martineau who wrote: "The circumstances connected with your removal from St. John's Wood College have rendered your name so well known that no other introduction is needed."[36] It was a *cause célèbre* for only a few months and was only one of many such dismissals or heresies in the period,[37] but the importance of the event on Hale White's life and thought can hardly be overestimated. Obliquely or directly he made frequent reference to this or similar expulsions in his journalistic writings, and the following excerpt from *The Aberdeen Herald* of January 15, 1863, is typical of the defensive pride with which he regarded them:

The Dissenters in England are always in trouble about their Colleges. They are constantly breaking out into heterodoxy. Not that there is ever any grand eruption to relieve the system of its foul humours once and for ever, but the disease is always coming up to the skin in pimples disfiguring the complexion exceedingly, and causing no small annoyance. Some years ago at New College, three or four young men were dismissed for some quibble about inspiration, and ever since that time there has been great constitutional irritation, much itching from pimples as aforesaid, inability consequently *to sleep*, and great tendency on the part of hands which had better have kept quiet, to scratch and make matters worse. Casually looking at the *British Standard* the other day, I perceived that some poor Dissenting student had been committing himself by using some phrase or other not found in the College vocabularly [*sic*], and that the whole religious Dissenting public had been, by an alarmed editor, summoned to arms to resist this outbreak of the heresy . . . Absurdity . . . reminded one of the picture in *Punch*, where the old gentleman, just waked out of his slumbers, is represented watching at his hall door, and exclaiming as he listens to the fancied murderers and thieves, that "there are three of 'em, if not four, by the footsteps;" while outside a jackass is sniffing through the keyhole. Seriously, though, what a mercy it is to be out of all this Colenso-Pentateuchal authenticity hubbub. What a mercy not to have every expression and almost every gesture watched and searched for any symptoms of unorthodoxy.

And even fifty-nine years after the dismissal, three years before his death, Hale White's bitterness over the proceedings was still fresh:

The Holy Office was never more scandalously indifferent to any pretense of justice or legality in its proceedings. We were not told what was the charge against us, nor

---

[36] Letter dated December 22, 1853. See *ibid.*, pp. 559–60.

[37] There were a number of such heretics among Hale White's friends. The closest of these was his own cousin, T. William Chignell, who trained for the Independent ministry at Homerton College (1843–49) and was ordained in the year Hale White began his training at Cheshunt. They were intimate friends until about 1890, when their correspondence declined—owing, perhaps, to a tactless letter Chignell wrote on the eve of Hale White's wife's death: ". . . there was no darkness in the world, otherwise God would not be God." (Unpublished letter to Mrs. Colenutt, January 16, 1890.) Hale White's scrapbooks are full of clippings from Chignell's lectures. He was a keen student of modern critical thought and science, and his influence on Hale White was profound. Soon after his ordination he became heterodox and separated from the Independents (See *E.L.*, p. 55) but managed to occupy a Unitarian pulpit at St. George's Chapel, Exeter, throughout his life. He introduced Hale White to the writings of Goethe.

Another heretic at the time was Macrae Moir, mentioned in Martineau's letter and very likely in *E.L.*, p. 81, and *A.*, p. 136. He was forced to resign as minister of a chapel in Worthing (where Hale White once preached) and came to London around 1852. He may have got Hale White his position on *The Aberdeen Herald*. (See Smith, "Life and Thought of William Hale White," pp. 229–30.)

what were the terms of the trust deed of the college, if such a document existed;[38] neither were we informed what was the meaning of the indictment, and yet the council must have been aware that nothing less than our ruin would probably be the result of our condemnation.[39]

The dismissal did come at a very inconvenient moment, for his father was at this time unable to help him financially (his business had fallen off and he was deeply in debt), but that "ruin" might result is something of an exaggeration. Testimonials to his good character were readily forthcoming from men like Maurice,[40] and he had many friends in London, Bedford, and elsewhere who were deeply sympathetic and were doubtless willing to help in any way they could. His father, furthermore, had a wide and influential circle of friends—some of them extremely wealthy.[41] And early in the next year—after a long vacation at Portsmouth[42]—Hale White readily found employment with John Chapman on *The Westminster Review*, where his heresy was a recommendation rather than a handicap.[43]

Externals will not, however, explain the effect of this experience on Hale White. Though he was not cut off from friends, though his father supported him with his sympathy and his pen, and though in his brief period of unemployment it is unlikely that many "Damn your eyes!"[44] rang in his ears, the dismissal brought him a sense of spiritual deprivation he was to feel all his life. The reason was that he could neither fully accept nor fully reject orthodoxy, just as throughout his life he could neither fully accept nor reject those who offered him love or praise or sympathy. If we can judge by his first sermon, he did not want to repudiate the church into which he had been born, but to invigorate it, to read fresh and vital meaning into the bibliolatry which was now its unsteady prop. But this path of constructive effort was cut off—partly by himself and partly by others—and he was "repulsed into self-reliance and reserve."[45] Instead of being allowed to assist the salvation of others, he was driven to be obsessively concerned with his own redemption; instead of

---

[38] On March 31, 1852, he, together with the two other expelled students, had written in *The Nonconformist*: ". . . and, being aware that a creed exists in the deeds of the institution."

[39] *E.L.*, pp. 68–69.

[40] See Stone, "Religion and Art of William Hale White" (Harvard thesis), Appendix A, p. 563.

[41] S. T. Whitbee, *British Weekly* (April 3, 1913), testifies to Bedford's sympathy for him. Other friends included Sarah and Richard Colenutt of Ryde, Isle of Wight; Mr. White of Portsmouth, father of the expelled student; Caleb Morris, the Welsh preacher at Fetter Lane Chapel, London (who was a profound shaping influence on Hale White—see "Caleb Morris," *L.P.*, p. 244 ff.); his mother's half-sister, Mrs. Elizabeth Street (see *Letter on the Death of Mrs. Elizabeth Street*); and, of course, William Chignell. His father was respected and loved by the Bedford Russells, the richest family in England, and well known to men like John Bright and G. J. Holyoake.

[42] See *G.D.*, p. 71.

[43] See *E.L.*, pp. 82–83. In *A.H.*, December 13, 1862, Hale White declared of Chapman that "anyone persecuted or in trouble was sure of attention and help from him."

[44] *R.T.L.*, p. 90.

[45] *A.*, p. 131.

being able to proclaim the truth with the emphasis of a Bunyan or even a
Carlyle, he was forced to discover it—and he had been given no training
in such free inquiry. He became haunted, not by the "real obvious danger" of his existence, but by a "vague, shapeless fear"[46]—a coward enemy
against which a strong will and an honest purpose were small defense. In
the *Autobiography* and elsewhere,[47] he tells of a terrible night at Stoke
Newington following his expulsion when he had his first experience of
"the horrors"—that panic fear of approaching an unseen and indefinable
abyss—which was to recur at intervals throughout his life. Like Catharine
Furze, he felt isolated in an indifferent world and longed for the companionship of a Christian community:

Poor Catharine! the world as it is now is no place for people so framed! When life
runs high and takes a common form men can walk together as the disciples walked
on the road to Emmaus. Christian and Hopeful can pour out their hearts to one
another as they travel towards the Celestial City and are knit together in everlasting bonds by the same Christ and the same salvation. But when each man is left
to shift for himself, to work out the answers to his own problems, the result is isolation. People who, if they were believers, would find the richest gift of life in utter
confidence and mutual help are now necessarily strangers. One turns to metaphysics;
another to science; one takes up with Rousseau's theory of existence, and another
with Kant's; they meet; they have nothing to say; they are of no use to one another
in trouble; one hears that the other is sick; what can be done? There is a nurse; he
does not go; his old friend dies, and as to the funeral—well, we are liable to catch
cold. Not so Christian and Hopeful! for when Christian was troubled "with appari-
tions of hobgoblins and evil spirits", even on the borderland of Heaven—oh, Bunyan!
"Hopeful kept his brother's head above water, and called upon him to turn his eyes
to the Gate and the men standing by it to receive him." My poor reader-friend, how
many times have you in this nineteenth century, when the billows have gone over
you—how many times have you felt the arm of man or woman under you raising
you to see the shining ones and the glory that is inexpressible?[48]

The desire to connect his troubles with the troubles of others, and to
relieve their misery and loneliness by describing his own, were at once the
motive and the excuse for Hale White's self-revelations. It was this
impulse that made him a novelist and that animated much of his thought.
And at the root of this impulse was that severed nerve, the pain—always
remembered—of that amputation he suffered in early life, that fundamental separation between himself and a community of belief.

[46] *R.T.L.*, p. 91.
[47] *A.*, pp. 133–34; *E.L.*, pp. 79–81; *G.D.*, pp. 72, 336–37.
[48] *C.F.*, pp. 125–26.

Chapter Three

NEGATION

In tracing Hale White's slow progress from the wilderness of doubt to a new land holding some kind of promise, our best references are his first two books, the *Autobiography* and the *Deliverance*. Though cast in semi-fictional form and departing widely at times from the actual facts of his external life, they record his inner experience in the years between, roughly, 1850 and 1885 with a passionate and merciless honesty bearing comparison, perhaps, only with Tennyson's *In Memoriam* and Newman's *Apologia*. His avowed purpose is to present in Mark Rutherford a "victim of the century"[1] and not a hero, but he does not disguise the fact that Mark Rutherford was a victim of himself as well—a self-persecutor imposing Puritan habits of self-contempt and self-discipline which, without their creedal support, were ill-suited for a mind and body striving to know the joys of freedom. But the final record of these books is of a progress, a deliverance. He wished, by sharing his own pain, to free others "from that sense of solitude which they find so depressing."[2]

What was the nature of that experience which Hale White felt could be so helpful? In what sense did it bring for him a "deliverance"? Willard L. Sperry has seen in these two books the record of a spiritual growth which follows the natural stages of a religious awakening: *negation, new birth, renunciation*, and *affirmation*.[3] While such terms are too conveniently descriptive to discard, and while we may profit from such suggestive labeling, we must remind ourselves that Hale White got out of the desert place not by a direct, but by a wandering route. His passage from desolation to life cannot be fixed by many dates nor marked by clear signposts. The *Autobiography* and the *Deliverance* have condensed that experience, but our attempt in this and ensuing chapters will be to see it in something of its original complexity. The forces which moved him from orthodoxy (of which we have seen but a few) were positive and negative at once: Wordsworth, Goethe, Carlyle, and Spinoza wrought in him that same "expansion"[4] which his father had also experienced, and helped to render the narrow confines of a decadent fundamentalism unbearable. But while these forces pulled him away from the church, he was

1 Letter to George Jacob Holyoake, January 20, 1882. In *P.N.b.*, p. 34. See also *D.*, p. 96.

2 *A.*, p. 2.

3 W. L. Sperry, "Mark Rutherford," *Harvard Theological Review*, VII (April 14, 1914), 166–92.

4 John Stuart Mill's experience was remarkably similar. See the *Autobiography* (New York, 1924), pp. 94–97, 102–6. See also Basil Willey, *Nineteenth Century Studies* (London, 1949), pp. 146–49.

simultaneously being pushed away by the critical rationalism which he read and overheard at John Chapman's and elsewhere. By degrees he renounced or modified the visionary hopes of his romantic "new birth" and blended what was left of them into a view of life more consonant with reality and more agreeable to his own capacities. His final affirmation, however, was uttered in a low and hesitant voice—so low, at times, that we are not always sure we have caught what he said or meant. He found no new system of dogma: he simply learned a kind of agnostic humility before the challenge of his own aspirations and the depth of his own suffering.

We are hardly justified in marking Hale White's progress by "stages," for though something like them undoubtedly existed, none of them was permanent. To the end of his days he was denying and affirming at once, doubting and believing, studying systems of thought and declaring the impossibility of any theory of life, asserting the romantic claims of emotion and exalting the stoic virtue of reason. Hellenism and Hebraism, Romanticism and Puritanism, existed side by side in him, conflicting, blending, co-operating, competing, in such subtle and unpredictable patterns that only by close examination can we see that such exchanges bring a final increase. "What a pest is the re-appearance in us of discarded conclusions!"[5] he writes in *Last Pages*; and it is with some assurance that we can say he never completely left one position for another. He got out of the waste place by routes which he hardly knew himself, and kept returning to it, fascinated by the effort to retrace old steps. But he never covered exactly the same country again; it became imperceptibly greener and greener. He remembered in these travels the mood of his early experiences, but he never could be sure of the tense.

I have never known much about epochs. I have had one or two, one especially when I first began to read and think; but after that, if I have changed, it has been slowly and imperceptibly.[6]

Though we do damage to the subtlety of these changes by placing them in a pattern, the pattern is nonetheless necessary. For notwithstanding the unsystematic nature of his pilgrimage, the pilgrim of fifty was a different man from the youthful heretic, and the older man had acquired, if not a serene faith from his experience, at least a familiarity with doubt and despair which lessened his fear of them.

. . . I had gradually learned the blessed lesson which is taught by familiarity with sorrow, that the greater part of what is dreadful in it lies in the imagination. The true Gorgon head is seldom seen in reality. That it exists I do not doubt, but it is not so commonly visible as we think. . . . Life to all of us is a narrow plank placed across a gulf, which yawns on either side, and if we were perpetually looking down into it we should fall.[7]

The first of these stages—negation—takes us into both a chapter of

[5] *M.P.*, p. 235.
[6] *D.*, p. 106.
[7] *Ibid.*, pp. 115–16.

Hale White's early career and into an aspect of his life's quality—a persistent and recurring mood. Hale White was never by temperament a lover of negations, and never enjoyed iconoclasm for its own sake. But in the period following his expulsion, that period when he "naturally thought nothing in the old religion worth retaining,"[8] he was forced to observe and share in the disheartening process of demolition. The old theological structure did not come down all at once, but only stubbornly yielded bit by bit under the critical hammers; and before it was completely leveled, Hale White had begun to suspect that any rebuilding must be done on the old foundations. With him it is hard to say where negation leaves off and where affirmation begins. As we have already suggested, the forces working to deny the validity of the old creed could also be seen as positive forces, making possible a fresher and more vital faith. But Hale White viewed most Biblical criticism (to take but one example) as primarily negative and, though this attitude was not always warranted or necessary, we must accept his emphasis. And we must make one more qualification. By studying these negative forces first we seem to imply that they came first chronologically. That is only partly true. The disintegrating of the old religion had, as we have already seen, begun in Bedford and had been accentuated in his college days, but actually the "new birth," the real conversion which Hale White experienced, came before most of the matters we are about to consider. The Everlasting Yea and the Everlasting Nay found, in him, almost simultaneous expression.

In the years between 1852 and 1860 Hale White still clung to the tattered habiliments of the old creed. Though deprived of a regular pulpit through his expulsion, and engaged in full-time secular employment, he preached frequently at Unitarian chapels and in the pulpits of friends. R. M. Theobald, in *The Westminster Gazette* for March 17, 1913, gives us the information that he preached frequently at Portsmouth for his cousin, T. W. Chignell, and in the diaries kept by Hale White's mother we learn of a trip to Portsmouth on June 8, 1860, which was most probably for this purpose. He seems to have occupied the pulpit of the Friar Street Chapel in Ipswich on two Sundays in 1853–54,[9] and to have had many engagements at Ditchling between the years 1855 and 1857, preaching there for the last time on March 15.[10] Sir W. Robertson Nicoll, in his

---

[8] *E.L.*, p. 78.

[9] W. J. Scopes, *The Inquirer*, January 31, 1914. Press cutting in possession of Dr. R. Hale-White.

[10] These dates are indefinite, and are gathered from press cuttings. *The Inquirer*, June 20, 1914, says he first went there in 1860, but the same paper on July 4, 1914, says his official connection with the church lasted a little over a year (1855–56). His mother, however, records in her diary that "Hale went to Ditchling for the last time" on March 15, 1857.

According to a newspaper article appearing in *The Birmingham Daily Mail* on March 29, 1913, Hale White "once or twice" preached at Zion Chapel in Birmingham for George Dawson (1821–76), a popular preacher, lecturer, and worker for liberal causes. "Dawson," the article reads, "was at that time editor of the 'Birmingham Morning News,' and as 'Mark Rutherford' wanted some means of a livelihood on the failure

Memories of Mark Rutherford, suggests that he officiated at a chapel in Billingshurst,[11] and his mother's diary records engagements at Caleb Morris' chapel in Little Portland Street, London, on March 25, 1855, February 13, 1859, February 27, 1859, March 13, 1859, October 16, 1859, and April 1, 1860, and doubtless he preached there more often. Although he never "settled" as a minister as he does in the *Autobiography*,[12] it is likely that his experience at the Unitarian chapel in the "straggling half-village, half-town of D——," referred to Ditchling, and that many of his experiences there were drawn from life.[13] One critic, taking this identification seriously, has written an interesting note on it:

> . . . Whose blame was it that they were all so "petrified" to him? I suspect that he was given to preaching over their heads, but as I looked in at the Meeting House window, and imagined him there in that poor little pulpit, I could not feel sure that his failure was due solely to this. Was there not an absence of human warmth on his part? Did he offer as much as he expected to receive? . . . Had he smiled upon little children and taken them by the hand in those meadow walks he tells us of, and spoken kind words to them, would they now in later life have forgotten him? Still, we must take a man of unique nature as we find him, and if Mark Rutherford failed in a quiet corner of Sussex, he succeeded brilliantly in the great realm of literature.[14]

However valid this supposition may be, it leaves out of account the fact that Hale White was suffering acutely from the realization that he could not really believe what he was preaching, or at least could not preach what he would like to believe. He was suffering also, no doubt, from the humiliation of finding Dr. Harris' prediction come true—that his sphere of influence would be among humble country folk. To save those laborers' souls seemed at the time a much less urgent occupation than saving his own.

The atheist Mardon serves in the *Autobiography* as a kind of symbol of the negative forces at work in him during this period. Possibly Mardon had a real existence, but we do not learn of it; the arguments, however, which are put in his mouth represented without a doubt the self-questionings which beset Hale White in this twilight period of religious faith. Mardon was a deeply religious thinker who, following logic to the limit, had been forced by honesty to do without the assurance of any belief. And he told Mark Rutherford, who was trying to believe in a "humanized" Christ and accept a liberal interpretation of the Bible, that he must give up this attempt to have his cake and eat it, that to accept the validity of

---

of his ministerial prospects, Dawson offered him work on his paper." This writer must have meant to say "The Church of the Saviour" instead of "Zion Chapel," for Dawson was at Mount Zion between August 4, 1844, and December 29, 1845, only. Even at the end of that period Hale White would have been only a little more than fourteen years of age. For a number of reasons it seems likely that Hale White's association with Dawson began after his expulsion in March 1852. Dawson was a friend of the Martineaus and of Chapman. In view of James Martineau's interest in Hale White's apostasy, it is quite likely that Martineau first brought Hale White to Dawson's attention.

11 P. 51.
12 *A.*, p. 113.
13 See *G.D.*, p. 463 n.
14 *The Inquirer*, June 20, 1914.

the "Christ-idea"[15] without concern for the real fact of his existence, was an impossibility.

"Pardon me," said Mardon, "but it does very much matter. It is all the matter whether we are dealing with a dream or with reality. I can dream about a man's dying on the cross in homage to what he believed, but I would not perhaps die there myself; and when I suffer from hesitation whether I ought to sacrifice myself for the truth, it is of immense assistance to me to know that a greater sacrifice . . . is possible. To know that somebody has poetically imagined that it is possible, and has very likely been altogether incapable of its achievement, is no help. Moreover, the commonplaces which even the most freethinking of Unitarians seem to consider as axiomatic, are to me far from certain, and even unthinkable. For example, they are always talking about the omnipotence of God. But power even of the supremest kind necessarily implies an object—that is to say, resistance. Without an object which resists it, it would be a blank, and what, then, is the meaning of omnipotence? It is not that it is merely inconceivable; it is nonsense, and so are all these abstract, illimitable, self-annihilative attributes of which God is made up."[16]

This "negative criticism," Mark Rutherford adds, was "all new to me," and "I was stunned, bewildered, out of the sphere of my own thoughts, and pained at the roughness with which he treated what I had cherished."[17]

By degrees, Mardon's criticism, coupled with the fictional controversy with Snale over the water supply, drove Mark Rutherford from the Independents (with whom he had first settled) to the Unitarians—that sect providing a last resort for many Victorian unbelievers attempting to maintain some kind of corporate Christianity while retaining only the bare bones of a creed. And Hale White's account of Mark's first Sunday at Ditchling—if not accurate historically—sets unmistakably the mood which accompanied increasing negation. Few artists have found symbols more expressive of the stark emptiness following religious denial than Hale White did in the cold, empty chapel to which he came unwelcomed that Sunday morning, the stale water and empty glass in the fireless vestry, the faded green curtains in the windows, and the old funeral sermon which had been left behind—and had done service on several occasions—in the pulpit Bible.[18] After preaching to seventeen inattentive, unmoved listeners, he was invited to dinner in the household of one of the congregation. Here he found spiritual desolation in another form.

There was a neck of mutton (cold), potatoes, cabbage, a suet pudding, and some of the strangest-looking ale I ever saw—about the colour of lemon juice, but what it was really like I do not know, as I did not drink beer. I was somewhat surprised at being asked whether I would take potatoes *or* cabbage, but thinking it was the custom of the country not to indulge in both at once, and remembering that I was on probation, I said "cabbage."[19]

[15] Obviously a reflection from Strauss or Hegel in Hale White's thought. See pp. 51–56 and 71–74 below.

[16] *A.*, pp. 60–61. These last arguments are repeated by Hale White in his essay, "Ixion," *The Secular Review* (September 11, 1880).

[17] *Ibid.*, p. 61. See also pp. 103–5.

[18] *Ibid.*, pp. 110–11.

[19] *Ibid.*, p. 112.

Potatoes *or* cabbage in a sense symbolized the choice between the spiritual fare offered by an Independency professing a sterile creed and Unitarianism professing almost none.

Before leaving the Independents he had written:

Nakeder and nakeder had I become with the passage of every year, and I trembled to anticipate the complete emptiness to which before long I should be reduced. . . . God was obviously not a person in the clouds, and what more was really firm under my feet than this—that the universe is governed by immutable laws? These laws were not what is commonly understood as God. Nor could I discern any ultimate tendency in them. Everything was full of contradiction.[20]

"A Satan we might conquer," he writes later in *Miriam's Schooling*, ". . . but what can we do against this leaden 'order of things' which makes our nerves ministers of madness?"[21]

Stripping off one theological garment after another, he was left increasingly defenseless against those nervous devils which preyed upon his health, and was increasingly haunted, like one of Kafka's heroes, by the fear that his spiritual nakedness was of interest neither to man nor to God. The congregation he found at Ditchling doubtless seemed to him part of that indifferent, leaden "order of things," and he unquestionably took out some of his frustration on them. While he craved self-expression and longed for influence, it seemed like hypocrisy to move an audience with interpretations of a dogma which could not move him. Hale White was not expert in detecting logical shortcomings in a theological system, but he was exceedingly quick in detecting a lowering of spiritual enthusiasm. A religion without passion was for him no religion, and these provincial tradesmen and farmers seemed in their own lives to be dramatizing the negations of their creed.

Although my congregation had a freethought lineage, I do not think that I ever had anything to do with a more petrified set. With one exception, they were meagre in the extreme. They were perfectly orthodox, except that they denied a few orthodox doctrines. Their method was as strict as that of the most rigid Calvinist. They plumed themselves, however, greatly on their intellectual superiority over the Wesleyans and Baptists round them; and so far as I could make out, the only topics they delighted in, were demonstrations of the unity of God from texts in the Bible, and polemics against tri-theism. Sympathy with the great problems then beginning to agitate men, they had none. Socially they were cold, and the entertainment at their houses was pale and penurious. They never considered themselves bound to contribute a shilling to my support. . . . They had no enthusiasm for their chapel, and came or stayed away on the Sunday just as it suited them, and without caring to assign any reason.[22]

The inevitable break from the Unitarians of course came. This form of theological negation could provide for Mark Rutherford neither any center for belief nor any sanction for morals. It left him only a mechanical universe run, like Paley's watch, by a cold, indifferent, abstracted God.

20 *Ibid.*, p. 99.
21 *M.S.*, p. 113.
22 *A.*, pp. 118–19.

The doctrine of the unity of God was the one positive element in the Unitarian creed and, as we shall later see, Hale White tried, with the help of Spinoza, to make a living religion out of it. But to use the doctrine as it existed with the Unitarians as a basis for corporate action was hopeless, and he eventually turned from it in revulsion.

As for a message of negations, emancipating a number of persons from the dogma of the Trinity or future punishment, and spending my strength in merely demonstrating the nonsense of orthodoxy, my soul sickened at the very thought of it. Wherein would men be helped, and wherein should I be helped?[23]

In this period and later Hale White was also introduced to the open iconoclasm of the "Secularists" under the leadership of Bradlaugh, who would hold forth at the Hall of Science against all believers who would engage in debate. This form of negation was less dangerous because it was more open, but it was nevertheless a variety of profanity which was exceedingly distressing to Hale White. In the *Deliverance* he describes one such meeting which has some of the characteristics of the Bryan-Darrow debates at the Scopes trial. The old priest who came to oppose Bradlaugh argued for Christianity by engaging in prayer (which was applauded by the audience), and he was answered by a characteristic Secularist polemic against the morality of Old Testament characters. Being a married man, the speaker said, he should not

. . . feel particularly at ease if he had to leave his wife with David. David certainly ought to have got beyond all that kind of thing, considering it must be over 3000 years since he first saw Bathsheba; but we are told that the saints are for ever young in heaven, and this treacherous villain, who would have been tried by a jury of twelve men and hung outside Newgate if he had lived in the nineteenth century, might be dangerous now. He was an amorous old gentleman up to the very last. (Roars of laughter.)[24]

While Hale White could appreciate the humor of this and recognized that the priest had by far the worst of it, as he deserved, he was nevertheless depressed by the spectacle. On the one hand

. . . the eminent Christian was nothing but an ordinary minister, who, when he was prepared for his profession, had never been allowed to see what are the historical difficulties of Christianity, lest he should be overcome by them. On the other hand, his sceptical opponents were almost devoid of the faculty for appreciating the great remains of antiquity, and would probably have considered the machinery of the Prometheus Bound or of the Iliad a sufficient reason for a sneer. That they should spend their time in picking the Bible to pieces when there was so much positive work for them to do, seemed to me as melancholy as if they had spent themselves upon theology.[25]

There were, however, in this early period of Hale White's life negative influences at work unconnected with any religious body, most of which centered about the circle of freethinkers and liberal critics who wrote for

23 *Ibid.*, p. 101. See p. 129 for a veiled reference to Spinoza.
24 *D.*, p. 15.
25 *Ibid.*, pp. 16–17.

The Westminster Review or who gathered at the home of Dr. John Chapman, the editor. Hale White found his way to Chapman sometime in the fall of 1852,[26] and was lodged in his house at 142 Strand, in a room above that of the *Westminster*'s new assistant editor, Miss Marian Evans.

> As the New College council had tested my orthodoxy, so Chapman tested my heresy and found that I was fit for the propagandist work in No. 142 and for its society. He asked me if I believed in miracles. I said "Yes and no". I did not believe that an actual Curtius leaped into the gulf in the Forum and saved Rome, but I did believe in the spiritual truth set forth in the legend. This reply was allowed to pass, although my scepticism would have been more satisfactory and more useful if it had been a little more thorough.[27]

Hale White was thus as a young man placed in a clearinghouse for radical thought unequaled anywhere in London, and was given an enviable opportunity for personal acquaintance with some of the most stimulating thinkers of his generation. But he does not seem to have made much of an impression on his colleagues. George Eliot never mentions him in the letters published in Cross's *Life*, and the recently issued Chapman diaries have no reference to him.[28] No doubt he felt overwhelmed—and somewhat shocked—by the freethinking and radical literature which found its way in and out of the *Westminster* office. But the experience there nonetheless left its mark on him, and from the record he has given us in the *Autobiography*, the *Early Life*, and elsewhere,[29] we can ascertain with some certainty the books and people who influenced him most deeply. His work did not take him into the main stream of the intellectual life at Chapman's, for he was not long on the *Westminster* itself, and was engaged most of the time in work of a personal and routine nature for Chapman— writing letters, keeping accounts, and "subscribing" publications.[30] But,

[26] Sir William Hale-White in *P.N.b.* gives the date simply as 1852, but it was most likely October or November of that year, for the following reasons. After the expulsion in March, Hale White took a six months' vacation in Portsmouth with his friends, T. William Chignell, Frederic White, and Sarah and Richard Colenutt; at the "beginning of the term" he was engaged at the Stoke Newington School for one day only (*E.L.*, p. 81) and, after calling on "several publishers" (*E.L.*, p. 82) he found work. Though he dilates upon the agonies of unemployment (*A.*, p. 140 ff.) this does not mean that he wandered the streets very long. To a man of his proud and introspective temper, one such refusal could be an immensely painful experience. October, therefore, seems the most likely date.

[27] *E.L.*, pp. 82–83.

[28] See Gordon S. Haight, *George Eliot & John Chapman with Chapman's Diaries* (New Haven, 1940).

[29] For convenience, these references may be listed here. *E.L.*, pp. 82–85; *A.*, pp. 141–57; "Dr. John Chapman," *The Athenaeum* (December 8, 1894); "George Eliot as I Knew Her," *The Bookman* (London) (August 1902), reprinted in *L.P.*, pp. 131–37; *A.H.*, March 8, 1862, August 1, 1863, August 12, 1865; *N.N.*, January 1, 1881, February 24, 1883; *B.P.*, August 8, 1873. A further interesting article mentioning Hale White and Chapman is found in *S.B.b.* by T. P. O'Connor, *T.P.'s Weekly* (July 26, 1924), pp. 455–56.

[30] *E.L.*, p. 83. Some of the important critical publications issuing from 142 Strand before 1852 which Hale White doubtless "subscribed" were: F. Foxton, *Popular Christianity: Its Transition State and Probable Development*; W. R. Greg, *The Creed of Christendom*; J. A. Froude, *The Nemesis of Faith*; C. C. Hennell, *Christian Theism*; W. Maccall, *The Elements of Individualism*; *The Agents of Civilization*; *The Education of*

living in the same house and taking meals with Miss Evans and the Chapmans, he had ample opportunity to hear good conversation[31] and, on one occasion at least, to attend one of Chapman's "Wednesday evenings." In *The Norfolk News* of January 1, 1881, Hale White writes:

Mr. and Mrs. Chapman were in the habit of giving Wednesday evenings, when they were glad to see their friends; and on one memorable Wednesday evening your correspondent was present, and recollects distinctly who were there. Miss Evans was there; together with Miss Helen Faucit, Mr. Herbert Spencer, Mr. G. H. Lewes, and others . . .[32]

To these names we must add those, mentioned elsewhere by Hale White, who either wrote for the *Westminster* or had their books published in Chapman's "Catholic Series." The list given below may be taken as indicating the people he was most aware of, though it does not, of course, indicate that they were all aware of him.[33]

Amongst Mr. Chapman's authors were Mr. Herbert Spencer, George Eliot, Harriet Martineau, Dr. Martineau, Mr. J. A. Froude, Mr. Francis W. Newman, Emerson, and that strangely gifted and wayward man of genius, William Maccall. "The Nemesis of Faith", of which the first edition, by the way, is not in the British Museum catalogue, was issued from 142, Strand.[34]

If we take from this assortment of intellect the names of Eliot, Froude, Newman, Emerson, and Maccall, we shall have those whose work was certainly known by Hale White and of more or less influence in shaping his mind.[35]

But these people did not alone—or primarily—give to Chapman's circle what Hale White considered its characteristic intellectual coloring. The book which any mention of Chapman immediately brought to Hale White's mind was Strauss's *Life of Jesus*, translated in 1846 by Miss Evans, and probably the most controversial book of the mid-century. Doubtless it was this book, together with the kind of thinking and writing

---

Taste; R. W. Mackay, *The Progress of the Intellect*; J. Martineau, *The Rationale of Religious Inquiry*; *Endeavours after the Christian Life*; F. W. Newman, *The Soul: Her Sorrows and Aspirations*; *Phases of Faith*; *History of the Hebrew Monarchy*; *Lectures on Political Economy*; Theodore Parker, *A Discourse of Matters Pertaining to Religion.* (All taken from Chapman's *Descriptive Catalogue*, 1852.)

31 Sometimes, however, it must not have been too inspiring. In his *B.N.B.*, p. 100, he records: "When I was at Chapman's there was a German boarding in the house who had written a book 'Die Religion der That'. It was a materialistic gospel. Expatiating at dinner one day on the baselessness and folly of the belief in immortality, he exclaimed dramatically in his broken English 'I do tink it is a glorious ting to die and have a bad small'. He sent his book to Carlyle, but he heard that Carlyle had given orders to his servant not to take delivery of any more new religions." This man was a Dr. A. Stamm, and his book was published at Hamburg in 1852.

32 George Eliot remembered this evening as well, though she does not seem to have remembered Hale White. See J. W. Cross, *George Eliot's Life* (London, 1885), I, 308.

33 "Dr. John Chapman," *The Athenaeum* (December 8, 1894), p. 790.

34 The second edition, issued in the same year (1849), is there.

35 His life at Chapman's was not, however, a leisurely one and he doubtless had little time for careful critical study of many books. (See *A.*, p. 149.) In *A.H.*, December 10, 1864, he mentions also Greg's *Creeds of Christendom* (1851) and in *N.N.*, December 9, 1882, refers again to *The Nemesis of Faith*.

it inspired in the *Westminster* and "Catholic Series" critics, which led Hale White to feel that the emphasis at Chapman's was primarily nega-tive and unsatisfying. On May 3, 1853, he wrote a long and important letter to his father, part of which read as follows:

With all that you say I most cordially agree, most especially with what you say about *cold negativism*. Mr Chapman is nothing so much of a negation merely as many of his books are, but I see, and must see infinitely more of this heartliness [*sic*] emptiness both in books and men than I ever saw before, and this drives me back again to all my old eternal friends who appear more than ever perfect, and Jesus above them all. Granted that all that the Strausses, Foxtons, and Newmans have made out is correct—that there is no miracle, that Palestine's laws of nature were really England's, and so on, yet I turn round on them and say "You cannot deceive my eyes". Here are words in these gospels in black and white, and such words I maintain were never spoken before. No literary world here full of attempts at book and sentence making, no writing for the sake of writing, no thought of publishing here, no vain empty cleverness, attempted merely for the purpose of glorifying the writer in the reader's eyes, but simple solemn words, spoken as by one conscious of eternity round him and over him, to beings whose life is an awful thing "coming from eternity and going to eternity again"—Oh, after all the soul rests only in calm satisfaction *on* the *soul* nothing short of this—and if you feel in a book that the writer's *heart*, his own real truest thought is not present, there is no rest but a vague dis-satisfaction and disquiet. But on the Bible I can repose. . . . The writer's *soul* is there, his own most real experience and consequently on that I rest. In nine tenths of the books I read, I feel just as a magnet I should think feels when there is a card put between it and a piece of steel, as if it would long to pierce through the covering and get at the real true metal . . . In the Bible I feel now at length do I see the real soul. Here I am heart to heart, hand to hand with a real human being. I embrace no clothed, disguised man but feel the blood beating and the touch of the warm flesh.[36]

Hale White had a remarkably close understanding and love of the Bible as a human document—which he had primarily gained from the Reverend Caleb Morris[37]—and he was pained by books which studied it as a text-book. All these people we have named did not, by any means, offer merely messages of negation, but those whose main concern was Biblical criti-cism—like Foxton, Strauss, and Newman—were doubtless felt by Hale White to be tampering critically with what should either be treated as a source of inspiration or else left strictly alone. While he did not question the validity of the new historical discoveries, he thought that emphasis on such matters rather than on the vitality still remaining in the Bible as literature was impertinent and irreverent. "I cannot endure negative criticism," he writes; "it does me no good, and I find that I have enough to do in the extraction of one thousandth part of the positive value of the Bible or any other great book. . . ."[38] This statement made in Febru-ary 1908 was, as we have seen from his letter to his father, one which he could have made in 1853 as well.

[36] *P.N.b.*, pp. 29–30.

[37] See *E.L.*, p. 87, and essay, "Caleb Morris," in *L.P.*, pp. 244–50. See also *G.D.*, pp. 27–28, and *C.F.*, pp. 72–73.

[38] *G.D.*, p. 3.

Only once in his writing does he seem to reveal any sympathy with the "negative" critics, and this was in a letter to *The Exeter and Plymouth Gazette* on January 6, 1864, replying to an Anglican clergyman of the old school who had violently abused William Chignell, Hale White's cousin, for a lecture he had delivered a short time before. The lecture had been based on a talk by one Mr. Pengelly, a naturalist who had expatiated before an Exeter audience on "The Antiquity of Man," and had provided Chignell with the materials for a discourse on the historical inconsistencies in the Bible and other related matters. Hale White came to Chignell's defense partly, one suspects, because he loved his cousin, but more because he hated the hypocritical impercipience of this conventional Anglican who, in Hale White's eyes, was a typical representative of his class. When the issue was strictly that between the Established Church and the new thought, however distasteful the latter might be to him, Hale White always took up the cudgels against the Church. That old sectarian prejudice is reflected in the following words:

When a new fact, or a supposed new fact, is presented to us are we to reject it because it is not what our theological predilections would have it be? or are we to examine, and if necessary believe it, trusting that in the end no "discrepancy" whatever will be found between any of the works of the Almighty? The world, sir, notwithstanding the denunciations of Mr. ——— ——— and his friends, is every way pronouncing pretty strongly as to which side it will take, and marches on its own grand way, discovering new truth after truth, and leaving the so-called defenders of the faith to follow in the rear and find out, as they have done in the disputes about the seven days of the Mosaic creation, about the sun and moon standing still, about the arithmetic of the Pentateuch, and in earlier times about the discoveries of Galileo and Columbus, that if they can't get the new light to accommodate itself to their eyes, they must even accommodate their eyes to the new light. Does Mr. ——— ——— believe now that the world was made in seven days? does he believe that the sun and moon stood still? does he believe in the ante-Copernican philosophy? Assuredly not; and yet his forefathers would have considered him, for not doing so, guilty of a profanity far worse than that of Mr. Chignell. The Bible says as distinctly as words can say anything that the world *was* made in seven days, and that the sun and moon *did* stand still; and if Mr. ——— ——— chooses to call these plain statements poetry he does so by a "verdict of his understanding," which he who thinks so much of the Bible and so little of his understanding, ought not to allow to be passed on such a sacred subject.[39]

And he goes on, proving this priest's error by quoting against him the example of Bishop Colenso and the words of Bishop Thirlwall. Hale White's love of fact and reason made impossible any turning away from the new criticism, but he never delighted in it unless it was directed toward a deeper and more religious understanding of the book. He wrote to his young son, William, in 1874:

You make a mistake, which is not uncommon, in treating the Bible as if it were a mere bundle of texts strung together without any connection. The Bible, as you will see if you read it as a whole is a collection of distinct treatises, written at dif-

[39] "The Priesthood *versus* the Human Mind and Science," *The Exeter and Plymouth Gazette*, January 6, 1864.

ferent times, at different places, and upon all sorts of subjects. Some of these treatises have been lost; others have been considered unimportant and some centuries ago were cut out of the Bible and placed by themselves in the Apocrypha. Hence it is above everything necessary to know under what circumstances particular words were spoken in order to get at their meaning. The words to which you refer about two or three being gathered together, had no more reference to church going than they had to theatres. They were spoken by Jesus to his disciples when they were going out alone into the world and they were told by him not to be afraid, for wherever two or three were gathered together, he, that is to say the spirit of truth, would be with them and make them more than a match for all their enemies. . . .[40]

Strauss was always a painful subject to Hale White, and, though he does not mention him often, he never brings up his name without revealing some bitterness or disappointment. Thanks to Strauss and others like him, Hale White could never again enjoy the naïve religious faith and calm peace of mind, which, for example, Miss Tippit of *Miriam's Schooling* still knew:

She contrived, through what she heard, and what she sang, and what she prayed, not only to provide herself with an explanation which she did not doubt of the here and hereafter—an explanation which would not probably have been secure against Strauss—but she obtained a few principles by which she regulated this present life—principles of extreme importance, which scepticism must admit if the world is not to go to ruin.[41]

Hale White was drawn to George Eliot partly because, "With all her freedom and wit, she was deeply religious,"[42] and the pain she suffered while translating Strauss indicated a sensitivity to sacred things (together with a tough-minded critical sense) which Hale White could deeply appreciate. On February 14, 1846, Mrs. Bray wrote to Sara Hennell that Miss Evans

says she is Strauss-sick—it makes her ill dissecting the beautiful story of the cruci-fixion, and only the sight of the Christ image and picture make her endure it.[43]

That Hale White shared something of the same revulsion is indicated by his calling Strauss "a known enemy of Christianity" to whom we go "forti-fied and prepared," and by referring to the *Leben Jesu* as "that horrid book by Dr. Strauss to whom [*sic*] Mr. Gladstone has so ingenuously di-rected us all."[44]

---

[40] *P.N.b.*, p. 22. Letter dated March 12, 1874. Another statement relevant in this connection is one quoted by Sir W. Robertson Nicoll in *An Introduction to the Novels of Mark Rutherford* (London, 1924), p. 12: "Any fool can buy a Bible and grin at it, and apparently get his folly printed. We cannot put down, and nobody would attempt to put down, Gibbon or a translation of Strauss; but somehow there is an instinctive desire to call out for a policeman when one sees the guilty daub which is supposed to contradict the *Book of Genesis* by depicting an old man making a human being out of mud."

[41] *M.S.*, p. 78.

[42] *N.N.*, January 1, 1881.

[43] Cross, *Life*, I, 139.

[44] *N.N.*, December 28, 1872. He adds, however, that the Church journals, which dif-fer among themselves more than they hate their common enemy, distill a more subtle poison than Strauss and succeed in discrediting Christianity more effectively.

The act of Biblical dissection was, to one with small appetite for such surgery, frightening and disgusting. Could the old book ever be seen again in its beautiful wholeness after such mutilation? Would people not brought up on the Bible think it, after such criticism, not worth looking into at all? Would the Philistines, understanding neither Strauss nor the Gospels, make this their vulgar excuse for condemning all morality and all religion alike? Such considerations as these motivated Hale White, not to deny the validity of Strauss's criticism, but to turn away from it and concentrate, as Caleb Morris did, on the "indwelling Christ of the Gospels"—on that Christ who could be recaptured ideally in the individual conscience and did not rest on historical proof or disproof. In describing Morris' position, Hale White is also clarifying his own:

. . . Christianity was not assent to certain propositions, nor external obedience to its precepts. It was an indwelling of the Christ of the Gospels, shaping thought, speech, and life. Hence he [Caleb Morris] was not strictly orthodox, for orthodoxy is system, and system is something artificial and restrictive. He believed undoubtedly in the chief doctrines of Christianity, but he was one of the freest of men, if freedom is largeness of the space in which we move and live. We may deny that Leviticus was written before the Captivity, or dispute the authenticity of the Gospel of St. John, and be narrower than a rigid Calvinist. Thomas à Kempis and Bunyan were infinitely free.[45]

The events in the life of Christ were, to Hale White and to Morris, not so much facts as truths; whether or not they actually occurred in history was of less importance than the knowledge that they could recur in the spiritual experience of all men in all time.

Now, strangely enough, this emphasis—which was part of the idealism conditioning much of Hale White's thought—had in reality a marked similarity to Strauss's teaching. Strauss had written in the Preface to the *Life of Jesus*:

The supernatural birth of Christ, his miracles, his resurrection and ascension, remain eternal truths, whatever doubts may be cast on their reality as historical facts. The certainty of this can alone give calmness and dignity to our criticism, and distinguish it from the naturalistic criticism of the last century, the design of which was, with the historical fact, to subvert also the religious truth. . . .[46]

But for Hale White, Strauss had destroyed more than he had preserved. The discussion between Mardon and Mark Rutherford, already indicated, is essentially that between a man claiming that Strauss has destroyed the basis of Christian belief and one who thought a faith was possible in spite of—and even because of—the new light. A preacher, says Mardon

. . . must base himself upon the Bible, and above all upon Christ, and how can he base himself upon a *myth*?[47] We do not know that Christ ever lived, or that if He lived His life was anything like what is attributed to Him. A mere juxtaposition

---

[45] "Caleb Morris," *L.P.*, pp. 247–48.
[46] *The Life of Jesus, Critically Examined*, translated by Marian Evans (New York, 1855), "Preface to the first German edition," p. 4.
[47] My italics.

of the Gospels shows how the accounts of His words and deeds differ according to the tradition followed by each of His biographers.[48]

We have seen this argument before, and it has obvious reference to Strauss's famous mythical theory, which explained all the miraculous and supernatural elements in the life of Christ by the natural tendency of a people to build legends about their heroes and objects of veneration. At this stage in the conversation Mark Rutherford seems to be defending Strauss, but a few pages later he has taken Mardon's criticism wholly to heart, and remarks:

The dissolution of Jesus into mythologic vapour was nothing less than the death of a friend dearer to me then than any other friend whom I knew.[49]

To reduce Christ to "mythologic vapour" in the sense Hale White uses the phrase—implying a fictionalizing of the roots of the Christian religion— was, as we have already seen, very far from Strauss's purpose. But it is nevertheless true that for many readers Strauss did accomplish the destruction of everything supernatural and most of what had been regarded as historical in the Gospel story.[50] To men like Hale White who had been trained from childhood to refer constantly to the Bible, and to link with it many of their fondest associations, this was the destruction of the one stable reference point in his life, the one thing which could still give continuity to a religious tradition. And he never abandoned it. It was always for him something more than great literature, though he did not, of course, take it as the literal word of God. To him it was enough to take the truth —or what seemed to be the truth—and let the rest alone. "Publish your convictions, but not your doubts"[51]—this was always his advice where the Bible was concerned, and explains as well as anything can why he found in Strauss only a negative message.[52]

And we must rely partly on that same explanation in understanding why Hale White, in the letter to his father, regarded Francis W. Newman and Frederick Foxton as carriers of a negative message. For, while these men were certainly no profane idol smashers, they spent considerable time and effort in publishing their doubts and in attacking the inadequacies of dogmatic Christianity. It may seem paradoxical that a man who was

---

[48] *A.*, p. 60.   [49] *A.*, p. 64.
[50] Storr, *Development of Theology*, p. 224.   [51] *L.3F.*, p. 173.
[52] Hale White regarded Renan, however, with approval. In the *A.H.* for August 29, 1863, he mentions having read Renan's *Vie de Jésus* while spending a holiday in a little French town. He said he must be silent and let readers judge the "theological portion of the work, that which deals with the supposed legends and accretions of time in the received accounts of the life of our Saviour." But he remarks that it has a "singular attractive style" and calls it "novel and interesting as if it were for the first time being told, instead of having been for centuries, the basis of the faith of Christendom." In 1906 he read Renan's *Antechrist* also with approval. (See *L.3F.*, p. 250.) Hale White was doubtless attracted by Renan's passionate feeling for the humanity of Christ and his attempt to recapture—through historical imagination—the personal magnetism and suffering of Christ. Though Albert Schweitzer has called this book an "erotic romance," the romanticizing of religion was appealing rather than offensive to Hale White, as long as the writer was sincere.

later to publish his own doubt, as Hale White did, and whose writing offended some critics by its lack of "faith,"[53] would find in the work of those two men anything to complain about. For they were, of course, pointing the way to a more vital faith and not merely dwelling on negations. The explanation lies, no doubt, in the fact that Hale White felt himself to be teaching by *example* in his novels, and not by precept; to be showing the way of deliverance, as Bunyan did, by sharing with the reader a purifying emotional experience instead of rationally discrediting an old and delineating a new faith. Again and again we return to this same point with Hale White: he wanted to assert the truth and not to find it; and he was impatient with those who could laboriously dissect their religion and then logically try piecing it, like Humpty Dumpty, together again. No religious feeling was evident for him unless one could pronounce his convictions like a Jeremiah or a Carlyle.[54] And from the intensity of this religious need, together with his incapacity for prolonged theological inquiry, came a feeling that men like Foxton and Newman could have nothing to say to a lonely, suffering individual like himself. How could anyone who had come near sharing his own experience speak about the agony of unbelief in such dispassionate terms?

The book of Foxton's which Hale White most likely knew was his *Popular Christianity: Its Transition State and Probable Development*, published by Chapman in 1849, but he might very well have known also *The Priesthood and the People* which Trübner issued in 1862. Foxton had been an Anglican clergyman who had gradually renounced, not merely certain doctrines of the Church, but dogmatic Christianity in general. His main purpose, however, was to bring the churches "into correspondence with the intelligence of the age, and to form a truly Catholic Christianity."[55] To this end *Popular Christianity* argues for a revision of belief relating to the inspiration of Scripture, miracles and prophecy, the divinity of Christ, and the teaching of Christianity by dogmatic creeds and articles. Most of the book is taken up with demonstrations of the superstitious character of those beliefs, and it ends by proclaiming that these falsehoods can be replaced by a genuinely spiritual faith only through *general education*.[56] "That *worship of the Bible* which the Reformers substituted for the idolatries they denounced" must now cease, and we must give up living in a world of "outward signs and symbols" and return to a religious philosophy aiding the development of "the inner and individual life of man."[57] Carlyle's ideas and vocabulary saturate this book.[58]

The tendency of the human soul to rise to the adoration of the God of the universe is constantly checked by the imperfection of our knowledge, and the errors of educa-

[53] *Sunday School Chronicle*, March 20, 1913. [54] See *M.P.*, p. 233.
[55] *An Analytical Catalogue of Mr. Chapman's Publications* (London, 1852), p. 3.
[56] *Popular Christianity* (London, 1849), p. 201.
[57] *Ibid.*, p. 218.
[58] Frequent references are also made to Strauss, Emerson, and Novalis. See p. 136. The quotation is found on pp. 200–201.

tion. Unable to worship in the great temple of the universe, and, by a familiarity with nature, to realize the idea of harmony and unity that pervades it, and therefore requiring a material object of worship, man, in the earliest ages, has been found to worship the most perfect of his own species.[59] He turns in despair from the open volume of nature as too profound for investigation, has no faith in the "divine significance of life," and readily conceives that God may have shut up all wisdom and all knowledge in the bosom of a priest, or "in the words of a book." . . . The cultus of every nation and every sect . . . enshrines in its unmeaning ceremonies, and consecrates in its dogmatical absurdities, the purest elements of natural piety. *A general education is the only path to a spiritual faith.*

As we shall presently see, this attempt to find a religion based on individual experience and finding support in Carlylean Natural-Supernaturalism was shared by Hale White. But he preferred the master to the disciple and doubtless felt that *general education* was a cold and sterile recommendation for one seeking present relief from gloom and self-despisings.

In F. W. Newman,[60] however, we might have expected that Hale White would find a doubter more congenial and more helpful. Here was a man deeply religious, possessing an intense veneration for the Bible, whose passage from Anglican orthodoxy to "natural" religion was marked by many of the same trials as those in Hale White's own pilgrimage. All of F. W. Newman's most important books were published by Chapman : *History of the Hebrew Monarchy* (1847), *The Soul, Her Sorrows and Aspirations* (1849), and *Phases of Faith* (1850), but it is probably this last, most recently published and most famous book, which Hale White had in mind in the letter to his father. Two elements in Newman's book may have been offensive to him. In the first place, Newman maintains that Jesus' one desire was to get people to believe in him, regardless of the grounds for their belief.[61] This, of course, implied that Christ was something of a religious demagogue and self-seeker. In the second place, Newman placed more emphasis on a *reasonable* belief than, one suspects, was pleasing to Hale White.

Religion was created by the inward instincts of the soul : it had afterwards to be pruned and chastened by the sceptical understanding. For its perfection, the co-operation of these two parts of man is essential. While religious persons dread critical and searching thought, and critics despise instinctive religion, each side remains imperfect and curtailed.[62]

This cannot, certainly, be called a negative doctrine, but doubtless it was to Hale White depressing, for he was ill-disposed toward such "critical and searching thought"[63] and needed a more poetic stimulus to religious

[59] Acknowledgment is made to *Heroes and Hero Worship*, Lect. I.

[60] Hale White refers to F. W. Newman in *L.3F.*, p. 68, and in *A.H.*, December 13, 1862.

[61] *Phases of Faith*, p. 190. See also Storr, *Development of Theology*, p. 377. It is interesting to note, however, that Hale White praised Newman's *The Relation of Physiology to Sexual Morals* very highly in his *R.O.* article for August 2, 1870.

[62] *Phases of Faith*, p. 232.

[63] It should be noted, however, that men like T. H. Huxley, who were primarily scientific in their emphasis, he deeply admired. In *A.H.*, October 11, 1862, he answers a

experience. And even this following statement by Newman—which super-ficially suggests an attitude of veneration toward the Bible similar to Hale White's—could have smacked too much of Anglican sentiment for his taste, and not enough of painful longing.

Meanwhile, it did begin to appear to myself remarkable;—that I continued to love and have pleasure in so much that I certainly disbelieved. I perused a chapter of Paul or Luke, or some verses of a hymn, and although they appeared to me to abound with error, I found satisfaction and profit in them. Why was this? was it all fond prejudice,—an absurd clinging to old associations?

A little self-examination enabled me to reply, that it was no ill-grounded feel-ing or ghost of past opinions; but that my religion always had been, and still was, *a state of sentiment* toward God, far less dependent on articles of a creed, than once I had unhesitatingly believed. The Bible is pervaded by a sentiment, which is im-plied everywhere,—viz. *the intimate sympathy of the Pure and Perfect God with the heart of each faithful worshipper.* This is that which is wanting in Greek philosophers, English Deists, German Pantheists, and all formalists. This is that which so often edifies me in Christian writers and speakers, when I ever so much disbelieve the letter of their sentences. Accordingly, though I saw more and more of moral and spiritual imperfection in the Bible, I by no means ceased to regard it as a quarry whence I might dig precious metal, though the ore needed a refining analysis. . . .[64]

After viewing this small evidence we might conclude that Hale White's statement to his father was not a considered one and should not be taken seriously. Undoubtedly it was the product of a mood and a moment, but such moods and moments recurred in his experience. "I long for the time when men will turn away from these most barren discussions on God, immortality, and their own souls,"[65] he writes in 1891, and this long-ing was active at the very moment he himself engaged in such discus-sions. As we have repeatedly seen, he was not seeking a new creed but a way out of the loneliness which derived partly from psychological and physiological maladjustments of a purely personal nature, and partly from his sense of homelessness in a critical and unbelieving age. His thinking—especially when it concerned himself or his own religious needs—almost always had emotional motivation, and when these personal chords were touched—as, for example, Dr. Harris touched them—he reacted quickly and sensitively and sometimes overstated his case. Hale White wanted someone to take him by the hand and lead him across the Slough of Despond. But the people around him were too busy with their money-making or publishing or book writing to notice his needs, and he was afraid that by reaching out his hand to them he would disclose his own weakness. This was, to no small degree, the reason he found negativism

---

Times assertion that, in regard to *The Origin of Species*, Huxley "can never teach us anything which it concerns us to know," by asking: "What then, does concern us?" See also *R.O.*, July 20, 1867.

[64] *Phases of Faith*, pp. 187-88. Cf. *L.P.*, p. 254: "I was surprised this morning when I reflected how large a stake I had in what was uncertain, in that for which I could but hope, and how little I live in that of which I am assured. The wise man should reverse the order."

[65] *L.3F.*, p. 48.

rather than affirmation around him at Chapman's. His relations with
George Eliot—the "Theresa" of the *Autobiography*—illustrate this point
clearly. She was the one bright spot in this experience for Hale White,
and she had the double virtue of being a woman and an intellectual. At
their first meeting, Hale White, "a mere youth, a stranger, awkward and
shy," was "grateful to her because she replied even with eagerness to a
trifling remark I happened to make, and gave it some importance,"[66] and
because of these and other attentions, he was shortly "entirely overcome
with unhesitating absorbing love for her."[67]

We shall later consider their relationship in more detail, but it serves
us here as a reminder that *cold negativism* was for Hale White likely to
be the only alternative to passionate attraction, and that a book which
bored him or an individual failing to see in him hidden funds of genius
could become in his eyes the very powers of darkness.[68] Cold negativism
was not an intellectual judgment so much as an expression of the fact that
in some peculiar way he felt not wanted. Religious problems could never
for him be understood except in intimately personal terms and we are
therefore forced, in extracting his thought, to return again and again
to the personality of the man himself. Like so many introverts, he longed
to go completely the other way, to escape completely from himself into
some non-self, into some new Celestial City. As Theresa once told him,
he liked Beethoven because "He encourages a luxurious revelling in the
incomprehensible and indefinably sublime. He is not good for you."[69]
He was, in other words, a passionate idealist whose deepest desire was
to transcend the negations and the "nicely calculated less or more" of an
impure and unfriendly world. The Chapman critics and men like Mardon
could not give him what he wanted, but, as we shall presently see, he
found in Wordsworth and the romantic poets the means of a genuine
religious awakening.

Before leaving this discussion we must mention the names of Jowett,
Kingsley, and Maurice, the Broad Churchmen, who, for all their positive
emphasis, came to be regarded by Hale White as propounding a form of
belief more dangerous than atheism. Maurice had been friendly and kind
to Hale White as a youth[70] and he repaid these favors by writing a warm
tribute to him at the time of his death in 1872;[71] but Kingsley and Jowett
were never treated so generously. Of Kingsley he wrote in *The Aberdeen
Herald* for April 4, 1863:

It is not for me to account for all the quips and oddities which an Oxford education
and strong temptations to remain in a wealthy church may have produced upon a

---

66 "George Eliot as I Knew Her," *L.P.*, pp. 131–32.   67 *A.*, p. 157.

68 See *A.*, p. 140. Here the indifference of the publisher became "mechanical brutality"—a reflection, one suspects, more of Hale White's sensitivity than of the actual
fact. Examples could be multiplied.

69 *A.*, p. 149.

70 See *G.D.*, pp. 3, 71. Maurice wrote a testimonial for Hale White after his expulsion.   71 *B.D.P.*, April 6, 1872. See below, pp. 158–59.

novel-writing, Neo-Platonistic, Christian-Socialist, semi-heretic, like the Professor of Modern History at Cambridge; but one thing is plain, that he is, as might have been expected after such a course of training as he has had, as full of irreconcileable [*sic*] antipathies and weak prejudices as any silly woman.

And in the *Letters to Three Friends,* writing to Miss Partridge in September 1897, he stated:

Let a candidate for holy orders, who wavers when he is asked to testify to that which is no longer a reality to him, consult any simple woman or even a child. Let him expel all conjectures as to what Maurice, Kingsley or, far worse, what Jowett would have advised. Jowett, by the way, is to me the representative of modern Infidelity.[72]

In spite of this severe criticism in late life, Hale White had as a youth been deeply influenced by Jowett, if we can trust the evidence of his scrapbooks, which are filled with clippings of Jowett's sermons. It is interesting to note, furthermore, that the clipping of Jowett's sermon reported in *The Christian World Pulpit* for June 16, 1880, is followed two pages later in the scrapbook by Hale White's article, "Ixion," which appeared in *The Secular Review* for September 11, 1880. The ideas expressed in the two articles are, in some cases, almost identical; and in 1881 Hale White could write:

. . . the real truth is that Dean Stanley's sayings and doings and those of Professor Jowett and one or two other clergymen of that school, are the only sayings and doings of clerical persons for which the world cares one atom. If Professor Jowett writes anything, all the cultivated classes in England listen.[73]

Why did this sympathy so decay that Hale White came finally to regard Jowett as "the representative of modern Infidelity"? The change was brought on partly, no doubt, by Jowett's remaining in the Church and reaping the material rewards of such allegiance when Hale White could not see how an honest freethinker could do so, and partly by what Hale White came to regard as his sloppy translating of Plato.[74] But it seems more likely that, from the beginning, some of Jowett's statements in *Essays and Reviews* and in his sermons had rung hollowly for Hale White, but that he supported Jowett simply because he was opposing the orthodox Church party.[75]

Though we have no proof of it, there is little doubt that Hale White read Jowett's essay, "On the Interpretation of Scripture," which was in-

72 Pp. 163–64.

73 *N.N.*, July 30, 1881. See also *N.N.*, July 22, 1882. Of tangential interest here is the fact that just before his article, "Marcus Antoninus," appeared in *The Secular Review* for July 3, 1880, he had read an article by Renan on this famous Stoic. It appeared in the *Times* of April 17, 1880, and was included in Hale White's scrapbook.

74 He praised it extravagantly in *N.N.*, July 2, 1881, but damned it utterly in *L.3F.*, pp. 257–58.

75 See *N.N.*, July 22, 1882: ". . . if the Church of England can hold a man like Professor Jowett, and if Professor Jowett can honestly say he is a member of that Church . . . then there is no reason why M. Renan should not be admitted . . . and Mr. Matthew Arnold. . . ."

cluded in *Essays and Reviews*. What in the following would Hale White have approved or disapproved?

> . . . any true doctrine of inspiration must conform to all well-ascertained facts of history or of science. The same fact cannot be true and untrue, any more than the same words can have two opposite meanings. The same fact cannot be true in religion when seen by the light of faith, and untrue in science when looked at through the medium of evidence or experiment. It is ridiculous to suppose that the sun goes round the earth in the same sense in which the earth goes round the sun; or the world appears to have existed, but has not existed during the vast epochs of which geology speaks to us. But if so, there is no need of elaborate reconcilements of revelation and science; they reconcile themselves the moment any scientific truth is distinctly ascertained. As the idea of nature enlarges, the idea of revelation also enlarges; it was a temporary misunderstanding which severed them. And as the knowledge of nature which is possessed by the few is communicated in its leading features at least to the many, they will receive it with a higher conception of the ways of God to man. It may hereafter appear as natural to the majority of mankind to see the providence of God in the order of the world, as it once was to appeal to interruptions of it.[76]

There is nothing here which would not have received Hale White's wholehearted intellectual assent, but his heart would have sunk at the absence of any expression of the *need* for a new faith. How to fill the emotional vacuum, the fear-filled emptiness, created by these amputating words? Jowett seemed to give no answer to Hale White's insistent question. And as the years passed, Hale White came to lose, not his respect for fact, but his respect for the instrument of reason alone in ascertaining fact. The sharp blade of reason could wound as well as heal; by itself it was the very instrument of negation, and its surgery alone was no substitute for the intuitive faith giving men inner resistance and a desire to live:

> Side by side with the reason there has always been in almost all nations, revelation. It is assumed that the conclusions of the reason are not sufficient. This assumption leads to all kinds of impostures, but, as a principle, there is truth in it. The results of what is usually called the reason require correction and a supplement by something which is not reason in the ordinary sense of the term. But it would be wrong to say that this something is contrary to reason or essentially a different faculty. It may be a method or process which is unusual or swifter than the customary processes or methods.[77]

This statement anticipates and introduces us to some of the attitudes we shall consider in the following chapters.

[76] *Essays and Reviews* (London, 1861), "On the Inspiration of Scripture," pp. 348–49.

[77] *L.P.*, pp. 264–65. See also *P.N.a.*, p. 14.

Chapter Four

NEW BIRTH

During his last year at Cheshunt and three years after his meaningless and hypocritical "conversion" at Bunyan Meeting, Hale White experienced a spiritual awakening which was both spontaneous and genuine. His first two years at college, he writes, had been "entirely external":

My heart was altogether untouched by anything I heard, read, or did, although I myself supposed that I took an interest in them.[1]

Unsatisfied with what he learned in the school, deprived of congenial friends within it, and restive under the narrow confines of a creed which fascinated while it oppressed him, he was preparing for revolt though hardly knowing it himself. His state of mind can be compared with that of Wordsworth as he crossed the flat middle ground between belief and disbelief in breaking with Godwin. The diseases peculiar to this area of experience Hale White knew intimately: they induce a hypochondriacal consciousness of illness but baffle attempts at diagnosis; they provoke a numbing dejection—"A grief without a pang, void, dark and drear"; and they heighten one's vulnerability to quack remedies. When one is in such a spiritual valley, he writes:

Hypochondriacal misery is apt to take an intellectual shape. The most hopeless metaphysics or theology which we happen to encounter fastens on us, and we mistake for an unbiased conviction the form which the disease assumes.[2]

This was written to explain Wordsworth's having "yielded up moral questions in despair"[3] recounted in *The Prelude*, but it undoubtedly fits Hale White's experience too.

As Hale White shared Wordsworth's experience of spiritual desolation, so also did he to a great extent discover through Wordsworth the way to escape from it. The escape came, not through unraveling metaphysical tangles, but through a new and almost explosive awakening. The following statement is one of the most significant self-revelations Hale White ever made:

But one day in my third year, a day I remember as well as Paul must have remembered afterwards the day on which he went to Damascus, I happened to find amongst a parcel of books a volume of poems in paper boards. It was called "Lyrical Ballads", and I read first one and then the whole book. It conveyed to me no new doctrine, and yet the change it wrought in me could only be compared with that which is said to have been wrought on Paul himself by the Divine apparition.

Looking over the "Lyrical Ballads" again, as I have looked over it a dozen times

[1] *A.*, p. 21.
[2] *M.P.*, p. 210.
[3] *Ibid.*, p. 211.

since then, I can hardly see what it was which stirred me so powerfully, nor do I believe that it communicated much to me which could be put in words. But it excited a movement and a growth which went on till, by degrees, all the systems which enveloped me like a body gradually decayed from me and fell away into nothing.[4]

In this important statement we are introduced to those forces of spiritual expansion, not derived from Wordsworth alone, which changed the whole direction of Hale White's life and which—though they had to be modified and calmed—never ceased to be operative. The seedtime for many of them was in the period shortly before his explusion:

> What days were those of the next few years before increasing age had presented preciser problems and demanded preciser answers; before all joy was darkened by the shadow of on-coming death, and when life seemed infinite! Those were the days when through the whole long summer's morning I wanted no companion but myself, provided only I was in the country, and when books were read with tears in the eyes.[5]

In this period of "new birth" negation took the form of affirmation—an affirmation which was by no means his final one, but which represented the first rapturous knowledge of the potent regenerating powers of romantic idealism. The writers and concepts contributing to this knowledge are our present concern.

Among the books devoured with such tearful enthusiasm at Cheshunt were, besides those of Wordsworth, samples of Goethe, Emerson, Byron, Coleridge, and, in particular, Carlyle. We cannot be certain that he read all these authors at this particular time, but he knew them all at an early period and through them received many of the basic concepts contributing to his spiritual awakening. It will repay us, before examining the nature of the awakening itself, to view what evidence is available of his early reading.

By his own statement we know that he was introduced to Goethe by his cousin, William Chignell, while he was still at Cheshunt,[6] and we have the further information from his second son that his "knowledge of German was thorough, and he had studied Goethe profoundly."[7] In *The Aberdeen Herald* of August 23, 1862, we find him maintaining that *Faust*, *Egmont*, and *Wilhelm Meister* had exercised an influence on the mind of Europe paralleled only by that of Bacon,[8] a statement suggesting that these were the books he read in the Hertfordshire fields. In later years, recollecting his visit to Weimar in 1862, Hale White answered his wife's question, "What do you think of him?" [Goethe] by saying: "You might just as well ask me, 'What do I think of the sea or the sky?'"[9] And we can add to

---

[4] *A.*, pp. 21–22.   [5] *Ibid.*, p. 23.   [6] *E.L.*, p. 55.

[7] *P.N.a.*, p. 8.

[8] Hale White's profound love of Bacon was doubtless inspired by Caleb Morris. See "Caleb Morris," *The British Weekly* (March 6, 1902), p. 532.

[9] *G.D.*, p. 318. Other references to Goethe are: *G.D.*, pp. 246, 318, 377, 388–89; *L.3F.*, pp. 147, 170, 173, 228, 278–79, 317, 332, 368; *P.J.*, pp. 133–48; *N.N.*, February 12, 1881; *B.N.B., passim.*

this evidence the statement by R. M. Theobald, one of the students expelled with Hale White, that

Hale White when he was expelled from New College was certainly very unorthodox. His favourite authors were Carlyle, Emerson, Goethe, and some other German authors.[10]

This statement provides the only evidence we have that he knew Emerson at this early date, but that he admired and read Emerson in later years is confirmed again and again in his writings. On April 25, 1873, he had an interview with him,[11] but the impulse for this visit long antedated the event. In 1846 the second volume of Emerson's *Essays* was published in Chapman's "Catholic Series" and in 1847 Emerson was lecturing in England on "Representative Men." Though Hale White in his newspaper articles makes more direct mention of the serene aspect of Emerson's face than of his work, we can gain some sense of Emerson's influence by such general statements as these:

I hear from Concord, United States, that Mr. Emerson is in good health, but he can no longer see to do any work. He was born in 1803. Carlyle was born in 1795 and Tennyson in 1809. When these three men shall have departed *absit omen*, the era—perhaps one of the greatest and brightest in literature for the English-speaking race—the era following the great French Revolution—will finally close. Byron, Shelley, Coleridge, Wordsworth have already gone; these three, Carlyle, Tennyson, and Emerson, who have altogether shaped the spiritual tendencies of thousands of us, are still here, and long may they remain.[12]

Hale White had been introduced to Byron long before leaving Bedford, and in the revolutionary printer of *The Revolution in Tanner's Lane*, Zachariah Coleman, we get a lover of Byron patterned after Hale White's own father, who as he "stood at the composing desk in his printing office . . . used to declaim Byron by heart."[13] In this period of new birth Byron's poetic message held for Hale White a fresh significance and a new power, as we shall presently see in more detail. Coleridge, of course, was met in the *Lyrical Ballads*, along with Wordsworth, and, though his metaphysics and later orthodoxy aroused Hale White's disaffection,[14] his

[10] *The Westminster Gazette*, March 17, 1913.

[11] The date of this visit has provoked considerable research. Herr Klinke demonstrated on pp. 64–66 of his thesis that the visit was on this date, and Dr. Smith confirms it by referring to Hale White's article in *The Birmingham Post* of the following day. Klinke never looked at the newspaper articles, hence the need for the heavy German scholarship. The evidence, briefly, is this: Mrs. D. V. White has a note dated April 24 (1873) from Emerson's secretary asking him to call at 9:30 the next morning. The newspaper articles confirm that the visit took place.

[12] *N.N.*, June 26, 1880. See also *N.N.*, December 31, 1881.

[13] *E.L.*, p. 37. See essay, "Byron, Goethe and Mr. Matthew Arnold," reprinted in *P.J.*, pp. 133–48.

[14] In a letter to his second son, John, dated October 16, 1893 (*P.L.*, p. 14), he said: "The Aids to Reflection are not Coleridge's best work. They are too theological. There is a seductive side to him against which it is always necessary to be on one's guard. 'The procreator of strange Centaure, spectral Puseyismus, monstrous illusory hybrids and ecclesiastical chimeres' [*sic*] was the immortal verdict of Carlyle and it is *true*. I like Coleridge best when he gets away from the Vernunft and Verstand and the Logos and his mediated

poetry—especially *Christabel* and *The Ancient Mariner*[15]—met with a deep response in him. There is a possibility that Hale White also knew his *Confessions of an Inquiring Spirit*, from which his father quotes in *To Think or Not to Think*, but this was not likely one of the books bringing tears to his eyes—at least not tears of joy.[16]

But of all these writers and poets, none was more surely a part of Hale White's experience of "new birth" than Carlyle. Hale White's life and work were saturated with the influence of this Victorian prophet. He bought the *Life of Sterling* on the day it was published in 1851,[17] and was awaiting eagerly the appearance of *Frederick* in August 1861.[18] In *The Groombridge Diary* Mrs. White gives the information that as a lad of nineteen he "devoured" the original volume of the *Latter Day Pamphlets*.[19] And in recounting the visit to Carlyle with his father in March 1868 he remembers the "howl of execration" the *Pamphlets* brought from the reviewers and his own "eager journey to the bookseller for each successive number."[20] In this same essay telling of the visit, Hale White writes of Carlyle's influence on his early life in much the same ecstatic vein that he applied to Wordsworth:

I remembered what Carlyle was to the young men of thirty or forty years ago, in the days of that new birth, which was so strange a characteristic of the time. His books were read with excitement, with tears of joy, on lonely hills, by the seashore and in London streets, and the readers were thankful that it was their privilege to live when he also was alive.[21]

Nor should we forget that it was Carlyle through *Heroes and Hero Worship* and *Sartor Resartus* who wrought that "expansion" in William White which finally pushed him out of the church. Though Hale White's "renascence of wonder" was made possible by the combined influence of all these romantic idealists, Carlyle's power over him remained longest and was the most pervasive. Hale White's final statement is unqualified:

Carlyle remains to me—this is my now irreversible verdict on him—the voice which in our century came from the deepest depths. In nobody do I find the immovable rock as I find it in him.[22]

German metaphysics. One arrowy word on a play of Shakespeare has more *Vernunft* in it to me than all his Kantian-Schellingian disquisitions on the faculty itself."

[15] See "September, 1798," *P.J.*, pp. 105–8.

[16] Other references by Hale White to Coleridge are: *P.J.*, pp. 99–109; *L.P.*, p. 169; *M.P.*, pp. 190–95; *L.3F.*, pp. 90, 92, 117, 163, 174, 183; *G.D.*, pp. 28, 46, 97, 169, 216, 465, 466, 479; Introduction to Carlyle's *Life of Sterling*, pp. x–xii; in Hutchinson correspondence, 1896–1907, now in the Brotherton Library, Leeds.

[17] *N.N.*, February 19, 1881.

[18] *A.H.*, August 17, 1861. Other references to Carlyle in newspaper articles are: *A.H.*, March 28, 1863, August 1, 1863, August 8, 1863, March 11, 1865, November 18, 1865, December 16, 1865, November 26, 1870; *N.N.*, November 20, 1875, June 26, 1880, February 12, 1881, February 19, 1881.

[19] *G.D.*, p. 190.

[20] *P.J.*, "A Visit to Carlyle in 1868," p. 2.

[21] *Ibid.*, p. 12.

[22] *L.3F.*, p. 107. During the American Civil War, however, Hale White strongly opposed Carlyle's support of slavery. See *A.H.*, August 8, 1863.

What was the message that these authors brought? It would be futile to attempt tracing their influence individually, for they were all caught up in a single idealist tendency in Hale White and cannot be disentangled. Moreover, Hale White is usually much more explicit in telling us *who* contributed to his spiritual changes than in how they contributed. But the spiritual awakening itself had certain dominant and recognizable characteristics which we need to understand, and which can only be illustrated by reference to these writers. Wordsworth provided the first loosening of the mortar holding him to the old church and creed, but these others helped in sustaining and clarifying this new vision when the first flush of enthusiasm had cooled. One may say that the awakening itself was characterized by three changes in habits of belief: (1) a new sense of the immanence of God or of a divine spirit in the material world and in the lives of men; (2) a development or accentuation of a habit of inner reference which directed to the conscience or intuitive faculty those moral and spiritual problems formerly solved by external authority; and (3) a trust in the unifying power of emotion, or energy, or vitality. Those three articles of faith were in reality of one piece, but we can see them most clearly by giving them separate emphasis.

The idea that an infinite something existed and was at work in the visible world, and not apart or remote from it, was, of course, a fundamental presupposition of most of the romantics. Wordsworth described it as

> A motion and a spirit that impels
> All thinking things, all objects of all thought,
> And rolls through all things;

and Carlyle as the "Divine Idea," interpenetrating the outer vestments of man and society, and making the Universe in truth the "living garment of God." The romantic rebellion against fixed orthodoxies, political as well as religious, had as one of its most significant results (or causes?) a transference of value and meaning from externals to internals, from the transcendent to the immanent, from dogma to experience. The divine presence was within man and the natural order and not outside them, and he who would find God needed as church and priest and sacrament only an open heart and a sensitively tuned spirit. Religious institutions were not necessarily repudiated, but they were no longer, to many of the romantics, the essential clearinghouses of man's spiritual life. Such a faith, obviously, could provide succor for the rebel already separated from orthodoxy, but it could also—by providing substitute channels of belief—encourage and prompt such rebellion, be heresy itself. But whatever form the faith might take or whatever its possible effects, it involved a fundamental change of emphasis: from theology to psychology, from authority to self-discovery, from miracle to nature.

In exactly what form Hale White made this emphasis in his own religious life it is hard to say; he never abandoned the term God in favor of

spirit, force, idea, tendency, or any of the other more scientific words often
employed by his teachers; but it is certain that he caught something of the
same vision. In the passage describing the effect of the *Lyrical Ballads*
upon him he writes:

There is, of course, a definite explanation to be given of one effect produced by the
"Lyrical Ballads." God is nowhere formally deposed, and Wordsworth would have
been the last man to say that he had lost his faith in the God of his fathers. But his
real God is not the God of the Church, but the God of the hills, the abstraction Nature,
and to this my reverence was transferred. Instead of an object of worship which was
altogether artificial, remote, never coming into genuine contact with me, I now had one
which I thought to be real, one in which literally I could live and move and have my
being, an actual fact present before my eyes. God was brought from that heaven of
the books, and dwelt on the downs in the far-away distances, and in every cloud-
shadow which wandered across the valley. Wordsworth unconsciously did for me
what every religious reformer has done—he re-created my Supreme Divinity; substi-
tuting a new and living spirit for the old deity, once alive, but gradually hardened into
an idol.[23]

Through Wordsworth Hale White first came to feel a sense of the
"miraculous inherent in the commonplace," and to see through the "film
of familiarity" to the spiritual life and meaning inhering in everyday
things.[24] And this led him, not merely to a deep and reverent love of
nature, but, like Wordsworth, to a romantic idealization of the virtues of
commonplace people. We say "romantic idealization" because he had, in
reality, no deep love of the common people in their commonness, and he
was always a democrat more on principle than in spirit; but in his novels
we are frequently introduced to those rocky natural forms like Mrs. Joll of
Miriam's Schooling who, in their elemental simplicity, declare their own
salvation.[25]

A rude, stout, hard person, we say, was Mrs. Joll, fond of her beer, rather grimy, given
to quarrel a little with her husband, could use strong language at times, had the defects
which might be supposed to arise from constant traffic with the inhabitants of the
Borough, and was utterly unintelligent so far as book learning went. Nevertheless
she was well read in departments more important perhaps than books in the conduct
of human life, and in her there was the one thing needful—the one thing which, if
ever there is to be a Judgment Day, will put her on the right hand;[26] when all sorts
of scientific people, religious people, students of poetry, people with exquisite emotions,
will go on the left and be damned everlastingly.

Though Hale White would not claim the same election for the people of
his chapel at Ditchling and though, we suspect, he would not have been
happy for one day in such a household as Mrs. Joll kept, he could, ideally,
see in such people the immanent manifestation of a divine spirit. Like the
stars, the sea, and the sky she derived her virtue from the essential unity

23 *A.*, pp. 22–23.
24 See *P.J.*, p. 107.
25 *M.S.*, p. 107.
26 These Hebrew old clothes persisted in Hale White's vocabulary even though he
held no literal belief in the symbolism.

of her nature and from the refreshing simplicity of being of one elemental pattern. Mrs. Lane of the *Autobiography* was almost of the same family. She, more sensitively tuned than Mrs. Joll, achieved an almost Goethean tolerance and disinterestedness toward the affairs of the world by quietly living in harmony with the universal, by seeing the petty things of life in their ordered proportion:

At all points her path was her own, intersecting at every conceivable angle the paths of her acquaintances, and never straying along them except just so far as they might happen to be hers. . . . the world of books in which I lived was almost altogether shut to her, but yet she was the only person in the village whose conversation was lifted out of the petty and personal into the region of the universal.[27]

Hale White later modified many of the concepts he received from Wordsworth and the other romantics, but this habit of believing that at the core of every human personality lay an unmodified spiritual essence never left him. It was the germ lending hope to his search for a religion of experience, and it also fed his bitterness and despair, for how many there were who never saw this inner light!

To Hale White, such people as Mrs. Joll or Mrs. Lane were, in the age in which he lived, rare and isolated. Not only in the high noon of his romantic new birth, but throughout his life, Hale White found the great elemental forces of nature more easy of approach than human beings, more certain to be there when he needed them, more generous in revealing their spiritual heart. Introverted and ingrown as he was, he seems often to have used nature as a substitute for human companionship and, if we may borrow Newton P. Stallknecht's terms, his new birth even in its first flush was based partly on a philosophy of "self-defence" rather than on one of "self-confidence."[28] George Allen of *The Revolution in Tanner's Lane* found, when all else had failed, that nature was his truest friend and most effective physician:

There is one religious teacher, however, which seldom fails those who are in health, and, at last, did not fail him. He was helped by no priest and by no philosophy; but Nature helped him, the beneficent Power which heals the burn or scar and covers it with new skin.[29]

The God of the hills, though Hale White could never define exactly what he or Wordsworth meant by it, always remained in some sense a reality for him long after the heat of his first enthusiasm had passed. "I believe that mind never worships anything but mind," he writes in the *Autobiography*, "and that you worship it when you admire the level bars of cloud over the setting sun."[30] And again, in agreement with Coleridge, "If the supernatural becomes natural and the natural becomes supernatural,

27 *A.*, pp. 120–21.
28 Newton P. Stallknecht, "Tragic Flaw in Wordsworth's Philosophy," in *Wordsworth and Coleridge* (Princeton, 1939), p. 55.
29 *R.T.L.*, p. 244.
30 *A.*, p. 104.

the world regains its splendour and charm."[31] Natural-supernaturalism in its pietistic aspects made a strong appeal to Hale White, for it allowed him to indulge his scientific passion for hard facts while enriching them with religious meanings and suggestions. The following are some of Hale White's most characteristic statements, and can be found in any period of his life and work:

The Infinite fascinates us and we call it God, but in reality God is the Finite. The Infinite as Infinite is nothing.[32]

And again:

Man is the revelation of the Infinite, and it does not become finite in him. It remains the Infinite.[33]

But serious metaphysics probably played little part in Hale White's nature worship. His longing for the infinite was a longing for personal security more than for a reasonable explanation of the universe. He loved the beauties of natural forms and colors mainly because he found in them certain restorative powers—objectifications, perhaps, of beauties he desired to find in himself. And this simple emotional response to nature has inspired some of Hale White's finest prose. Those small essays on the seasons in *Pages from a Journal* and pieces like "An Afternoon Walk in October"—both products of old age—have lavished on them a tender delicacy and a passionate restraint which betray a love of natural things intensified, rather than diminished, in the passage of fifty years. He was a profound admirer of Richard Jefferies and much of their descriptive writing has almost precisely the same touch.[34] It was the product not merely of a disciplined talent but of a disciplined habit of reverence—an instrument tooled as a kind of prayer for searching out virtue in the commonplace and divinity in the subtle passages of experience. It was primarily to Wordsworth that he was indebted for this habit of reverence, and for the descriptive impulse springing from it.

The modern love of scenery was not known in Cowfold, and still less was that worship of landscape and nature known which . . . is peculiar to the generation born under the influence of Wordsworth.[35]

But though Hale White was fortunately so born, he does not express his love of nature only in precious prose poems or in descriptions of landscapes. The muscularity of his talent is revealed in such passages as the following, where he is describing the longing of lonely city-pent people,

---

[31] "September 1798," *P.J.*, p. 108.

[32] *L.P.*, p. 283. See also *G.D.*, pp. 139–40

[33] *M.P.*, p. 251. In *M.P.*, p. 240, he says it is "strangely limited by that which is finite and personal." He believed that human love was based, essentially, on the recognition of this infinite something in another. Thus human love became a link with God.

[34] See *L.3F.*, pp. 36–38, 43. See also *L.P.*, p. 314.

[35] *R.T.L.*, p. 165.

like Caillaud and Pauline of the *Revolution*, for the small evidences of "nature" penetrating the smoky alleys of the man-made town:

The workroom faced the north, and was exactly on a level with an innumerable multitude of red chimney-pots pouring forth stinking smoke which, for the six winter months, generally darkened the air during the whole day. But occasionally Nature resumed her rights, and it was possible to feel that sky, stars, sun, and moon still existed, and were not blotted out by the obscurations of what is called civilised life. There came, occasionally, wild nights in October or November, with a gale from the south-west, and then, when almost everybody had gone to bed and the fires were out, the clouds, illuminated by the moon, rushed across the heavens, and the Great Bear hung over the dismal waste of smutty tiles with the same solemnity with which it hangs over the mountain, the sea, or the desert. Early in the morning, too, in summer, between three and four o'clock in June, there were sights to be seen worth seeing. The distance was clear for miles, and the heights of Highgate were visible, proclaiming the gospel of a beyond and beyond even to Kent's Court, and that its immediate surroundings were mercifully not infinite.[36]

But this concept of the universal realizing itself in the particular, the immaterial in the material, the infinite in the finite, was not necessarily derived only from Wordsworth—who illustrated it in his poetry—or from Coleridge and Carlyle, who in various ways explained it and made it part of a philosophical scheme. Hale White was himself a good German scholar and had, according to his second son, read both Kant and Hegel.[37] Though he professed to eschew metaphysics as "a path which leads to madness,"[38] he could, writes his son, "no more escape from the urge towards philosophical enquiry than a bird can help flying."[39] And we may be sure that the *philosophical* premise underlying his experience of "new birth" received at an early stage his devout attention. In *The Norfolk News* for April 8, 1882, Hale White spoke of his friend, James Hutchison Stirling, the author of *The Secret of Hegel* and the *Text-Book to Kant* as the "man who, more than any other, has made us acquainted with the thought of Kant and Hegel." These could very well have been his own textbooks. In his *John Bunyan*, Hale White quotes at some length from *The Critique of Pure Reason*, following it with a significant claim that "Kant has regained that reverence which the Puritan felt for something supernatural," for that "necessary connexion of the infinite with ourselves."[40]

---

[36] *Ibid.*, p. 43.
[37] *P.N.a.*, p. 11.
[38] *A.*, p. 127. Spoken by a fictional character, but with obvious approval.
[39] *P.N.a.*, p. 14.
[40] *B.*, p. 244. Quotation on pp. 242–44. Hale White also profoundly admired Kant's *Über Pädagogik*. In a letter to his son, John, dated March 21, 1899 (*P.L.*, p. 29), he wrote: "Of one thing I am sure that if the Pädagogik could be made a manual and could be acted on, the world in thirty years would be a place to be left with much more regret than I shall leave it when my time comes."

It is noteworthy that A. W. Benn in *The History of English Rationalism in the Nineteenth Century* (London, 1906), II, 399, criticizes Dr. Stirling's *The Secret of Hegel* severely. Stirling made such remarks as these in the book: "Kant and Hegel have no object but to restore Faith—Faith in God—Faith in the immortality of the Soul and the Freedom of the Will—nay, Faith in Christianity as the Revealed Religion—and that, too, in perfect harmony with the Right of Private Judgment." Writes Benn: "That Kant

Two things fill the mind with ever new and increasing admiration and awe, the oftener and the more steadily we reflect on them: *the starry heavens above and the moral law within*. I have not to search for them and conjecture them as though they were veiled in darkness or were in the transcendent region beyond my horizon; I see them before me and connect them directly with the consciousness of my existence. The former begins from the place I occupy in the external world of sense, and enlarges my connexion therein to an unbounded extent with worlds upon worlds and systems of systems, and moreover into limitless times of their periodic motion, its beginning and continuance. The second begins from my invisible self, my personality, and exhibits me in a world which has true infinity, but which is traceable only by the understanding, and with which I discern that I am not in a merely contingent, but in a universal and necessary connexion, as I am also thereby with all those visible worlds. The former view of a countless multitude of worlds annihilates as it were my importance as an *animal creature*, which, after it has been for a short time provided with vital power, one knows not how, must again give back the matter of which it was formed to the planet it inhabits (a mere speck in the universe). The second, on the contrary, infinitely elevates my worth as an *intelligence* by my personality, in which the moral law reveals to me a life independent on animality and even on the whole sensible world, at least so far as may be inferred from the destination assigned to my existence by this law, a destination not restricted to conditions and limits of this life, but reaching into the infinite.

The concept described here, with its psychological and cosmological implications, was a discovery Hale White made (like many of the early romantics) in his own experience and for which he found his own terms. In his novels the "starry heavens above" and the "moral law within" are the two forces operating with dramatic effectiveness upon his characters. But these characters are not Kantians; they are simply people like Hale White himself who had been infected with romantic aspirations and who found, experientially, this explanation for them. Hale White doubtless read Kant long after he had learned all Kant had to teach him, but it is not without significance that he knew this source book of romantic idealism.

Though his second son says that Hale White lamented the time he had "wasted"[41] on Hegel, there are almost unmistakable evidences in his novels of Hegelian language and thought. We can profitably view them here, not only because they show how the idea of divine immanence was extended and developed in Hale White's thinking, but because they tell us something of the way he applied this idea to his reading of the Bible as well as of Nature. The German thinkers following Kant's lead, notably Fichte, Schelling, and Hegel, all dealt in one way or another with the problem of the Incarnation. They were all necessarily concerned with the manner in which the human and the divine achieved union, and with explaining the supreme example of such a union in the person of Christ. Hegel, of course, went a step further than these others and explained the union in terms of an historical process analogous to the Christian idea of the Trinity: "God

---

and Hegel . . . had hopelessly failed to convince their own countrymen of those dogmas does not seem to have at all shaken their Scottish interpreter's confidence in their ability to convince the unbelieving portion of the British public." It is not, however, difficult to understand why this interpretation would have appealed to Hale White.

41 *P.N.a.*, p. 11.

the Father is God as He is in Himself eternally. God the Son is God objectified in nature and history . . . God the Spirit is the finite returning to the infinite, God taking back . . . His otherness into His own being again."[42] God and the universe being essential to each other, the one unable to exist without the other, Incarnation was, naturally, a vital element to the life of both.[43]

Since the whole process of the finite is the channel through which the life of the Absolute flows, it may be said that incarnation is the very *raison d'être* of God's existence. But Christianity does not speak of incarnation in general, but of a unique act of incarnation in the Person of Christ. How does Hegel deal with the problem of the historical Jesus? He argues that man is conscious of division and alienation from God, and craves for reconciliation. Though he is essentially one with God, he requires sensible proof of the fact. Hence arises the necessity for an atonement manifested in sensuous form. The God-man Jesus dies for men in order to demonstrate to them their oneness with God.

Just how seriously Hale White took this conception we cannot tell. But in his search for a "human" religion, for a faith based on experience instead of revelation—combined with his love of the Gospel story—Hegel could have seemed to save what was best in both worlds. If the Incarnation was simply the supreme flowering in the person of Christ of that *Idea* which existed in the composition of all men and all matter, then one could indeed by searching find out God. Then one could, after Thomas a Kempis, realize the "imitation" of Christ as an actual fact. The *Imitation of Christ* was the book Zachariah Coleman read to George Allen, and the thoughts it evoked found expression in Hegelian terminology:

He turned over the leaves again—"*He to whom the Eternal Word speaketh is delivered from a world of unnecessary conceptions.*" Zachariah bent his head near him and gently expounded the texts. As the exposition grew George's heart dilated, and he was carried beyond his troubles. It was the birth in him—even in him, a Cowfold ironmonger, not a scholar by any means—of what philosophers call *the idea,* that Incarnation which has ever been our Redemption.[44]

And again in the *Deliverance* Hale White describes how faith in the realizable *Idea* is sustained by Christ's example.[45]

In the Gospel of Luke, also, Mrs. Butts read that she was to hope for nothing again from her love,[46] and that she was to be merciful, as her Father in heaven is merciful. That is really the expression of the *idea* in morality, and incalculable is the blessing that our great religious teacher should have been bold enough to teach the idea, and not any limitation of it. . . . He always trusted it; He did not deal in exceptions;

---

[42] Storr, *Development of Theology*, p. 213.

[43] *Ibid.*, pp. 213–14. In *B.N.B.*, p. 12, Hale White writes: "Suppose . . . we could consider Christ's expiation mythologically; we should be awe-struck by the idea of a super-Divine justice which must be satisfied; for the Justice which demands the sacrifice of Christ is obviously something which God himself cannot resist, something *above* Him."

[44] *R.T.L.*, p. 229.

[45] *D.*, pp. 63–64.

[46] Spinoza's words, "Whoso truly loves God must not expect God to love him in return" had been quoted by Goethe in his *Autobiography* and found frequent re-expression from both sources in Hale White's letters and novels. See *G.D.*, p. 118, and *R.T.L.*, p. 100. See also F. Pollock, *Spinoza: His Life and Philosophy* (London, 1880), p. 369.

He relied on it to the uttermost, never despairing. This has always seemed to me to be the real meaning of the word faith. It is permanent confidence in the idea, a confidence never to be broken down by apparent failure, or by examples by which ordinary people prove that qualification is necessary. It was precisely because Jesus taught the idea, and nothing below it, that He had such authority over a soul like my friend's, and the effect produced by Him could not have been produced by anybody nearer to ordinary humanity.

We have already quoted from the dispute between Mark Rutherford and Mardon in the *Autobiography* where we found a similar statement: "What the four evangelists recorded was eternally true, and the Christ-idea was true whether it was ever incarnated or not in a being bearing His name."[47]

Now, as we have before emphasized, these ideas may or may not have been Hegelian in origin—he could have received much the same notion from Schleiermacher, for example—but we can be quite sure that Hale White did not stop at a mere intuitive appreciation of this germinal idea. His early training had made him too eager for explanations of religious experience, and too accustomed to connecting divine events to a system of redemption and retribution. He was, however, no philosopher. He thought more in terms of symbols than in terms of ideas; his religion was rather the explanation of *felt* needs than a consideration of the whole human problem; and when it achieved universality it was because, in the depth of his own experience, he found a deeply representative microcosm. In the *Autobiography* he writes:

I was always singularly feeble in laying hold of an idea, and in the ability to compel myself to dwell upon a thing for any lengthened period in continuous exhaustive reflection. But, nevertheless, ideas would frequently lay hold of *me* with such relentless tenacity that I was passive in their grasp.[48]

And we may be certain that the idea of divine immanence which led to his love of nature and his appreciation of the infinite in particular humanity came to him variously through the sources we have indicated, and served him variously in creating a "human" religion. But, as we shall gradually see, this knowledge also gave him a certain sense of superiority to his less perceptive neighbors, a new sense of "election" to spiritual eminence, which fed a damning pride that nearly destroyed him. The heavy hand of Calvinism and of Puritanism remained on him, and his youthful leap into the empyrean—though he always looked on it with favor[49]—brought soon afterward a return into something very like the dark place from which he had issued.

A second part of Hale White's new birth—one intimately involved in the first and already suggested—is indicated by him in that crucial passage from which we have already quoted:

Of more importance . . . than the decay of systems was the birth of a habit of inner reference and a dislike to occupy myself with anything which did not in some way

---

[47] *A.*, p. 60.   [48] *Ibid.*, p. 90.   [49] See *A.*, p. 23, and *C.F.*, p. 124.

or other touch the soul, or was not the illustration or embodiment of some spiritual law.[50]

When one has lost the support of external dogma, or is losing it, he almost inevitably will try to believe more in himself, and to discover in the conscience or intuition some inward monitor to replace the authority of the creed. Hale White had not, of course, come to Wordsworth with this faculty undeveloped, but he had never before been given such an opportunity to use it. The Bedford Calvinism he had known encouraged rather a blind conformity to dead forms than that moral individualism Puritanism had once encouraged; but here, under this new dispensation, every man was once again called upon to be his own priest. And Hale White developed these habits of introspection into something like a fine art. Joan of Arc,[51] George Fox,[52] John Wesley,[53] and Father Tyrrell[54] are only a few of the people he admired because they had experienced that transfer of faith from an outer church or creed to an inner light; but none of them had developed the habit of instinctive perception more perfectly than his aunt, Mrs. Elizabeth Street. In the *Letter* written on her death, he describes the processes of training and discipline which brought the faculty to perfection:

I used to wonder at her instinctive perception in difficult cases of the proper thing to be done; especially where any relationship of persons was involved. It was swifter than any reasoning process, and much more accurate. Her ability to arrive at this instinctive perception was due to primary genius, but also to constant loyalty to previous perceptions. It is an undeniable law of nature, that by faithfully doing the thing which we see proper to be done, we come to see more keenly next time what is proper to be done; and by not doing it, we lose altogether the power of discerning it. Especially is this true of all the finer gifts of the soul, and if a man be loyal and faithful, he will in time possess an instantaneous oracle, which will seldom fail him. Nothing is easier than to reason it down. You must be perfectly still to hear it, and although it has a divine commission, it yields if you remonstrate with it, and seems a mere idle phantom or disappears altogether. People will tell you that by this doctrine prejudice is preached; and that by it all the follies of the bigot can be justified. It is altogether untrue. Because the voice may be simulated, it is no proof that it has no authority, and everybody who has listened to it, knows well enough that he can distinguish between it and any meaner suggestions. I observed that continually your aunt . . . came at last to say "you ought" when other people would say "it would be better." This was significant, because it showed that the more refined indications of what was becoming and beautiful had acquired the sanction of law and conscience.[55]

This was, essentially, what other romantics referred to as "reason" or "imaginative faith," but Hale White's expression of it contains a coloring from Quakerism and no little admixture of his own Puritan insistence on the absolute in disciplined veracity. Few aspects of his

[50] *A.*, p. 22.
[51] *L.P.*, pp. 214–18.
[52] *B.N.B.*, pp. 6, 10.
[53] *Ibid.*, pp. 69–71.
[54] *L.3F.*, pp. 236–37, 240, 257, 285, 287.
[55] *A Letter Written on the Death of Mrs. Elizabeth Street* (London, 1877), pp. 12–13.

thought show a more subtle blending of Puritanism and Romanticism than this: here was an inner monitor mysterious, oracular, nonrational in its working, yet less the fruit of original genius than the final reward of arduous self-discipline and moral probity. While it could provide an entrance into mystical experience, it does not seem to have been valued primarily for this purpose, but as a monitor for ethical conduct; while, to borrow Koestler's terms, it was a faculty to be envied by a yogi, it was employed for the purposes of a commissar. As we shall see in the next chapter, Hale White never learned to trust in himself or his own intuitions to the perfect degree his aunt did,[56] but the achievement of such an ideal was his persistent ambition, and in many of his novels he studied with great insight the psychological difficulties of acquiring such self-confidence. The inner drama of many of his heroines can almost be said to revolve around E. A. Robinson's words:

> . . . That was the curse prepared
> For me: I would not listen to my voices.
>
> (*The Glory of the Nightingales*, Pt. V.)

Moral election is usually reserved for those who do so listen, and Catharine Furze, for example, is finally saved by following her inner light. But part of the tragedy of her childhood lay in the fact that she had never been "shaped" by her own particular daemon or genius; she had never been given the help of Wordsworth in channeling her habits of inner reference into constructive lines of action. Wordsworth, writes Hale White,

. . . would have turned much that was vague in her into definite shape; it would have enabled her to recognise herself; it would have given an orthodox expression to cloudy singularity, and she would have seen that she was a part of humanity in her most extravagant and personal emotions.[57]

"An orthodox expression to cloudy singularity" was part of the vital contribution Wordsworth, for one, also made to Hale White; he seized at the very opportunity poor Catharine had lacked. Deprived of outer guides, bewildered and revolted by the discordant voices of philosophies, sects, and creeds, he welcomed this new sanction for trusting his own conscience—for finding in the simple clear voice of emotionally charged instinct a substitute for dogma. The perfection of this inner monitor was a way of synthesizing a fragmented personality by a single act of faith rather than by rules. "Oh, what a privilege it is to meet with anybody who is controlled into unity, whose actions are all directed by one consistent force!"[58] he writes in *Catharine Furze*, and we can almost believe he had his Aunt Street in mind as he wrote it.

---

56 See *B.N.B.*, p. 95.

57 *C.F.*, p. 126. Hale White says "a book" and not Wordsworth, but from the context Wordsworth is clearly indicated.

58 *C.F.*, p. 71. See also "Ourselves," *M.P.*, p. 177.

Though in his own life Hale White's habit of inner reference some-times brought only a bitter return into the dark cul-de-sac of his own personality instead of an entrance to the bright avenue of faith, he held extravagant claims for moral individualism throughout his novels:

It is much more important to believe earnestly that something is morally right than that it should be really right, and he who attempts to displace a belief runs a certain risk, because he is not sure that what he substitutes can be held with equal force. Besides, each person's belief, or proposed course of action, is a part of himself, and if he be diverted from it and takes up with that which is not himself, the unity of his nature is impaired, and he loses himself.[59]

There is much in Hale White's faith in this intuitive sense reminding us of Newman's "Illative Sense," that faculty by which certainty is reached without logical proof, and by which conclusions can be held defying logical demonstration. In his *Black Notebook* he writes, for example:

We want some word to express a condition for which not only "belief," but "assent" or even "acquiescence" are too strong, a condition in which something is undoubtingly *taken on* or assumed to be our own without any mental *act* whatever.[60]

And again in his short story, "Michael Trevanion," he gently circum-navigates Newman's position and describes once more his faith in a fac-ulty which can yield, not definitions, but a certainty above and stronger than proof:

Mere assent is nothing; the question of importance is whether the figuration of the creed is dull or vivid—as vivid as the shadows of a June sun on a white house. Bril-liance of impression is not altogether dependent on mere processes of proof, and a faultless logical demonstration of something which is of eternal import may lie utterly uninfluential and never disturb us.[61]

A supporting element in this individualism based on intuitive self-knowledge was a faith, which Hale White shared with most of the roman-tics, in the power of emotion to purify and ennoble. John Hale-White writes that "emotion, in him, ensued upon intellectual conviction, either reasoned, or intuitive,"[62] but in many spheres of experience he seems, like Keats or Hazlitt, to have trusted to the *intensity* of emotion as a criterion of truth. He writes in the *Autobiography*, "Passion may burn like a devouring flame; and in a few moments, like flame, may bring down a temple to dust and ashes, but it is earnest as flame, and essentially pure."[63] We have already seen that those who could treat the Bible dis-passionately were regarded by him as little better than profaners, and we shall increasingly see that the presence of deeply felt, controlled emo-

---

[59] *C.H.*, p. 107.
[60] *B.N.B.*, p. 51. Again in *B.N.B.*, p. 64, he says: "No man can understand a religion unless he has believed it. I have been struck with this truth when I have listened to sincere Roman Catholics."
[61] *M.S.*, p. 161. See also *A.*, p. 105.
[62] *P.N.a.*, p. 13.
[63] *A.*, p. 21.

tion was for him a critical touchstone by which, to a great extent, poetry, men, politics, and religion were alike judged. Vitality, strength, passion— when these three combined in a man or a poem, all shortcomings could be forgiven. "Vitality means passion," claimed Hale White, and because of this fact he pardoned, for example, the indiscretions of David with Bathsheba in the Bible story, and even saw in the contradictions of David's personality evidences of his greatness.[64]

"Great minds are never wrong but in consequence of being right . . . ,"[65] he quotes approvingly from Coleridge, and Hale White was particularly drawn to Byron and Carlyle because they evidenced to a supreme degree the passionate vitality and strength of great men. In his essay, "Byron, Goethe, and Mr. Matthew Arnold," he writes:

Energy, power, is the one thing after which we pine in this sickly age. We do not want carefully and consciously constructed poems of mosaic. Strength is what we need and what will heal us. Strength is true morality, and true beauty.[66]

And again he voices this belief in "The Morality of Byron's Poetry":

We do not understand how moral it is to yield unreservedly to enthusiasm, to the impression which great objects would fain make upon us, and to embody that impression in worthy language.[67]

In a general way, Hale White believed that an age of vitality and energy, prophets and heroes, strong loves and hates was, because of these things, healthy and righteous, and that an age of compromise and cold reason was decadent. They were not only symptoms of an inner health; they were largely that health itself. "It is supposed that truth lies in the mean. More often perhaps it lies in the extremes. The worship of the mean is real idolatry."[68] He deplored the fact that Tory and Whig in the House of Commons could, after being bitter enemies in the Chamber, let their hatred evaporate in a handshake afterward: "Blessed is love, less blessed is hatred, but thrice accursed is that indifference which is neither one nor the other, the muddy mess which men call friendship."[69]

And this same prejudice is extended into the realm of personal life. In the *Autobiography*, for example, where he is describing Mark Rutherford's futile love for Mary Mardon, he clearly emphasizes that it is better to have loved and lost:

It was a hopeless love, but to be in love hopelessly is more akin to sanity than careless, melancholy indifference to the world.[70]

With such a dedication to a "hopeless love" one can satisfy both a romantic taste for the absolute and the Puritan's conviction that life is a vale of tears. One can be at once great in aspiration and noble in failure. Hale

64 *C.F.*, p. 95.   65 *M.P.*, p. 250.
66 *P.J.*, p. 147. First published in *The Contemporary Review* (August 1881).
67 *P.J.*, p. 130.
68 *B.N.B.*, p. 54. See also *R.T.L.*, p. 40.
69 *D.*, p. 11.   70 *A.*, p. 116.

White persistently and cruelly demanded both experiences of himself simultaneously, and the result was in part that bifurcation of his character we have already noted. But if half of one's philosophy involves a faith in the efficacy of passion for its own sake, that faith cannot be expressed in tempered or qualified terms, and in many of his statements Hale White betrays a love of excess that found small expression in his real life. Sorrow was good, for when shared, it "welds souls,"[71] and even avarice had things to recommend it:

The strongest characters are those which are most strongly motived. Motives are strength and willing without motives (if such a thing be possible) is weakness. But is then an avaricious man strong? Certainly so far as this one passion goes. There is no condition more painful than that in which motives do not operate.[72]

Few men have lived more bitterly than Hale White with the knowledge that they were timid and withdrawn. Lacking the courage of his own emotions, he often vented his frustration by favoring extremes—love or hate, full life or absolute death—and condemning all tepid moods as cowardly and evil. Nothing was worse than being a "prey of reasons,"[73] the melancholy victim of one's own indecision. He was drawn to people who, like himself, "had in some form or other an enthusiastic stage in their history,"[74] and such characters in his books always receive the most sympathetic treatment. Catharine Furze, for example,

. . . was one of those creatures whose life is not uniform from sixteen to sixty, a simple progressive accumulation of experiences, the addition of a ring of wood each year. There had come a time to her when she had suddenly opened. The sun shone with new light, a new lustre lay on river and meadow, the stars became something more than mere luminous points in the sky, she asked herself strange questions . . . This phenomenon of a new birth is more often seen at some epochs than at others. When a nation is stirred by any religious movement it is common, but it is also common in a different shape during certain periods of spiritual activity, such as the latter part of the eighteenth century and the first half of the nineteenth in England and Germany.[75]

And, having known in his own period of "new birth" precisely this experience, he lets some of the characters of his novels entertain the hope of welding not only individual souls, but a whole society by the sudden spreading of inspiration.

M'Kay had been brought up upon the Bible. He had before him, not only there, but in the history of all great religious movements, a record of the improvement of the human race . . . not merely by gradual civilisation, but by inspiration spreading itself suddenly.[76]

The instinctive outpouring of the divine spirit! The transformation of men and society by a blaze of righteousness! It was a great vision

[71] *Ibid.*, p. 161.
[72] *B.N.B.*, p. 43.
[73] *R.T.L.*, p. 40. "A sane, strong person is not the prey of reasons. . . ."
[74] *A.*, p. 23.   [75] *C.F.*, p. 124.   [76] *D.*, p. 24.

and one which could, in uneasy fashion, be accommodated both to the Puritan's dedication to high causes and the romantic's faith in passionate aspiration. But Hale White was only half a romantic, and as increasing age brought "preciser problems" and demanded "preciser answers,"[77] he was forced to qualify—sadly and slowly—the enthusiastic idealism of his "new birth."

But again and again throughout his life the old passionate dream reasserts itself, and the old fire brightens in a momentary glow. While he never saw society regenerated, he did to a degree find the dream realized in his personal life in his very last years. In knowing and loving the woman who became his second wife he had probably the deepest religious experience of his life.

My love of God, I speak it with reverence, is the love of Dorothy. I do not mean altogether that. What shall we call the emotion with which on a spring morning, early, we watch Venus rise out of the silent sea? Love of beauty! Nothing more?[78]

Thus he knew a "new birth" on the very eve of his death, and this was merely the most conspicuous of his many turnings back, recapitulations, of these experiences we are trying to see in terms of a "progress." But this last was an "Indian Summer" love and one which was made possible to no small degree by the almost superhuman patience of a devoted woman. And one suspects, after reading *The Groombridge Diary*, that Hale White—closing a lifetime strewn with the wrecks of shattered ideals— could scarcely believe that what he had dreamed of and hoped for all these years could thus be actually coming true.

Powerful though his romantic impulses were, Hale White made an early acquaintance with that despair which comes from seeking absolutes too insistently. For him, writes his second son, "every conquest of Science, every creation of Literature and Art, every heroism of conduct became an additional revelation."[79] But to seek the "omnipresent divine" in so many passages of experience was to invite discouragement and contradiction.

I have been reading the Revised Version diligently. . . . I have also been reading the Origin of Species; Jehovah and Darwin, it is a curious mixture. Both Gods, though, the God after the Pentateuch, and the God of the development are good, very good in their ways.[80]

They remained, however, *different* Gods. And thus it was as Hale White continued throughout his life to search the human record, he again and again discovered not one great absolute, but a multitude of irreconcilable particulars. By degrees he substituted the question, "What will help me?" for the question, "What is true?" The linkage between man and God was too subtle to be investigated on other terms. God was, to be sure, mani-

---

[77] See above, p. 64.
[78] *G.D.*, p. 147. Her maiden name was Dorothy Vernon Horace Smith.
[79] *P.N.a.*, p. 14.
[80] *Ibid.*, p. 9.

fested everywhere. But there was *eros* as well as *caritas*, human as well as divine love; there were the rival claims of reason and emotion as the monitors of human conduct. There were, too, those conflicts in his own life between the desire for heroic action and a love for metaphysical specula-tion, between the ideal of human life he first caught in the Hertfordshire fields from Wordsworth and the realities of a society in which the evi-dences of a divine spirit were more and more difficult to discover.

We shall study these conflicts in later pages, but the things we have seen in this chapter cannot be forgotten, for the romantic side of the man asserted its dominance again and again. After quoting from Wordsworth's "The Ruined Cottage," he once remarked: "Because this religion is in-definite, it is not therefore less supporting."[81] In some sense his romantic vision, however vaguely delineated, continued to support him throughout his life. The craving for knowledge of elemental things, whether of the spirit or of nature, whether in the search for God or the examination of the stars, was a lure and a temptation for Hale White almost deeper than his own consciousness. He was led to elemental experience as Doughty was led to "fanatic Arabia" among "men who believed fiercely and loved and hated simply—men who were truly of one substance with the earth wherein they lived."[82] But obsessed though he was with these cravings, he never became a fanatic. He never let his longing for high spiritual ad-venture blind him to the facts that his starting point was solid earth and that moral earnestness is never, by itself, an adequate substitute for knowl-edge and intelligence.

[81] *P.N.a.*, p. 15.
[82] J. M. Murray, *Countries of the Mind* (London, 1931), p. 106. Hale White was a profound admirer of Doughty. See *G.D.*, pp. 457, 458, and *L.3F.*, p. 295.

Chapter Five

RENUNCIATION

At some time or other in his life each item in the gospel of idealism we have just delineated was retired or modified by Hale White. By degrees he discovered that such a romantic vision was neither entirely consonant with the realities of life nor entirely agreeable to his own temper; as an ideal he continued to believe it, but as a way of life much of it had to be renounced. We are here dealing with that stage in his experience which he describes in the *Autobiography*:

The struggle was not felt just then. It came later, when the first enthusiasm of a new purpose had faded away, and I had to fall back on mere force of will.[1]

And with a fading of the first enthusiasm came not merely a renunciation of certain doctrines he had hitherto sanguinely held, but a recognition that *renunciation itself*, self-denial, was a good the virtues of which he had underemphasized. When "mere force of will" became his essential resource, and when he met with situations where it seemed most important, his religious philosophy began, like Wordsworth's, to turn from one of self-confidence into one of self-defense, from one of aspiration to one of fortitude. Renunciation, then, was not simply another form of negation; it was a positive element in his religion, and a necessary corrective to the excesses of his idealism. While Hale White never became a pessimist in any usual sense of the word,[2] he developed a profound sense of the tragic nature of human life, and became dominated by the conviction that man's salvation could only be achieved through an intent concentration on that tragic aspect.

The repudiation of the Wordsworthian vision began, most probably, with a wavering of his faith in the divinity of nature:

When first I read Wordsworth I saw God in Nature.
As I grew older I felt a difficulty in saying so much.[3]

The difficulty was dramatized most forcibly when Mark Rutherford first experienced the squalor of the London slums. Hale White's own experience in those quarters was not a close or prolonged one, but he reacted sensitively to the filth and misery which he discovered. What could these people know of nature? How could God be a reality to them if the natural world were the body in which he manifested himself to men?

When I was living in the country, the pure sky and the landscape formed a large portion of my existence, so large that much of myself depended on it, and I wondered

---

[1] *A.*, p. 45.
[2] See E. V. Tempest, "Optimism in 'Mark Rutherford,'" *The Westminster Review*, CLXXX (August 1913), 174–84.　　　[3] "Revolution," *L.P.*, p. 94.

how men could be worth anything if they could never see the face of nature. For this belief my early training on the "Lyrical Ballads" is answerable. When I came to London the same creed survived, and I was for ever thirsting for intercourse with my ancient friend. Hope, faith, and God seemed impossible amidst the smoke of the streets. It was now very difficult for me, except at rare opportunities, to leave London, and it was necessary for me, therefore, to understand that all that was essential for me was obtainable there, even though I should never see anything more than was to be seen in journeying through the High Street, Camden Town, Tottenham Court Road, the Seven Dials, and Whitehall. I should have been guilty of a simple surrender to despair if I had not forced myself to make this discovery. I cannot help saying, with all my love for the literature of my own day, that it has an evil side to it which none know except the millions of sensitive persons who are condemned to exist in great towns. It might be imagined from much of this literature that true humanity and a belief in God are the offspring of the hills or the ocean; and by implication, if not expressly, the vast multitudes who hardly ever see the hills or the ocean must be without a religion. The long poems which turn altogether upon scenery, perhaps in foreign lands, and the passionate devotion to it which they breathe, may perhaps do good in keeping alive in the hearts of men a determination to preserve air, earth, and water from pollution; but speaking from experience as a Londoner, I can testify that they are most depressing, and I would counsel everybody whose position is what mine was to avoid these books and to associate with those which will help him in his own circumstances.[4]

Not only did nature's inaccessibility to millions of men impress itself on Hale White, and not only did he come to feel that the slum dweller's salvation must be prefaced by sanitation rather than by sermons, but by degrees he found it less and less easy to discover God in nature when he did have the opportunity to associate with it. More and more the scientific description of natural processes suggested themselves as the true description and, although beauty remained, it gave only enigmatic answers to questions of ultimate truth.

On the one hand was infinite misery; on the other there were exquisite adaptations producing the highest pleasure: on the one hand the mystery of life-long disease, and on the other the equal mystery of the unspeakable glory of the sunrise on a summer's morning over a quiet summer sea.[5]

Like Tennyson,[6] Hale White was distressed over the evolutionary doctrine revealing a nature which was "careful of the type," but "careless of the single life," and which gave no answer to the problem of personal immortality.[7] This was a problem of crucial importance to him, and none of the solace romantic poetry could give had the power to deny the verdict of his common sense:

. . . the greatest difficulty was the inability to believe that the Almighty intended to preserve all the mass of human beings, all the countless millions of barbaric half-bestial forms which, since the appearance of man, had wandered upon the earth,

[4] *D.*, pp. 4–6.
[5] *A.*, pp. 99–100.
[6] Hale White was a profound and sensitive admirer of Tennyson. See *L.3F.*, pp. 165–73.
[7] The question of immortality in Hale White's religious thought will be more fully discussed in the chapter on Spinoza.

savage or civilised. Is it like Nature's way to be so careful about individuals, and is it to be supposed that, having produced, millions of years ago, a creature scarcely nobler than the animals he tore with his fingers, she should take pains to maintain him in existence for evermore? The law of the universe everywhere is rather the perpetual rise from the lower to the higher; an immortality of aspiration after more perfect types; a suppression and happy forgetfulness of its comparative failures. There was nevertheless an obstacle to the acceptance of this negation in a faintness of heart which I could not overcome. Why this ceaseless struggle, if in a few short years I was to be asleep for ever? The position of mortal man seemed to me infinitely tragic. He is born into the world, beholds its grandeur and beauty, is filled with unquenchable longings, and knows that in a few inevitable revolutions of the earth he will cease.[8]

To alleviate the faintness of heart was a need more pressing for Hale White than to solve the riddle of the universe, and was the dominant force forming his religious beliefs; but, nevertheless, the impersonality of natural laws presented an obstacle to faith which, in all the urgency to believe, he could not ignore. Like Wordsworth, who frequently resorted to the term "goings-on" to describe the processes of nature, thus revealing "how he felt" about nature if not "what he felt," Hale White grew to know a strange fear and loneliness before "those elemental transactions taking place in indifference to man,"[9] where before he had felt only joy and kinship. In *The Groombridge Diary* we learn that he was moved to something like terror at the fact that "the stars . . . blindly run." His second wife writes:

Hale said there was something very human about the study of the Heavens—man, as it were, controlling the stars through his telescope, marshalling them before him, naming them, dictating their courses for years to come. He said it produced the strangest effect upon him when he sat watching for some transit or eclipse, and just at the very second predicted the shadow slipped into its place. On the other hand, as Goethe had said, there was something "dreadfully *in*human". He was much moved as he said these words, gasped as if on the brink of some horror.[10]

Hale White's renunciation of nature was not a denial of its beauty[11] nor of its restorative power over him, but of that intimate, warm, personal something he had once found there. Of that he was no longer sure. Gradually, as in the *Book of Job*, nature was seen to stand in its own right, a symbol still of the unity underlying the universe, a corrective still of man's unhealthy egotistical concerns, but mute and indifferent to the irrelevant questions arising from human needs. Over the passage of years nature reasserted for him its independence of man, and Hale White increasingly felt that he was in Job's universe and must submit to it with Job's resignation.

And as nature began to draw away from the realm of intimate per-

---

[8] *A.*, pp. 89–90. In Hale White's scrapbooks are clippings revealing his interest in evolution, e.g., "Professor Clifford on Natural Religion," *Devon Evening Express*, October 10, 1877. See also the Chignell controversy, above, p. 53.

[9] Willard L. Sperry, *Wordsworth's Anti-Climax* (Cambridge, Mass., 1935), p. 170.

[10] *G.D.*, p. 246. See also pp. 400–401.

[11] See *ibid.*, p. 107.

sonal experience so did some of that confidence in himself, in "self-reference" as a monitor of conduct. Like Wordsworth, Hale White came to know the "weight of chance desires" and increasingly felt the need of some protection against the anarchy of personal moods.

> I, loving freedom, and untried;
> No sport of every random gust,
> Yet being to myself a guide,
> Too blindly have reposed my trust:
> And oft, when in my heart was heard
> The timely mandate, I deferred
> The task, in smoother walks to stray;
> But thee I now would serve more strictly, if I may.

In seeing the universe of souls as a manifold expression of the one, and in feeling his kinship with it, he had discovered a religion but he had not discovered an ethic to go with it. Unlike his aunt, he had never developed his inward monitor until it was a reliable substitute for duty; and as he became aware of the division between man and nature, he became also aware of division in himself. Hale White, like many of the romantics, was brought face to face with what Albert Schweitzer has described as a perennial moral paradox faced by those adopting a nature philosophy:

He recognizes that from the standpoint of logical thought all ethical conduct can be only an expression of the relation of the individual to the universe. But when ethics has become universal in this sense it is brought up short by the question how and in what way the relation of the individual to the universe is comprehensible as action on the universe. On the answer to this question depends whether it can establish a real activist ethic or whether it offers only so much ethic as can ever be secured by presenting a philosophy of resignation in the garb of ethics. This is the rock on which all real nature-philosophy is liable to come to grief.[12]

Hale White felt the need of a moral program, but he was not sure about the method of finding it. Was instinct or reason the most to be trusted? Was it safe to follow the inner light or should one find his moral anchorage in principles discovered by others—in the best that has been thought and said? These questions were provoked by some clashes between his romantic idealism and the world of experience, and it will repay us to examine some of them carefully, for they show a basic pattern in the development of his religious philosophy and in the growth of his personality.

Hale White confessed that one of the evils of Calvinism was that "it concentrated my thoughts upon myself, and made me of great importance."[13] This is a vital admission, for it gives support to what is only too evident: that in the habit of "self-reference" which Wordsworth had

---

12 Albert Schweitzer, *Civilization and Ethics* (London, 1923), p. 125. In his *Eighteenth Century Background*, p. 272, Basil Willey writes: "It is perhaps worthy of remark that those who have felt most powerfully the healing influence of 'Nature' have often been those who were most subject, in their ordinary moments, to gloom and nervous depression."

13 *E.L.*, p. 59.

stimulated there was no little admixture of the egotism which had been part of his Puritan heritage. He was concerned not merely with *the* soul, but very particularly with *his* soul; and when that soul began to feel the workings of the spirit it was likely to become infected with a spiritual pride which in his case could be rightly claimed as the first of the deadly sins. For it led him—at least for a time—to be tolerant of others only if they too showed evidence of such spiritual refinement, and it made him choose loneliness before accepting companionship with the unillumined. In his search for a "perfect friend," and the quarantine of a "real" from an "other" self (see Introduction, pp. 5, 8) we have but two examples of his attempt to impose absolutes upon himself and his society. In these acts we can detect a mixture of self-pity and aspiration, of self-defense and self-confidence. He wanted a perfect friendship, yet he could not keep from envying the popularity and worldly successes of baser souls; he cherished a high ideal which, by definition, would place him above other men, yet he wanted the world to love and praise him because he possessed such spiritual superiority. He tried to keep his eyes on the heavens, but he could not resist looking back to see if men were awed by his eminence, and condemning them when he saw they looked another way. Such ambivalence is not unusual in the Puritan character, but in Hale White the rival claims of the absolute and the finite, the ideal and the real, were peculiarly accentuated. He had, however, in a very deep sense cast in his lot with humanity, and in his final affirmation he proclaimed a way of living on easier terms. But at the moment of high conflict, when he saw that his ideal of a perfect friendship could find no consummation in the world of experience, it seemed a painful likelihood that the hope of incorporating absolutes into an "activist" ethic was doomed in all phases of human life. What then could be done? Schweitzer's prediction that a philosophy of resignation could arise from such despair seems to have been fulfilled in Hale White's case. Failing in friendship, he drew in upon himself, encased himself in a shell which protected while it isolated. In the *Deliverance* he reveals a characteristic strategem for meeting what was to him the brutal vulgarity of his employer:

I dreaded, as I have always dreaded beyond what I can tell, the chaos and wreck which, with me, follows subjugation by anger, and I held to my resolve under all provocation. It was very difficult, but how many times I have blessed myself for adhesion to it. Instead of going home undone with excitement, and trembling with fear of dismissal, I have walked out of my dungeon having had to bite my lips till the blood came, but still conqueror, and with peace of mind.[14]

Thus, while the ideal was not scrapped, it was retired; self-confidence withered before the need for self-defense.

This failure, and others like it, turned his attention more and more to developing those powers which would assist in the problem of survival, to finding an ethic and a religion existentially valid. The sense of

14 *D.*, pp. 109–10. See also p. 118.

division between himself and the world brought home to him again with renewed force the truth of those dualisms that Calvinism had taught, those divisions between higher and lower, right and wrong, flesh and spirit. And especially did it remind him that Calvinism was not far wrong in emphasizing patience and fortitude in bearing the burdens of life. But, while many of the moral definitions which Calvinism had provided could be taken over without alteration, there were many which required redefinition, which had to be tailored to meet a modern situation and to embody the knowledge about men and the universe which science and enlightenment had provided. Which, for example, was the valid instrument for moral inquiry: reason or emotion? Having found his confidence in the authority of his own intuitions severely shaken, he made this inquiry with a desperate urgency, and we are shown, in Clara and Madge Hopgood, advocates for both sides of the argument. Clara, the exponent of reason, deliberation, analysis, does not "believe in oracles which are supposed to prove their divinity by giving no reasons for their commands;"[15] while Madge, supporting impulse, instinct, emotion, declares that this "balancing, see-saw method would be fatal."[16] We shall study this little morality play in more detail later, but it serves us here by suggesting something of the division which existed in Hale White himself after romantic idealism began to fail him, and something of the futility of his efforts to find answers to such metaphysical and psychological problems. While he was fascinated by them, he was nevertheless an amateur in moral inquiry, and his final affirmation never would have emerged had he always faced his problems in this way.

Another method which he employed in his search for an "activist" ethic was even less promising. That was a gathering up the best of what had been thought and said into a collection of maxims and principles, from which he could make an appropriate selection at the appropriate time:

I have at my command any number of maxims, all of them good, but I am powerless to select the one which ought to be applied. A general principle, a fine saying, is nothing but a tool, and the wit of man is shown not in his possession of a well-furnished tool-chest, but in the ability to pick out the proper instrument and use it.[17]

A better way of getting nowhere could hardly be devised, but it is again an illustration of the devices which this man, cut off from his native faith, forced to renounce the romantic ideals which for a time sustained him, would employ in order to discover a stable reference point outside himself and an anchorage in the world of experience where he could rest.

But though he found few final answers after the renunciation of his idealism, and though he never perfected a method for moral inquiry, of one thing he became relatively sure: that no religion and no ethic could be effective unless it took account of human suffering and unless it de-

[15] *C.H.*, p. 21.   [16] *Ibid.*   [17] *A.*, p. 69. See also "Principles," *D.*, pp. 163–71.

manded self-denial and sacrifice. Though one's faith was only a dim spot of hope and though no moral program issued clearly from it, one must nevertheless suffer for that hope as if it were a clear issue calling for heroic action. What one suffered *for* was important, of course, but not so important as the resolution itself. Hale White was certain that life to be righteous must not be too pleasant, that a "flowery" religion was a sure indication that "no good was being done." In Carlyle, Hale White found—perhaps unwarrantably—the correct emphasis.[18]

> Carlyle is the champion of morals, ethics, law—call it what you like—of that which says we must not always do a thing because it is pleasant. There are two great ethical parties in the world, and, in the main, but two. One of them asserts the claims of the senses. Its doctrine is seductive because it is so right. It is necessary that we should in a measure believe it, in order that life may be sweet. But nature has heavily weighted the scale in its favour; its acceptance requires no effort. It is easily perverted and becomes a snare. In our day nearly all genius has gone over to it, and preaching it is rather superfluous. The other party affirms what has been the soul of all religions worth having, that it is by repression and self-negation that men and States live.

And again, in the *Autobiography*, he writes:

> . . . I hanker sometimes after the old prohibitions and penalties. Physiological penalties are too remote, and the subtler penalties—the degradation, the growth of callousness to finer pleasures, the loss of sensitiveness . . . —are too feeble to withstand temptation when it lies in ambush like a garrotter, and has the reason stunned in a moment.[19]

Like Carlyle, who gave a "puritanically ascetic twist" to the notion of Olympian tolerance which he had received from Goethe,[20] Hale White in subtle ways transformed his romantic idealism into a gospel of self-renunciation and repression. Most Victorian moralists, in forging a union of the two extremes, left the Goethean position (Arnold, for example, felt Goethe to be escapist) and let their ethical concerns revolve more about the concrete facts of life as they found it. Hale White followed much the same course, but the modifications he wrought in his earlier idealism were peculiarly his own and deserve our special study.

In his method for making a "human" religion out of the reinterpreted Gospel story we get, perhaps, the clearest example of how he retained a Calvinistic rigor in the emancipating doctrines of idealism. It had been demonstrated by Hegel and others that Christ's incarnation was not a unique act in history, but merely a supreme example of how the divine idea could be realized in any human being. If this is so, Hale White seemed to argue, and if Christ is the perfect exemplar in history of the fruition of this process, let us turn to Him to discover what is expected, in terms of

---

[18] "A Visit to Carlyle in 1868," *P.J.*, pp. 8–9.

[19] *A.*, p. 9. See also *R.T.L.*, p. 88: ". . . suffering, actual personal suffering, is the mother of innumerable beneficial experiences. . . ."

[20] See Samuel C. Chew, "The Nineteenth Century and After (1789–1939)," *A Literary History of England* (New York, 1948), p. 1316.

realistic human experience, of the God-infected man. It is claimed that He died *for* us. How can this be understood in terms of human experience? Why, it is simply an illustration of the fact that everywhere and in all time the innocent must suffer for the guilty, the just for the unjust. And not only is this so, but it is *right* that it is so, for Christ can be taken as a symbol of what is eternally true even though he was himself only an ordinary individual. Furthermore, it is no exaggeration to say that Hale White would reverse the expression and maintain that a man cannot be innocent unless he does suffer. We may be freed from all the superstitious paraphernalia of orthodox Christianity, but we do not thereby escape to blessed freedom; we reread the Gospel in the light of our new insights, and it becomes a Gospel of blood, sweat, and tears for all of us and not just for one man. In his early sermon Hale White clearly showed this doctrine in the process of development:

I remember, for example, discoursing about the death of Christ. There was not a single word which was ordinarily used in the pulpit which I did not use,—satisfaction for sin, penalty, redeeming blood, they were all there,—but I began by saying that in this world there was no redemption for man but by blood; furthermore, the innocent had everywhere and in all time to suffer for the guilty. It had been objected that it was contrary to our notion of an all-loving Being that He should demand such a sacrifice; but, contrary or not, in this world it was true, quite apart from Jesus, that virtue was martyred every day, unknown and unconsoled, in order that the wicked might somehow be saved. This was part of the scheme of the world, and we might dislike it or not, we could not get rid of it. The consequences of my sin, moreover, are rendered less terrible by virtues not my own. I am literally saved from penalties because another pays the penalty for me. The atonement, and what it accomplished for man, were therefore a sublime summing up as it were of what sublime men have to do for their race; an exemplification, rather than a contradiction, of Nature herself, as we know her in our own experience.[21]

This was a terrible doctrine, because it was not merely a recognition, drawn from the facts, of the tragic nature of human life, or of the suffering he himself had experienced; it was in itself an ideal providing Hale White with a compulsion to seek suffering, to enjoy self-denial for its own sake. Craving to be one of those "sublime men," he went through his life not only carrying crosses, but seeking crosses to carry. Where the facts of the *Autobiography* and the *Deliverance* do not square with the facts of his own life, the alterations are without exception devised to make his sufferings appear worse than they actually were. Mark Rutherford is pictured as a man persecuted by his employer and virtually living with the poor in Drury Lane; Hale White had a congenial[22] and well-paid[23] position in the

21 *A.*, pp. 25–26. It is interesting to note that Aldous Huxley in his essay, "On Grace," in *Music at Night* (London, 1950), pp. 59–68, advances a similar—remarkably similar—restatement in humanistic terms of the doctrines of Calvinism, notably of the doctrines of Predestination and Election.

22 Jack writes in *P.N.a.*, p. 2: "His work in the Contract and Purchase Department was much more congenial to him than journalism, and he left his mark there, I believe, in the shape of improved organization." See "Mr. Whittaker's Retirement," *M.P.*, pp. 87 ff. See also *G.D.*, p. 352.

23 Dr. R. Hale-White tells me he was retired on a £500 pension.

Admiralty, and his connection with Drury Lane was only that of an occasional observer. The truth seems to be that his compulsions to suffer
were not always commensurate with the actual facts of his existence, and
where this was so he often displayed something like an evil genius in
devising ways of torturing himself and, without conscious intent, torturing
others. We shall see more of this instinct as we proceed. The need to renounce the pleasures of life was, with him, often deeper than consciousness;
there was, to be sure, an opposing instinct, but it never became strong
enough to constitute the dominant coloring of his life.

In his last years, he seems to have recognized this habit of "damping"
(Mrs. White's expression) very clearly, but even then he does not seem
to have overcome it very effectively. She writes in *The Groombridge
Diary*:

> It is strange that he sees now a strain in his nature which I am convinced he
> never saw before; a wretchedness in himself which seems as if it *must* vent itself in
> making wretchedness for others; not with any cruel intention, but just from sheer
> misery; an instinctive desire to damp enthusiasm or joy. The odd thing is that this
> instinct lies so closely and comfortably side by side with an instinct for those very
> qualities which he damps; he loves joy and enthusiasm as well as hates them spite-
> fully. I said: "You sometimes feel wretched." He said "Yes"; he was making up
> the fire. I said: "And you feel as if you must make other people wretched." "Yes,"
> he said bitterly, "it's damnable," and he gave the fire a savage poke.[24]

And then, with unusual insight, she goes on to diagnose this disease in the
man she loved:

> It has been a merciful thing that some instinct, equally inherent in one, and of a
> diametrically opposite kind, should have from the first withstood *his* instinct. I have
> clung passionately, obstinately, to exuberant joy and health and happiness all through
> these three years; and I suppose the whole time, though I did not realize it (except
> bit by bit, slowly, unconsciously, and as it were with resolutely shut eyes), the whole
> time he was instinctively at war with me trying to wreck his happiness and my own.
> As by degrees his nature has straightened out—here and there it was very much
> curled up, fold within fold—this instinct has become plainer to himself.

Now this habit grew, we believe, not simply from a personal and temperamental idiosyncrasy, but partly from his failure to find any sure positive pole which could draw him out of himself into confident, assertive
action. It was part of the awful heritage of a Puritan whose only strength
and joy lay in belief and who was deprived of that belief, partly by the
conditions of the age in which he lived, and partly by his own honesty—
which prevented his accepting an assurance merely because he needed it.
At one time the burden of original sin had been very largely carried on the
shoulders of a Redeemer, but now, for those who would accept the responsibility, it was carried by individual men. Hale White accepted this burden
and was nearly prostrated by its weight; he was bitter at a world which
cheerfully let him carry it and, instead of giving him praise or honor for
his sacrifice, seemed rather to be repelled by it.

[24] *G.D.*, pp. 393–94.

His hypochondria, therefore, had its roots largely in religious doubt, in the need to find psychological expression for what had once been expressed theologically. Christianity for him was "the religion of the man who goes through life thinking much, but who makes few friends and sees nothing come of his thoughts."[25] Christianity had no message for those who were happy, healthy, or rich, but only for those who were melancholy, suffering, and poor:

There is no Saviour for us like the hero who has passed triumphantly through the distress which troubles *us*. Salvation is the spectacle of a victory by another over foes like our own. The story of Jesus is the story of the poor and forgotten. He is not the Saviour for the rich and prosperous, for they want no Saviour. The healthy, active, and well-to-do need Him not, and require nothing more than is given by their own health and prosperity. But every one who has walked in sadness because his destiny has not fitted his aspirations; every one who, having no opportunity to lift himself out of his little narrow town or village circle of acquaintances, has thirsted for something beyond what they could give him; everybody who, with nothing but a dull, daily round of mechanical routine before him, would welcome death, if it were martyrdom for a cause; every humblest creature, in the obscurity of great cities or remote hamlets, who silently does his or her duty without recognition—all these turn to Jesus, and find themselves in Him. He died, faithful to the end, with infinitely higher hopes, purposes, and capacity than mine, and with almost no promise of anything to come of them.[26]

There is no little amount of self-pity and worldly ambition betrayed here, but nevertheless this is as passionate a confession of loneliness and despair as our literature has to show. And few writers have celebrated the cause of the world's *déracinés* with more poignancy and honest feeling. But he was aware of their suffering because he was obsessed with his own; he could never in his life or writing achieve that complete sympathy, that *Einfühlung* which the romantics had preached, and he could never overcome that extravagant pride which brought him almost to the brink of suicide at relatively slight affronts. He loved Christ because Christ had suffered, and he understood that suffering, not by imaginative projection, but by feeling his own pulse. The words of Emily Dickinson remind us strongly of Hale White's self-imprisonment:

> Adventure most unto itself
> The Soul condemned to be;
> Attended by a Single Hound—
> Its own Identity.[27]

Hale White could experience remorse over the pain his self-obsession indirectly brought to others, but that remorse did not usually indicate a change in his habit or an alteration in the half-conscious belief that pain itself was somehow good. In the *Autobiography*, for example, he confesses himself with perfect honesty, but underneath the confession lies the

[25] *A.*, p. 41.
[26] *Ibid.*, p. 56.
[27] *The Poems of Emily Dickinson*, ed. M. D. Bianchi and A. L. Hamson (London, 1933), p. 223.

deep desire to draw attention to himself, to be honored for his honest self-criticism. He had judged Mary Mardon harshly because of her silence during a conversation Mark Rutherford had had with her father. Then he discovered she had silently been suffering from neuralgia:

I thought how rash I had been in judging her as I continually judged other people, . . . and I thought, too, that if I had a fit of neuralgia, everybody near me would know it, and be almost as much annoyed by me as I myself should be by the pain. It is curious, also, that when thus proclaiming my troubles I often considered my eloquence meritorious, or, at least, a kind of talent for which I ought to praise God, contemning rather my silent friends as something nearer than myself to the expressionless animals. To parade my toothache, describing it with unusual adjectives, making it felt by all the company in which I might happen to be, was to me an assertion of my superior nature.[28]

Examples of how Hale White in real life thus advertised his suffering are readily obtainable from his letters. Though, according to Dr. R. Hale-White, his grandson, he was an extraordinarily healthy man physically, he nearly always shared what pain he had with his friends and very often made some moral generalization about it, attempting to view it in a cosmic relationship. This is an example:

One more screw! I met somebody this morning to whom I complained with some bitterness that I should not mind so much all this agony if I could feel that it did me any good; made me more tolerable to my friends or improved my morals. It would also be partly explicable and bearable if I knew that it saved some other person any suffering. As far as I could see, however, it was gratuitous, useless, and most mischievous.[29]

Though Hale White could be equally aware of beauty and joy, we should never see him fairly unless we recognize this compulsion to impose his own ego on the world around him, to demand in others the same pain and melancholy he felt, and to feel lonely and left out unless others accepted his religion of suffering and drank from the same bitter cup. It is no exaggeration to say that throughout much of his life he *hated* to see other people happy, for that had not been his experience and it was not, therefore, the right of anyone else. When, for example, his eldest son announced his engagement (and Hale White would attend none of the marriages of his children), he wrote to him, "It is not all bliss to us—simply because your joy reminds us of a whole life's joy missed through her illness."[30] And in a later letter on August 8, 1884, he writes:

It is so much more difficult to sympathise with a person's joys than with his sorrows, the reason being that the spectacle of another's joy wakes the contrast with our own unhappiness, and that of his sorrows with our pleasure.[31]

---

[28] *A.*, p. 62. His own wife's suffering from disseminated sclerosis might have suggested this incident. Cf. Dostoevsky's statement in *Notes from Underground* where the toothache is used as a symbol very much as Hale White uses it here.

[29] *L.3F.*, p. 159. According to the letter, he had neuritis at the time. Ursula C. Buchmann [*William Hale White* (Zürich, 1950), p. 24] says "William Hale White was ever shy of 'talking about his troubles'." This is a mistaken judgment.

[30] *P.N.b.*, p. 22. Letter dated July 28, 1884.   [31] *Ibid.*, p. 23.

Though we are not attempting primarily a psychological study of Hale White, we cannot understand his renunciations simply on a theological or metaphysical plane, for they were deeply personal. His moral and religious generalizations were always conditioned by his particular needs and frustrations, and much of his melancholy and despair was rooted in the fact that he felt unloved and uncared for : unloved by a secular society which granted him little recognition and gave him no place of great power ; unloved by the religious society of his childhood ; unloved in an active sense by a wife who was confined to a chair or bed for nearly twenty-five years of their married life.[32] To regard Hale White's melancholia[33] as in any real sense pathological is quite false—he conquered it to a great extent by his own prescription : "susceptibility to nobler joys"[34]—but we are nevertheless helped in understanding it by Karl Menninger's description of the disease in its more virulent forms :

But in melancholia the loss of a loved one, not necessarily by death, in fact more often by jilting, results in a different sort of reaction . . . It is not the world that seems poor and empty, it is something inside of the individual himself. He complains that he feels worthless, miserable, and wretched . . .

In such a person, it may be seen . . . that such an individual hates himself only a little more than he loves himself. In spite of his talk of how unworthy he is, he demands from those about him an inordinate amount of attention, sympathy, anxiety, and care.[35]

We may say that Hale White had felt "jilted" by his world and his church and by the high promise that had once been held out to him by romantic idealism; and over the hurt he nursed a lifelong resentment, which kept it fresh, while at the same time he desperately longed for some balm to soothe it. His problems were personal, but they were also part of a *mal de siècle* with which he had been so seriously infected that he is almost the epitomization of it. His son, John, has diagnosed his trouble with objectivity and insight :

The melancholy of which I speak and which was such a pronounced feature of my father's life, had other causes [than his wife's illness]. He himself attributed it principally to incurable dyspepsia producing insomnia with all its train of evils. It is certain that it did spring largely from such troubles, but no reader of the "Autobiography of Mark Rutherford" can, I think, fail to realize that his melancholia had other roots as well ; in the unsolved problems of the age ; the decay of religious faith ; the ugliness of the industrial development ; the terrible contrast of poverty and riches. It was a symptom of the age. The great Victorian moralists were characterized by no nobler quality than their profound sense of the troubles of the time, and the courage with which they faced the current orthodoxies and insisted on the need of fundamental solutions. Their melancholy may have been the measure of their sense of failure, but their courage and intellectual integrity remained unaffected. My father had not the

[32] John Hale-White writes in *P.N.a.*, p. 5 : "At the time when my recollections of her begin, she was already an invalid." He was born October 23, 1861, so that must have been around 1865 or 1866. She died June 1, 1891.

[33] For an important confession of his melancholy, see *A.*, p. 43.

[34] *A.*, p. 45.

[35] *Man Against Himself* (New York, 1938), pp. 41–42.

rich genius of such men as Carlyle and Ruskin, but he was of their epoch and their school, suffered as they, and showed the same unswerving refusal to compromise.[36]

We have thus traced Hale White's renunciation of certain doctrines of romantic idealism until we have seen it become a *habit* of renunciation coloring and shaping his attitudes toward things great and small, religious and secular. The habit of renunciation was a relatively permanent acquisition, but his denial of romantic idealism was neither final nor complete: it was only the blighting by a heavy frost of a youthful and overenthusiastic faith. It remains now to see what positive affirmations were matured from these complicated inheritances of Hale White's personal and religious life.

[36] *P.N.a.*, p. 6. There is also evidence indicating that he felt unloved by his mother. See below, pp. 140–42.

Chapter Six

AFFIRMATION

In the 1883 Preface to his translation of Spinoza Hale White wrote:

The power to go from one ascertained point to another . . . is what makes the strength of the human mind. It is this which creates for us principles, or at least the only principles worth the name. Our usual habit is something quite different. We pick up one rule to-day and act upon it, and we pick up another to-morrow and act upon that. To-day we discern that our only safety lies in self-government as strict as that of the Stoics, and to-morrow we incline to a belief in the natural man and in the divinity of all our passions . . .[1]

His recognition that he could not solve the moral problem or bring into any system all the diverse forces in the universe and human experience, was for Hale White the beginning of his affirmation. When he arrived at this wisdom the vacillation described above lost something of its painful urgency.

No theory of the world is possible. The storm, the rain slowly rotting the harvest, children sickening in cellars are obvious; but equally obvious are an evening in June, the delight of men and women in one another, in music, and in the exercise of thought. There can surely be no question that the sum of satisfaction is increasing, not merely in the gross but for each human being, as the earth from which we sprang is being worked out of the race, and a higher type is being developed. I may observe, too, that although it is usually supposed, it is erroneously supposed, that it is pure doubt which disturbs or depresses us. Simple suspense is in fact very rare, for there are few persons so constituted as to be able to remain in it. It is dogmatism under the cloak of doubt which pulls us down. It is the dogmatism of death, for example, which we have to avoid. The open grave is dogmatic, and we say *that man has gone*, but this is as much a transgression of the limits of certitude as if we were to say *he is an angel in bliss*. The proper attitude, the attitude enjoined by the severest exercise of the reason is, *I do not know*; and in this there is an element of hope, now rising and now falling, but always sufficient to prevent that blank despair which we must feel if we consider it as settled that when we lie down under the grass there is an absolute end.[2]

In statements such as this Hale White's true greatness lies. Nearly every sentence holds observations on life which, at one time or another, dominated his existence, but—though no philosophy was wrought from them—a way of life in which they received a balanced emphasis was discovered. Hale White's affirmation was rooted in agnosticism and (in a curious way) anti-intellectualism, but it was not obscurantist. He continued to admit the most contrary facts into his thought and to let them remain unresolved side by side. One can read the *Black Notebook* and be baffled by the contradictions resting there. For example, in almost direct

[1] *Ethic* (1883), p. ix.
[2] *D.*, pp. 89–90.

95

opposition to the opening sentence of the statement just quoted, he writes (in a note which was reprinted in *Last Pages*) :

> If a man holds sincerely any theory of life it is better than none. Any system which gives unity and subordinates motives is an advantage.[3]

It is nonetheless true, however, that Hale White never adopted such a theory of life, and that he learned to concern himself with that circumscribed area of experience which he could know and understand. This meant, of course, that his affirmation was exactly what Albert Schweitzer warns against—"a gospel of resignation in the garb of ethics." It was certainly not an "activist" ethic and certainly owed its existence very largely to a deep, habitual sense of frustration and despair. But it was a solution which fitted him like a garment, and which had grown out of an honest appraisal of his own shortcomings and strength :

> I had discovered that my appetite was far larger than my powers. Consumed by a longing for continuous intercourse with the best, I had no ability whatever to maintain it, and I had accepted as a fact, however mysterious it might be, that the human mind is created with the impulses of a seraph and the strength of a man.[4]

Like everything in his life, the affirmation was held with difficulty, but when he reminded himself of such truths as these, he was learning a discipline truly appropriate to his character and its needs. When he admitted he was ordinary and commonplace, he became great and distinctive.

> Masses of human energy have no proper outlet. Great genius will make one for itself, but for ordinary gifts, enormous in volume there is none. Shall I write history? There are men who will devote their whole lives to half a dozen disputed points in a biography. Science? There are laboratories and observatories armed with the most expensive instruments wielded by specialists each of whom has a minute department. Politics? The condition of politics is such that no man with any self-respect will touch it. The consequence is an expression of energy in any direction and at all cost, which is productive of infinite mischief, or a suppression of it which is just as bad. What is wanted is an organization of energy, a true CHURCH.[5]

Thus despair had taught him that it was no longer possible to make all knowledge one's province, and the specialization which characterized modern life—dangerous though he saw it to be—forced humility upon this honest man. The departmentalization of human life and society made a simple, passionate belief impossible, and there was little to do but vaguely trust a larger hope (the evolutionary progress expressed above) and to cultivate your own corner of knowledge as best you knew how. He admitted that there may be those new Bacons who could attempt the synthesis, but the little man had better leave such matters alone. This may

---

[3] *L.P.*, p. 266. See "Principles," *D.*, pp. 163–71.   [4] *D.*, p. 2.

[5] *B.N.B.*, p. 23. In *N.N.*, February 19, 1881, he writes : "Every day the burden of life becomes greater, because we have so much to learn. Every day it becomes more and more imperative that a child should know German and French and the sciences, and a hundred other things, from theology to gymnastics. Surely a reduction in the number of items in the fearful programme ought to be hailed as a blessing of blessings."

seem to be nothing but a slightly new expression of negativism and despair, but actually it was not. There was a core of positive belief in all of Hale White's maturest thought, and it will repay us to try to understand it.

This positive hope can best be described, perhaps, as the grim hanging-on of a drowning man who finds one last resource of strength which saves him. Such an escape from drowning was an experience of Hale White's own life,[6] and it became a deep and significant symbol for him. He gives it to us again in his short story, "Michael Trevanion":

> He was on the point of sinking, when he bethought himself that if he was to die, he might just as well die after having put forth all his strength; and in an instant, as if touched by some divine spell the agitation ceased, and he was himself again.[7]

Much the same sort of experience forms the illustrative background of the short story, "Faith," in *Pages from a Journal*, but the most striking illustration of this "reasonable hope" which contains such saving grace is found in the story, "Two Martyrs," published in *The Bookman* for February 1893. It is in two parts, contrasting the martyrdom by death of an early Christian hero in the arena at Rome, with the living martyrdom of a nineteenth-century middle-class English girl. The second part of the story concerns a young schoolteacher who has just reached her twenty-eighth birthday. She lives, unmarried and unloved, in a mean, middle-class apartment and, as the story opens, she is shown being left alone by the landlady whose parting request is: "If anybody comes—but I don't suppose as anybody will—you won't mind going to the door yourself?" Her reply is, "I don't think anybody will come." The story is neither skillfully constructed nor subtle in its psychologizing, but seldom has stark despair been more relentlessly portrayed. From the books in the room we learn that she has been reading Renan, Strauss, and Helmholtz; and thus, presumably, we may assume that her unhappiness has been abetted by the "advanced" thinking of these nineteenth-century critics and scholars. Lonely, sexually frustrated, intellectually confused by her reading, bored with her schoolwork, she is about to commit suicide.[8]

> "Duty! What is duty? To whom do I owe it? Who prescribes it? A hundred years hence, what will it matter? Reproach! how will it touch me when I am quiet under the grass?"
> She goes to the mantlepiece, on which is a bottle labelled—"Two teaspoonful to be taken at bed-time."
> "An overdose of this and I am at rest!"
> She takes up the bottle, but stops. To this has it come! The law on Mt. Sinai, the vision of the saint, are represented by a scarcely heard "No" which presents no credentials. It has to be taken absolutely on trust; it has nothing to say to the tremendous argument on the other side. Why should she listen?

> The fog meanwhile shifts itself uneasily, and a just perceptible ray from the sun setting over the Hampstead Road falls on her face.[9]

---

[6] *E.L.*, pp. 52–54.   [7] *M.S.*, p. 160.   [8] P. 154.

[9] There are elements in the style of this story which we shall meet with later; but we should note the attenuated sketching in of the background as if for a stage direction;

The faith restraining this girl from the fatal act is neither cheerful nor one offering much stimulus to great deeds. But for Hale White the problem became not so much the finding of such stimulus as the problem of spiritual survival. Out of such pin points of hope, out of the slight shift in the fog or the last desperate stroke against death, could grow a new strength and faith not by any means devoid of joy and love. It was a faith without credentials and without definition, but it was enough to turn an Empedocles into a Job.

One must simply live, and find rewards in the living and not the explanation of life. "Do not, my love," he writes to his second wife, "enter this dark wood of metaphysics and theology. Be satisfied with the Love of God, a different thing altogether from the science of God and theology."[10] Do not, he writes in effect to another correspondent, assign limits to the unknowable or indulge in that passion for definition which has about it the "dogmatism of death":

> The passion for definite statement, like the passion of men for women and women for men, is no doubt implanted in us for a good reason, but what fearful mischief does not the one as well as the other breed! We carry our desire for logical completeness into a region where no logical completeness is possible, and shape out of the void all kinds of illusory phantoms. . . . I wholly agree . . . that the precision which is considered to be indispensable in view not only of life but more particularly of death is useless. There is no steel in that breastplate, and the arrow will pierce it as if it were paper.[11]

Do not, he finally told himself, expect to find happiness or love by remaining locked in the dark cave of your own personality. This simple discovery came to him in his last years with the force of a revelation, and a lifetime of tragic suffering is shadowed in his words:

> It has dawned on me that my duty is to strive after your happiness and not after my own. What a simple discovery! and yet these simple discoveries are often those which are last made and are the most important. This, in particular, came like a flash—"not yours but hers." The moment it became real to me the whole aspect of things was altered. And perhaps your happiness is the road to mine: perhaps if I do not think about my own happiness, but about yours, I shall be happy.[12]

But his affirmation was not simply a product of his last years, though it became increasingly enriched as his experience deepened. He had already traveled through the psychological stages of the process we have been delineating by the time he wrote his first book, and in the Preface to the second edition of the *Autobiography* he sums up his affirmation in a simple statement we cannot improve upon:

> It is all very well that remarkable persons should occupy themselves with exalted subjects, which are out of the ordinary road which ordinary humanity treads; but we who are not remarkable make a very great mistake if we have anything to do with

---

the clumsily contrived dramatic effects; the long quotations; the subjugation of any fullness or color in the character to the *idea* prompting the story. All these are fairly typical of his novelistic habits, though they are here exaggerated. In spite of these faults, however, the story is powerful in its pointedness.

10 *G.D.*, p. 147.   11 *L.3F.*, p. 191.   12 *G.D.*, p. 338.

them. If we wish to be happy, and have to live with average men and women, as most of us have to live, we must learn to take an interest in the topics which concern average men and women. We think too much of ourselves. We ought not to sacrifice a single moment's pleasure in our attempt to do something which is too big for us, and as a rule, men and women are always attempting what is too big for them. . . . Great men do the world much good, but not without some harm, and we have no business to be troubling ourselves with their dreams if we have duties which lie nearer home amongst persons to whom these dreams are incomprehensible. Many a man goes into his study, shuts himself up with his poetry or his psychology, comes out, half understanding what he has read, is miserable because he cannot find anybody with whom he can talk about it, and misses altogether the far more genuine joy which he could have obtained from a game with his children, or listening to what his wife had to tell him about her neighbours. . . .

Metaphysics, and theology, including all speculations on the why and the wherefore, optimism, pessimism, freedom, necessity, causality, and so forth, are not only for the most part loss of time, but frequently ruinous. It is no answer to say that these things force themselves upon us, and that to every question we are bound to give or try to give an answer. It is true, although strange, that there are multitudes of burning questions which we must do our best to ignore, to forget their existence; and it is not more strange, after all, than many other facts in this wonderfully mysterious and defective existence of ours. One fourth of life is intelligible, the other three fourths is unintelligible darkness; and our earliest duty is to cultivate the habit of not looking round the corner.

"Go thy way, eat thy bread with joy, and drink thy wine with a merry heart; for God hath already accepted thy works. Let thy garments be always white, and let not thy head lack ointment. Live joyfully with the wife whom thou lovest all the days of the life of thy vanity, which He hath given thee under the sun, all the days of thy vanity: for that is thy portion in life."[13]

Hale White never rested serenely in this resolve, but in so far as he ever came to any religious harbor, this was it. The note of quiet surrender to the inevitable, the low note of untroubled resignation and peace which is suggested in this passage, is quite alien to most of his actual experience, for he was as imperfect a Stoic as he was a romantic. This statement is that of a man talking to himself, telling himself that he must stop trying to be God and be a man; that here was the ideal embodying the greatest wisdom and he must try to live up to it. This stoical deliverance may seem unsatisfactory to us, too quiescent and too defeatist, but it has much to recommend it: it avoids dogmatism[14] and sentimentality; it holds fast to the facts as one man saw and felt them and never indulges in the dishonest luxury of easy assurances; it reminds us (if we need any longer such reminding) that the more perceptive Victorians were aware of the tragic abyss beneath the thin crust of civilization upon which their generation confidently walked.

One critic has brilliantly summed up the affirmation which grew out of Hale White's life and books, and we can profitably conclude with it:

What we call morbid in the sensations of Mark Rutherford is simply an unusual power of feeling those aspects of life which most people forget. The horror of life, never so

---

13 *A.*, pp. xxxiii–xxxvi.
14 See *D.*, p. 94. "Nature is Rhadamanthine . . .," etc.

much as perceived by persons of cheerful dulness, beats upon the naked nerve of this man. He has never learned the art, as George Eliot puts it, of being well wadded with stupidity. He refuses the myrrh and wine, and endures his cross without narcotics. No doubt it were wiser to drink the deadening cup, to let the mind be subdued to the element in which it works; but this is impossible to him. And so he prefers to find his way out of suffering by suffering: to master death by dying; an expert in pain, who selects nothing, omits nothing, rejects nothing, but tells the whole truth about life as he knows it.[15]

His tragic view of life grew, we may believe, from the same root that had originally given Calvinism to the world and which seemed to explain reasonably to millions of people the truth about human existence. But it was for Hale White a sad rediscovery, for we suspect that he entertained a secret hope that Calvinism could be cast away forever.

[15] "Mark Rutherford," *The Bookman* (London) XXVI (August 1904), 163.

Chapter Seven

SPINOZA

The major scholarly effort of Hale White's life was his work on Spinoza. His translation of Spinoza's *Ethic*,[1] which appeared in 1883 and went through three revised editions (1894, 1899, 1910),[2] was the first reliable translation to be published in English.[3] And his edition of the *Tractatus de Intellectus Emendatione* (1895) made available to English readers a minor work of Spinoza which had long been neglected. In addition to the translations, Hale White contributed an article entitled "Spinoza's Doctrine of the Relationship between Mind and Body" to *The International Journal of Ethics* (July 4, 1896), some reviews of other translations, and several essays[4] dealing in whole or part with the Jewish philosopher. As a commentator upon Spinoza's work, Hale White provided to philosophy little enlightenment, for not only did he lack the equipment for close philosophical inquiry but his criticism is extremely meager in quantity as well. To the student of Hale White, however, these slight contributions are of paramount interest—especially his two prefaces to the *Ethic* appearing in 1883 and 1894,[5] and his essay entitled "Revo-

---

1 Hale White always writes *Ethic* rather than *Ethics*. It has been suggested that he was following the ignorant conception of *ethica* from a neuter plural to a feminine singular. See A. S. Oko, *William Hale White* (Cincinnati, 1922), p. 239.

In his Preface to the 1883 edition of the *Ethic* Hale White wrote: "The present translation . . . was completed more than twenty years ago . . ." It is likely, however, that his interest had been aroused earlier, during his years at Chapman's and his association with George Eliot.

2 The translation was carefully revised by Hale White and his collaborator, Miss Amelia Hutchison Stirling, for the second edition. In the third edition mistakes pointed out to Hale White by Sir Frederick Pollock and Dr. J. P. N. Land were corrected. The fourth edition remained substantially the same. In an article entitled, "Some Reminiscences of the Author of 'Mark Rutherford,' " *The British Weekly* (March 20, 1913), Miss Stirling wrote: ". . . he saw that I had more knowledge of Latin than he had had the opportunity of acquiring, and he weighed and almost invariably accepted my suggested alterations without any personal feeling." Her influence can no doubt also be detected in the second Preface to the *Ethic* (1894).

3 In the Introduction to his 1899 edition of *Spinoza, His Life and Philosophy*, Sir Frederick Pollock declared that at the time of the first edition there had been no adequate or complete translation of Spinoza, but that the need had since been met by the work of two men: R. H. M. Elwes (*Works*, London, 1883–84) and W. Hale White. Of the two he termed Hale White's version as "rather the more elegant," but added that both were reliable. Actually, Hale White's translation appeared slightly earlier than Elwes', by a narrow margin. George Eliot's translation, completed in 1856, was never published.

4 Review of H. H. Joachim's *A Study of the Ethics of Spinoza* (1901) in *The Bookman* (January 1902), p. 137. Review of Henri de Boulainvilliers' *Éthique* (1907), edited by F. C. d'Istria, in *The Athenaeum* (October 5, 1907), pp. 398–99. "Spinoza," *Pages from a Journal*, pp. 32–61. "Coleridge on Spinoza," *The Athenaeum* (May 22, 1897), pp. 680–81.

5 The hortatory and in many ways inadequate Preface of the first edition was replaced in the second by an elaborate and comprehensive introduction of 105 pages as against 38 pages of the former. This new Preface contained a life of Spinoza, an account

lution," in *Last Pages from a Journal*.[6] They are of interest because in Spinoza Hale White found a body of thought which came as close to accommodating all the moral and intellectual antagonisms of his life as he was ever to discover. What these discoveries were and why Hale White could not fully accept them are of vital importance in understanding Hale White's life and work.

Spinoza has been called "the patron saint of unbelievers."[7] If this seems a strange title for a philosopher to wear, we should remind ourselves that from the time Lessing revived the interest in Spinoza among late eighteenth-century German romantics until his adoption by mid-nineteenth-century "unbelievers" in England, Spinoza had taught a habit of mind rather than a philosophy, and tended to inspire passionate discipleship more than scholarly curiosity. At the time Hale White's translation of the *Ethic* appeared, a renaissance of interest among scholars and philosophers was in full swing,[8] but to Shelley, Coleridge, Goethe, Maurice, Froude, Lewes, Arnold, George Eliot and many other nineteenth-century writers who were influenced by him,[9] Spinoza brought a religious rather than an academic message. Sir Frederick Pollock writes:

The truth is that the strength of Spinozism is not in the system as such, but in its method and habit of mind. Hostile critics have attacked the system ever since it was made known, some with real power, some with desperate captiousness; but even when they are successful the spirit eludes them. Not only will it not be driven from philosophy, but in like manner it works its way into regions where formal philosophy is unwelcome or unknown. Religion and poetry become its carriers unawares, and it might not be too fanciful to trace its presence even in the fine arts. It is more or less true of every great philosopher, but it is eminently true of Spinoza, that the history of his philosophy is interwoven with the general history of culture.[10]

---

of his works, and an analysis of the *Ethic* in the light of the *Short Treatise* and the *Letters*. Here too the *Tractatus Theologico-Politicus* is considered at some length and a list of parallel passages from Giordano Bruno is appended. The Preface to the third edition remained about the same and failed to take into account the new facts learned about Spinoza since 1894. The Preface to the fourth edition remedied these faults by additions drawn from Freudenthal's *Lebensgeschichte Spinozas* (1899) and by some revisions in the later part.

[6] It is interesting to note that this was the last essay Hale White ever published, originally appearing in the *Nation* (August 9, 1913), pp. 708–9, and reprinted in *Last Pages from a Journal*, pp. 88–94.

[7] Review of *Spinoza Essays*, ed. Prof. Knight, *The Athenaeum* (October 20, 1883), p. 493.

[8] In 1877 the bicentenary of Spinoza's death had been celebrated at The Hague. This event inspired a number of translations and studies besides the authorized Van Vloten and Land edition (1882–83) which was in part subsidized by commemoration funds. Among them were: Sir Frederick Pollock, *Spinoza, His Life and Philosophy* (1880); W. Knight, *Spinoza, Four Essays* (1882); James Martineau, *Study of Spinoza* (1882); A. B. Moss, *Bruno and Spinoza* (1885); H. H. Friedländer, *Spinoza, His Life and Philosophy* (1887); John Caird, *Spinoza* (1888); and W. J. Collins, *Spinoza, A Short Account of His Life and Philosophy* (1889).

[9] No thoroughgoing study of Spinoza's influence on nineteenth-century literature has been made. Sir Frederick Pollock has sketched in the main outlines and Sophie Bernthsen in *Der Spinozismus in Shelleys Weltanschauung* (Heidelberg, 1900) has made a beginning. But the main task remains to be done.

[10] Sir Frederick Pollock, *Spinoza, His Life and Philosophy* (London, 1899), p. 349.

Those apostates who, like Hale White, found themselves lonely and rudderless in their new-found independence from old creeds, could take heart in the example of the Amsterdam Jew of pure and blameless life who had also been maligned and persecuted for his beliefs.[11] Those whose faith had been shaken by the new Biblical criticism could be reminded, perhaps through their reading of Schleiermacher,[12] that Spinoza himself could be regarded as the father of modern Biblical criticism—that he, in the *Tractatus Theologico-Politicus* (1670) nearly two centuries earlier, had submitted Scripture to reason without any apparent damage to his moral character or any fracture of his religious peace. And those whose belief had fallen under the blows of the new science could find in Spinoza the sanction for a scientific appraisal of reality which, instead of being a cold and negative empiricism, was actually the prop and passport to a living faith. All these reasons and more combined to make Spinoza by the middle 'sixties an accepted and beloved figure—at least to liberal thinkers—instead of the child of Satan he had formerly been held to be.[13] G. H. Lewes, writing in *The Fortnightly Review* for April 1, 1866, said:

> But the temper of opinion has changed. The detested atheist is now commonly spoken of as if he were a saint; the "devil's ambassador" is listened to as if he were a prophet. Men vie with each other in exaggeration of his merits . . . We owe the change to Lessing and Mendelssohn, whose sincerity and penetration at once discerned in the execrated writings a massive grandeur and a lucid depth, and in the man a moral elevation and serenity which claimed all honour. Herder, Goethe, Novalis, Schleiermacher, Schelling, Hegel—each had his emphatic protest to utter against the vulgar outcry . . . it would now be deemed as great a mark of ignorance to speak with reprobation of Spinoza as to shudder at the heresy of Galileo.[14]

Hale White was just one of the many who seized upon Spinoza as a possible way of deliverance from dead forms to spirit in religion, from dogmas to the free exercise of intuition and conscience.

Hale White, however, was no Spinozist. Like most of the other artists and critics who embraced Spinoza, he was an eclectic reader. In his 1883 Preface to the *Ethic* he makes little attempt to elucidate the metaphysics, but instead deals with those parts of the philosopher's message which answered for him the question: *"Wherein can you help me?"* "One cannot help feeling," writes a critic in *The Westminster Review*, "that he has been impelled to the study and translation of the 'Ethic,' not as a student of philosophy, but by the motives which led him to write 'Mark Rutherford.' "[15] That this is true we shall presently see in more detail, and our

11 G. H. Lewes, "Spinoza's Life and Works," *The Westminster Review*, XXXIX (May 1843), 372–81.

12 For a comment on Spinoza's influence on Schleiermacher's *Christian Faith* (1821–22) see Storr, *Development of Theology*, p. 236.

13 See J. T. Merz, *A History of European Thought in the Nineteenth Century* (London, 1907), III, 121–22.

14 "Spinoza," *The Fortnightly Review*, IV (April 1, 1866), 389.

15 Review of Spinoza's *Ethic*, transl. W. H. White, *The Westminster Review*, LXIV (July 1883), 209.

purpose here is to examine those aspects of Spinoza's thought that Hale White felt to be important and not attempt a review of the philosophy in its entirety.

Actually, Spinoza defined for Hale White, much as he had for Goethe, a mood rather than a metaphysic, an attitude rather than a system. In his second Preface to the *Ethic* (1894) Hale White quotes from Goethe's *Autobiography*, and in these words of a man who shared a profound spiritual kinship with Hale White and who likewise did not read Spinoza philosophically, we may detect some of the qualities of Hale White's own discipleship:

After looking through the world in vain to find a means of development for my strange nature, I at last fell upon the *Ethic* of this man. Of what I read out of the work and of what I read into it, I can give no account. Enough that here I found a sedative for my passions, and that a free, wide view over the material world seemed to open before me. But what especially bound me to him, was the great disinterestedness which shone from every proposition. That wonderful expression, "who loves God truly must not desire God to love him in return," with all the preliminary propositions on which it rests, and all the consequences that follow from it, filled my whole mind. To be disinterested in everything, but the most so in love and friendship, was my highest desire, my maxim, my practice, and so that audacious saying of mine afterwards, "If I love thee, what is that to thee?" was spoken right out of my heart. Moreover, it must not here be denied that the most inward unions are those of opposites. The all-composing calmness of Spinoza was in striking contrast with my all-disturbing activity, his mathematical method was the opposite of my poetic imagination and way of writing, and the very precision which was thought not adapted to moral subjects made me his enthusiastic disciple, his most decided worshipper. Mind and heart, understanding and feeling sought each other with an eager affinity, binding together the most different natures.[16]

Of all the lovers of Spinoza, Goethe was probably the most perfectly equipped to understand and to follow him in that attitude of "disinterestedness" which he engenders in true believers. And the fact that Hale White quotes (and translates) this passage suggests that he understood Goethe's meaning and that he found, or wanted to find, something of the same inspiration.

In another place Hale White had written that the works of Spinoza were "productive beyond those of almost any man I know of that *acquiescentia mentis* which enables us to live."[17] But what he perhaps never quite understood was that the *"acquiescentia mentis* which enables us to live" is not quite the same as Goethean "disinterestedness." The one indicates a peace in the face of pain and hardship while the other indicates a rising above pain and hardship; the one suggests stoic fortitude while the other suggests almost mystical aspiration. In earlier chapters we have traced Hale White's struggle to maintain some sort of absolute idealism within the frame of life's realities, and how from this struggle emerged a gospel of resignation. We shall see something of the same transition in his rela-

---

16 *Sp.b.*, pp. lxxxix-xc.
17 "Spinoza," *P.J.*, p. 58.

tions with Spinoza. Hale White could doubtless understand what was meant by "disinterestedness," but, as we have already noted, he was no more able to translate it into a habit of life than was Carlyle. The world was too much with him; its mud clung to his boots and prevented such ascension. But he envied the Goethean achievement as he loved the Spinozistic dream and, in his intense awareness of the demands made by life for renunciation and self-denial, it seems likely that he was fascinated by this Olympian denial which escaped the danger of deteriorating into mere masochism or gratuitous self-torture. Spinoza offered a way clear of this danger, and Pollock describes how Goethe grasped at it:

> The whole of our education and experience bids us to renounce and resign: "Dass wir entsagen sollen." The problem of man's life is to reconcile himself to this. One ready way is the superficial way of the many, to proclaim that all things are vanity. But the path of wisdom, sought only by a few, is to cut short the pains of resignation in detail by a resignation once for all; to rest one's mind on that which is eternal, necessary, and uniform, and possess ideas which remain undisturbed by the contemplation of a transitory world. This was the secret of Spinoza for Goethe.[18]

To achieve such resignation is at the same time to know a supreme and absolute spiritual consummation. But although Hale White was religious, he was never religious in quite the way Spinoza was, and in his attempts to be a Spinozist we witness once again a futile effort to force his personality into an alien frame. He could never muster the self-confidence to make a resignation "once for all" to the inevitable; he could not be at ease in those open places of Spinozistic experience where duality has faded into a blessed oneness; he could never feel certain that morality was possible when the words "will" and "pain" and "right" and "wrong" were erased from one's ethical vocabulary. Yet Spinoza demanded all of these things. Their lure was great, but their seductiveness competed in Hale White with a whole set of Puritan inhibitions and prejudices. To study the drama of this conflict (which Hale White never seems clearly to have recognized himself) is to witness a spiritual dénouement epitomizing not only the changes in a man but something of the spiritual struggles of a century.

In an essay entitled, "Revolution,"[19] published on the very eve of his death, Hale White told of those ideas and doctrines which, in retrospect, he felt had wrought the most fundamental changes in his life. Among them were three principles from Spinoza's *Ethic* pertaining to (1) his doctrine of immortality, (2) his concept of the union of mind and body, and (3) his formula for the control of the passions by "adequate" ideas.

The first of these doctrines was taken from Part 5 of the *Ethic*, Proposition XXIII:

> *The human mind cannot be absolutely destroyed with the body, but something of it remains which is eternal.*[20]

[18] Pollock, *Spinoza*, p. 370.
[19] *L.P.*, pp. 88–94.   [20] *Ibid.*, 90–91.

Following this, Hale White remarks:

This proposition with its demonstration and those connected with it contain everything which I have ever found to be a reality touching the so-called immortality of
the soul. The ground does not shake.

That Hale White keenly missed the assurance of immortality—missed it,
perhaps, more keenly than any other item in his childhood faith—is revealed in the peculiar emphasis he places upon his fear of death, and the
number of times in his work that we find the subject discussed. "Death
has always been a terror to me," he writes on the second page of his *Autobiography*; "and at times, nay generally, religion and philosophy have
been altogether unavailing to mitigate the terror in any way."[21] Later on,
he makes an even clearer confession:

But the worst stroke of all was that which fell upon the doctrine of a life beyond
the grave. In theory I had long despised the notion that we should govern our conduct
here by hope of reward or fear of punishment hereafter. But under Mardon's remorseless criticism, when he insisted on asking for the where and how, and pointed
out that all attempts to say where and how ended in nonsense, my hope began to fail,
and I was surprised to find myself incapable of living with proper serenity if there was
nothing but blank darkness before me at the end of a few years. As I got older I
became aware of the folly of this perpetual reaching after the future, and of drawing
from to-morrow, and from to-morrow only, a reason for the joyfulness of to-day. I
learned, when, alas! it was almost too late, to live in each moment as it passed over
my head, believing that the sun as it is now rising is as good as it will ever be, and
blinding myself as much as possible to what may follow. But when I was young I was
the victim of that illusion, implanted for some purpose or other in us by Nature, which
causes us, on the brightest morning in June, to think immediately of a brighter morning which is to come in July. I say nothing, now, for or against the doctrine of
immortality. All I say is, that men have been happy without it, even under the pressure of disaster, and that to make immortality a sole spring of action here is an exaggeration of the folly which deludes us all through life with endless expectation, and
leaves us at death without the thorough enjoyment of a single hour.[22]

Without going deeply into Spinoza's doctrine of immortality, it should
be realized, as Pollock points out, that

Spinoza's eternal life is not a continuance of existence but a manner of existence;
something which can be realized here and now as much as at any other time and
place; not a future reward of the soul's perfection but the soul's perfection itself.[23]

Now the substitution, for a man of Hale White's Nonconformist upbringing, of a psychological for a cosmological hereafter was as essential for
his deliverance as it was difficult. It was essential because he had been
trained to place an enormous value on spiritual survival, and it was difficult[24] because abandoning the hope of *personal* immortality, in which
memory abides, involved a serious wrenching of that individualistic pride

21 *A.*, p. 2. Cf. Spinoza, *Ethic*, Pt. 4, Prop. LXVII: *"A free man thinks of nothing
less than of death . . ."*
22 *A.*, pp. 64–65. See also *Sp.a.*, pp. xxx–xxxi.
23 Pollock, *Spinoza*, p. 275.
24 See *A.*, p. 89, for an excellent statement of this difficulty.

which was one of his most marked characteristics.. Nevertheless, Hale White seems to have tried to accept Spinoza's guidance in this matter more completely than in almost any other, and it was with intense earnestness— once the old notions of reward beyond the grave had been discarded—that he set about learning these new paths across the Sloughs of Despond and monomania.

He writes in the *Deliverance*:

Our aim ought not so much to be the salvation of this poor petty self, but of that in me which alone makes it worth while to save me; of that alone which I hope will be saved, immortal truth. The very centre of the existence of the ordinary chapel-goer and church-goer needs to be shifted from self to what is outside self. . . . If the truth lives, *we* live, and if it dies, we are dead. Our theology stands in need of a reformation greater than that of Luther's [*sic*]. It may be said that the attempt to replace the care for self in us by a care for the universal is ridiculous. Man cannot rise to that height. I do not believe it. I believe we can rise to it. Every ordinary unselfish act is a proof of the capacity to rise to it; and the mother's denial of all care for her own happiness, if she can but make her child happy, is a sublime anticipation. It may be called an instinct, but in the course of time it will be possible to develop a wider instinct in us, so that our love for the truth shall be even maternally passionate and self-forgetting.[25]

In voicing this ideal Hale White may have been, more than he perhaps realized, whistling to keep up his courage; but that the ideal itself was in-spired in no small degree by Spinoza cannot be doubted, for the exposition of Spinoza's doctrine given us in the Preface to the *Ethic* reveals the same characteristics:

Spinoza believes that the more *reasonable* we are the better will it be for us both here and hereafter; for *us* in some sense, although in what sense *us* is obscure. There is no heaven for him but this. Heaven is not a hereafter of reward: it is the here and hereafter of the intellectual love of God. In so far as the mind is capable of intellectual love, it is not only eternal but a part of God Himself. Man perceiving things under the form of eternity is not a thing down here created by a Being up there, of whom he knows nothing, save what has been revealed to him, but he is actually one with the God who has created Arcturus, Orion, the Pleiades, and the chambers of the south, and in a sense may be said to have had a share in their crea-tion. Spinoza never goes nearer to inspiration than in the propositions on the rela-tionship between God and man, and there is an unmistakeable heat in them which shows that they were dear to him.[26]

In the effort to attain a "really human religion" Hale White was never helped by Spinoza more than in this. The conception of the presence and working out in the individual of the element of eternity[27] (though the conception received various expressions in Hale White's work) is with him an unwavering faith.[28]

To achieve immortality on Spinoza's terms became, for Hale White, the problem of overcoming his own self-absorption. God was now lodged

[25] *D.*, pp. 91–92.
[26] *Sp.b.*, p. xcviii.
[27] See also Hegel's influence in this regard, pp. 71–74, 88 above.
[28] See *M.P.*, p. 251.

not in the heavens, but in ordinary men in society; immortality was to be found in a psychological condition, not in a posthumous reward. But to know this God or immortality one must not defensively isolate himself from the universe of which he is a part; he who would find his life must lose it. "All depends," writes George Santayana in describing the challenge of Spinoza, "in not being afraid to confess that the universe is non-human, and that man is relative."[29]

Let a man once overcome his selfish terror at his own finitude, and his finitude itself is, in one sense, overcome. A part of his soul, in sympathy with the infinite, has accepted the natural status of all the rest of his being. Perhaps the only true dignity of man is his capacity to despise himself. When he attains this dignity all things lose what was threatening and sinister about them, without needing to change their material form or their material influence. Man's intellectual part and his worshipping part have made their peace with the world.

The self-despising of which Santayana speaks is really a form of self-love and not self-hate, an abandonment inspired by confidence and not by fear. Often, as we have seen before, Hale White struggled in vain to achieve such self-immolation, and one of his characteristic statements is that found in the *Autobiography*: "Blessed are they who *heal*[30] us of self-despisings."[31] But on the occasion which inspired that statement he had simply been relieved of an acute sense of inferiority and failure by some kind words from George Eliot. He had not been despising himself in the manner Santayana has described; he had been ignobly and bitterly hating himself.

But there were nevertheless moments when Hale White achieved—at least in fantasy—an otherness which was precisely what Santayana described and Spinoza desired. Such a moment is given us in the *Deliverance*:

The instinct which leads us perpetually to compare what we are with what we might be is no doubt of enormous value, and is the spring which prompts all action, but, like every instinct, it is the source of greatest danger. I remember the day and the very spot on which it flashed into me, like a sudden burst of the sun's rays, that I had no right to this or that—to so much happiness, or even so much virtue. What title-deeds could I show for such a right? Straightway it seemed as if the centre of a whole system of dissatisfaction were removed, and as if the system collapsed. God, creating from His infinite resources a whole infinitude of beings, had created me with a definite position on the scale, and that position only could I claim. Cease the trick of contrast. If I can by any means get myself to consider myself alone without reference to others, discontent will vanish.[32]

To destroy self-pity and envy of the petty advantages of his fellow-beings by accepting his own relativity in the universe God has made most certainly has a Spinozistic ring to it. The absolute elimination of the "trick

---

[29] George Santayana, Introduction to *Spinoza's Ethics* (London, 1910), p. viii.

[30] My italics.

[31] *A.*, p. 157.

[32] *D.*, p. 119. Perhaps there are echoes of Carlyle in *Sartor Resartus*, Bk. II, Chap. IX: "Foolish soul! What Act of Legislature was there that *thou* shouldst be Happy?"

of contrast" was, of course, the inevitable reward to anyone who followed Spinoza all the way. Whether or not Hale White owed this wisdom to Spinoza cannot be determined, but it is certain that his journals are full of observations with which Spinoza would have been in full agreement. "If we desire peace," he writes in *More Pages*, "we must get beyond the notion of personality. Nothing of any value is bound up with it: it is an illusion."[33] And again, in *More Pages*: "As we move higher, personality becomes of less consequence. We do not live in the 'I,' but in truths."[34]

But the most remarkable evidence that Hale White was at times capable of a full abnegation in the Spinozistic sense is provided in the essay, "An Epoch," in *More Pages*. This was written in late life, between 1907 and 1910, in those Groombridge years which were among the most contemplative of his existence.

One morning when I was in the wood something happened which was nothing less than a transformation of myself and the world, although I "believed" nothing new. I was looking at a great, spreading, bursting oak. The first tinge from the greenish-yellow buds was just visible. It seemed to be no longer a tree away from me and apart from me. The enclosing barriers of consciousness were removed and the text came into my mind, *Thou in me and I in thee.* The distinction of self and not-self was an illusion. I could feel the rising sap; in me also sprang the fountain of life uprushing from its roots, and the joy of its outbreak at the extremity of each twig right up to the summit was my own: that which kept me apart was nothing. I do not argue; I cannot explain; it will be easy to prove me absurd, but nothing can shake me. *Thou in me and I in thee.* Death! what is death? There is no death: *in thee* it is impossible, absurd.[35]

This is consummation.[36] Though it represents a rare and temporary event rather than any final peace, it is a striking revelation of the degree to which Hale White could at times catch Spinoza's spirit.

But Hale White was no mystic, and in the normal run of his life he seldom achieved self-escape by a fearless immersion in the spiritual and material oneness of a God-given universe. His was not entirely, in a Spinozistic sense, a facing of reality but an escape from it, away—as Spinoza would say—from the inevitable perfection of things as they are.[37] However violent his aspirations, Hale White could never permanently rid himself of an earth-bound conscience or of the slavery of immediate human needs. To live happily in the wide arena of Spinozistic emancipation would require an almost godlike largeness of mind, and Hale White is not peculiar in lacking it. The attempt to "despise" the self brought Hale White hard up against a paradox which a man of his emotional equipment could

---

[33] *M.P.*, p. 236.
[34] *Ibid.*, p. 232.
[35] *Ibid.*, pp. 182–83.
[36] Not only does this statement provoke comparison with the vitalism of D. H. Lawrence and Henri Bergson, but it records an experience remarkably paralleled by the Existentialist, Jean-Paul Sartre. See "The Root of the Chestnut Tree," *The Partisan Review* (Winter, 1946), pp. 25–33. The date of composition of this story is probably around April 1, 1908. See *G.D.*, pp. 7–8.
[37] See *Ethic*, Part 4, "Of Human Bondage."

not transcend: the denial of the self gave a value to the self, intellectual emancipation from the tyranny of natural law brought a proud sense that man was no mere piece of materialistic clay, but above it and apart from it. In his essay, "Spinoza," he writes:

> The sorrow of life is the rigidity of the material universe in which we are placed. We are bound by physical laws, and there is a constant pressure of matter-of-fact evidence to prove that we are nothing but common and cheap products of the earth to which in a few moments or years we return. Spinoza's chief aim is to free us from this sorrow, and to free us from it by *thinking*.[38]

If we read *brooding* here instead of *thinking*, we are perhaps describing more accurately Hale White's application of Spinoza's formula, and the reason why it failed him. Though he was convinced that there was "nothing of any worth" in what we call "personality," it was always for him more of a sobering reminder that "there is no health in us" than a joyful freeing of his selfhood. The trick of contrast kept reasserting itself, and while his egotism became softer in its demands, it had the last word. In 1910 he admitted he had not fully learned Spinoza's lesson:

> It is impossible totally to exclude the "I" in our most unselfish acts. We ought not to torment ourselves because we cannot exclude it. We must not set pleasure so sharply over against unselfishness.[39]

Perhaps, if we change the wording, this was actually much closer to what Spinoza meant anyway.

Thus the full realization of a Spinozistic immortality proved beyond his powers of self-denial, his reach for it always exceeded any firm grasp. At the end of his life he seems to have rested in a compromise, containing something of Spinoza still but more of a longing for an older faith which was rooted in dualism and provided a richer promise for the satisfaction of the ego.

> I should like to die not entirely. I should like that part of me to live that rejoices in these clouds, this field of barley, these surrounding trees. But there is another part which I so heartily wish were dead that in order to annihilate it I would joyfully sacrifice the first.[40]

And again:

> We cannot help feeling that it makes *some* difference if in a few more years we are no longer to be witnesses to the evolution of all that is now stirring amongst mankind, and our own development and ascent are to be suddenly arrested.[41]

The second doctrine, that of the unity of body and mind, is caught up in two passages quoted by Hale White from Part 2 of the *Ethic*.[42]

> *The mind and the body are one and the same individual, which at one time is considered under the attribute of thought, and at another under that of extension.* (Prop. XXI, Pt. 2, *Schol.*)

[38] *P.J.*, pp. 33–34.
[39] *L.P.*, p. 297.
[40] *Ibid.*, pp. 303–4.   [41] *Sp.a.*, p. xxxi.   [42] *L.P.*, pp. 89–90.

And this follows from the proposition that

substance thinking and substance extended are one and the same substance, which is now comprehended under this attribute and now under that. (Prop. VII, *Schol.*)

After quoting these, Hale White says, "These scholia loosened each difficulty which arose from considering matter as a thing by itself set over against thought as a thing by itself." The nature of these difficulties is investigated at some length by Hale White in his article, "Spinoza's Doctrine of the Relationship Between Mind and Body."[43] The essay is not very satisfactory, but it indicates with some clarity Hale White's understanding of this crucial Spinozistic doctrine.

Spinoza had said (Prop. XIII, Pt. 2) : *"The object of the idea constituting the human mind is a body, or a certain mode of extension actually existing, and nothing else."* In explaining this and other propositions, Hale White wrote:

It is evident, therefore . . . that to Spinoza the body is not the object of the mind, in the sense that the mind is its separate, but exact reflection or counterpart. . . . What Spinoza intends by "object" is in fact *ob-jected*. He denies the existence of two utterly diverse entities, mind and body. How, he thinks, if this be true, are we to pass from one to the other? . . . The body and mind *are the same thing* considered under two different attributes. . . . there is no such thing as an abstract mind issuing its orders to the body, and no such thing as an abstract body controlling the mind . . . Man thinking *in time and existent* is this particular body as thought: man's body is the mind as extension.[44]

Hale White was, doubtless, not particularly entranced by the metaphysical difficulties of his subject and is definitely somewhat puzzled by them. But the central idea here dealt with—the idea that mind and body were not to be considered dualistically but monistically—was certainly of deep interest to him even though the chemistry of the union remained beyond his comprehension. The ethical implications, at least, caught his imagination, if the metaphysical did not. For on no point would Spinoza be more likely to give a wrench to Hale White's Puritan set of mind. It was Spinoza, he wrote, who "relieved men, or who did his best to relieve them, from the trouble and despair consequent upon . . . a dual government of the world."[45] The qualification, ". . . or who did his best" is an extremely revealing one, for it seems to suggest that Hale White—at the very moment when Spinoza most absorbed his attention—did not cease believing that duality and all its consequences were here to stay. He did not seem to understand that Spinoza *really believed* that a "dual government of the world" was a fundamental misconception, that it did in plain fact not exist. But Hale White's mental block against this idea is understandable. For if Spinoza relieved men's despair, he did so by wiping

43 Published in *The International Journal of Ethics*, VI (July 1896), 515–18.
44 *Ibid.*, 516. See discussion of this problem in Stuart Hampshire, *Spinoza* (Harmondsworth, England, 1951), pp. 58–69.
45 *Sp.b.*, pp. xcix–c.

out not only theological and rationalistic distinctions, but the ethical assumptions traditionally based on those distinctions: the differences between right and wrong, sin and punishment. Formerly, as Blake would say, the body was of the Devil and called evil, the mind was of Heaven and called good. Now the very notion of evil itself—as orthodoxy had understood it—was dissolved. Adam sinned, declared Spinoza, through "privation" of knowledge—mere "absence" of something—which absence cannot be called anything positive. So, with scant justice to Spinoza's ingenuity, runs his argument.[46] Why, therefore, if sin is "nothing positive" or, in other words, nonexistent, should we punish or be punished for so-called wrongdoing? Hale White was deeply impressed by this argument and wrote at length about it in his 1894 Preface:

We . . . may say at least as much as this—that when once we have made Spinoza real to us, our attitude towards human beings and our conception of what punishment should be will be entirely altered. All that portion of man which was considered by theology as the domain of the devil becomes as truly man as his virtues. We may even affirm that we are saved as much by our sins as our virtues. "In the stringed instrument of man," says Jean Paul, "there is no string to be cut out; it needs but to be tuned." All vindictiveness also at once disappears: we shall never punish in order to gratify revenge, or because we imagine any penalty to be divinely attached to crime, except for the purpose of reformation. Nature knows nothing of penalties. She corrects in order to obtain a result. The practical effect of the teaching, duly laid to heart, will in fact be immense. . . . the mother and father will see limitation where they would otherwise have seen sin, and will chastise merely in order to amend. They will recognise that the creature thus limited and the very limitation itself are the work of God. Hell, to put it briefly, is forthwith abolished, understanding by hell all retribution which is retribution and nothing more; for many of us who have ceased to believe in hell as a dogma of the Church, continue to believe in it essentially by inflicting pain simply because wrong is supposed to deserve it. The desert of the wrongdoer is henceforth discovered to be nothing more than the desert to be put right . . . Spinoza, it will be observed, was distinctly led to think of human nature in the way in which he thought of it because he thought of God in a certain way. It is a remarkable instance of the effect which a metaphysical doctrine can have upon daily life.[47]

This was Blake's "marriage" of Heaven and Hell, of evil and good, body and mind, instinct and reason. And it provided a formula which, perhaps, could have brought unity to the divisions of Hale White's personality. But certain aspects of this doctrine distressed him. Again and again, in a dozen different contexts, he asks this insistent question: if all things are good in this God-made, God-infested world, how can one account for the fact of pain?[48]

. . . of pain we have no explanation. Pain is not lessened by understanding it, nor is its mystery penetrated if we see that to God material could not have been wanting for the creation of men or animals who have to endure it all their lives.

[46] See Pollock, *Spinoza*, p. 47. Based on Spinoza's letter to Blyenburgh, Jan. 28, 1665.

[47] *Sp.b.*, pp. lxxviii–lxxix.

[48] "Spinoza," *P.J.*, p. 52.

And finding no answer, we find him again returning to the solution of Job for comfort:

But if Spinoza is silent in the presence of pain, so also is every religion and philosophy which the world has seen. Silence is the only conclusion of the Book of Job, and patient fortitude in the hope of future enlightenment is the conclusion of Christianity. It is a weak mistake, however, to put aside what religions and philosophies tell us because it is insufficient. To Job it is not revealed why suffering is apportioned so unequally or why it exists, but the answer of the Almighty from the whirlwind he cannot dispute. . . .[49]

The fact of pain was a barrier between the mind and the body which Hale White could never permanently lower. Not only was he too accustomed to thinking of the body as the base and separate lodging of the essential self, the soul, but the habit of mortifying its demands had too long been associated in his mind with virtue itself. He could hate the body but he could not completely join forces with it; he could meet with fortitude its pains and with discipline its pleasures, but it remained always apart and always in some sense a threat.

Closely tied in with this difficulty was a notion of which he could never quite rid himself that pain is always part of some kind of retributive justice. Among the "Notes" of *Last Pages*, for example, he makes such assertions as these:

All religions have said that if we do wrong we must not only amend and offer reparation but that there must be expiation. Modern philosophy [doubtless Spinoza is meant] denies it. I cannot rid myself of what seems to me an instinct that wrongdoing demands a penalty.[50]

And again:

It is a shallow notion that the suffering of another for our transgressions is injustice and a moral wrong. We are saved by the sacrifice of the Just. Never is individualism more completely mistaken than in proclaiming the horror of redemption from evil by the death of him who is not guilty.[51]

If the "humanizing" of the Gospel story is to be taken seriously, then this is a logical consequent. As the innocent, but human, Christ died and suffered for us, so those of us who would follow his example must also suffer (and even die) for the guilty. How far this is from Spinoza's meaning and spirit needs no comment, but Hale White never completely seemed to realize that one cannot be a Spinozist and a Puritan at the same time.

But the most striking comment Hale White makes on the necessity of painful punishment for wrongdoing is found in his short story, "Atonement." Here we are presented with a man who, in a mood of desperate melancholy and ill temper, rages out of his house one Saturday afternoon and nearly stumbles over his dog on the threshold. "God damn you!" he cried, and viciously kicked the animal, who faithfully followed his master

---

[49] *Ibid.*, pp. 52–53.
[50] *L.P.*, p. 285.
[51] *Ibid.*, pp. 319–20.

along the street until it dropped dead in the gutter, killed by the injuries it had received. The man's remorse was terrible, the more so because he could not rationally account for his anger nor for the fact that the spectacle of his loving and ever-patient wife had seemed to increase rather than allay it.[52]

A separate consciousness seemed to establish itself in this foot; there was nothing to be seen and no pain, but there was a dull sort of pressure of which I could not rid myself. If I slept I dreamed of the dog, and generally dreamed I was caressing him, waking up to the dreadful truth of the corpse on the path in the rain. I got it into my head—for I was half-crazy—that only by some expiation I should be restored to health and peace; but how to make any expiation I could not tell.

The opportunity came not long after. A fire had broken out in a neighboring house, and all the inhabitants had been rescued except a mongrel cur. The man saved the dog, but in jumping from a window fell on *that* foot, which subsequently had to be amputated. His cheerful fortitude during the operation amazed the doctors, and the dog's owner—who made him a gift of the animal—could not understand the eagerness and joy with which he received it.

How can this be explained? It is, to no small degree, a parable drawn from Hale White's own inner experience. The volcanic intensity of the man's temper might very well be a reflection of Hale White's own mood during those bitterly prolonged years of his first wife's long illness, when her saintly patience could seem a perpetual rebuke to his acute frustration. The dog could be a symbol for the wife, and the story as a whole a study in the processes of expiating an irrational hatred which, to Hale White, must have seemed strangely akin to original sin itself. Hypochondria, monomania, melancholia—these were the modern names for an ancient heritage. Orthodoxy would have provided safety valves; apostasy burdened the sinner with the problem of finding his own atonement. Spinoza would have provided the man in this story a way of expiation which did not demand the cutting out of the offending member, a purification which was as alien to such masochism as love is to hate. But the man in the story, wrestling like Hale White himself against the impulse to destroy what he loved,[53] could find his atonement only after exacting of his own body, in the manner of an older code, an eye for an eye and a tooth for a tooth.

Spinoza's admonition to forget the problem of sin entirely and to rise above the idea of good and evil, reward and punishment, demanded an Olympian disinterestedness Hale White could never for long attain. As George Moore has said, ". . . a withdrawing from all commerce with

---

[52] *P.J.*, p. 177. An article in the *Illustrated London News* for May 9, 1885, about the heroic death of Miss Alice Ayres in a fire, from which she had tried to save three children, was included in Hale White's scrapbook, and may have suggested the background of this story.

[53] In conversations with the present author at Sherborne, October 17, 1949, Mrs. D. V. White remarked upon this instinct in her husband. See also *G.D.*, p. 393.

virtue and vice is, it would seem, a licentiousness more curiously subtle
and penetrating than any other . . ."[54] Hale White's books are the record
of how he kept returning to the commerce with vice and virtue, to the
dualities of normal Christian experience, which could divide and conquer
the licentiousness of which Moore speaks. To wander undecidedly between
the claims of the flesh and the spirit, instinct and reason, was better than
not acknowledging the rival claims at all.

We read our Bible, Thomas à Kempis, and Bunyan, and we are persuaded that our
salvation lies in the perpetual struggle of the higher against the lower self, the
spirit against the flesh, and that the success of the flesh is damnation. We take
down Horace and Rabelais and we admit that the body also has its claims. We have
no power to dominate both sets of books, and consequently they supersede one another alternately.[55]

Needless to say, Spinoza could have given him that power had he been
able to accept him fully. But Hale White, following his essay entitled,
"Spinoza," appends an almost ludicrously irrelevant "Supplementary
Note on the Devil."[56] The philosopher had removed the Devil, but the
ex-Calvinist felt ill at ease without his threatening presence.

On whatever lines the world may be framed, there must be *distinction, difference,*
a higher and a lower; and the lower, relatively to the higher, must always be an
evil. The *scale* upon which the higher and lower both are, makes no difference. . . .
Perfectly uninterrupted, infinite light, without shadow, is a physical absurdity. I
see a thing because it is lighted, but also because of the differences of light, or, in
other words, because of shade, and without shade the universe would be objectless,
and in fact invisible. The atheist was dreaming of shadowless light, a contradiction
in terms.[57]

If Spinoza was meant by "atheist" here (and it was a tag he had long
worn), then this is rejection indeed. For few men ever dreamed of "shadowless light" more passionately or denied with more determination this
alignment of moral values. And if, in the following passage, we read
"philosophy" to mean that of the Amsterdam Jew, we have an even clearer
repudiation:

Philosophy proclaims the unity of our nature. To philosophy every passion is as
natural as every act of saintlike negation, and one of the usual effects of thinking
or philosophising is to bring together all that is apparently contrary in man, and to
show how it proceeds really from one centre. But Christianity had not to propound
a theory of man; it had to redeem the world. It laid awful stress on the duality in
us, and the stress laid on that duality is the world's salvation. The words right and
wrong are not felt now as they were felt by Paul. They shade off one into the other.
Nevertheless, if mankind is not to be lost, the ancient antagonism must be maintained.[58]

With Rabelais and Spinoza on his left, and Bunyan and the Bible on
his right, Hale White read on throughout his life. At the end of it all we

---

[54] George Moore, *Confessions of a Young Man* (London, 1928), p. 65.
[55] *P.J.*, p. 76.
[56] *Ibid.*, pp. 58–61.   [57] *A.*, pp. 100–101.   [58] *D.*, pp. 94–95.

realize that these two sets of volumes symbolized a dualism he never resolved, but the right-hand books were the better thumbed and the better marked.

The third and last doctrine quoted by Hale White in "Revolution" concerns the control of the passions by "adequate" ideas.[59]

The actions of the mind arise from adequate ideas alone, but the passions depend upon those alone which are inadequate. (Prop. III, Pt. 3.)

From this it follows by direct deduction:

. . . the more perfection a thing possesses, the more it acts and the less it suffers, and conversely the more it acts the more perfect it is. (Prop. XL, Pt. 5.)

In these specific doctrines—which might be viewed at some distance from Spinoza's main premise—Hale White could find more that was sympathetic and helpful to him. The particular kind of clear thinking and truthfulness involved in Spinoza's doctrine of "adequate" ideas could appeal strongly to a man with Hale White's passion for veracity and objective hardheadedness, who was also something of a scientist.

Spinoza explained what he meant by an "adequate" idea in a letter to Hugo Boxel, clarifying the matter by explaining what it meant to have an "adequate" idea of God:

To your question, Whether I have as clear an idea of God as I have of a triangle? I answer, Yes. But if you ask me whether I have as clear an image of God as I have of a triangle, I shall say, No; for we cannot imagine God, but we can understand Him.[60]

On Spinoza's premises, a man can have an adequate idea of God because the human mind is part of the mind of God and because that human mind has the power to perceive itself. Hale White was much impressed by this notion, for it was a support to his belief that human beings possess an essence (or soul) which is not represented by their actions or speech but which partakes of the eternal.[61] And it further supported his contention that the failure to imagine a thing (say God) is no proof of its nonexistence. Baruch Cohen in *Clara Hopgood* speaks right from the *Ethic*:

"I believe that inability to imagine a thing is not a reason for its non-existence. If the infinite is a conclusion which is forced upon me, the fact that I cannot picture it does not disprove it . . .

"You will be surprised, perhaps, to hear that mathematics, which, of course, I had to learn for my own business, have supplied something for a foundation. They lead to ideas which are inconsistent with the notion that the imagination is a measure of all things."[62]

Hale White frequently employs Spinoza's mathematical illustration to support his own convictions. In *Last Pages* he writes:

A man learns that the three angles of a triangle are equal to two right angles. What has happened? Something has been added to his personality, for what is his

59 *L.P.*, p. 90.   60 *Sp.b.*, p. lxvii.
61 *Ibid.*, p. lxviii.   62 *C.H.*, pp. 175–76.

personality but ideas? Secondly, the Universal, Eternal Truth has incarnated itself in a person. Everlastingly this process goes on . . .[63]

To see the truth clear, without body or metaphor, as pure *idea* with no admixture of an *image*, was an intellectual prejudice of profound implication both in Hale White's writing and thought. With him as with Spinoza truth was synonymous with absolute clarity and simplicity. Those "Notes" written between 1892 and 1894 are full of expressions of this belief:

> I pray for a gift which perhaps would be miraculous: simply to be able to see that field of waving grass as I should see it if association and the "film of custom" did not obscure it.[64]

Again he tells us:

> Clear vision is not often the cause of distress. It is rather the cloud of imagination distorting what is before us and preventing distinct view. Science, removing the heavens to an infinite distance, destroying traditions, abolishing our little theologies, does not disturb our peace so seriously as that vague dreaming in which there is no thinking.[65]

Both Hale White and Spinoza would agree that to form an adequate idea of a triangle, for example, we must divest the mind of the *image* of the triangle and conceive of it as pure idea. The image is a distortion, and makes the idea inadequate, because considerations irrelevant to the reality of the idea are caught up in it. In a letter to Miss Mabel Marsh on September 1, 1899—dealing mainly with the problem of children's education— Hale White's remarks reveal a strong Spinozistic coloring:

> . . . you cannot too soon exercise children in abstracting. You may prove of any particular triangle by measurement that its three angles = two rt. ∠s, but to prove that the three angles of *every* triangle *must* = 2 rt. ∠s, you must use the ideal point and the ideal line. On the *every* and *must* depend the whole educational importance of geometry. . . . What is gained by sensuous picturing of material points and lines? Nothing. The child will soon enough pick up a serviceable acquaintance with them, and if you authorize him to think that this thing • is really a point of which the smallest use can be made scientifically, the passage from the false conception to the true will be made more and not less difficult. . . . It would be no exaggeration to affirm that correct notions as to the foundations of geometry are inseparably connected with correct notions as to theology and ethics.[66]

Hale White often declared to his son, John, that "the objective life of scientific investigation would have suited him better than any other, and that, if he had been given the necessary training in his youth, he would have given up everything for science."[67] In 1892, while living at High Wickham, Hastings, he bought an astronomical telescope and, though limited in his knowledge of mathematics,[68] became a proficient amateur, delivering a lecture to the British Astronomical Association in 1895 on the "Wilsonian Theory of Sunspots" and making many investigations into the

---

[63] *L.P.*, p. 275.   [64] *M.P.*, p. 231.   [65] *Ibid.*, p. 230.
[66] Unpublished letter in possession of Mrs. D. V. White. Cf. also *L.P.*, pp. 138–52.
[67] *P.N.a.*, p. 9. See also *L.P.*, p. 91 and *P.N.b.*, p. 37.
[68] *Ibid.*, p. 92.

astronomical accuracy of poets and novelists.[69] The sketches of his observations, which have been preserved by his second wife, reveal a draftsman-like neatness and precision, together with a clear knowledge of scientific classification. But, in regard to his declared penchant for science, his son adds: ". . . in some moods he felt like this no doubt, but the intuitive and poetic element in him was likewise strong and I have heard him declare with equal enthusiasm that of all things he would have liked to be the organist to a cathedral."[70]

There were unquestionably these two sides of his nature, but what particularly interests us here is the fact that Spinoza not only left room in his philosophy for such diverse interests, but gave warrant for their simultaneous expression. In Spinoza, writes Pollock, "we find almost everywhere . . . scientific and essentially modern thought clothed in the semblance of scholastic forms."[71] In Spinoza the poet and the scientist could come to terms, for all matter in his conception was God-filled, all was pregnant with idea, and to understand it "adequately" was to achieve that joyous surrender: the intellectual love of God. As we have already seen, Hale White strained in this direction. All his scientific and scholarly work was originally motivated by a deeply felt emotional, if not religious, attraction. His second wife reports him as saying that "he looked at the stars to increase his awe, not to increase his knowledge."[72] And in his *Black Notebook* he gives us this significant confession:

I am afraid that at one point I am not scientific. I am apt to rejoice when explanation is stopped by the incomprehensible. The true man of science, although he may admit the incomprehensible, hates it and perpetually endeavours to repel and restrict it.[73]

To get an adequate idea of anything was to consider it in itself, without reference to anything else. To see it completely in full terms of its own reality was to see it perfectly, for imperfection was, with Spinoza, merely negation. Now this did not mean seeing a sunset in terms of mathematics or a flower in terms of biologic laws; it meant seeing these objects in terms of *all* their attributes, of *all* the qualities imbedded in them. Regarding a triangle as an abstraction is valid because it *is* only an abstraction, an idea; but we must, Spinoza insists, derive our ideas from physical or really existing things and not pass over into abstract and universal notions. This seems to be contradictory, but it is not really, for the "constant and eternal" things to which Spinoza refers are themselves particular, present, and operative everywhere.[74]

If we examine Hale White's notebooks, we find abundant evidence that this method of investigating in the particular for the meaning of life was his as well. And the emotional excitement accompanying such discovery gives much of Hale White's writing a strong Spinozistic flavor:

Intense feeling gives intellectual precision. The man who feels profoundly the

[69] See Bibliography.   [70] *P.N.a.*, p. 10.
[71] Pollock, *Spinoza*, p. 147. See also p. 138.
[72] *G.D.*, p. 87.   [73] *B.N.B.*, p. 35.   [74] Pollock, *Spinoza*, p. 141.

beauty of a cloud is the man who can describe it. But the first effect of intense feeling is often to break up false precision. The ideas of God, life, personality, right and wrong, are examples.[75]

And again, in *Last Pages*, we find this remarkable instance of his ability to see clearly and deeply the full nature of an object in and of itself:

I was lost the other day looking into a wild, red rose, its colour, the bareness of its beauty lying open to the sun, unreserved in all its loveliness. I thought of our disguises and masquerades. We talk of the scale in creation, lower to the higher, that is to say to man, but this definite progression is false, for in the flower is a revelation on its own account which is not superseded nor is subsequently attainable. What man or woman can match my red rose in its own way?[76]

Is there more hypnotic entrancement here than clear vision? Perhaps; but the investigating method Hale White displays, and the habit of mind which seeks for moral and spiritual value in the concrete, come very close to what Spinoza recommended. While Hale White was scientific, he could not approve of the a-religious tendencies of modern science; while he loved objectivity, he could not sympathize with that objectivity which sees the outline and not the full body. The scientist fades off into the poet in Hale White, and the objective thinker into the man of deep moral prejudice. But the intensity and honesty of his method cannot be denied, nor can the fact that Spinoza contributed largely to what was best in it.

The main corollary of Spinoza's doctrine of adequate ideas involves their use in controlling the passions. To achieve serenity, to allay the furious heat of his inner contentions, was, as we have already seen, one of Hale White's most fundamental needs and ambitions. Spinoza offered an ingenious solution:

. . . the abstract of the whole matter is that it is possible to think of any passion as we think of a crystal or a triangle, and when we do so it is no longer injurious. A man, for example, suffers an insult, and is hurried by passion to avenge it. He is a *victim* for the time being (*patitur*). A stream of images passes before him, over which he exercises no authority. But it is possible to break that series of images,— to reflect, to put the insult from him, to consider it as if it were an effect of gravitation or electricity, to place himself outside it, to look at it as God looks at it. This is to refer it to God's idea or to have an adequate idea of it.[77]

Briefly, a passion was anything operating on the individual of which he was not the adequate cause. When the passion is removed he can act; otherwise he is acted upon. Action brings joy; passion brings suffering.

When Hale White came to apply this doctrine to his own life, he was once again faced with a conflict we have seen before. To view one's anger or jealousy objectively, as a God might view it, offered a means of purgation far less exhausting than the one delineated in the story, "Atonement." But to do so required that one expunge from the mind all thought of the *cause* of the anger, to see it only in terms of its own reality. Here was a

[75] *M.P.*, p. 236.
[76] *L.P.*, p. 313.
[77] *Sp.a.*, pp. xvii–xviii.

formula that would, indeed, have allowed Hale White to cease that "trick of contrast" which throughout his life so insistently triggered his sense of inferiority.

But, save in rare moments, he was unable to rise to such heights of Olympian disinterestedness. In discussing his grandfather, Dr. Reginald Hale-White declared: "Like most introverts he wanted to be God, and like most introverts he saw external things or people as the impediments— his wife, society, or the nature of the universe. This meant that essentially he was devoid of sympathy."[78] And when we find such statements as these in Hale White's work, we can never be certain that the enlightened self-interest expressed is exactly what Spinoza meant:

> It is of the greatest importance continually to bear in mind that the violation of a law personal to myself is as immoral as the violation of a general law, and may be more mischievous.[79]

This was Spinoza's recommendation too: to consider oneself by oneself, in terms of the reality of one's own being. But a man like Hale White, so conscious of his own suffering, was likely to find those laws dictated by a need of self-protection rather than self-negation.[80]

> The worst effect of disordered mind and body is that it makes one incapable of sympathy unless it be self sympathy, a most poisonous emotion which is self-intensifying.

The man who could write those words was fatally equipped to make the superhuman effort of self-forgetfulness that Spinoza recommended. The attempt would only increase his torment. It would remind him with renewed sharpness that he was a *victim* of outside forces and not the master of his own destiny. It would breed melancholy rather than joy.

And because Hale White's eye was usually turned inward and because he was, perhaps, unable ever to view his own passions as objectively as crystals or triangles, he continued throughout his life to be acted upon rather than acting, suffering rather than finding happiness. It was Spinoza's contention that the primary "effects" (joy, sorrow, desire)[81] could, if viewed "adequately," aid rather than impede action—for they would then free the body from its slavery to baser passions. But the "invading cares" in Hale White's experience kept asserting their dominance. The Spinozistic cure was always in his mind, but even as he thought of it he seemed to be feeling his own pulse.

> Annihilation of this swarm of petty invading cares by adoration! They possess and distract, not by their inherent strength but through the absence of a dominant power. The lover is absorbed in the desire to be with his mistress and keeps his

---

[78] Private conversation, February 21, 1950. (Dr. R. Hale-White has read and approved this text.)

[79] *M.P.*, p. 226.

[80] *P.L.*, p. 5.

[81] *Ethic*, Pt. 3, Prop. XV and LIX. Or "affects." See *The Athenaeum* (October 27, 1883), p. 534 for Hale White's discussion of the term.

appointment with her, breaking all hindrances like threads. Who shall deliver me from the body of this death? The answer was not difficult to St. Paul, but how is it with me?[82]

To overcome hate by love, anger by reason, to rearrange intellectually the primary "effects" was essentially the Spinozistic treatment. Again and again Hale White diagnosed his problem in these terms:

> We cannot obtain happiness by direct effort to obtain it. We can make a direct effort to avoid what prevents happiness. We can do more: we can, with effort, turn ourselves towards that which is happy rather than towards that which is wretched. . . . Some people are so made that it is their nature to dwell on the brilliant night. Others seem unable even to think of it in presence of the dull day. I do not believe that for any heroic act greater resolution is necessary than that which is needed by these others, constitutionally sad, but who rightly consider it their duty to affirm the stars rather than the gloom, even if it be impenetrable.[83]

When Hale White affirmed the stars it was usually, one suspects, out of just such a sense of duty as here described. Had the Spinozistic germ penetrated more deeply his encysted introspective nature, he might have known a fuller deliverance into a world less melancholy and more inviting to positive action. But he remained the sufferer rather than the actor and, with a kind of narcissistic discontent, worried about his own moral sanitation.

But we must end by reminding ourselves that the gloom and despondency pervading much of Hale White's thought cannot be explained by his psychological maladjustments alone. To do so would be to underestimate the strength of the spiritual calamity which befell not only Hale White, but the Victorians in general, and their frustration and balked instincts in a hostile world. The habit of looking heavenward for justice and truth had to be reversed and qualified in such a way that the habit was no longer spontaneous or free from self-consciousness. This brought pain, as the learning of new habits in maturity is bound to do. And men like Hale White who had lost their old faith felt as though they had been cheated, cheated of emotional security and of their spiritual home. They sought revenge, either by becoming critics of society or critics of themselves, or both. No man is more critical of himself than the stoic, no man more aware of his depravity, no man more proud of the conquest of what is base in him. But the story of suffering man was formerly written in the law; now it was written obscurely in individual nervous systems. And while Hale White could say: "There is so much unaccountable, undeserved misery in the world, that I find the only thing to be done is not to think about it,"[84] it was his tragedy that he could never quite stop thinking about it and could never quite accept the relief which Spinoza, for one, could have offered.

[82] *L.P.*, pp. 290–91.
[83] *Ibid.*, pp. 320–21.
[84] *L.3F.*, p. 80.

Chapter Eight

MASKING AND UNMASKING: THE *AUTOBIOGRAPHY* AND *DELIVERANCE*

Hale White's importance to English literature derives primarily from his six "novels": *The Autobiography of Mark Rutherford* (1881), *Mark Rutherford's Deliverance* (1885), *The Revolution in Tanner's Lane* (1887), *Miriam's Schooling* (1890), *Catharine Furze* (1893), and *Clara Hopgood* (1896). They are all referred to as novels in the advertisements of the set issued in 1936 by the Oxford University Press, but in reality some of them have small claim to the title. The first two, as we already know, are spiritual autobiography rather than novels and possess but slight fictional coloring and no invention of plot. *Miriam's Schooling*, a little over one hundred pages in length, is hardly more than a short story; and *Clara Hopgood*, while it can claim both length and plot, is primarily nothing but a series of conversation pieces on some of Hale White's favorite philosophical, political, and literary subjects. In considering the twenty-five or so "short stories" in Hale White's canon, we meet the same problem of definition: some of them fade off into essays and many are little more than meager *exempla*, briefly illustrating points of moral instruction or bodying forth in a slightly sketched framework something of the particular life behind a *pensée*.

Our quotations from these works have already given some notion of their quality, but most of their virtues as well as faults are apparent only on closer examination, and both derive from the motives which led him to write. He never thought of himself as a literary artist. In his books and letters he nearly always spoke contemptuously of his writings,[1] scorned the literary market place, despised "literary men," and even declared that he thought writing stories to be "somewhat of a degradation."[2] It was his purpose to teach, not to entertain, and if art assisted his message it was almost an accidental accretion, the happy by-product of an effort to declare himself clearly, pointedly, forcefully. Mrs. White writes in *The Groombridge Diary*:

Hale tells me most emphatically that he was never in the literary world; not educated for literature; not trained for literature; has known hardly any literary people.[3]

These facts would not seem to promise the aesthetic reader much of a feast. But the miracle is that in spite of their manifest faults his novels

[1] See *G.D.*, p. 36.
[2] *Ibid.*, p. 176.
[3] *Ibid.*, p. 33. See also p. 15.

are so extraordinarily good. Arnold Bennett has declared that he "simply cannot construct . . . I think that he must have constructed as he went along."[4] And he himself confessed to his first son that "he could never satisfactorily form a plot himself."[5] He relies heavily, for example, on death, accident, and (that favorite Victorian device) emigration for disposing of his characters; he sets the stage for a seduction scene by using such melodramatic devices as a sudden thunderstorm and a convenient shelter; and, in one case at least, divides his plot directly in the middle, leaving the reader to make his own transition.[6] Moreover, in descriptive passages sometimes the essayist is more in evidence than the novelist, providing us with beautifully finished set pieces which, though superbly written, often possess little organic relation to the action. And, like most Victorian writers, he frequently intrudes as the helpful author to comment on the behavior of his characters and, at times, injects full-length sermons or stories which they have composed.[7]

Through these and other shortcomings the modern reader can detect the hand of the amateur, but the reader familiar with the minor fiction of the last half of the nineteenth century can see these faults as the foil to some unique and extraordinary virtues. Here is a prose style unequaled, perhaps, in the century for lucid, incisive statement; a brevity which is a refreshing change from the "three-deckers" which taxed the eyes and the patience of readers in the 'eighties; and, above all, a degree of psychological insight into the lives of his characters which was the fruit of a lifetime spent in analyzing with merciless honesty and shrewd intelligence his own nature and its needs. Hale White, in spite of his protestations to the contrary, cared immensely about the quality of his writing and the degree of its success. He would not claim status as a "literary man" because he wanted others to give him the title—force it upon him—while he humbly bowed his head in acquiescence to the inevitable results of his genius. He refused to compete with what he regarded as the "fencing and trifling" of the popular novelist. But in following his own bent—which he perversely refused to call "artistic"—he proved himself a more effective competitor than any aping of current fashions could possibly have made him.

Hale White cared and did not care about his art. To profess caring about it too much would mean, in the event of failure, a crushing humiliation. It was much simpler and safer to wear the mask of the humble, shy, and anonymous citizen who simply got the notion one day—at the age of fifty—of writing a book. But in a letter he wrote to William Dean Howells, following a favorable review of the *Autobiography* and the *Deliverance* in

---

[4] Arnold Bennett, *Journal 1921–1928* (New York, 1933), p. 28.

[5] *P.N.b.*, p. 37. See *M.P.*, p. 138: "I could supply conversation and description, but it was very difficult to invent a plot, and still more difficult to invent one which of itself would speak."

[6] *R.T.L.*

[7] See, for example, *C.F.*, p. 96 ff., and pp. 70–73.

Harper's Monthly of February 1886, we can see the mask being removed.[8]

I am not an author by profession, but a man immersed in other work and long past middle life. I do not know how to make a book, so as to give it a beginning, a middle and an end and never should have dreamed of publishing anything if it had not struck me when I was fifty that perhaps some of my experiences were worth recording for the sake of those who were brought up as I was. Consequently I know perfectly well that those little volumes are crammed with all sorts of literary and other blunders. The only thing I can say for them is that they are true—but then what is *my* truth—and were not manufactured for money.

My reasons for publishing anonymously, or rather under an assumed name, were mainly that I did not desire praise, blame or any talk in fact about what I had done from anybody near me. I have felt too much and am too old to care for notoriety of any kind and wanted to be quiet. Consequently nobody who knows me ever says a word to me about the autobiography. This is what I like, but nevertheless I should be less than human did I not feel gladdened and exalted by such a criticism as that now before me from a man in your position and with such a name.

Again I thank you, thank you with—to me—unaccustomed emotion; and as to such a friend I cannot wear a mask I beg to subscribe myself—

devotedly yours
W. HALE WHITE

This letter has value as a piece of characteristically honest self-appraisal, but it is more valuable for what it suggests than what it says—especially in the way of offering a clue to his motives for novel writing. Under the pressure of a great name and high praise Hale White readily dropped his mask. This is a significant fact when we remember that his own wife at the time did not know he wrote novels and never in her lifetime read one of them.[9]

Why was he willing to reveal himself in the one case and not in the other? Part of the answer is, obviously, that marital incompatibility is a dominant theme in many of the books and stories and was clearly drawn in whole or part from his own experience. But a more important reason was that he needed an *external* reference point, an *outside* source of confidence which would encourage him to believe in himself. In his own words, he had expected from men "a sympathy which proceeds from the

---

[8] From letter dated February 25, 1886. In Houghton Library, Howells Collection. (MS. Am. 800.20.) Howells' review was one of the few notices of his first books.

[9] John Hale-White in *P.N.a.*, p. 6, declares that, at a later date, "He confided to her . . . that he had published books under an assumed name, telling her that I could read them to her some day—. So much she told me afterwards, but I had then left home and the opportunity never came to me."

Hale White's youngest daughter, Mary Theodora, told the present author on November 28, 1949, that she did not know he had written books until her twenty-first birthday. She was born December 14, 1869.

In an anonymous article, "Some Reminiscences of Mark Rutherford," appearing in *The Westminster Gazette* of March 17, 1913, was the following: "W. Hale White was singularly reticent regarding his literary work. An inquiry addressed to his daughter [Mary Theodora] in 1887 elicited the following reply: 'I am sorry to say I know nothing of the books to which you refer, and I do not think my father, if he were able to write to you, could help you. Your note apparently should have been addressed to a publisher, for I am not aware that my father's name has appeared on the title-page of any book save one written some years ago.' The book referred to is, of course, 'The Epic [*sic*] of Spinoza.' "

Invisible only."[10] Though he condemns such ambition in the *Autobiography*, he never quite gave up hoping for it. And in Howells ("a man in your position and with such a name") he found something very close to an earthly substitute—a "friend" to whom his "real" self had been exposed and who seemed to love him for it. Here was one of those rare opportunities to bring Mark Rutherford and Hale White into the same person. He could feel safe in admitting the identification—not only because the intimacy was separated by an ocean but because Howells, unlike his wife, was great and strong enough to need nothing of Hale White's pity or affection.

In response to another critic who praised the *Autobiography,* Hale White wrote:

> The only good which has come to me through that book is that it has revealed to me here and there the existence of one or two human beings who, to my surprise, have spoken to me out of darkness, and convinced me that, even in this epoch of disintegration and isolation, we are not solitary.[11]

His dominant motive for writing was not, therefore, to achieve popularity nor to achieve status as a novelist. It was primarily to draw unto himself a small circle of admirers with whom he could talk about his troubles (the title of one of his essays) and who would sympathize with his effort to redress the balance of justice in the world.

For Hale White it was impossible to write his *apologia* without at the same time writing his indictment, for he wanted praise as much as he wanted to confess his guilt. The writing of books became for him, therefore, a means of therapy—a new ceremony of exorcism. In late life he asked his second wife to give up writing fiction: "I wish I had never written stories. . . . If I had been given you as a wife when I was thirty I would never have let the public hear a syllable from me."[12] Whatever this means, it certainly indicates that Hale White found in his writing a compensation for living which he had missed, and that it was an appeal for sympathy which personal happiness would have rendered unnecessary.

Perhaps one of Hale White's most significant confessions is found in the following words from the *Autobiography*. The "excess of communicativeness" of which he speaks might never have found its way into books had he found people who could adequately have absorbed it.[13]

> It occurs to me here to offer an explanation of a failing of which I have been accused in later years, and that is secrecy and reserve. The real truth is, that nobody more than myself could desire self-revelation; but owing to peculiar tendencies in me, and peculiarity of education, I was always prone to say things in conversation which I found produced blank silence in the majority of those who listened to me, and immediate opportunity was taken by my hearers to turn to something trivial. Hence

---

10 *A.*, p. 54.
11 Alfred Gardner, "Mark Rutherford," *The British Weekly*, LIII (March 27, 1913), 746.
12 *G.D.*, p. 176.
13 *A.*, pp. 27–28.

it came to pass that only when tempted by unmistakable sympathy could I be induced to express my real self on any topic of importance. It is a curious instance of the difficulty of diagnosing (to use a doctor's word) any spiritual disease, if disease this shyness may be called. People would ordinarily set it down to self-reliance, with no healthy need of intercourse. It was nothing of the kind. It was an excess of communicativeness, an eagerness to show what was most at my heart . . . which made me incapable of mere fencing and trifling, and so often caused me to retreat into myself when I found absolute absence of response.

These impulses toward self-expression were clearly evident in his first two books, where the experiences of Mark Rutherford closely parallel those of Hale White himself. But why, in the later books, did his confessions take the form of novels? Part of the impulse came no doubt from the example of George Eliot whom he loved and respected, and whose moral habit of mind found rich expression in this medium. Part of it came, also, we suspect, from a long-postponed desire to try his hand at creative expression. The fact that he was long past fifty when he first turned to fiction does not necessarily mean that he was indifferent to this medium before then; it may simply mean that he was able to fulfill a long-frustrated dream. Only after 1879, when he was promoted to the position of Assistant Director of Contracts at the Admiralty,[14] was he sufficiently relieved of financial anxiety to relinquish entirely his hated journalistic work as London correspondent. This work was enormously time-consuming, and it is significant that his books did not appear until he had rid himself of it. But there is another motive driving him to fiction which should probably be given more weight than any of these. The first two books might be said to have "written themselves"—the direct, clear exposition of all the sorrows and bitterness and wisdom that had accumulated over fifty years. If he were to go on writing, if these were not to be his only books, then he must find a way to express more objectively his religious problem and deliverance; he must, in short, picture them in the experience of people other than that one individual, Mark Rutherford. And in thus turning from an absorbed examination of himself to an examination of others, in attempting to objectify his subjective drama, he followed in his writing a pattern of development which paralleled the method of "deliverance" set forth in the books.

Because Hale White's novels proper were only a continuation, under a further disguise, of the message of his autobiographical books, it will profit us to determine as best we can the sources for his materials and the manner in which he turned his personal experience into fiction. Lord David Cecil has claimed that "The Victorian novelists may miss the heights and depths, but they cast their nets very wide."[15] Something almost the opposite must be said of Hale White. His range was extremely narrow and his inventive faculty very meager, but within those limits he exercised an intense penetration and a profound understanding of the spiritual and

[14] *P.N.b.*, p. 12.
[15] Lord David Cecil, *Early Victorian Novelists* (Penguin, 1948), p. 17.

psychological problems he dealt with. All his art was literal and deeply personal. Mrs. White writes, "Hale tells me now that he never *created* a character in his life, never sat down to write without having somebody before his mind's eye."[16] We have already noticed that characters like Broad, Allen, and Mrs. Furze had their originals in Hale White's Bedford experience, and the truth of Mrs. White's statement will become increasingly apparent as we study the novels individually. Although many of his characters are composites, they are unquestionably pieced together out of people he had known, and in many cases the pieces can be identified with some assurance. And a great number of them are mere stenographic projections of Hale White's own personality. Sympathetic characters like Zachariah and Pauline Coleman, Catharine Furze, Clara and Madge Hopgood, Baruch Cohen, and Miriam Tacchi—while they may have had other originals—all to some degree remind us of Mark Rutherford himself. They are all exiles in their own country, poetic sensitive natures who eschew the society of their Philistine neighbors and who learn at last that life is posited on the renunciation of what their pride loves. All of them experience that moment—as Hale White did at the Stoke Newington school—when "the circumstance of the external world presses on us like the air upon an exhausted glass ball,"[17] and they all in their several ways find Mark Rutherford's deliverance. None would take exception to the lesson taught Catharine Furze by Doctor Cardew:

"Nothing is more dangerous, physically and mentally, than to imagine we are not as other people. Strive to consider yourself, not as Catharine Furze, a young woman apart, but as a piece of common humanity and bound by its laws. It is infinitely healthier for you. Never, under any pretext whatever, allow yourself to do what is exceptional. If you have any originality, it will better come out in an improved performance of what everybody ought to do, than in the indulgence of singularity. For one person, who, being a person of genius, has been injured by what is called conventionality—I do not, of course, mean foolish conformity to what is absurd—thousands have been saved by it, and self-separation means mischief."[18]

But it is not in character drawing alone that Hale White reveals the personal and literal nature of his art. His settings as well are all remembered and painted with the eye of a social historian rather than with that of an imaginative artist. To record a passing phase of social history, though not a primary motive in his novel writing, was a prominent one. In the opening pages of the *Autobiography* he claims that the book has "some little historic value"[19] as the record of a Dissenting race fast passing away, and H. W. Massingham in his "Memorial Introduction" to the first book

---

[16] *G.D.*, p. 66 n.

[17] *R.T.L.*, p. 132.

[18] *C.F.*, p. 222. This belief, central to Hale White's spiritual affirmation, also had an effect on his novel writing. He felt he had no license as a novelist that he did not possess as a man; there was the same necessity to stick close to observed fact, the feeling that "invention" was something like lying, the same compulsion to expunge all "singularity" in favor of a clear, direct statement, as colorless and pure as fresh water.

[19] *A.*, p. 1.

asserted that "Hale White is . . . the only great modern English writer sufficiently interested in provincial Dissent, and knowing enough about it, to give it a serious place in fiction. . . ."[20]

Hale White's geographical and social facts are almost always dependable. To this day one can find his way about Bedford—in spite of the ravages of industrialism—with his books as a guide. And if we follow him to London, especially to the area around Holborn, the reliability and literalness of his descriptions are even more striking. The present writer made the experiment of taking the following directions seriously:

If the explorer goes up a court nearly opposite Bouverie Street, he will emerge from a covered ditch into one that is open, about six feet wide. Presently the ditch ends in another and wider ditch running east and west. The western one turns northward, and then westward again, roofs itself over, squeezes itself till it becomes little less than a rectangular pipe, and finally discharges itself under an oil and colourman's house in Fetter Lane. The eastern arm, strange to say, suddenly expands, and one side of it, for no earthly reason, is set back with an open space in front of it, partitioned by low palings. Immediately beyond, as if in a fit of sudden contrition for such extravagance, the passage or gutter contracts itself to its very narrowest, and, diving under a printing-office, shows itself in Shoe Lane.[21]

Though some of the tops are gone from the "ditches" and though time and German bombs have wrought many changes, that itinerary can still be followed and will bring the explorer at length to Shoe Lane.

With these indications to encourage us, let us investigate each of his books in turn for evidences of personal reminiscence and to see how this remembered material was employed. In doing so we shall discover not only a dominant feature of his art, but a dominant feature of the author's mind—the literalness which was part of his intellectual honesty, and the fear of departing far from observed fact and experience which was part of his self-absorption and self-distrust.

The *Autobiography* and the *Deliverance* are, of course, more obviously records of Hale White's own experience than the other books. But even these depart in some significant ways from Hale White's true biography. Mark Rutherford left college with a diploma in his hand and not by expulsion, and, though his faith was shaken just as Hale White's was, he nevertheless assumed a full-time pulpit in Water Lane. We can only guess why this alteration of the facts was made, but it seems probable that Hale White feared the expulsion incident would be too obvious a clue to the authorship and that he would seem to be too patently seeking sympathy and self-justification. Moreover, by placing Mark Rutherford as a regular minister, first in an Independent and then in a Unitarian pulpit, he gave himself the opportunity of satirizing and deploring the spiritual condition of the churches and of paying off old scores on pharisees like Snale, whoever his original may have been. Of course, as we have already seen, Hale

---

[20] *Ibid.*, p. ix.
[21] *R.T.L.*, pp. 42–43.

White did preach widely after he left college, but he was never the full-time minister pictured in the memoirs, and he was certainly not dependent for financial support on preaching a faith he had ceased to believe.

Except for these facts and the broken engagement with Ellen, for which there is no autobiographical evidence, the other incidents in the first book follow closely those of Hale White's real life. For example, he makes the statement that "My old nurse, who took care of me as a child, had got a place in London as housekeeper in a large shop in the Strand."[22] The old nurse was a Jane Reed (later Mrs. Evis) who had actually taken care of Hale White as a child and who came to London afterward. Small though this point is, it serves to indicate Hale White's faithfulness to fact even in those minor details which would be most easy to invent. His youngest daughter, Mary Theodora, penned a comment in Sir William's *Notes* about this old woman:

She died on 9th April 1894 aged 78 years. After she ceased to be the family nurse to the Whites, she became caretaker at the offices of the Athenaeum newspaper in Wellington Street, Strand which was curious for she could neither read nor write. I remember going to see her there.[23]

Wollaston in the *Autobiography* is, of course, Dr. John Chapman; Theresa, who appears as his niece, is his young assistant editor, George Eliot; and Mary Mardon may very well be a disguised picture of Hale White's first wife. Though in the book Hale White does not marry Mary Mardon and though she catches a chill and follows her father to the grave, we cannot consider these as definite identifying details any more than we can take as fact Theresa's emigration to America.[24] John Hale-White writes in his *Notes*:

The fact is that if he drew any character from her [his first wife] it was that of Mary Mardon to whom Mark Rutherford was *not* married in the story, and who is one of his most sympathetic creations.[25]

While Mary Mardon is unquestionably a sympathetic character and while Mark Rutherford's emotional need for her was very great, there are, nevertheless, indications that she was not just what he hoped for in a woman. On one occasion he writes: "This, I know, was not pure love for her; it was a selfish passion for relief. But then I have never known what is meant by a perfectly pure love."[26] And on an earlier occasion he had felt momentarily contemptuous of her intellectual "slightness" and "inability to talk upon the subjects which interested Mardon and myself. . . ."[27] Now although this feeling was immediately followed by remorse, it

---

[22] *A.*, p. 80.

[23] *P.N.b.*, p. 12. See also *E.L.*, p. 40.

[24] See *D.*, p. vi. The "butterfly collector" pictured in *A.*, pp. 123–28, is almost certainly a portrait of Selwyn Image, whom Hale White probably met between 1855 and 1857.

[25] *P.N.a.*, p. 6.

[26] *A.*, p. 139.

[27] *Ibid.*, p. 62.

was there, and it was exactly the feeling which became the separating wedge between most of the incompatible couples which he paints in his novels. And in these other cases, though the women are sometimes violently unsympathetic, a feeling of remorse is invariably the sequel to the man's intemperate or hasty judgment. There seems little reason to doubt that the material for these studies was provided by the relation with his own wife. Though he recognized the saintly qualities of Mary Mardon, there was an ambiguity in his love for her which, we may suppose, existed in the same form in Hale White's real life. This was contributed by the fact that he was in love with Theresa at the same time he was courting Mary. His confession becomes very significant once we know the real people behind the fictional names:

I was distressed to find that, in the very height of my love for Theresa, my love for Mary continued unabated. Had it been otherwise, had my affection for Mary grown dim, I should not have been so much perplexed, but it did not. It may be ignominious to confess it, but so it was; I simply record the fact.[28]

In later years he spoke frequently, in glowing terms, of George Eliot, but almost never mentioned his wife. The second Mrs. White records in *The Groombridge Diary*:

Of George Eliot he spoke with such devotion, such humility, such peace. He said she was a sweet, gentle creature; he said: "I could worship that woman."[29]

These confessions do not, of course, indicate that Hale White ever entertained a serious notion of proposing marriage to George Eliot, but they do suggest that she was to him an ideal—a woman both intellectual and (to him) personally attractive who could provide mental stimulation as well as devotion. She was that particular kind of "new woman," so unlike the "clucking fowls" of Bedford society and so remarkably like his sympathetic heroines, whom he celebrated in various ways throughout his life. Her resemblance, for example, to Pauline Coleman is striking in this regard:

In his own Calvinistic Dissenting society, the pious women who were members of the church took little or no interest in the mental life of their husbands. They read no books, knew nothing of politics, were astonishingly ignorant, and lived in their household duties. To be with a woman who could stand up against him was a new experience. Here was a girl to whom every thought her father possessed was familiar![30]

This matter warrants emphasis because in this contrast between the unattainable sibyl, the goddess of wisdom, and the attainable woman, the woman of his own class before whom he was not awe-struck (however much she differed from the typical Bedford *hausfrau*), we have another of those dichotomies between the ideal and the real which were so central in Hale White's experience.[31] It seems unquestionable that in real life

---

[28] *Ibid.*, p. 158.   [29] *G.D.*, p. 72. See also *M.P.*, pp. 117–23.
[30] *R.T.L.*, p. 51.
[31] It is interesting to note that, in his books, Hale White frequently pictures a

he married Mary Mardon, or someone much like her, and that always in his mind was the image of that "other woman," not tempting him, but destroying his peace and goading his discontent. The whole direction of his spiritual deliverance was, as we have already seen, toward learning contentment with one's hard lot, toward the renunciation of what one would like to love in favor of what one can find to love, toward ameliorating the painful claims of a high ideal by accepting as joyfully as possible the imperfect reality. But while Hale White could arrive at this stoical insight, he could not, as we know, rest in it. He could know moments of serene reconciliation (such as those recorded in the last pages of the *Deliverance*), but there were other moments succeeding these when the dream of what might have been reasserted itself, causing him to despise those around him and, brooding, enter his study, shut the door, and curse his cowardly compromise with the ideal. George Eliot was, doubtless, always more real to him as a symbol than as a person; but though her real image may have faded from his consciousness as the years passed, the symbol to which she was a major contributor never did. Mary and Theresa in the *Autobiography*, even if we regard the book as pure fiction, embody a type of conflict prevailing in his studies of theological and social as well as marital incompatibility. And our interest in this conflict is increased when we know, what the casual reader cannot, that these symbols are drawn remarkably close to life and that only a few disguising lines have been drawn to obscure the guilt and shame which they embodied for their creator.

The *Deliverance* is, in general, the record of Hale White's experience after leaving his employment at Chapman's until the time of writing, but here again there are important departures from actual fact. The separation and reunion of Mark Rutherford with Ellen Butts has no basis in his own experience, for he was married to Harriet Arthur[32] on December 22, 1856, after an unbroken engagement dating from 1854 if not earlier. Their courtship was apparently a smooth one, for Hale White's mother records in her diaries many visits from Harriet to Hale's family in the intervening years,[33] and she certainly had not been married before, as Ellen Butts had been in the *Deliverance*. But the comments made in the book on their relations after marriage are, no doubt, drawn from life:

> My love for Ellen was great, but I discovered that even such love as this could not be left to itself. It wanted perpetual cherishing. The lamp, if it was to burn brightly, required daily trimming, for people become estranged and indifferent, not so much by open quarrel or serious difference, as by the intervention of trifles which need but the smallest, although continuous effort for their removal.[34]

man, at the moment of his new love, recalling to mind an earlier love ideal. Baruch Cohen, for example, felt shame when he realized "It was not Clara Hopgood who was before him, it was hair, lips, eyes, just as it was twenty years ago. . . ." (*C.H.*, p. 148.)

[32] Mrs. Elizabeth Street, whose death was celebrated by Hale White in the published *Letter*, was Harriet's half-sister.

[33] *P.N.b.*, pp. 14–20.

[34] *D.*, p. 117.

This suggestion of strain on the relationship corresponds to the tensions which must have existed in his actual married life (of which we shall learn more later), and provokes the suspicion that Harriet Arthur may have contributed something to the portrait of Ellen Butts as well as to that of Mary Mardon.

But the greatest divergence from actual fact in this book is its ending. At the close of the *Deliverance* Mark Rutherford, instead of appearing as the prosperous and respected civil servant which Hale White was and continued to be until his retirement on March 31, 1892, is pictured as literally worked to death by tyrannical employers. Thus was his demise celebrated by his associates:

The next morning his salary up to the day of his death came in an envelope to his widow, without a single word from his employers save a request for acknowledgement. Towards midday, his office coat, and a book found in his drawer, arrived in a brown paper parcel, carriage unpaid.[35]

That last little turn of the screw was quite gratuitous indeed, for upon retirement Hale White received a letter of appreciation for his services (which he always proudly cherished) and a handsome pension. Sir William Hale-White writes: "He took great pride in the Civil Service, he never said anything against it, often praised it and himself set a high standard."[36]

What were actually the conditions of Hale White's employment and his salary during the years recorded in the *Deliverance*? Two days[37] after leaving *The Westminster Review* on February 18, 1854, he was appointed clerk in the Registrar General's office in Somerset House.[38] On March 12, 1857, he was appointed Registrar of Births, Deaths and Marriages for St. Marylebone, performing the work of this office in the evenings, after his duties at Somerset House were completed. On December 23, 1858, he was given a clerkship in the Accountant General's office by Sir Edwin Reed, chief constructor to the Navy;[39] in 1869 he was transferred to the Contract Department of the Admiralty, and in 1879 became Assistant Director of Contracts. Probably his early salary was not more than £130 a year, but by 1869, when he was transferred to the Contract Department, it was between £200 and £300 per year. After he became Assistant Director it was considerably more. While these salaries were not munificent, they were sufficient to give him a solid middle-class standing in the community[40]

---

[35] *Ibid.*, p. 133.   [36] *P.N.b.*, p. 36.

[37] For date see George Jackson, "Mark Rutherford's Scrapbooks," *London Quarterly and Holborn Review*, CXXXI (April 1919), 203.

[38] See mention of Somerset House in *D.*, p. 69.

[39] See R. M. Theobald, "Some Reminiscences of Hale White," *The Westminster Gazette*, March 17, 1913.

[40] G. D. H. Cole and Raymond Postgate in *The British People, 1746–1946* (London, 1949) quote from a survey of income distribution made in 1867 and covering ten million people. According to these figures only 199,000 people in this group earned more than £300 per annum; they were listed as "middle" class and above. Only slightly over a million people earned more than £100.

and enabled him to take frequent holidays, both in England and abroad.

Until 1879, however, Hale White had to supplement his income by serving as London correspondent for a number of provincial journals, reporting Parliamentary debates and commenting on political and social events of importance in the city. These writings extended from May 11, 1861, until March 17, 1883, and the papers to which he contributed were *The Morning Star* (1865), *The Aberdeen Herald* (1861–72), *The Birmingham Post and Journal* (1866–80), *The Rochdale Observer* (1867–72), *The Nonconformist* (1872–73), and *The Norfolk News* (1872–83). This work, from which we have frequently quoted, made unconscionable demands on his time and energy, but the complaint of poverty recorded in *The Groombridge Diary*[41] seems to be something of an exaggeration. His second son gives a vivid account[42] of his father's journalistic labors and the pressure under which they were accomplished:

His duties as London Correspondent made it necessary for him to go frequently to the House of Commons after Office hours.[43] I see him now coming home between 6 and 7 in the evening and running upstairs to prepare for the evening meal, after which he could [*sic*] often work upon his articles. He retired generally quite early, slept badly, and rose early; often by 4 'clock [*sic*]. The fire place in his study had a row of gas jets round the base to enable him to light the fire easily; after his bath he made himself a cup of cocoa in an aetna, and then, in those early morning hours, he read and wrote as his own spirit moved him, not as the journalist from whom a weekly task was exacted. Nevertheless, when he had an article to finish, even these hours were invaded, and he would rouse me up at 6 o'clock to meet the newspaper train on its arrival at the station, and bring him the morning's papers. Sometimes the article was finished in the waiting room at Victoria Station on his way to the Admiralty.

The description in the *Deliverance* of his journalistic travails and their heavy strain on his nerves is, therefore, supported by the facts. In the book, however, they precede his office work and even his marriage; actually his marriage came earlier and he never, as in the book, supported himself by journalism alone. And there are other minor divergencies. His writing simultaneously for two papers which "circulated in the same district"[44] seems to be somewhat of a variation of the facts. Only *The Nonconformist* and *The Morning Star*, both London journals, could possibly meet that

41 *G.D.*, p. 72.

42 *P.N.a.*, p. 2. In his articles he frequently complains of the hard life of a correspondent. Examples are *R.O.*, August 26, 1871, and *A.H.*, August 19, 1865, and February 6, 1864. On this last date he wrote, for example: "The last words I shall write before Parliament opens are at this moment being written, and henceforth nothing remains but late nights, worry, eternal gossip and discussion upon matters upon which one is compelled, alas! to talk and write so much, and which one loves so little . . . All the while, though, to me, during the coming storm of pseudo-eager discussion, tempestuous argument, and rain of scribble thereupon consequent, may the Fates be gracious! While Schleswig rages, while the firmament shudders, while Palmerston and D'Israeli shake the welkin, may the evening, or may-be the morning, pipe, and the accompanying quiet moments, never fail till the blessed August re-appear, and with it once more the deep autumnal peace."

43 Note the book entitled "After Office Hours," mentioned in *C.H.*, p. 109.

44 *D.*, p. 1.

description, but nearly a decade separated his contributions to them. And though *The Nonconformist*[45] circulated to Dissenting areas outside of London, it is unlikely that it competed with these other journals, for though they all had a liberal and Dissenting bias, *The Nonconformist* was given over almost entirely to sectarian gossip.

The character M'Kay who figures so largely in the *Deliverance* undoubtedly had an original, but he cannot now be identified unless he was the "friend" mentioned in the following comment by Hale White in *The Norfolk News* of October 12, 1872. The friend referred to wrote for *The Standard*, a notorious Tory organ, and M'Kay also wrote for a Tory paper. Furthermore, M'Kay had acquired an "extraordinarily extravagant style" which seems to be the issue in this comment; and, finally, M'Kay wrote London "specials," "a dignity to which," says Mark Rutherford, "I never attained."[46]

A friend of mine was once asked to write for a London daily newspaper. He wrote accordingly and took the article to the office. The editor looked at it for a second and threw it on one side. "That will not do," he said. "But," replied my friend, "you have not read a line of it." "Perfectly true," was the answer, "but I can tell by the absence of *'glitter'* without reading it that it is not the article that suits us." Where shall we be when it becomes the fashion to describe a stoppage in Cheapside, not as a "block," but as "An intertangled mass of vehicular traffic impervious to the most persistent of Jehus."

M'Kay's dislike of jargon in any form would seem further to identify him with this portrait.[47] His importance in the book does not rest, however, on his newspaper work but on his interest in religious and social reform among London slum dwellers, and in that connection we shall presently uncover a more suggestive clue to his identity and, perhaps, even learn his proper name.

"Never, but once or twice at the most," writes Hale White in the *Deliverance*, "did my labours meet with the slightest recognition beyond payment."[48] This seems to be an exact statement, for the available evidence indicates only two cases where his journalistic work was noticed. He "scored" once in accusing the M.P., C. P. Villiers, of supporting the Civil Service Pension Bill in order to provide himself with a handsome endowment."[49] Villiers' rejoinder and White's own reply to it were printed in *The Birmingham Post* of July 10 and July 17, 1869. And on the second occasion he "ventured, by way of filling up my allotted space, to say a word on behalf of a now utterly forgotten novel." He goes on to say:

I was tempted by this one novel to look into others which I found she had written, and I discovered that they were altogether silly. The attraction of the one of which

45 The editor of this paper was Mr. Edward Miall, later M.P., who had supported Hale White in his dispute with New College. Hale White frequently praises him in his column.

46 *D.*, p. 8.

47 See *ibid.*, p. 10.

48 *Ibid.*, p. 7.

49 *B.D.P.J.*, July 10, 1869.

I thought so highly, was not due to any real merit which it possessed, but to something I had put into it.[50]

By examining his newspaper columns we learn that these remarks in the *Deliverance* are literally true. The novel referred to was *The True History of Joshua Davidson* by Eliza Lynn Linton, an agitator for women's rights whose brash self-confidence was hardly equaled by her literary talents, and the article Hale White mentioned appeared in *The Norfolk News* for December 21, 1872:

The present column is hardly one for the recommendation of books, and yet it is impossible for anybody who has read "The True History of Joshua Davidson" to avoid saying a word or two about it. It is the story of an ardent young religious enthusiast, who has a dream that the Christianity of the Gospels can be realised on earth, and who treats men and women as he believes Christ would have treated them . . . he becomes an Internationalist, and goes over to Paris in the days of the Commune. Coming back to England to justify the Commune . . . he is brutally murdered by an excited mob at a public lecture which he is giving. The character of the man is one altogether new, and yet it is instantaneously recognized as true and as likely to be typical in the future. The story of the constant collision between the living, acted Christianity of the genuine believer in it, and the dead, traditional profession of it, is told with great pathos. Some of the subordinates of the tale are living portraits, which almost speak from their frames and tell their names. There is one of a politico-economical M.P., a confirmed sceptic, but who never acknowledges his scepticism and goes to Church every Sunday—a gentleman who writes perpetual tracts, makes perpetual speeches without a trace of Christianity in them, and who yet hits out fiercely and cries "Prove it," when charged with heterodoxy. It needs no very profound acquaintance with M.P.'s to label that picture. The author of the book is a lady well known to literature; but as she wishes to remain anonymous, it is not for me to say who she is, although her name has been communicated to me.[51]

In response to this notice Hale White received the following letter:[52]

HAYTER HOUSE 238 MARYLEBONE RD. N.W.
Jany 20 '73

MY DEAR SIR:

I hope I am not doing anything wrong in writing to thank you in my own name for the kind notice you gave of "Joshua Davidson." I am very very glad you approved of this child of my deepest heart & faith, & thank you cordially for your notice. The book is coming into a second edition, & that without any of the three great papers—Times, Sat. Rev: & P.M. Gazette—having touched it—So I think that is well for an anonymous book published not more than two months ago?

I hope you will not think this letter intrusive, & that you will still keep my secret. It is creeping out that I wrote the books but I stop it where ever I can.

Most faithfully your obliged
E. LYNN LINTON

I see by the date of your note that it was written at the end of December. Owing to a mistake on the part of the friend to whom *our* friend, Mr. Holyoake, entrusted the packet, I received it only the end of last week.

E.L.L.

---

50 *D.*, p. 7.
51 The book appeared under the pseudonym, "Annie Ogle."
52 This letter is in the possession of Mrs. D. V. White.

This book, strangely enough, went through six editions in the two years following its publication.[53] While it has almost no literary merit, it has definite historical interest in showing the passage of an ardent Calvinist from religious Dissent to political Dissent. With Joshua, translating Christianity into positive action took the form of an alliance with international communism—a fact of profound significance in understanding one aspect of nineteenth-century liberalism. Hale White rejected this political doctrine, but he was doubtless attracted by the hero's tough-minded religion and by his need to fill with some positive assertion the vacuum left by a departed creed. But the resemblance between Joshua and Mark Rutherford cannot be pushed very far. Joshua shows none of that delicate awareness of spiritual complexities, none of the subtle intelligence of Mark Rutherford. He is a "muscular" Christian, as brave as he is stupid. The book is really more of a polemical tract than a novel, more of an essay than fiction, reminding one somewhat of Upton Sinclair's *Call Me Carpenter*. The characters are only vehicles for ideas, and Joshua is the only one possessing—even in slight degree—flesh and blood. Some of the living portraits the authoress presented are those of Disraeli and Karl Marx, who appears under the name of Felix Pyat. Hale White may have been temporarily excited by Joshua's character as a humanized Christ, but his later disaffection for this crude work was as justified as it was inevitable.

A more interesting problem presented by the *Deliverance* is to discover if there is any basis in fact for the work of Mark and M'Kay in the slums of Drury Lane. To satisfy ourselves on this point is important, for this incident is the only hint we ever get from the books that Hale White might have actually engaged in a program of social reform—that he ever did more than criticize society as a frustrated and indecisive onlooker. Did he, we wonder, ever break his chrysalis of self-absorption and self-pity by losing himself—like Robert Elsmere or Joshua Davidson—in one of the many movements of moral rehabilitation to which many people in this period were turning as a substitute for lost faith? The only evidence we have of his association with Drury Lane is provided in his newspaper columns.

We quote the two following statements because they illustrate not only this point, but also the complaint he makes in the *Deliverance* that in his articles he "was obliged, with infinite pains, to vary, so that it could not be recognised, the form of what, at bottom, was essentially the same matter."[54] In *The Norfolk News* of December 28, 1878, he writes:

One day this week being tired with wandering about London in the cold, I evidently longed for a cup of hot coffee. There was no railway station near, and I was in a part of the world where cafés and restaurants do not abound. Fortunately I caught sight of the Coffee Tavern in Drury Lane, erected by the Coffee Taverns Company. For one penny only, I had a cup of good strong coffee; and a large one too, with the

---

[53] For a comment on its success see Walter de la Mare, "Women Novelists of the 'Seventies," *The Eighteen Seventies*, ed. H. Granville-Barker (Cambridge, 1929), p. 65.
[54] *D.*, p. 1. The Jamesian punctuation of this is not typical of Hale White's writing.

privilege of sitting to drink it in a warm well-lighted room, and the additional privilege of smoking had I so desired. I asked the number of the customers daily, and was told that although the tavern was only just opened the average was about 2000. There were several very decent-looking men there drinking coffee or cocoa and reading the newspapers, but what pleased me more than anything was to see a dirty slatternly woman come in, precisely of the Drury Lane gin-shop type, the kind of creature that shuffles along in her rags out of Parker Street to the palace at the corner, shuffles in, takes her quartern of fire and damnation, comes out, wipes her mouth on her dirty black tatters and then shuffles off again—who knows whither—ultimately of course to the devil. Doubtless she was not reformed, nor would be reformed, by the coffee tavern, but at any rate so far as the substitution of one cup of coffee for one quartern of gin went, so far the tavern did good. All success to Mr. Cowper Temple and his friends in their enterprize. It is rare in these days to find a gospel which all can agree to preach, but here surely is one.

In *The Birmingham Daily Post* for December 28, 1878, he writes on the same subject:

Wandering about this week in the unaccustomed neighborhood of Drury Lane, cold and tired, I happened to espy a coffee tavern. I went in, and for one penny I had a large cup of coffee, hot and good. The Tavern was just open, and the average number of customers hitherto had been 2,000 daily. There were several decent persons there drinking and smoking, but what pleased me better than anything was to see a perfect specimen of the Drury Lane slattern come in with her mud-coloured rags and rusty-black thin shawl. She swallowed her coffee, and departed hastily. Perhaps she is not to be reformed by coffee, but the substitution of half-a-pint of it that morning for half-a-quartern of Drury Lane liquid fire was so far a distinct gain. There are few gospels now-a-days which we can all believe, but assuredly this of Mr. Cowper-Temple's is one, and as much as in me lies I mean to preach it.

The "unaccustomed neighborhood of Drury Lane" would seem to indicate that Hale White was no active partner in the socio-religious experiment pictured in the *Deliverance*. But it seems likely that he wished he had been, and that perhaps he is thinking of Mr. Cowper Temple[55] or "his friends" in drawing the character of M'Kay. There is no doubt, however, that when Hale White did wander in that quarter of the city, he was a sensitive and shocked observer of the conditions he witnessed. The

[55] In 1875 Mr. Cowper Temple was a Member of Parliament and is mentioned by Hale White in the *N.N.* column for November 20, 1875, as a warm friend of Ruskin and an admirer of the *Fors Clavigera*. Hale White was also a friend of Ruskin, and a description of his Carshalton house appeared in Ruskin's book. These common interests, together with their Parliamentary connections, could very well have brought them together. Also, Hale White's father was, as doorkeeper, known to all the members and highly esteemed by them throughout his term of office.

Included among Hale White's literary remains were copies of a number of letters sent to a Reverend C. Anderson from Matthew Arnold, Stopford Brooke, Selwyn Image, and Brooke Lambert. In a letter dated March 9 [1874?], Arnold said, "My best wishes go with you to the East of London" and went on to congratulate Anderson as one of those "who, renouncing the old taste of employing with the multitude a false but powerful fairy-tale in the way of religion, do yet not renounce the taste of conveying *religion* to the multitude. They are the time civilisers. . . ."

Brooke Lambert was a prominent worker among the poor of London's East End, a clergyman who saw the gospel more in terms of soup kitchens and workingmen's clubs than in words. The Reverend Anderson, Vicar of St. John's, Limehouse, was a sympathetic associate in this religious social work. It seems likely, therefore, that one or both of them might also have shared in Hale White's portrait of M'Kay.

case histories of the Drury Lane characters, Taylor, John, Cardinal, and Clark, which he gives us in the *Deliverance*, are sociological studies which could have been drawn only from life. The realism and almost clinical details of the portraits are proof enough, but we have additional evidence from comments in his articles. On many occasions, especially in the years between 1875 and 1882, he voices an almost prophetic foreboding over the submerged violence and brutality residing in the London slums:

It is a fact, and a melancholy fact, that in London there is an enormous mass of brutality, ready to seize any opportunity for wreckage and violence. It is a fact as solemn as Ireland. . . . Underneath the smoothness of the ordinary aspect of ordinary life in London lies simple chaos, and it is ever augmenting with the growth of this great city. It is like the central cesspool of Dante's Hell, into which flows the blackguardism of four millions of people, and it daily rises higher and higher. Some day or other it may break out and overwhelm us.[56]

Though Hale White was temperamentally a fugitive from all dirt and slovenliness,[57] his concern for the poor showed none of the sentimental "do-goodism" which often characterized the slum visitor from the suburbs. While there is small reason to believe that he ever dirtied his own hands in their service, and considerable evidence to indicate that he assumed unquestioningly a somewhat patronizing middle-class superiority in his relations with these unfortunates, his sincere shock over their condition is unmistakable.

In *The Norfolk News* of August 20, 1881, he tells of visiting one of these slum dwellers—who might have modeled for one of the portraits in the *Deliverance*:

This very morning my duty took me to a slum, one of the most slummish of the slums hereabouts. About a dozen children were playing about the entrance of a court and not one of them had shoes or stockings. There was a muckheap opposite a row of cottages and the little imps swarming over it and at play on it. One of them followed me. He was about ten or eleven years old and he spoke to grown women words of filthy debauchery. He bawled them out openly and they took not the slightest notice. The man whom I wanted to see is a drunkard and beats his wife. I pushed open the door, but could not find anybody. Rags, the remains of a supper, boots, dirt of all kinds were huddled up together on the floor and on the table. Most likely the owner was asleep up above—with the sleep of gin or beer. I walked on and the next object which attracted my attention was a magnificent new church, dedicated to St. Michael and all Angels, and about three-parts finished. It is like a little cathedral, and if it costs a penny will cost thirty or forty thousand pounds. . . . This is the way in which it is proposed to meet the problem of the slum. It is absurd and pre-posterous. Does anybody suppose that the inhabitants of that slum will venture in their rags into such a building as that and seat themselves by the side of the exquisite young ladies, devotees in curate worship?

Hale White was firmly convinced that the ministrations of orthodox religion were ineffectual and even pernicious means of meeting the moral problems of Drury Lane and London blackguardism. More needed than

[56] *N.N.*, February 11, 1882.
[57] See *G.D.*, pp. 48 and 456.

sermons and fancy churches were good drainage, decent housing, light, fresh air, and—as a beginning—coffee instead of gin. Only through such reforms could a soil suitable for the growth of Christianity be prepared. How far the Established Church was from recognizing this plain fact is the subject of some of his must abusive journalistic comment. In *The Norfolk News* of January 15, 1876, for example, he tells of a High Church quarrel over the question of whether or not some "dirty children" were to be allowed to attend services at St. Anne's, Highgate. A few "volunteer missionaries" had invited them, but other members of the congregation objected on the grounds that "the children stank and had fleas."

Therefore the churchwardens, having to choose between the salvation of the clean and those who were unclean, and thinking that if they gained the clean they would lose the unclean, declared in favor of the former. From this point of view the ejectment of the children . . . will appear capable of Christian justification. Some members of the congregation, recollecting, however, certain awkward passages in the New Testament about the poor, felt aggrieved, and the result was a secession and the building of a new church.

Hale White himself had no love of stinks and fleas ("Hale . . . is so beautifully clean . . . he imagines dirt much worse than it is!"[58]) and one suspects that he invokes them in order to shock the smugly orthodox more than from any deep love of their possessors. But he was percipient enough to realize that his society regarded their poverty itself as a crime and—however little he himself shared the qualities of a St. Francis—he was keenly sensitive to the ironic contrasts between Christianity and Churchianity.

The debate between a freethinker and a "celebrated Christian" in the early pages of the *Deliverance* is a leaf we have already seen from Hale White's true biography.[59] The episode was suggested by a discussion between Father Ignatius and Charles Bradlaugh at the New Hall of Science in December 1872, which Hale White reported in *The Birmingham Post* of December 21, 1872, and later recalled in *The Norfolk News* of August 6, 1881, and March 17, 1883. In this last piece he writes:

I shall never forget an argument—if argument it can be called—which I once heard between him [Father Ignatius] and Mr. Bradlaugh. The reverend hermit came with a rope around his body and thought that prayer was sufficient without any further proceedings for the instantaneous conviction of the whole audience in the Hall of Science. It was a most lamentable exhibition, lamentable because the majority of his hearers evidently thought that no better defense of Christianity was possible.

Though this is the only time Mr. Bradlaugh appeared in the *Deliverance*, Hale White followed his career in the House fairly closely. "I venture to say," he writes in *The Norfolk News* of March 19, 1881, "that the only difference between Mr. Bradlaugh and many other members whom I have known is that Mr. Bradlaugh has the courage to avow his convic-

---

58 *Ibid.*, p. 48.
59 *D.*, pp. 13–17. See above, p. 49.

tions." Though Hale White had small sympathy for his freethinking and atheism, he had even less for those members of the House who tried to eject him because he refused, on grounds of religious disagreement, to take the oath of membership. Their hypocrisy was infinitely more despicable than his honest skepticism.

The third chapter of the *Deliverance* is an abrupt digression, returning us to his native Bedford and recounting the story of Miss Leroy, the daughter of a French emigré, and George Butts, the man who became her husband. The evidence that this couple were Hale White's own uncle and aunt from Colchester—at least in all major details—is overwhelming. In the *Early Life* he writes:

> I had an aunt in Colchester, a woman of singular originality, which none of her neighbours could interpret, and consequently they misliked it, and ventured upon distant insinuations against her. She had married a baker, a good kind of man, but tame. In summer-time she not infrequently walked at five o'clock in the morning to a pretty church about a mile and a half away, and read *George Herbert* in the porch. She was no relation of mine, except by marriage to my uncle, but she was most affectionate to me, and always loaded me with nice things whenever I went to see her. The survival in my memory of her cakes, gingerbread, and kisses, has done me more good, moral good—if you have a fancy for this word—than sermons or punishment.[60]

Mrs. Butts was, writes Mark Rutherford, "one of the very, very few whom I have ever seen who knew how to love a child,"[61] and she too used to walk to a church porch at four o'clock on a summer's morning and read, not George Herbert, but *De Imitatione Christi*; and George Butts was the "tame" creature Hale White describes his uncle as being: "He was a big, soft, quiet, plump-faced, awkward youth, very good, but nothing more."[62] Hale White's mother was, apparently, offended by this woman's shocking French ways and freedom of talk; at least Mark Rutherford's mother reacted in this way to Miss Leroy and, as we shall presently see, there is little reason to doubt the identifications. This is what we are told in the *Deliverance*:

> Miss Leroy told a male person once, and told him to his face, that if she loved him and he loved her, and they agreed to sign one another's foreheads with a cross as a ceremony, it would be as good to her as marriage. This may seem a trifle, but nobody now can imagine what was thought of it at the time it was spoken. My mother repeated it every now and then for fifty years.[63]

That a woman so emancipated from the prevailing conventions of his youthful environment should also be "one of the very, very few . . . who knew how to love a child," is a fact of the greatest significance in Hale White's life. We cannot help feeling that her love planted the seeds of rebellion in him at an early age, and that the frequent trips to Colchester were made as much to escape the company of his mother as to taste strange

60 *E.L.*, pp. 11–12.
61 *D.*, p. 43.
62 *Ibid.*, p. 38.
63 *Ibid.*, p. 34. From this one suspects that she read Feuerbach as well!

gingerbread and kisses. For there are grounds to believe that Hale White's mother was foremost among those who "ventured distant insinuations" against his aunt. The marriage between this strikingly original woman of foreign extraction and the dull provincial miller aroused in the *Deliverance* just the sort of gossip Hale White attributes to his mother in the *Early Life*:

My mother was stunned, and never completely recovered. I have seen her, forty years after George Butts' wedding-day, lift up her hands, and have heard her call out with emotion, as fresh as if the event were of yesterday, "What made that girl have George I can *not* think—but there!"[64]

That girl had loved Hale White as, one can only suppose, his mother never had, and it must have been with a strange sense of guilt and frustration that he listened to his mother's words.

These suppositions are enforced by the evidence from another book, *The Revolution in Tanner's Lane*. There the characters of Mrs. Coleman and Pauline and the relationship between them correspond closely with those of Hale White's mother and aunt. Pauline is French, free in her ways, unconventional, pious but not orthodox, and, like Miss Leroy, caring nothing for "the linen-closet, the spotless bed-hangings, and the bright poker, which were the true household gods of the respectable women of those days."[65] In all these things she was Miss Leroy's double. Mrs. Coleman is a conventional, severe, gossipy, formalistic Calvinist, an impeccably clean housekeeper, strict Sabbatarian, possessing a keen nose for the moral shortcomings of her neighbors. In these things she seems to correspond to Hale White's mother. The words Hale White chooses with which to describe Mrs. Butts and Pauline make their identification almost conclusive; and the fact that Mrs. Zachariah Coleman's criticisms are almost paraphrases of those of Mark Rutherford's mother suggests strongly that they were both drawn from the same original. These are the words from the *Deliverance*:

Thus did Mrs. Butts live among us, as an Arabian bird with its peculiar habits, cries, and plumage might live in one of our barnyards with the ordinary barn-door fowls.[66]

And thus—illustrating again Hale White's tendency to dress up the same matter in slightly different guise, as he had learned to do in his journalism—is Pauline presented in the *Revolution*:

Pauline surprised Mrs. Zachariah considerably. A woman, and more particularly a young woman, even supposing her to be quite orthodox, who behaved in that style amongst the members of Pike Street [a Dissenting chapel], would have been like a wild seagull in a farm-yard of peaceful, clucking, brown-speckled fowls.[67]

We have already seen in Mrs. Furze a similarity to Hale White's

[64] *Ibid.*, p. 39.
[65] *Ibid.*, pp. 34–35. Cf. *R.T.L.*, p. 46.
[66] *Ibid.*, p. 42.
[67] *R.T.L.*, p. 57.

mother, and we shall see her image again and again throughout the novels. There is general agreement among Hale White's relatives that his mother was of a highly nervous temperament and that Hale White inherited his nerves from her. However valid such a line of psychological descent may be, it seems obvious that his memories of her were by no means entirely pleasant. Can it be that in his books the son sought to avenge her failure to love him as his aunt and uncle did and as he longed to be loved? Can this lack of maternal love account, in part at least, for his lifelong need to seek affection *outside* his home? These things seem likely, and may be important clues in understanding that malignant anxiety with which he sought a spiritual home.

In reading the *Autobiography* and the *Deliverance* we are, therefore, virtually examining Hale White's family album—but one annotated rather more freely than is usually the case with a record which some members of the immediate family might examine. In a strict historical sense, it is not in all details a true account. But though the photography is sometimes blurred and formalistic—as is usual in such Victorian memorials—the commentary, once we learn to read it, is extremely lucid and revealing.

Chapter Nine

THE NOVELS: FACT AND FICTION

When we turn from the two autobiographical books to the novels proper, the correspondences between fact and fiction are, of course, more difficult to determine and fewer in number. *The Revolution in Tanner's Lane* cannot, for example, have been entirely a record of personal experience, for the first half of the book treats of a period of history preceding Hale White's birth—those closing years of the Napoleonic Wars, when England was oppressed by high taxes, labor unrest, and the callous Toryism of George III and Lord Liverpool. Hale White had not known this era, but his grandfather had been "Radical, and almost Republican,"[1] and Hale White's ancestral sympathies were very strong. He reminds us in the *Early Life* that his grandfather with two neighbors "refused to illuminate for our victories over the French, and he had his windows smashed by a Tory mob,"[2] an incident which is also recounted in the *Deliverance*.[3]

Hale White made this period of history peculiarly his own, and imaginatively he belonged very much to it. He loved its heroism, vitality, and fighting spirit; he loved the vigor of its political and religious conviction, its clear causes, its ardent affirmation of right and wrong. To understand the temper of that time Hale White had only to feel his own pulse when it was beating high, for he had inherited the longings and—to a degree—the equipment of a romantic revolutionary. Thus does he write in his essay, "Our Debt to France":

> What is the meaning of the Revolution? Externally it is political, but it is more than that. It is the reference of all institutions to first principles, to man. It means the application of primary standards to the whole of life; but the miracle is not so much the judgement as the re-erection of the Court by which it is pronounced; the re-appearance in flashing splendour of Conscience and Justice. There is still something more. The sudden apparition of these celestial figures produces intoxication. Such is the temper of the time that men and women, even ordinary men and women, are drunk with the beauty and majesty of the new world revealed to them. Heroes like those in the barricade scene in *Les Misérables* become possible and even common, and from the very gutter, from parents like the Thénardiers, can be evolved the almost supernatural purity and devotion of an Eponine. All life at such a season wears a new aspect, the earth again becomes exquisite, heaven infinite, and hence arises a new language and hitherto undiscovered melodies.[4]

To recapture the history of this period was, therefore, almost to remember a personal experience, so thoroughly had Hale White absorbed

[1] *E.L.*, p. 21.
[2] *Ibid.*
[3] *D.*, p. 38.
[4] *The Bookman*, II (August 1892), 140. See also "Notes on Shelley's Birthplace," *The Bookman*, XLII (June 1912), 67.

its temper. And just as he rebuked the wealthy of Victorian England by revealing to them the poverty of Drury Lane, so in the *Revolution* he rebuked an age of political opportunism and religious decay—of Jukes and Broads and Snales—by contrasting it with an age of Colemans, Bradshaws, and Major Cartwrights. The two halves of *The Revolution in Tanner's Lane* point up this very contrast, and it is an ironic comment on the differences between old and new, vitality and passivity, revolution and compromise, health and sickness, courage and cowardice, and—almost—right and wrong. As H. W. Massingham remarked, Hale White is telling the old story: "One generation of mankind bind a doctrine to their hearts; their children wear it as a phylactery round their foreheads."[5] Hale White, as we know, tore off the phylactery but found no new doctrine which he could, with enthusiasm, bind to his heart. The wars of the mid-nineteenth century were for him wars of nerves in which moral courage and passionate conviction were less called for than stoic patience and tireless intellectual watching. He was never content with his obscure desk job in that half-idle army. This book is, therefore, not only the record of two periods of history; it is the objectification of an inner conflict suffered by its author.

The ironic contrast between England of the early century and of the mid-century is not, however, entirely effective. In the first place, the earlier half of the book concerns itself with centers of political agitation, Manchester and London, while the second half is entirely set in Bedford, a comparatively obscure Midland town. The political and religious indifference infecting Bedford was, to no small degree, typical of the country as a whole, but Hale White does not show us that this is so. Furthermore, the connection between the two halves is secured only by the reappearance, in minor roles, of Zachariah and Bradshaw in the second part, leaving the suggestion in the reader's mind that the relative absence of heroism in the closing section was due simply to the increased age of the protagonists and not to the character of the *age* itself. In the second place, the title is confusing and inadequate. The "revolution" in Tanner's Lane was a revolution only in the sense that a radical change had come over the spiritual condition of the people of Bedford. But inasmuch as we are not shown Bedford's earlier condition, we witness the retirement of Broad in favor of a somewhat better successor and the departure of the Allens—the last of the town's true spiritual heroes—with some confusion. What is symbolized in these acts becomes clear only after we have studied the book, and, indeed, Hale White's work in general.

What is the reason for this failure? To no small degree it is attributable to the very nature of Hale White's art. He was here more of an historian than a novelist. The hard facts were too sacred to be tampered with, and Hale White was seldom able to summon that creative passion which would control the structure of an entire work, enlisting his data in the service of a central creative conception. This inability can be seen both as a virtue

---

[5] *A.*, "Memorial Introduction," p. xviii.

and a fault. It is a virtue if we value his refusal to bring the multiplicity of life into an artificial or contrived unity, his restless insistence upon resting *in* the fact and eschewing easy syntheses. But it is a fault, both in his art and life, in that this honest and courageous facing of the complexities of human experience left him, very largely, impotent before a concrete situation demanding action or unified expression. He could write the answers no more effectively than he could live them, a fact which is reflected in both the form and style of his novels. He could not carefully select his materials, for such selection might mean distortion; he could not really fictionalize his work, for that was something close to lying; he could not seriously concern himself with technique—except within individual sentences and paragraphs—for that smacked of ordering things from outside in rather than from the inside out. Life for Hale White was made of fragments. He trusted that a unity could be achieved and that a genius might achieve it imaginatively even in the mid-nineteenth century, but—though he tentatively found something he could call his own "truth," or at least a method for finding it—he could never be presumptuous enough to proclaim it as a truth for all men.

Thus the tenuous unity of the *Revolution* reflects the tenuous unity of the man himself. And part of the excitement of reading this book comes from observing that struggle between fact and fiction which is never quite resolved but which, when once noticed, depicts a drama transcending that consciously conceived by its author. Because the *Revolution* suggests these faults more clearly than the other novels—except perhaps *Clara Hopgood*—it has seemed necessary to dilate upon them here. But they are, to a degree, characteristic of all his work, for there was in him no possible divorce between aesthetics and morality and hardly any between the didactic and the imaginative statement.

In a letter to his second son he gives as clear an expression to the principles of his art as we can find:

Art is art in proportion to its distinctness. Noble art is distinguished from base art by the perfect clearness of the conception which it aims to embody. . . . The sum and substance, to put it in other words, is *realization*. Whatever we have to speak, let it be bounded by a precise limiting line, so that the thing spoken is marked off from the vague, from chaos, from all other things with absolute precision. . . . Perhaps I could have concluded all I had to say in one word. Our actual *experience*, not what we can invent or dream: and no step a hair's breadth beyond what is real and solid for us, proved and again proved.[6]

While this passion for distinctness may have harmed the book's structure as a whole, it lent color and vigor to individual scenes and characters. The first half of the *Revolution* is by far the most alive and dramatic of all his novels. There is more action and less comment, and its historical setting is so vividly recaptured that the reader is led to believe that Hale White would have been a greater artist had he more often stood away from

[6] *P.L.*, p. 14. Letter dated August 29, 1893.

his canvas. But though the events of this book belong largely to history, many of the characters—as we already know—are remembered. In major features Mrs. Zachariah Coleman is Hale White's mother and Pauline is his aunt. And there can be little doubt that Zachariah Coleman is more than half patterned after Hale White's father. These last were both printers, both lovers of Byron, both political radicals in their youth—and both experienced the same liberalization of their native Calvinism.[7] But Hale White's emotional identification with his father was so close that we cannot separate with any distinctness or assurance those qualities which he gave of himself to the portrait of Zachariah and those obviously borrowed from William White. Major Maitland is the one disguised historical character whom we can identify with some certainty. His association with "The Friends of the People" and his emphasis on peaceful reform rather than open revolt suggest very strongly Major Cartwright[8] who, together with Sir Francis Burdett, is mentioned by name several times in the book.

The real characters and incidents animating the second half of the novel have already been examined.[9] We need only add here that Priscilla Broad is formed on the pattern of all Hale White's conventional, silly, intellectually restricted women. She is one of the "brown-speckled fowls," and makes life miserable for her politically conscious and somewhat literary husband, George Allen. This man is the son of Isaac Allen, who again bears a strong resemblance to Hale White's father. Could it be that the son is Hale White himself in major details and that he is recalling his own married experience or that of his father?[10] Their marital fortunes, we suspect, were not too dissimilar; and women like Priscilla very likely have their originals—like Mrs. Coleman—in Hale White's mother. No concrete proof of such conjecture is possible, but as the reader becomes more familiar with Hale White's novels the feeling grows that he has met most of these people before—in either the *Early Life*, the *Autobiography*, or the *Deliverance*—and he is increasingly inclined to take seriously Hale White's remark that he "never *created* a character in his life."

Miriam's Schooling was published in early June 1890, one year before the death of Hale White's wife, and nearly two before his retirement from the Admiralty. Written as a story, without chapter divisions, it has a unity that the *Revolution* lacks, and strikes the reader as one of Hale White's most intimate and powerful self-revelations. Certainly none of his books, except the autobiographies, displays a more single-minded concern with the psychology of suffering and the method of salvation from it. In later

---

[7] Hale White's grandfather could not have directly stood for the portrait, since he was killed in a riding accident before Hale White's birth.

[8] See Graham Wallas, *The Life of Francis Place* (London, 1898); F. D. Cartwright (ed.), *Major John Cartwright: His Life and Correspondence*, 2 vols. (London, 1826); and E. Halevy, *England in 1815* (London, 1924).

[9] See above, pp. 21–24, 28–30.

[10] For a discussion of these matters see "Mark Rutherford Centenary," *The Bedfordshire Times and Independent*, December 18, 1931.

chapters we shall view in more detail the correspondences between the spiritual condition of Miriam Tacchi, the heroine, and Hale White.[11] But it should be noted here that the years between 1885 and 1892, to estimate roughly, were for Hale White particularly lonely and trying ones. His sons were one by one marrying or leaving home;[12] his wife was nearing her death from an incurable disease; his office work involved greater responsibility and had grown heavier owing to the Sudan War and the prospect of war with Russia;[13] and in this period his complaints of nervous dyspepsia and insomnia were incessant.[14] While few of these matters are directly included in this book, they are obliquely reflected in the peculiar intensity and near savagery of Miriam's mental and physical suffering.

After 1892 more serene moods were possible for Hale White, but this was the heat of the day. In 1886 he writes to his second son:

For years I have not suffered from such continued gloom. I have hardly been able to open my lips except at the office, and at times I have scarcely known what I have been doing. What is the cause of it all, I cannot conjecture, save that it is some internal disorder which, as I get older, naturally gets worse.[15]

While Miriam's career differs in externals from Hale White's, her spiritual passage across the valley of the shadow can be called almost a literal transcript of her creator's experience. In most of his books Hale White is remembering his past, but in this he mainly seems to be registering a present state of mind. Though Miriam attains peace at last, it is the peace of an anesthesia rather than of health, a peace achieved during suffering rather than after it. In later years Hale White told his second wife that *Miriam's Schooling* was "the only one of his books he remembers, and of that . . . only one scene . . ."[16] Though we need not accept this statement literally—for his memory was strong to the end—it does suggest that this story was born of a particularly intimate personal experience and that he valued it in a special way.

Many of the autobiographical elements in this book are, therefore, drawn from Hale White's own "buried life" and are not easily isolated, though they are easily recognizable. But some of the events are clear transcriptions of the author's experience. The most obvious is the visit to Stonehenge—an event marking the beginning of Miriam's convalescence and, one suspects, an important turning point in Hale White's own spiritual history. Perhaps this is the "one scene" he remembered.

11 See below, pp. 165–69, 187.

12 William married in 1886; John left home to begin his career in 1882.

13 *P.L.*, p. 5. Letter dated April 19, 1885. "The strain at the office in consequence of the prospect of war has been awful."

14 *P.N.b.*, pp. 39–40.

15 *P.L.*, pp. 6–7. Letter dated May 27, 1886.

16 *G.D.*, pp. 48–49. He spoke seldom about his books but seemed to mention this one quite often. See *G.D.*, pp. 36–37. In a letter to the present author on March 28, 1950, Mrs. D. V. White remarked that she felt there was something "peculiarly 'close' " in this book.

In two letters preserved by his second son we learn of Hale White's visit there in July 1888 with his old friends, Mr. and Mrs. Colenutt. On July 9 he writes:

Stonehenge, after you get acquainted with it, is wonderful, but I find that it disposes me to indefinite, vague misty sentiment, and this I try as much as possible to avoid. It is bad for anybody; trebly bad for me, and I would rather acquire some distinct piece of information about Stonehenge than be the victim of the shapeless emotion which almost overpowers me as I look at it.[17]

He continues the record in a letter of July 13:

I have just returned from a trip to Stonehenge . . . with Mr. and Mrs. Colenutt. Amesbury is Tennyson's Almesbury; where was the holy house to which Queen Guinevere went. The village or little town is not particularly remarkable, but it is a very pleasant characteristic English cluster of houses and the valley of the Avon is extremely beautiful. Stonehenge and more especially its vast plain struck me *harder* than anything I have ever seen, but these hoary stones, about which nothing is known, gave rise to thoughts not particularly profitable. A monument like this so easily lends itself to the very simple, but perfectly worthless depression begotten by the idea of the transitory passage of generations across the planet . . .[18]

Miriam too "knew nothing of the history of the Amesbury valley, but she was sensible—as who must not be?—to its exquisite beauty and the delicacy of the contrasts between the downs and the richly-foliaged fields through which the Avon winds."[19] And her reaction to Stonehenge itself was exactly like Hale White's:

One day she contrived to reach Stonehenge. She was driven there by the farmer with whom she was staying, and she asked to be left there while he went forward. He was to fetch her when he returned. It was a clear but gray day, and she sat outside the outer circle on the turf looking northwards over the almost illimitable expanse. She had been told as much as is known about that mysterious monument,— that it had been built ages before any record, and that not only were the names of the builders forgotten, but their purpose in building it was forgotten too. She was oppressed with a sense of her own nothingness and the nothingness of man. If those who raised that temple had so utterly passed away, for how long would the memory of her existence last? Stonehenge itself too would pass. The wind and the rain had already worn perhaps half of it, and the place that now knows it will know it no more save by vague tradition, which also will be extinguished.[20]

A few pages after this experience is recounted, Hale White writes of "A man now old and nearing his end" who "is known to Miriam's biographer . . ."[21] This man is without a doubt White's ancient friend, Mr. Colenutt, whose conversations during the trip would likely be associated with his memories of the holiday. But the degree of stenography in this scene is not nearly so significant as the evident fact that Hale White is making of Miriam his emotional representative. Her oppression over

[17] *P.L.*, p. 8.
[18] *Ibid.*
[19] *M.S.*, p. 116.
[20] *Ibid.*, p. 117.
[21] *Ibid.*, p. 119.

human mutability and "the nothingness of man" is a direct reflection of her creator's mood, and we can therefore suppose that her method of overcoming despair was Hale White's solution as well.

Another episode drawn from Hale White's recent history in *Miriam's Schooling* was that of Mr. Armstrong and his astronomical telescope. The original of Mr. Armstrong was doubtless the minister of a chapel in Newport-Pagnell, who is mentioned by Hale White in a letter to Miss Sophia S. Partridge in December 1906.[22] For both Miriam and Hale White contemplation of the heavens brought that relief from self-absorption they both craved and needed, and it was a healthier release than the "vague, misty sentiment" inspired by the mystery and vastness of Stonehenge. About Stonehenge nothing definite could be known, but a study of the stars demanded mathematical precision, thus providing these insecure souls with a safe intellectual base for their spiritual reveries. Mr. Armstrong gave to Miriam a piece of advice which Hale White never tired of repeating:

If you can once from your own observation *realise* the way the stars revolve—why some near the pole never set—why some never rise, and why Venus is seen both before the sun and after it—you will have done yourselves more real good than if you were to dream for years of immeasurable distances, and what is beyond and beyond and beyond, and all that nonsense. The great beauty of astronomy is not what is incomprehensible in it, but its comprehensibility—its geometrical exactitude.[23]

The setting of *Miriam's Schooling* opens and closes in the Cowfold we have seen before, and centers in a familiar London. In none of his books is the contrast between country and city developed so explicitly as here, and nowhere does he make such symbolic use of it. With Hale White as with Thomas Hardy, the contrast was not merely geographical but moral and cultural as well. The city was modernity, with all its brash commercial newness; the country was age, with its richness and warmth of tradition. The city was complexity and bigness, breeding indifference to the value and uniqueness of the individual; the country was simplicity, affording room for human eccentricity and nonconformity. In this gray period of Hale White's life, he increasingly sought emotional peace by remembering the scenes and persons of his childhood home, and in his next book— *Catharine Furze*—his nostalgia is unmistakable.

The most striking instance of direct reminiscence in *Miriam's Schooling* is his portrait of Mr. Fitchew, one of those Bedford primitives whose crude exterior hides genuine virtues. Hale White brings not only his character but his proper name into the book. In the story Fitchew appears as an intransigent creature, a "rough and coarse" man-of-all-work who

22 See *L.3F.*, p. 249. See also pp. 44–45.

23 *M.S.*, pp. 140–41. The motto under the frontispiece of this book is *Nihil Aliud Quam Bene Ausus Vana Contemnere* ("There is nothing better than a brave attempt to ignore vain imaginings"). This is virtually the theme of the book as it is, to a lesser degree, of *Catharine Furze*. See *C.F.*, p. 79.

was "grasping in his dealings . . . not so much because he was naturally mean, but because he was always determined that well-dressed folk should not 'put on him.' "[24] He refused to attend church or chapel, and resisted attempts at conversion with the pointed argument: " 'I don't see as them that goes to church are any better than them as don't. What's *he* [the minister or parson] know about it?' "[25] He had a wife, "hard as flint" and "most particularly clean."[26]

They had married late in life—why, nobody could tell—and had one child, a girl, whom the mother seemed to disregard just as she did her husband, saving that she dressed her and washed her with the same care which she bestowed on her kettle and candlesticks.

This man is unquestionably the same Bill Fitchew whom Hale White describes in the *Early Life* as a debtor to his uncle, Samuel Lovell, and who made unconscionable use of his daughter—dressed in her "white, Sunday frock with red ribbons"[27]—as a means of softening his creditor's demands for payment. Thus would the conversation run at the door of Fitchew's house:

"Hullo, my pretty dear, what's your name? Dear, what's your name?"

"Say Keziah Fitchew, sir," prompts Mrs. Fitchew, appearing suddenly at the side door as if she had come to fetch her child who had run out unawares.

After much hesitation: "Keziah Fitchew, sir."

"Are you a good little girl? Do you say your prayers every morning and every evening?"

"Yes, sir."

"Would you know what to do with sixpence, if I gave it you? You'd put it in the missionary box, wouldn't you?"

Keziah thinks, but does not reply. It is a problem of immense importance. Uncle turns to Bill, so that Keziah cannot see him, puts up his left hand to the side of his face and winks violently.[28]

The upshot of this interview is that Lovell gets a promise of £10 within a fortnight and Fitchew is invited, as is the annual custom, to join with the other debtors in sharing a drink (at Mr. Lovell's expense) at the Red Lion.

But the importance of Fitchew (who is a minor character in the story) lies not alone in this identification. Miriam finds his simplicity and coarse honesty a corrective to her pride and snobbery; here was a man as absolutely in his orbit as the stars themselves, who did not try to deny his own essential being in the name of some vague spiritual ambition. He was an object lesson, walking evidence, that to *be oneself* involves *relaxing* into character rather than *striving* for character. Hale White, no less than Miriam, needed to learn that lesson, and it is not without significance that

24 *Ibid.*, pp. 150–51.
25 *Ibid.*, p. 150.
26 *Ibid.*, p. 152.
27 *E.L.*, p. 25.
28 *Ibid.*, pp. 25–26.

this book has a large cast of such whole and elemental people—Miss Tippit, Didymus Farrow, and Mrs. Jeremy Joll—all of whom, we suspect, were drawn from memories of Bedford. Mrs. Joll, he writes,

. . . was well read in departments more important perhaps than books in the conduct of human life, and in her there was the one thing needful—the one thing which, if ever there is to be a Judgment Day, will put her on the right hand; when all sorts of scientific people, religious people, students of poetry, people with exquisite emotions, will go on the left and be damned everlastingly.[29]

But the rude, unlettered people of the city—like Mr. and Mrs. Dabb— were of another stamp and their outsides were a clear advertisement of the quality of their souls. Dirt in the city was dirt, greed was greed, slovenliness was slovenliness; these things were man-made and no Wordsworthian apologetics could explain away their hateful reality.

This disillusionment with the city was, however, of gradual growth and is doubtless as much a reflection of Hale White's melancholy state of mind in this period as a cause of it. At any rate, when both he and Miriam passed for the first time through the Highgate archway into the city, they felt they were entering upon "the goal of all their aspirations, the promised land in which nothing but golden romance awaited them."[30] In *The Norfolk News* for May 6, 1876, Hale White recalled this event from his own experience in words that closely parallel those of the novel:

The toll gate on the archway-road up at Highgate, had gone, but thank goodness, the archway remains. To many Londoners it is a sacred spot. Five-and-thirty-years ago, when the present writer first saw London through it, the road underneath it was the great highway to the North, and a hundred coaches passed up and down it every day. Thousands of boys can call to mind the first glimpse of the city through that arch, and can remember the exultation with which they looked down from the coach-top upon what they thought to be the Land of Promise. The ruddy morning cloud may all have turned to wet drizzle since then, but the reminiscence of the emotion is still pleasant, and I for one should be intensely sorry to see the archway destroyed.

After thirty-five years Bedford once again seemed to be the Land of Promise and London a place of exile.

Before considering Hale White's next novel, some mention must be made of the companion piece to *Miriam's Schooling*, that remarkable production, *Michael Trevanion*. This tale, like *Miriam's Schooling*, was born of the period of despair and melancholy preceding his wife's death and, like that book, is preoccupied with the psychological development of one main character. Michael Trevanion is a Calvinist believer whose adamantine religious faith is equaled only by his emotional absorption in Robert, his one son. The father was "religious, upright, temperate, but given somewhat to moodiness and passion."[31] His servant, who had helped him at his trade of stonemason for twenty years, "knew perfectly well what these

29 *M.S.*, p. 107.
30 *Ibid.*, p. 70.
31 *Ibid.*, p. 155.

attacks of melancholy or wrath meant, and that, though their assigned cause lay in the block before them or the weather, the real cause was in-doors."[32] And part of that "indoor cause" lay in his domestic relations:

> His case was very simple and very common—the simplest, commonest case in life. He married, as we have said, when he was young, before he knew what he was doing, and after he had been married twelve months, he found he did not care for his wife. . . . He mistook passion for love . . . he made the one irretrievable false step and was ruined. No strong antipathy developed itself; there were no quarrels, but there was a complete absence of anything like confidence. Michael had never for years really consulted his wife in any difficulty, because he knew he could not get any advice worth a moment's consideration. . . .[33]

The comparison between Hale White's own situation (and the mood which went with it) and that of Michael is a striking one. But more important here are the relations between Michael and his son, Robert. Between these two silent people had grown a strong bond of love and respect—as stubborn and masculine as the rocky Cornish seacoast which is the setting for this drama. But in the very strength of the bond lies its weakness, for Michael lavishes on Robert all the fierce possessiveness of a lonely and frustrated man. Hardly realizing it himself, he had come to regard his son almost as a substitute for God. When, therefore, Robert falls in love with a girl—and one of another religious persuasion!—the father's religion is inadequate to sustain the shock. He resorts to a dishonest stratagem in order to cast suspicion on the girl's moral character, attempting by this means to draw Robert back to himself. The device fails, however, and at last, after the girl melodramatically saves the old man from drowning, he learns forgiveness and a reconciliation is effected. But the reconciliation is not merely the expression of his gratitude; it results from a transformation wrought in his inner nature. In that moment of being snatched away from the threshold of death, he learned what most of Hale White's main characters learn: that one must give in order to have, that life is posited upon renunciation.

This plot, so far as can be discovered, was entirely invented, but in the father-son relationship and in some details of setting we can detect a significant reflection of Hale White's own experience. From a letter he wrote to his second son, John, on July 1, 1887, we learn that they had just spent a holiday together in Cornwall and that this reunion had done much to assuage his loneliness and melancholy:

> I was very glad to have you with me, more glad than I can tell. I doubt if I should have gone or remained if you had not been there. I am afraid I was an unpleasant companion but at any rate I gave you the opportunity for a little self-sacrifice. It would be ungrateful and untrue to say I am no better but whether I shall ever recover my old health of mind I do not know. I must be patient and wait.[34]

Evidence accumulated by Mr. H. A. Smith indicates that "of all the chil-

[32] *Ibid.*
[33] *Ibid.*, pp. 156–57.
[34] *P.L.*, p. 8.

dren Jack was nearest his father in temperament and outlook,"[35] and it seems likely that Hale White had him in mind—or at least his love for him—when he wrote *Michael Trevanion*. But the very fact that John was a favorite son makes even more plausible the supposition that he provoked—at least in part—those feelings of resentment and bitterness which appear so openly in the story. For in March 1889 he became engaged to Miss Agnes Hughes, the daughter of the Pre-Raphaelite painter, Arthur Hughes, whom Hale White had known since about 1875.[36] The couple was married, as were all his children, in the Anglican Church; and Hale White, excusing himself on the grounds of distance or indisposition, refused to attend this ceremony as he had refused to witness his eldest son's marriage on December 30, 1886.[37] Possibly both of these "desertions" were in his mind as he wrote *Michael Trevanion* (sometime between 1887 and 1890), but it seems likely that the trip to Cornwall with John was the immediate event moving him to articulate his feelings. Hale White grew to have a deep affection for his sons' wives, much as Michael Trevanion learned to love Robert's Susan, but the initial abandonment doubtless registered a deep wound which, for the moment at least, caused him to feel something like rage against the fatal unkindness and brutality of life. In this tale, sheltered beyond his anonymity, Hale White seems to be letting his bitterness burn itself out, expressing himself in this medium with an emotional freedom forbidden in real life. What is the following statement but an attempt to purge self-pity by indulging it? It comes, significantly enough, at the very moment of reconciliation in the story—suggesting that its purgative uses for the author had not been entirely effective.[38]

Robert, as much moved as his father, fell on his neck as if he been a woman, and then led him gently down the slope, away from curious persons who had watched this remarkable greeting, and took Michael to be some strange person who had accidently met his child or a relative after long separation.

"Foreigners, most likely; that's their way. It looks odd to English people," remarked a lady to her daughter. It did look odd, and would have looked odd to most of us—to us who belong to a generation which sees in the relationship between father and son nothing more than in that between the most casual acquaintances with the disadvantage of inequality of age, a generation to whom the father is—often excusably—a person to be touched twice a day with the tips of the fingers,[39] a postponement of a full share in the business, a person to be treated with—respect? Good gracious! If it were not bad form, it would be a joke worth playing to slip the chair

[35] Smith, *Life and Thought*. Information from Mary Theodora, Hale White's youngest daughter. John was called "Jack" by the family. A third son, Ernest, is rarely mentioned in the family records.

[36] *P.N.a.*, p. 4.

[37] William, the eldest son, married Miss Jean Fripp at Tarrant Rushton, a remote village in Dorset. See *P.N.b.*, p. 24.

[38] *M.S.*, pp. 190–91.

[39] In a letter to Henry Arthur Jones, reprinted in D. A. Jones, *The Life and Letters of H. A. Jones* (London, 1930), p. 111, there is a remarkable repetition of this phrasing and sentiment: "The curse of curses nowadays is not that we don't keep the Law, although we do not do much in that line, but that we don't know what Love means and touch one another with the tips of gloved fingers." The letter was dated August 15, 1890, and is added evidence that this story was written around this date or before it.

away from the old man as he is going to sit down, and see him sprawl on the floor. Why, in the name of heaven, does he come up to the City every day? He ought to retire, and leave that expensive place at Clapham, and take a cottage in some cheap part, somewhere in Cambridgeshire or Essex.[40]

There can be little doubt that there were moments in this period of his life when, like Michael, he felt that "His human nature got the better of every other nature in him, divine or diabolic, and he was distracted," and when he felt like crying out with Michael, "My God! My God! why hast Thou forsaken me?"[41] However unjust these oblique representations against his children were, it was out of such passionate frustration that *Michael Trevanion* was forged. And it is a remarkably well-controlled and powerful expression, sharing something of the solemn beauty of Hawthorne's *Scarlet Letter* or of Gide's *Symphonie Pastorale*. In few of his writings has Hale White been more furtively or subtly self-revealing.

In August 1893, Hale White revisited Bedford,[42] partly to occupy the idle hours of unaccustomed retirement[43] by visiting old friends, but partly, no doubt, to freshen his memories of the place in preparation for writing *Catharine Furze*. Except for three chapters,[44] this story is entirely laid in his native town and provides the most detailed picture of Bedford's social and religious life that Hale White gives us. In a letter to his son following the visit[45] he writes:

We had two or three pleasant days at Bedford. The lowland river scenery there is as exquisite as it ever was and I went over to Oakley and saw two or three poor people there, old friends. One ancient lady who now keeps the little post-office on the munificent salary of 3/6 a week was servant in our house, about 50 years ago. It was very delightful, in a way, to wander about the familiar lanes and be greeted with such excitement by familiar faces and listen to old-world stories and recollections. I felt as if I had a right to be there. I have no right here and no ties.[46] But perhaps although delightful it was not healthy.

Nearly two years earlier, in November 1891, he had written that "for some reasons I dislike Bedford. My father's shade meets me at every corner when I go there."[47] The difference in tone is the measure of his returning health and good spirits. Though we meet many of the old problems and the old people in this book, that intense desperation which marked *Miriam's Schooling* has passed.

[40] In February 1889 Hale White moved from Park Hill, Carshalton (a house he had built himself) to Street Farm, Ashtead, Surrey. He had lived at Park Hill for over twenty years and was never long contented in any of his later residences. No doubt his children had suggested that he move and retire—sensible suggestions which he peevishly resented. His Ashtead house was more in the country, but about equally far from the office. Hale White moved there only one month before John's engagement was announced. See correspondence with the architect, Philip Webb, in *L.3F.*, pp. 297–396.

[41] *M.S.*, pp. 184–85.   [42] *P.L.*, p. 13. Letter dated August 26, 1893.

[43] He retired from the Admiralty on March 31, 1892. See "Mr. Whittaker's Retirement," *M.P.*, pp. 87–107.

[44] Chapters VI, VII, VIII.

[45] *P.L.*, p. 13. Letter dated August 26, 1893.

[46] He was then at 9, High Wickham, Hastings, whence he had moved in April 1892.

[47] *L.3F.*, p. 52.

The "ancient lady" referred to above was no doubt a member of the household of his old nurse Jane about whom he speaks at affectionate length in the *Early Life*.[48] She too lived in a "little thatched cottage at Oakley" and as children Hale and his sister had frequently accepted the rough but generous hospitality offered there. Throughout his life, Hale White remembered the simple, unpretentious life of this cottage as a damning contrast to the artificiality and loneliness of more favored homes. Here one had a "right" to be, as doubtless he felt he had no right in his new house at Hastings.[49]

Oh, for a house with this one room, a Homeric house! How much easier and how much more natural should we be if we watched the pot or peeled the potatoes as we talked, than it is now in a drawing-room, where we do not know what chair to choose amongst a dozen scattered about aimlessly; where there is no table to hide the legs or support the arms; a room which compels an uncomfortable awkwardness, and forced conversation. Would it not be more sincere if a saucepan took part in it than it is now, when, in evening clothes, tea-cup in hand, we discuss the show at the Royal Academy, while a lady at the piano sings a song from *Aida*?

While such sentimental primitivism sorts strangely with what we already know of Hale White's passion for comfort, cleanliness, and suburban middle-class respectability, there were certain things in that rude life which deeply appealed to him: the simple affection that prevailed in these close quarters, the intimate feeling of belonging. In this case, however, as in many others, his romanticism grew directly out of a sense of inferiority. The desire to hide arms and legs and to look away from his hearers when he talked was, with Hale White, inseparably connected with his longing for "sincerity." In situations demanding social poise, self-consciousness came flooding in, and he hated the masks he had to wear.

Though Phoebe Crowhurst's house at Abchurch in *Catharine Furze* is not particularly idealized, there can be no doubt that it was patterned after that of Nurse Jane. Phoebe, like Jane, had been a servant in Catharine's home in Bedford (Eastthorpe) and her house was also located "about a mile and a half out of the village."[50]

The living-room faced the north-east, the door opening direct on the little patch of garden, so that in winter, when the wind howled across the level fields, it was scarcely warmer indoors than outside, and rags and dish-clouts had to be laid on the door-sill to prevent the entrance of the snow and rain. At the back was a place, half outhouse, half kitchen, which had once had a brick floor, but the bricks had disappeared. Upstairs, over the living-room, was a bedroom, with no fireplace, and a very small casement window, where the mother and three children slept, the oldest a girl of about fourteen, the second a boy of twelve, and the third a girl of three or four, for the back bedroom over the outhouse had been given up to Phoebe since she was ill. . . . Just underneath the window was the pigstye.

Visitors in these parts thought the cottage "most picturesque," and in the

48 *E.L.*, pp. 40–44. See above, p. 129.
49 *Ibid.*, pp. 41–42.
50 *C.F.*, p. 208.

novel it had been made the subject of a water color which hung in the drawing room of the Honourable Mr. Eaton.[51]

"Lovely! What a dear old place!" said the guests.

"It makes one quite enamoured of the country," exclaimed Lady Fanshawe, one of the most determined diners-out in Mayfair. "I never look at a scene like that without wishing I could give up London altogether. I am sure I could be content. It would be so charming to get rid of conventionality and be perfectly natural. You really ought to send that drawing to the Academy, Miss Eaton."

Though the fictional Lady Fanshawe's fatigue with conventionality presumably springs from impulses slightly different from those of Hale White, her words come very close to parodying his own in the letter to his son. In Lady Fanshawe was embodied that easy social poise which made Hale White so uncomfortable, and that capacity to sentimentalize suffering which would always trigger his most violent antipathies. Her affection for the simplicity of humble life was a dilettante indulgence; she had no "right" to it. But for Hale White such simplicity was a burning need, and the cottage at Abchurch—however inadequate it may have been for a man who worried incessantly about the comforts of his dwelling place[52]—symbolized a life of "sincerity" and wholeness which he deeply craved. Phoebe served in the novel as a corrective to Catharine's self-absorption; her simple generosity was a marked contrast to the artificiality of "well-dressed" folk.

Catharine called to mind Phoebe's past life: it was all of a piece, and countless little incidents unnoticed at the time obtained a significance and were interpreted. She knew herself to be Phoebe's superior intellectually, and that much had been presented to her which was altogether over Phoebe's horizon. But in all her purposes, and in all her activity, she seemed to have had self for a centre, and she felt that she would gladly give up every single advantage she possessed if she could but depose that self and enthrone some other divinity in its place. Oh the bliss of waking up in the morning with the thoughts turned outwards instead of inwards![53]

This book is pregnant with such personal reminiscence, and much of it has been viewed earlier. Most obvious, of course, is the similarity between Catharine Furze's ingrown nature and Hale White's, but a host of minor characters provoke comparison with people mentioned in Hale White's memoirs and letters. Could Mr. Furze—a kindly, easygoing man—have been formed upon the model of Hale White's merchant uncle, Samuel Lovell, mentioned in the *Early Life*? And may not Dr. Turnbull, a professed materialist, be patterned after Dr. John Chapman? Turnbull "disbelieved in what he called the soap-bubble theory, that somewhere in us there is something like a bubble, which controls everything . . . and escapes invisible and gaseous to some other place after death."[54] Dr. Chapman was equally contemptuous of orthodox opinions about the soul and,

51 *Ibid.*, pp. 208–9.
52 See, for example, *L.3F.*, pp. 53–54, 100–101, 114.
53 *C.F.*, p. 217.
54 *Ibid.*, p. 203.

after abandoning the editorship of *The Westminster Review*, he "qualified himself as a doctor"[55] and became a very "advanced" physician indeed. The girls' school attended by Catharine which had been built by a Spital-fields silk manufacturer was another detail remembered from Hale White's childhood: this was none other than the "beautiful Georgian house"[56] built by Hale White's great uncle, William Hale, at Homerton, which was later turned into a school. The descriptions in the *Early Life* and *Catharine Furze* are virtually identical. And the author intrusion following Mr. Cardew's sermon in this book is a transparent allusion to Hale White's early friend and religious teacher, Caleb Morris:

> These notes, made by one who was present, are the mere ashes, cold and grey, of what was once afire. . . . The writer of this history remembers when it was his privilege to listen continually to a man whose power over his audience was so great that he could sway them unanimously by a passion which was sufficient for any heroic deed. The noblest resolutions were formed under that burning oratory, and were kept, too, for the voice of the dead preacher still vibrates in the ears of those who heard him.[57]

In the article, "Caleb Morris," reprinted in *Last Pages*, Hale White gives notes from Morris' sermons which correspond closely to those recorded in *Catharine Furze*, and he concludes them with this identifying remark: "These are but black cinders. They were once aglow, white with fire."[58]

But to the degree that *Catharine Furze* is a recollection of past experience and old friends, *Clara Hopgood* is the embodiment of present interests and current problems. The story opens in Fenmarket and moves to London, thus showing us familiar scenes, but the heroines of this story are not the typical Rutherfordian malcontents. Madge and her sister Clara are given advantages which are shared by none of Hale White's other leading ladies. Their suffocation in the provincial air of Fenmarket is not due to a "vague and aimless discontent," but to a malaise incurred by education abroad and by well-developed artistic and literary habits. They are both excellent talkers, and, like Shavian idea-women, represent clearly defined points of view. To find their prototypes we must look not among the "brown-speckled fowls" or Cinderellas of Bedford, but among the circle of cultivated friends who gathered in increasing numbers around Hale White during his years of residence at Hastings (1892–1900).[59] In the years following his retirement, Hale White turned more and more to liter-

---

55 See Hale White, "Dr. John Chapman," *The Athenaeum* (December 8, 1894), pp. 790–91, and *A.H.*, August 1, 1863.
56 *E.L.*, p. 12.   57 *C.F.*, pp. 73–74.   58 *L.P.*, p. 247.
59 Some of these friends were: Mrs. Dannreuther, whose husband was a composer and musician, and who was a friend of William Morris, Burne-Jones, and Rossetti; Miss Betham-Edwards, the novelist (*L.3F.*, p. 56); Miss Frances Low, the critic; Dr. Greenhill, the Oxford scholar; Coventry Patmore, the poet; Miss Maitland, principal of Somerville College; Julia Collingwood, Hale White's cousin and an able musician, and Miss Rose Paul, daughter of Louis Paul, the novelist. Older friends and acquaintances with whom he maintained relationships were: G. J. Holyoake (*L.3F.*,

ary and scholarly pursuits which had been neglected in the busy preceding years. This book is virtually a catalogue of those interests.

In the opening pages, however, reminiscence is obvious. Both of the girls had been educated at Weimar, near Goethe's home, and had brought back to Fenmarket many of those dangerous foreign ideas which had helped to undermine Hale White's own orthodoxy. Not only had they become enthusiasts for Goethe and "learned to know the poet as they would never have known him in England,"[60] but they had been attracted to the disquieting influences of German Biblical criticism and foreign culture in general.[61]

At Weimar, in the evening, they could see Egmont or hear Fidelio, or talk with friends about the last utterance upon the Leben Jesu; but the Fenmarket Egmont was a travelling wax-work show, its Fidelio psalm tunes, or at best some of Bishop's glees, performed by a few of the tradesfolk, who had never had an hour's instruction in music; and for theological criticism there were the parish church and the Ram Lane Chapel.

In sending these girls to Weimar, Hale White had doubtless remembered his own trip there in 1860 and drawn upon his memories in describing the city.[62] Although it was quite unusual for girls of the mid-century (the time of this story) to go abroad for their education, this slight anachronism arises from the fact that Hale White is here attempting, not always successfully, to interpolate present problems into a past setting.

Hale White is also recalling other early influences in making Frank Palmer, Madge's lover, a member of the Broad Church party and a particular disciple of Maurice and Sterling. Hale White, we remember, bought Carlyle's *Life of Sterling* on the day it was issued, and as a young man sat with respectful attention at the feet of Maurice when he preached at Lincoln's Inn Fields.[63] Frank Palmer was the embodiment of all the merits and weaknesses which Hale White, in later years, found in the Broad Church party. Though on the occasion of Maurice's death, Hale White praised him by saying that his "ecclesiasticism never perverted his humanity" and that "a sweeter, kinder gentleman never walked this earth,"[64] his deepest judgment was quite different. In *The Aberdeen Herald* for November 9, 1861, he wrote:

I pray most fervently that some means may be found to put an end to this jugglery and hocus-pocus by which men like Mr. Heath, Mr. Frederick Maurice, and Mr.

p. 68) ; George Allen, Ruskin's publisher (*L.3F.*, pp. 121, 141) ; Dykes-Campbell ; Miss Hutchison Sterling ; Mr. Hutchinson, the Wordsworth scholar ; William Morris ; Arthur Hughes ; Browning ; Ruskin ; Swinburne. His extensive correspondence with Miss Sophia S. Partridge began soon after his removal to Hastings and, in 1896, through Miss Partridge, he became acquainted with Miss Mabel Marsh, with whom he carried on an affectionate correspondence until 1910.

60 *C.H.*, p. 14.
61 *Ibid.*
62 See *G.D.*, p. 318. He made other visits to Germany in 1861 and 1883.
63 Maurice was chaplain of Lincoln's Inn Chapel from June 1846 until February 1858.
64 *B.D.P.*, April 6, 1872. See above, p. 60.

Kingsley, are allowed to stop in the Church. I have heard Mr. Maurice several times, and the impression he produces is so painful that I will not willingly hear him again. It is absolutely pitiable to see a man of great intellectual ability so cowed by the fear of saying what is not orthodox, and yet so anxious to be heterodox, that his sermons are an unintelligible chaos,—to me at least,—which the most dexterous and vehement striving will not make combine.

Frank Palmer's opinions were, in like manner, tailored to please Madge rather than to express his own deepest convictions, and he was more conspicuous for his kindness and generosity than—in Hale White's eyes—his intellectual integrity.[65] Madge saw him as gifted with "all that makes a man admirable, with courage, with perfect unselfishness!"[66] But he had one flaw—a certain "smiling latitudinarianism,"[67] a tendency to trim his opinions and interests to fit those of the people he liked. Hale White hints strongly that he picked up such habits from Maurice. On one occasion, for example, Frank learned of Madge's enthusiasm for Tennyson's *Oenone* and promised, *for her sake*, to learn the poem. This distressed Madge, for she wanted him to share her enthusiasms without such tutoring, and he was made uneasy by her displeasure. The conversation went as follows:

"I do greatly admire Tennyson," he said.
"What do you admire? You have hardly looked at him."
"I saw a very good review of him. I will look that review up, by the way, before I come down again. Mr. Maurice was talking about it."[68]

Though Frank Palmer is something of a catch-all for Hale White's ideas on the subject of the Broad Church, he was almost certainly patterned after a William Matheson whom Mrs. D. V. White mentions in *The Groombridge Diary* and identifies as the man who first guessed the authorship of the *Autobiography*.[69] Like Frank, Matheson was a "delightful companion" and employed by a manufacturing chemist. And just as Frank "almost worshipped Mr. Maurice,"[70] so Mr. Matheson's "religious affinities were with F. D. Maurice, whom he knew and revered."[71]

Again in this book Hale White pays a tribute to Caleb Morris who, interestingly enough, disliked Maurice.[72] Both Morris and Maurice were preachers in London at the time Hale White was a student at New College, and both were strong influences upon him. But in spite of the fact that Morris shared many of Maurice's heterodox notions and yet remained in the church, Hale White never condemned him for it. Doubtless the reason was that Morris concerned himself with preaching the Gospel and never tempered his statements in the interests of institutional solidarity. This is Hale White's obvious reference to him in *Clara Hopgood*:

I could take you to a little dissenting chapel not very far from Holborn where you would hear a young Welshman, with no education beyond that provided by a Welsh

---

[65] See Hale White's final severe judgment on Maurice in *L.3F.*, p. 164.
[66] *C.H.*, p. 55.   [67] *Ibid.*, p. 47.
[68] *Ibid.*, p. 53.   [69] *G.D.*, pp. 51–52 n.
[70] *C.H.*, p. 23.   [71] *G.D.*, p. 51.
[72] See Hale White, "Caleb Morris," *British Weekly*, XXXI (March 6, 1902), 532.

denominational college, who is a perfect orator and whose depth of insight is hardly to be matched, save by Thomas à Kempis, whom he much resembles.[73]

Another of Hale White's heroes who appears in this book is the Italian patriot, Mazzini. During the long years of Mazzini's English exile, Hale White visited him twice, once around 1862 and again around 1876, and mentions the fact frequently in his letters and articles. In a letter to Miss Partridge on December 25, 1899, he writes:

I spent one evening almost alone with Mazzini. He was living then under a feigned name in very humble lodgings in Brompton. He had much of the saint in him, and consequently it was difficult, for me at least, completely to sympathize with him. Imperfection of sympathy, however, did not prevent an admiration, almost enthusiastic, for him, especially for his sublime courage and for his faith in certain Ideals to which he gave the name of God. In his purity and simplicity of worship he was altogether un-English, admitting no compromises, a true believer in the celestial Kingdom of the New Testament. He was not a failure, although Italy is not yet a regenerate republic. Such as he are the salt of the earth, and the more impracticable they are, the more do they sweeten and preserve it.[74]

A similar visit is arranged in *Clara Hopgood*, and the man is described in almost the same words:

It was not the face of a conspirator, but that of a saint, although without that just perceptible touch of silliness which spoils the faces of most saints. It was the face of a saint of the Reason, of a man who could be ecstatic for rational ideals, rarest of all endowments.[75]

But most of the intellectual and moral subjects which Clara and Madge discuss with each other and their friends are direct reflections of matters which were occupying Hale White's mind at this period. On March 20, 1896, he wrote to his son, John:

My acquaintance with Mr. Dykes Campbell and Mr. Hutchinson led me to renewed, prolonged and patient study of Wordsworth. I have been reading the early reviews of him, biographies of him, all sorts of notices and memoranda of him and writing about him, although the writing I am afraid will come to nothing, and really after what Coleridge has written about him it does not much matter if not another word be spoken. I have always held that the essay in the Biographia Literaria is at the very summit of criticism.[76]

A brief glance at Hale White's bibliography will show the tremendous upsurge of his literary interests in this period, and most of these interests are shared on another level by Madge and Clara. Frank Palmer, trying hard to discover the key to Madge's complicated heart, memorized the *Intimations of Immortality* and recited the poem to her. But, unfortunately, her love for the poem was no greater than Hale White's. The title, she declared, was "unmeaning" to her, and she went on to deflate Frank further by saying:

". . . and as for the verse which is in everybody's mouth—
        Our birth is but a sleep and a forgetting;
and still worse the vision of 'that immortal sea,' and of the children who 'sport upon

---

[73] *C.H.*, p. 133.   [74] *L.3F.*, p. 193. See also *G.D.*, p. 299.
[75] *C.H.*, p. 170.   [76] *P.L.*, p. 21.

the shore,' they convey nothing whatever to me. I find though they are much admired by the clergy of the better sort, and by certain religiously-disposed people, to whom thinking is distasteful or impossible. Because they cannot definitely believe, they fling themselves with all the more fervour upon these cloudy Wordsworthian phrases, and imagine they see something solid in the coloured fog."[77]

We might suspect that Madge had just been reading Hale White's criticism of Professor William Knight's Eversley edition of Wordsworth in *The Athenaeum* of September 25, 1897 :

The "Ode" is popular because it hits the taste of a number of people to whom it is a pleasure to repose in dreams of pre-existence, and to strengthen their faith thereby in a life after death; but it is desultory, will not stand examination (as Coleridge pointed out) by the reason, and lacks the simplicity of such masterpieces as "The Ruined Cottage" or "Laodamia."[78]

The conversations between Madge and Baruch about Shelley are also a leaf from Hale White's own writing. In letters to Miss Partridge on December 30, 1897, and April 4, 1898, he confessed the passing of his early enthusiasm for Shelley, maintaining that the poet had become "enslaved by the ideals of the French Revolution."[79] Furthermore, Baruch's interest in the relations of Shelley and Harriet formed the matter of a conversation Hale White had with Browning on May 15, 1879, and may very well be remembered here.[80] And Madge's love of Tennyson follows that generally expressed by Hale White in two letters to Miss Partridge included in *Letters to Three Friends*.[81]

The figure of Baruch Cohen, who is a Jew and bears Spinoza's Hebrew name as well as his philosophical beliefs, is a reflection of Hale White's renewed interest in the philosopher in these years. Between 1892 and 1894 Hale White was hard at work on a second preface to his translation of the *Ethic*, a matter which required a rereading and a re-estimation of Spinoza's life and work. Thus is Spinoza's disciple described in *Clara Hopgood*:

Baruch Cohen was now a little over forty. He was half a Jew, for his father was a Jew and his mother a Gentile. The father had broken with Judaism, but had not been converted to any Christian church or sect. He was a diamond-cutter, originally from Holland, came over to England and married the daughter of a mathematical instrument maker, at whose house he lodged in Clerkenwell.[82]

Though Baruch is pictured as having been a widower for nineteen years, with one son, while Spinoza was never married (though probably engaged),[83] the external similarities between Baruch and Spinoza are obvious. Hale White, it would seem, merely took a page from his biographical sketch of the philosopher[84] and adapted it to an English setting and a later

[77] *C.H.*, pp. 58–59.   [78] P. 412.
[79] *C.H.*, p. 165. *L.3F.*, pp. 172, 178–79.
[80] See W. H. Stone, "Browning and 'Mark Rutherford'," *The Review of English Studies* (n.s.), IV (July 1953), 251–52.
[81] Pp. 164–73.   [82] *C.H.*, p. 111.
[83] *Sp.b.*, p. viii. It is very likely that the name of Clara was suggested by that of Clara Van den Ende whom Spinoza loved but never married.
[84] *Sp.b.*, pp. vi–xxv.

time. Baruch is the very embodiment of Spinoza's unorthodox Hebraism.

In nothing was he more Jewish than in a tendency to dwell upon the One, or what he called God, clinging still to the expression of his forefathers although departing so widely from them. In his ethics and his system of life, as well as in his religion, there was the same intolerance of a multiplicity which was not reducible to unity. He seldom explained his theory, but everybody who knew him recognised the difference which it wrought between him and other men. There was a certain concord in everything he said and did, as if it were directed by some enthroned but secret principle.[85]

But Hale White has given to Baruch characteristics which are perhaps as much reflections of his own character as of Spinoza's. Both Baruch and Hale White are lonely isolated souls who long for rich friendships but possess the fatal tendency to alienate people. Of Baruch, Hale White writes: "He had often made advances; people had called on him and had appeared interested in him, but they had dropped away."[86] This statement should be compared with the one Hale White makes in the *Deliverance* about himself:

. . . we went out of our way sometimes to induce people to call upon us whom we thought we should like; but, if they came once or twice, they invariably dropped off, and we saw no more of them. This behaviour was so universal that, without the least affectation, I acknowledge there must be something repellent in me. . . .[87]

And where Baruch's situation departs most widely from Spinoza's it becomes most like Hale White's. "After the death of his wife," writes Hale White, "Baruch's affection spent itself upon his son Benjamin,"[88] and this son, like Hale White's own children, had left home and could relieve the father's loneliness by only occasional visits. Here again Hale White is provided with the opportunity for expressing some of his characteristic feelings about the father-son relationship.

During one of Benjamin's visits, the pair, together with a girl they had casually met, are capsized while being ferried across a river in a small boat. Benjamin immediately makes for the girl and saves her, leaving his father—who could not swim—to be rescued by the boatman. Baruch was not, however, impressed by his son's instinctive chivalry, and his reflections following this event reveal that his Spinozism was vulnerable in much the same way that Hale White's was. He cannot think about the objective morality of the situation until the painful knowledge that he is not solely and exclusively loved has made its wound and been partly healed. Baruch's Spinozistic stoicism lacks detachment and serenity in precisely the same way Hale White's does. Thus did Baruch lick his wounds after this little episode:

Meanwhile, Baruch lay upstairs alone in no very happy temper. He heard the conversation below, and knew that his son had gone. In all genuine love there is something of ferocious selfishness. The perfectly divine nature knows how to keep it in check, and

---

[85] *C.H.*, p. 113.
[86] *Ibid.*, pp. 113–14.   [87] *D.*, p. 114.   [88] *C.H.*, p. 114.

is even capable—supposing it to be a woman's nature—of contentment if the loved one is happy, no matter with what or with whom; but the nature only a little less than divine cannot, without pain, endure the thought that it no longer owns privately and exclusively that which it loves, even when it loves a child, and Baruch was particularly excusable, considering his solitude. Nevertheless, he had learned a little wisdom, and, what was of much greater importance, had learned how to use it when he needed it. It had been forced upon him; it was an adjustment to circumstances, the wisest wisdom. It was not something without any particular connection with him; it was rather the external protection built up from within to shelter him where he was vulnerable; it was the answer to questions which had been put to *him*, and not to those which had been put to other people. So it came to pass that, when he said bitterly to himself that, if he were at that moment lying dead at the bottom of the river, Benjamin would have found consolation very near at hand, he was able to reflect upon the folly of self-laceration, and to rebuke himself for a complaint against what was simply the order of Nature, and not a personal failure. His self-conquest, however, was not very permanent.[89]

This was the formula for making of a spiritual defeat a kind of victory, and Baruch's effort to apply it corresponded precisely with that of Hale White. Though the victory was not permanent, it should not escape us that there is considerably more peace of mind manifested here than there was after a similar episode in *Michael Trevanion*. The distance between these two books is the measure of the Slough of Despond.

A final and most interesting illustration of the degree to which Hale White brought himself into *Clara Hopgood* appears in the discussion of the book called *After Office Hours* by an "unknown" author named Robinson. Baruch asked for the volume at the bookstore where Clara worked and, as she got it down, "she was . . . struck with a few sentences which caught her eye."[90] In characteristic fashion, Hale White then proceeds to fill a page with quotations from the book, and we are somewhat surprised to discover that they are all taken directly—with almost no alterations— from Hale White's own *Black Notebook*, and that many of them were reprinted in *More Pages from a Journal*. The first of these *pensées*, for example, goes as follows:

A mere dream, a vague hope, ought in some cases to be more potent than a certainty in regulating our action. The faintest vision of God should be more determinative than the grossest earthly assurance.[91]

The same maxim appears in *More Pages* only slightly altered:

A mere dream, a vague hope may be more potent than certainty in a lesser matter. The faintest vision of God is more determinative of life than a gross earthly certainty.[92]

But more significant than these literal transcriptions (one might almost say, advertisements) is the conversation of Baruch and Clara about the

[89] *Ibid.*, pp. 117–18. Compare Spinoza's method for control of the passions, above, pp. 119–21.

[90] *Ibid.*, p. 110. Needless to say, Clara must have read it with phenomenal rapidity.

[91] *Ibid.*

[92] *M.P.*, p. 220.

obscure and neglected author. He was known to Baruch, and Clara had remarked that she "should have thought that some notice would have been taken of him; he is so evidently worth it."[93] To this Baruch replies:

"Yes, but although he was original and reflective, he had no particular talent. His excellence lay in criticism and observation, often profound, on what came to him every day, and he was valueless in the literary market. A talent of some kind is necessary to genius if it is to be heard. So he died utterly unrecognised, save by one or two personal friends who loved him dearly. He was peculiar in the depth and intimacy of his friendships. Few men understand the meaning of the word friendship. They consort with certain companions and perhaps very earnestly admire them, because they possess intellectual gifts, but of friendship, such as we two, Morris and I (for that was his real name) understood it, they know nothing."[94]

This is obviously a self-criticism and a self-confession. And it returns us, if we remember, very nearly to the same point where we came in at the beginning of the last chapter. The humble, retiring man, hiding behind his anonymity, could write:

I like privacy for its own sake. I do not care for a window close to and level with the street. It is not because I am ashamed to be seen, but because I prefer not to be seen. It is pleasant to me to feel if I wander through some lovely wood that nobody knows where I am; and when I go home I do not explain too particularly where I have been.[95]

But, in reality, he was longing for his genius to be recognized, longing to be seen if he could be worshiped as a sage. Though he did not, perhaps, explain too particularly where he had been, he took care to drop enough tell-tale clues and to leave enough prints so that those sufficiently interested could rediscover the route. His books are strewn with boyish attempts at disguise, and his masks are so crude and transparent that one might suppose their only reason for being was to provoke us to take them off. And when we remove them the tragic character of the face they partly hid tells us that this man took no joy in games of counterfeit identity, but wanted to be known and loved for what he was.

---

[93] *C.H.*, p. 133.

[94] *Ibid.* The name Morris indicates, no doubt, that Hale White had again his old friend Caleb Morris in mind, for the reference to him quoted above follows immediately on the same page.

Hale White's intense possessiveness of friends is clearly illustrated in his relationships with the women he knew in later life: Mabel Marsh, Sophia S. Partridge, Gladys Easedale, and Miss Dorothy Horace V. Smith, who became his second wife. In some of his letters to Mabel Marsh, for example, he is quite imperious in his demands for attention. See also *G.D.*, *passim*.

[95] *L.P.*, pp. 259–60.

Chapter Ten

THEMES IN THE NOVELS: DELIVERANCE

Continually and insistently, and in a thousand different phrasings, Hale White throughout his lifetime repeated the questions: "Who am I?" "How can I know myself?" "How can I act as one personality?" In an earlier time the problem would have been put more succinctly: "What must I do to be saved?" Though occasionally he employs that earlier vocabulary, he is deeply aware that for him it is now archaic, that not only the terms but the methods of salvation must—in a secular world—be altered. To discover these new methods was the major effort of his life, and to advertise them was a fundamental use of his novels. His books were for him a therapy, but they also proclaimed a therapy—a formula for spiritual wholeness in a fragmented age. None of his characters is permitted to relieve the travail of self-discovery by a return to Calvin, just as none of them, of course, can enlist the aid of Freud. But, with the formulations neither of theology nor of psychology, of old or new priests, they learn ways of deliverance. Their solutions may, perhaps, seem inadequate to us today, but we should remember that the characters Hale White depicts knew much more about living with God than with themselves or their fellow men.

In *Miriam's Schooling* we find, perhaps, the clearest and most forceful presentation of this pattern of salvation. Miriam's spiritual pilgrimage was marked by those periods of negation, new birth, renunciation, and affirmation which we have discovered in Hale White's, and they are so clearly delineated that this book reads almost like an allegorization of his autobiography. Miriam's act of negation expressed itself in an angry rejection of her father and her Cowfold home when her father, after many years as a widower, decided to marry again. Incensed at what she regarded as a betrayal, she refused to share her father's affections with another. In particular, she resented the "displacement of her own mother." "She never knew her, and owed her nothing except her birth; but she was *her* mother, and she took sides with her, and considered her insulted, and became her partisan with perfect fury."[1]

Perhaps, too, Miriam was slightly jealous that her father, who was now nearing his half century, should show himself not altogether dead to love. She would have liked to find him insensible, leaving all love affairs to his children, and she once even went so far as to use the word "disgusting" in conversing with Andrew on the subject.

This rupture and the ensuing self-imposed exile lay at the bottom of all her subsequent psychological difficulties.

[1] *M.S.*, p. 65. Compare this with Hale White's own attitude toward second marriage. See below, pp. 194–96.

Accompanied by her brother, Andrew, she ran off to London; but the Land of Promise soon proved a vale of tears. Her brother, under the competitive tensions and temptations of London life, became, by degrees, a drunkard. Miriam, falling in love with a music-hall singer named George Montgomery, made the bitter discovery that he was a common philanderer. On every side the corrupting influences of the great city closed in, breeding spiritual restlessness, closing off human sympathies, blunting sensibilities, and exaggerating one's sense of isolation and impotence. Hale White almost joins the company of the naturalists—of Zola or Gissing or Richard Whiteing—when he treats of the effects of urban squalor on human beings. George Montgomery, for example, was as much sinned against as sinning, the unconscious victim of an evil environment.

> . . . a man who had lived as he had lived in London is not likely to admire any woman with much fervour, and indeed the incapacity for genuine admiration of women is one of the strongest arguments against such a life.[2]

And even well-meaning people like Miriam's aunt, Mrs. Dabb, had been rendered insensible to human need by their long association with the impersonal city. The only way she could think of to assist in the salvation of Andrew was to suggest that he cultivate the "finer emotions"[3] by reading a volume of Mrs. Hemans' poetry. Miriam found herself, therefore, "face to face with a great trouble, and she had to encounter it alone, and with no weapons and with no armour save those which Nature provides."[4] With Hale White, these were always the terms on which spiritual battle was waged.

Gradually Miriam's capacity for affection also became infected. Her brother's failure provoked her contempt rather than her sympathy.

> The affection of Miriam for her brother, never very strong, was not increased by his ill-luck. She began, in fact, to dislike him because he was unfortunate. She imagined that her dislike was due to his faults, and every now and then she abused him for them; but his faults would have been forgotten if he had been prosperous. She hated misery, and not only misery in the abstract, but miserable weak creatures. She was ready enough, as we have seen, to right a wrong, especially if the wrong was championed by those whom she despised; but for simple infirmity, at least in human beings, she had no more mercy than the wild animals which destroy any one of their tribe whom they find disabled.[5]

As her hatred grew in intensity, she became more and more ingrown, more and more encased in her own "self-sympathy." Finally the crisis came. Overcome by the same sense of despair that Hale White knew on that critical night in Stoke Newington,[6] she was tempted by suicide:

> . . . this was her first acquaintance with an experience not rare, alas! but below it humanity cannot go, when all life ebbs from us, when we stretch out our arms in vain,

2 *Ibid.*, p. 84. (Cf. *A.*, p. 9.)
3 *Ibid.*, p. 97.
4 *Ibid.*, p. 98.   5 *Ibid.*, p. 99.   6 See *A.*, pp. 133–34.

when there is no God—nothing but a brazen Moloch, worse than the Satan of theology ten thousand times, because it is dead. A Satan we might conquer, or at least we should feel the delight of combat in resisting him; but what can we do against this leaden "order of things" which makes our nerves ministers of madness? Miriam did not know that her misery was partly a London misery, due to the change from fresh air and wholesome living to foul air and unnatural living. If she had known it, it would not have helped her. She could not have believed it, for it is the peculiarity of certain physical disorders that their physical character does not appear, and that they disguise themselves under purely mental shapes.[7]

By the same instinct which saved the heroine of "Two Martyrs," she "held back and passed on."[8] The first wedge had been driven. Salvation was now possible because she had been cleansed in the fire of primary human knowledge; she had learned life's first premise—that death and life are the elemental facts. As always in Hale White's religion of experience, this is the point from which we must start in building a new life. Miriam had been turned away from the fatal act by an inner strength and not by any external compulsion. In Hale White's catechism, this was a fact of great importance. For, he declares, a man is guiltless who sins in his heart (even if the sin be adultery) provided he does not sin in action and is not restrained from doing so by force or fear of detection; "if the restraint, although he may not be conscious of it, is self-imposed, he is not guilty."[9] Can this modification of Christian doctrine represent, in reality, a rationalization—an apology not so much for Miriam as for himself? From what we already know of the closeness of this book to his own experience, such a conjecture seems plausible.

Miriam's "new birth" dawned on the day she visited Stonehenge. In a vision like that of Paul on the road to Damascus, "it came into Miriam's mind that she must do something for her fellow-creatures."[10] This was precisely the resolve of the Mark Rutherford of the *Autobiography* when he left the Unitarian Chapel,[11] and there was the same quality of spiritual pride mixed up in it. Like Mark, she made a wrong choice of her first mission. Idealistically she decided to become a nurse, imagining that "she would at once be asked to watch over grateful patients, to give them medicine, and read to them."[12] Instead, for three probationary months she was assigned to scrubbing floors. Naturally untidy, and blind to the connection between the dust in the corner and the ideal of service she yearned to fulfill, she was soon afterward discharged by the "experienced, professional superintendent" who "knew perfectly well that the smart, neat, methodical girl, with no motive in her but the desire of succeeding and earning a good living, was worth a dozen who were self-sacrificing but not soldierly."[13]

Following this failure, she returned in despair and humiliation to Cow-

---

[7] *M.S.*, p. 113.
[8] *Ibid.*, p. 114.
[9] *Ibid.*
[10] *Ibid.*, p. 117. See also p. 119.
[11] See *A.*, pp. 131–32.
[12] *M.S.*, p. 122.   [13] *Ibid.*, p. 124.

fold—not, like the repentant prodigal, to ask forgiveness, but to lick her wounds.

She cursed the constitution with which she was born. She wished she had been endowed with . . . blessed thoughtlessness, and that she could be taken out of herself with an interest in pigs, pie-dishes, and Cowfold affairs generally.[14]

She finally attempted to achieve such self-release by marrying, out of boredom, a Cowfold basketmaker named Didymus Farrow. He was the typical half-peasant type we have seen before: practical, loyal, uncommunicative, unread, and—in a clumsy way—gentle and affectionate. Almost from the first, Miriam held him in secret contempt. As she yielded to him, we are told, she shut her eyes and "purposely strove to think an imaginary Romeo's head was on her neck," and, like a high-minded Madame Bovary, sought with such illusions to paint provincial drabness with an idealistic coloring.[15] She soon came to hate openly this man whom she had victimized by marriage, but it was he, strangely enough, who finally showed her the way to salvation.

Under the influence of Mr. Armstrong, Didymus became interested in astronomy, and together they built an orrery to demonstrate the movements of the stars. Miriam, at first indifferent, became increasingly interested as the machine took shape and increasingly impressed with her husband's ability to grasp the mathematical intricacies of the problem. There was, she finally decided, something almost poetic in the precision with which he carved the cogwheels of the delicate device and in the loving care he lavished on every small detail. And when, added to these awarenesses, Didymus patiently impressed upon her a conception of the stellar universe, he quietly drew her out of herself and out of her selfish judgment of him. He, the humble and unsophisticated one, was the teacher. He unconsciously taught her what all of Hale White's heroines in one way or another learn: how to find virtue in the commonplace. To acquiesce in such knowledge was no joyous surrender for either Miriam or Hale White, but it provided a sedative to discontent which might, with cherishing, last a lifetime.

The mood of the last scene of this book—meditative and rather sad— is exactly the gray tone belonging to Hale White's own affirmation in that period of his life around 1890 and earlier:

Miriam fell on her knees against the little seat and sobbed, and the dog, wondering, came and sat by her and licked her face with tender pity. Presently she recovered, rose, went home, let herself in softly before her husband was downstairs, and prepared the breakfast. He soon appeared, was in the best of spirits, and laughed at her being able to leave the room without waking him. She looked happy, but was rather quiet at their meal; and after he had caressed the cat for a little while, he pitched her, as he had done before, on Miriam's lap. She was about to get up to cut some bread and butter, and she went behind him and kissed the top of his head. He turned round, his eyes sparkling, and tried to lay hold of her, but she stepped backward and eluded

14 *Ibid.*, p. 133.
15 *Ibid.*, p. 132.

him. He mused a little, and when she sat down he said in a tone which for him was strangely serious—

"Thank you, my dear; that was very, very sweet."[16]

We feel that such a deliverance must be won again and again, that it is not permanent but subject to mood and circumstance. But Hale White is telling us that, while this is so, there is also demonstrated in Miriam's self-conquest a formula, which if applied early enough, could transform a life. She made a beginning, in Kant's terms, of joining "the starry heavens above and the moral law within."[17] And the moral law became increasingly for Hale White simply this: look outward, not inward; love others, not oneself.

In *Clara Hopgood* the path to salvation follows a somewhat different course. Madge, after being quite willingly seduced by Frank Palmer, follows an instinctive voice telling her that their love is not genuine and rejects him. His affection is unwavering and he begs her to let him save her good name; but her inner voices cannot be moved. She writes:

Forgiveness! Who is to be forgiven? Not you. You believed you loved me, but I doubted my love, and I know now that no true love for you exists. We must part, and part forever. Whatever wrong may have been done, marriage to avoid disgrace would be a wrong to both of us infinitely greater. I owe you an expiation; your release is all I can offer, and it is insufficient. I can only plead that I was deaf and blind. By some miracle, I cannot tell how, my ears and eyes are opened, and I hear and see. It is not the first time in my life that the truth has been revealed to me suddenly, supernaturally, I may say, as if in a vision, and I know the revelation is authentic.[18]

Madge combines the qualities of a Quaker and a "new woman," and while there is more than a touch of histrionics and posturing in her self-denial, she is a true representative of certain qualities in her creator. In her moral individualism, she follows Hale White's own principle of living for the "right" that is her "own" right. In her rebellion against society's conventions (and what the reader continues to feel were her best interests) she caught something of that insurrectionary spirit which animated Hale White's heroes of an earlier day. She is the most unconventional and daring of all his characters, and perhaps in drawing her Hale White was encouraged by Ibsen, in whom he had taken a deep interest.[19] Although she, like Miriam, had to find her salvation through renunciation, the terms of her problem are radically different. Her moral problem is not how to abandon her claims to singularity, but how to fully believe in them. Her renunciation consists of the rejection of those "enemy voices" which tell her to distrust her inner light—which keep reminding her of such comparatively irrelevant matters as her fatherless child! It is a hard struggle, and the unsophisticated insights of the warmhearted Mrs. Caffyn do not add to her serenity:

"If you can't love a man, that is to say if you can't *abear* him, it's wrong to have him, but if there's a child that does make a difference, for one has to think of the child

16 *Ibid.*, p. 154. 17 *B.*, p. 242. 18 *C.H.*, pp. 62–63. 19 See *L.3F.*, pp. 44–48.

and of being respectable. . . . I'd put up with a goodish bit to marry the man whose child wor mine."[20]

But more disturbing were the arguments presented by her sister, Clara:

> "I have sometimes wondered whether you have not demanded a little too much of yourself and Frank. It is always a question of how much. There is no human truth which is altogether true, no love which is altogether perfect. You may possibly have neglected virtue or devotion such as you could not find elsewhere, overlooking it because some failing, or lack of sympathy on some unimportant point, may at the moment have been prominent. Frank loved you, Madge."[21]

The reader, too, wonders if Madge is not the victim of perverse self-deception, for in the early pages of the book Hale White makes her love for Frank very convincing indeed—a love that could quite obliterate from her consciousness Frank's intellectual shortcomings. Is not her "inner voice" in reality nothing but another name for the same pride and snobbery which, with Miriam, was a besetting sin? Hale White would not have us believe so, but the reader is led to feel that he is enmeshed in a problem of motivation, which neither as a novelist nor as a man could he quite solve.

As the plot works out, however, Madge is saved by her refusal to listen to any voices but her own. But *her* renunciation is not the main point of the story. The novel is entitled *Clara Hopgood*, not *Madge Hopgood*, and it is Clara's double sacrifice on behalf of her sister that Hale White wants us to note in particular. Not only does Clara submit herself to unpleasant employment in a Holborn bookstore in order to support Madge during her pregnancy, but she conceals her love for Baruch Cohen (whom she might have married) in order that Madge may have him. Though Clara's conduct was regulated by rules and reason as against Madge's impulse and instinct, she was aware that her sister's peculiar genius needed its own monitor of conduct, and she was, from the first, sympathetic and indulgent. By her self-sacrifice she brought happiness to Madge and Baruch and, presumably, found in her own heroic spinsterhood a happiness she could not have attained in any other way. Once freed from the burden of supporting Madge, she enlisted in Mazzini's service and, some eighteen months later, died in Italy. In later years Madge answered her daughter's questions about the legendary Aunt Clara by saying that ". . . 'she wanted to free the poor people of Italy who were slaves.' "[22]

Clara's peculiar genius lay in living heroically to free others, Madge's in living for herself. Neither course was a mistaken one as Hale White draws it: both girls were passionate idealists and both won because they refused to compromise. They molded circumstance rather than being molded by it. They both had to suffer, but such suffering as theirs was, with Hale White, a form of gratification and a path of deliverance.

---

[20] *C.H.*, p. 122.   [21] *Ibid.*, p. 108.   [22] *Ibid.*, p. 188.

Hale White has here given us an extremely interesting little morality play. He was both Madge and Clara: one half of him wanted to go off and suffer a martyr's death in the name of some righteous and *reasonable* ideal;[23] the other wanted to settle down with a devoted, passionate, and intellectually congenial woman and be happy. This book is, therefore, both a kind of self-analysis and a wish fulfillment: he never fully realized their ideals in his own life, but he needed both kinds of peace which these girls found. In *Pages from a Journal* he has virtually declared the theme of this book. The question raised here is: how can I be both Madge and Clara at the same time?[24]

I envy Jack's unhesitating ardour. How I curse this omnipresent doubt which gnaws the root of action! I am not lazy or self-indulgent, but I am paralyzed by scepticism. It is weakness, although it looks like wisdom. The greatest men are not affected by it. I sometimes distrust my reason. Was it intended to be the guide of life? Its main office seems to be the generation of melancholy and despair. Possibly impulse is surer than reason, impulse which pays no attention to rational suggestion. The wave does not hesitate to break upon the shore, but hurls itself headlong in magnificent blindness.

In spite of the importance of many of the ethical problems presented in this story, it is, as a literary production, contrived and unconvincing. Hale White is here working a problem in moral casuistry rather than with human experience directly, as in *Miriam's Schooling*. The two heroines are stubborn saints who are aided in their salvation by quite fortuitous circumstances. The lucky appearance of Baruch Cohen, for example, who would not be bothered by Madge's past indiscretions, can hardly be said to have arisen necessarily out of her moral decisions or to represent the typical fortunes of a Victorian young lady. And Clara's discovery of a Mazzini near at hand who was waiting for her services and could provide her with a "good cause" of the first importance is surely not the fortune of every would-be martyr, and was certainly not the luck of Hale White himself. With other people and in other situations might they not have been destroyed by their spiritual individualism? If Hale White had an answer to this question, he could not answer it within the frame of the novel.

But this book, interestingly enough, is the only one Hale White ever defended in print. In one of his articles written under the pseudonym of "Claudius Clear" in *The British Weekly*, W. Robertson Nicoll (usually one of Hale White's strongest admirers) had adversely criticized the book, and Hale White wrote a reply in its defense. Nicoll had, one suspects, been shocked by what seemed its advocacy of sexual license.[25]

I shall content myself with saying that his last book, "Clara Hopgood," appears to be utterly unworthy of him from every point of view. There are sentences in it that none [sic] but he could have written, but, on the whole, it is unsatisfactory even in style,

---

[23] See above, pp. 30–31.
[24] "Some Letters," *P.J.*, p. 343.
[25] W. R. Nicoll, "Mark Rutherford," *The British Weekly*, XX (July 9, 1896), 185. For an intelligent criticism of this book see *The Athenaeum* (August 15, 1896), p. 220.

while the moral teaching is in sad contrast with that of his early books. It has been received with profound disappointment by all in the circle of his admirers that I am able to communicate with. His reputation, and it is a very secure reputation, rests on those two noble and memorable books, "The Autobiography of Mark Rutherford" and "The Revolution in Tanner's Lane."

To this Hale White replied in *The British Weekly* of July 30, 1896:

I am silent, of course, upon your correspondent's criticism, which mostly errs on the side of generosity, but I cannot help a protest against the charge of immorality brought against "Clara Hopgood." The accusation is another proof that, even in a country which calls the New Testament a sacred book and professes to read it, the distinction between real and sham morality is almost unknown.[26]

Hale White leaves no hint as to whether the plot of Madge's unconventional emancipation was his own invention or whether it was suggested by his reading or observation. One conjecture is, however, tempting. In his article on Dr. Chapman in *The Athenaeum* of December 8, 1894, he makes particular mention of Froude's *Nemesis of Faith*, a self-confessional book very like his own *Autobiography*. A. W. Harrison, writing in *The London Quarterly and Holborn Review*, has pointed out numerous similarities between *The Nemesis of Faith* and the "method, subject matter, temper and style" of Hale White's work. He writes:

Is there anything more striking in all Mark Rutherford's work than his remarkable women who affirm so passionately that the sin against the Holy Ghost is the sin against love? We have Miss Arbour in the *Autobiography* with the strange story of her flight from a loveless marriage and Miss Leroy in the *Deliverance* who "told a male person once . . . that if she loved him and he loved her, and they agreed to sign one another's forehead with a cross as ceremony, it would be as good . . . as marriage."[27]

But Mr. Harrison failed to mention the most "remarkable" woman of all—Madge Hopgood. Unlike most of those others, we know of no clear original for Madge among Hale White's acquaintances, but her similarity to Froude's Mrs. Leonard of the *Nemesis* is striking. Mrs. Leonard, neglected by her fox-hunting husband, falls in love with a young man named Markham. After several months of idyllic love, they learn that the squire is returning home for a visit. Mrs. Leonard was torn between two alternatives: running away with Markham and bearing his child, or remaining alone at home with her first child, Annie, who, before Markham came on the scene, was the one thing in life she had ever loved. The dilemma is partly resolved when Annie catches a chill and dies. But after the little girl's death, Mrs. Leonard makes this surprising statement:

"Markham," she said, "it is for my sin. Would, oh, would it had been myself, not she, who has been taken! It is for my sin in marrying her father. It was an offense against earth and Heaven. . . ."[28]

[26] Untitled letter to the editor, p. 232, signed "Reuben Shapcott." See also Willard L. Sperry's comment in *The Harvard Theological Review*, VII (April 14, 1914), 190.

[27] A. W. Harrison, "Mark Rutherford and J. A. Froude," *The London Quarterly and Holborn Review*, CLXIV (January 1939), 43.

[28] J. A. Froude, *The Nemesis of Faith* (Chicago, 1879), pp. 217–18.

Seeing the sin in the loveless marriage rather than in the passionate adultery is a point of view Madge would have perfectly understood. And she would have been further won to Mrs. Leonard by the fact that she too based her actions on an intuitive rather than reasoned awareness of the right. Froude's heroine was more of a naïve innocent than Madge, but she was equally equipped to believe that the passion of love was the voice of God:

> The windings, wheel within wheel, of the untrue spirit's self-deceptions, were all strange to her, for she had always been too natural to think about herself at all.[29]

Both of these books present the same argument for ethical individualism. The moral of *Clara Hopgood* is simply this: "The worth of the right to you is that it is your right, and that you arrive at it in your own way."[30] But with Hale White there was always the law of society as well as the law of his own being, and he looked now here and now there. He hated anarchy as much as he admired independence, he despised disorder but loved rebels. And he never managed quite to reconcile these antithetical impulses.

The heroine of *Catharine Furze* comes much closer to embodying (in one person) the qualities of Hale White himself. Like most of Hale White's feminine leads, she is unhappy and maladjusted in her native environment, ". . . she felt as a pent-up lake might feel if the weight of its waters were used in threading needles. . . ."[31] In Eastthorpe, he writes,

> . . . Catharine felt that her strength would have to occupy itself in twisting straws. It is really this which is the root of many a poor girl's suffering. As the world is arranged at present, there is too much power for the mills which have to be turned by it.[32]

"Had Catharine been born two hundred years earlier," says Hale White, "life would have been easy,"[33] for she would have found self-expression in the faith of her ancestors; had she been born later, she would have found other, if not equal, compensations:

> She would perhaps have been able to distract herself with the thousand and one subjects which are now got up for examinations. . . . She was, however, in Eastthorpe before the new education, as it is called, had been invented. There was no elaborate system of needle points, Roman and Greek history, plain and spherical trigonometry, political economy, ethics, literature, chemistry, conic sections, music, English history, and mental philosophy, to draw off the electricity within her. . . .[34]

Catharine found herself in that middle ground where action is impossible because society provides no orthodox channel for it, and where intellectual expansion was impossible because of the Philistine indifference of her neighbors. Like Madge, Clara, and Miriam, Catharine took her "singularity" very seriously; and this led her into contempt for those

---

29 *Ibid.*, p. 246.   30 *C.H.*, p. 36.
31 *C.F.*, p. 127.   32 *Ibid.*, p. 200.
33 *Ibid.*, p. 124.   34 *Ibid.*, p. 126.

about her who were unable to draw out the "best" in her. She could love a just cause, she could champion the poor and love them in—and because of?—their misery, but she found it very difficult to symphathize with "average" people or issues; ". . . one of her defects was a certain hardness to persons for whom she had small respect,"[35] and her mother did not escape the judgment born of this "defect." She wanted the companionship of those whose lives could in some way be defined in absolutes—in extremities of idealism, poverty, simplicity, courage, or love. But life seemed to deny such things, and "her position was critical because she stood by herself, affiliated to nothing, an individual belonging to no species, so far as she knew."[36]

But Catharine received her awakening, her "new birth," through the Reverend Mr. Cardew, a married preacher who was lonely with his wife in the same way Catharine was lonely with her Eastthorpe companions. "It was through him the word was spoken to her, and he was the interpreter of the new world to her."[37] Her love for him was "the very life of all that was Catharine, senses, heart, and intellect, a summing-up and projection of her whole selfhood."[38] But this love wrought a strange transformation in both of them. In touching the "absolute" through it, they were made aware that this very love had led them to neglect their earthly responsibilities to their fellow men. In their transcendent experience they gained a perspective (an "adequate" conception, in Spinoza's terms) enabling them to see the commonplace in a new light and revealing to them the selfishness and intolerance which had been bound up in their personal ideal.

Mr. Cardew reached this realization himself, but it was implanted in Catharine by the words of Dr. Turnbull. He, the practical physician, knowing nothing of Catharine's love for Cardew, spoke of the minister in terms of frank disapproval:

"A remarkable man in many ways, and yet not a man whom I much admire. He thinks a good deal, and when I am in company with him I am unaccountably stimulated, but his thinking is not directed upon life. My notion is that our intellect is intended to solve real difficulties which confront us, and that all intellectual exercise upon what does not concern us is worse than foolish."[39]

Catharine tried to argue that his needs were special and peculiar, requiring untypical fulfillment and entitling him to his own rules of behavior. The doctor replied with an admonition against cultivating singularity, which we have already quoted,[40] and then proceeded to praise Cardew's wife and condemn his neglect of her:

While he is luxuriating amongst the cowslips, in what he calls thinking, she is teach-

---

[35] *Ibid.*, p. 161.
[36] *Ibid.*, p. 126.
[37] *Ibid.*, p. 127.
[38] *Ibid.*
[39] *Ibid.*, p. 221.   [40] See above, p. 127.

ing the sick people patience and nursing them. She is a saint, and he does not know half her worth.[41]

And then Dr. Turnbull speaks some words out of Hale White's own mouth in saying that a man can *train* himself to love by self-discipline, and that he has a clear duty so to master his affections once he has assumed the sacred responsibility of marrying a woman:

A man marries a woman whom he loves. . . . Is it likely that he would have selected this one woman if he had seen, say, fifty more before he had married her? Certainly not; and when he sees other women afterwards, better than the one he has chosen, he naturally admires them. If he does not he is a fool, but he is bound to check himself. He puts them aside and is obliged to be satisfied with his wife. If it were permissible in him in such a case to abandon her, a pretty chaos we should be in. It is clearly his duty, and quite as clearly in his power, to be thus contented—at least, in nine cases out of ten. He *may*—and this is my point—he *may* wilfully turn away from what is admirable in his own house, or he may turn towards it. He is as responsible for turning away from it, or turning towards it, as he is for any of his actions. If he says he cannot love a wife who is virtuous and good, I call him not only stupid, but wicked. . . .[42]

These words took effect upon Catharine and, by a miraculous coincidence, the same awareness—unprovoked by any external stimulus—impinged upon the consciousness of Mr. Cardew at the same time. "His eyes were opened; he crept into an outhouse in the fields, and there alone in an agony he prayed."[43] Both had been shown the blessed path of renunciation.

At a final meeting between the lovers at Catharine's deathbed, they acknowledge the debt they owe to each other:

"Mr. Cardew, I want to say something."
"Wait a moment, let me tell you—*you have saved me.*"
She smiled, her lips moved, and she whispered—"*You* have saved *me.*"[44]

And the author adds the almost inevitable word of explanation:

By their love for each other they were both saved. The disguises are manifold which the Immortal Son assumes in the work of our redemption.

Like Miriam, these two people have learned that high and vague ideals must be made to square with reality, and that human beings can know contentment only if they find the lodging of the absolute in the commonplace. They must submit. And here, though Catharine's love is never consummated in a physical sense, we do not feel that she is unfulfilled; rather we feel that through her suffering and renunciation she has attained a fulfillment which entirely satisfies her. And Hale White's power as a novelist partly lies in convincing us that this higher happiness

---

41 *C.F.*, p. 223. Dr. Turnbull's advice here is precisely the same as that rendered by the friend in the story, "The Sweetness of a Man's Friend," *L.P.*, pp. 37–46.
42 *C.F.*, pp. 223–24.
43 *Ibid.*, p. 227.
44 *Ibid.*, p. 244.

is, in her case, a psychological possibility and not just a sentimental fiction.

Catharine's salvation involved the achievement of an inner peace, but it also involved an adjustment of the laws of her own being to those of society. She was saved, at least in part, because she conformed. And this fact prompts a necessary digression. In all of the processes of deliverance we have traced, the conventions of Victorian society played an important part. Only in Madge Hopgood does outright rebellion seem to be condoned, and even she ends by being safely and respectably married. And it should not escape us that, while Hale White can bring himself to portray an illicit relationship, he never, in any of his books, shows a man or woman unfaithful except in spirit to a wife or husband. Though to the casual reader it might not appear so, Hale White is not primarily a social critic. He is first of all a moral psychologist, studying the weaknesses of the individual personality. This may seem doubtful to the reader of Mark Rutherford who has been impressed by his pictures of the London slums and has noted his careful following of political affairs and persons in his years as Parliamentary correspondent. And it may seem doubly doubtful to those who have listened to Marxist critics like Ralph Fox and A. L. Morton acclaiming Hale White as an advocate of revolution.[45] Unlike Hardy in *Jude the Obscure* or Ibsen in *The Doll's House* he is not leveling an attack on those social conventions which cramp true love and stifle freedom of the spirit. He is trying to demonstrate how love and freedom can exist realistically within the frame of society's laws. When he talks of "reality," he is as often thinking of the policeman on the corner as he is of spiritual facts or the processes of nature. This emphasis in his novels is a fundamental part of his political bias in general.

André Gide has called Hale White "apolitical, because there is no politics without fraud."[46] It is a just statement. And Hale White himself has declared:

For my own part I cannot be enthusiastic about politics, except on rare occasions when the issue is a very narrow one.[47]

His overwhelming interest is in discovering ways in which the individual can make an adjustment to existing society without compromising himself. M'Kay's whole purpose in his Drury Lane experiment, for example, was to teach stoical submission rather than revolt:

Our main object was to create in our hearers contentment with their lot, and even

---

[45] *The Novel and the People* (New York, 1945), pp. 93–94; and *Language of Men* (London, 1945), pp. 49–57.

[46] *The Journals of André Gide, 1928–1939* (New York, 1949), III, 338.

[47] *A.*, pp. 18–19. We have evidence that he engaged in what might be called political action on only three occasions: (1) in writing his pamphlet, *An Argument for an Extension of the Franchise* (1866) in support of the Reform Bill of 1867; (2) in his agitation to stop the enclosure of Banstead Downs—a matter recorded in a letter to the *Times*, October 31, 1876, and in an article, "A Victory on the Downs," *The Pall Mall Gazette*, August 16, 1886; (3) and in his effort to form a Liberal committee in 1880 "to promote a contest in his division of the county." (See *B.D.P.*, January 10, 1880).

some joy in it. That was our religion; that was the central thought of all we said and did, giving shape and tendency to everything.[48]

The point is not that Hale White approved of the status quo or preached the gospel of a Bolingbroke or Soame Jenyns, but he believed that the individual must achieve and maintain a private integrity before any mere political program would help him. Hale White could not be a social reformer—not only because he needed the stimulus of great spiritual causes which he could not find in his century, but because he feared infection from the very dirt he would have liked to cleanse. He distrusted, moreover, any action, personal or political, which was not shaped by a controlling principle, such as that which once had shaped Calvinism when it was a vital creed. Where in his day could he find such a program? Socialism, in so far as it was an *idea*, was a helpful substitute for the old religion, but it was not adequate.[49] Democracy, though he supported it at first, he came to fear as ushering in mere mob rule.[50]

In these latter days of anarchy and tumult, when there is no gospel of faith or morals . . . democracy seems bent on falsifying every prediction of earlier democratic enthusiasts by developing worse dangers to liberty than any which our forefathers had to encounter. . . .

. . . .

The disease is often obvious, but the remedies are doubtful. The accumulation of wealth in a few hands, generally by swindling, is shocking, but if it were distributed to-morrow we should gain nothing. The working man objects to the millionaire, but would gladly become a millionaire himself, even if his million could be piled up in no other way than by sweating thousands of his fellows. The usurpation of government by the ignorant will bring disaster, but how in these days could a wise man reign any longer than ignorance permitted him? The everlasting veerings of the majority . . . show that, except on rare occasions of excitement, the opinion of the voters is of no significance. But when we are asked what substitute for elections can be proposed, none can be found. So with the relationship between man and woman, the marriage laws and divorce. The calculus has not been invented which can deal with such complexities.

He therefore concludes that in the modern Babylon the individual does well to preserve his own integrity and keep his moral balance. And all his books, except perhaps *The Revolution in Tanner's Lane*, are permeated with this conviction. Catharine could find no outlet for her energies in "great causes." Miriam escaped from urban complexity into provincialism. Only Clara found her deliverance through political action, but her Mazzini represented the cause of another country and, in a sense, of an earlier day. In their several ways, these girls all realize that the Kingdom of God is within them and they cease demanding that it be found in Cowfold

48 *D.*, p. 87.
49 See *L.P.*, p. 248, and p. 254; *D.*, p. 25; and *P.J.*, p. 214. In this last place he writes: "The evils of Capitalism are so monstrous that any remedy is better than none. Socialism may not be the direct course: it may be a tremendously awkward tack, but it is only by tacking that we get along."
50 *P.J.*, pp. 78, 79–80.

or Eastthorpe or London. They, like their creator, seemed to agree that "Achilles is dead, and the turn of the Myrmidons has come."[51]

> Myrmidons, race féconde
> Myrmidons,
> Enfin nous commandons :
> Jupiter livre le monde
> Aux Myrmidons, aux Myrmidons.[52]

Since that "fatal divorce" between "politics and private sincerity,"[53] there is little that the noble individual can do but quietly resist evil, make the best of the people about him, and cultivate his own garden.

But in *The Revolution in Tanner's Lane* we are taken into a world where a politically minded race is in its own country—a world where it was something like treason to recognize that "the world is all wrong" and then confess—as Hale White does in "An Apology"[54]—inability or unwillingness to do something about it. Zachariah Coleman was born into an age of heroes and heroism. Though it was characterized by injustice, brutality, and misery, it was, we are made to feel, a happier and healthier age than that known by Hale White's other leading characters. "It was not yet God's time in 1817, but God's time was helped forward, as it generally is, by this anticipation of it."[55] Zachariah Coleman's salvation depends not upon *finding* his work but in *doing* it, not in finding an alien Mazzini but in being one himself.

The book exists as much to celebrate the political struggles of the revolution as to illustrate the moral progress of Zachariah. The history shares the stage with the actors, and we witness in the leading character certain changes which are, perhaps, more significant historically than they are psychologically. The story reveals the gradual weakening of Zachariah's affiliation to his wife and to his Calvinistic faith as his affiliations to a revolutionary movement and to the unbaptized radicals who lead it become stronger. It is a study of how social and religious orthodoxy can be undermined by an "expansion of spirit" rather than by outright rebellion. Zachariah is a microcosm of those liberating forces which were

[51] *Ibid.*, p. 81.

[52] *Ibid.*, pp. 81–82. These verses from Béranger are quoted again by John Hale-White in his annotations of his father's notes on Sir James Fitzjames Stephen's book, *Liberty, Equality, Fraternity.* He refers to the essay in which these lines are found by saying : "I may add that this Apology should not be taken as an abandonment of political principles previously held, but as the expression of a mood in which his own proper 'daimon' warned him, in advancing age, away from political and social problems and towards the secluded life of study for which he was best fitted." The verses are again quoted in *R.O.*, April 27, 1867.

[53] *B.J.*, March 21, 1868.

[54] *P.J.*, p. 79. See also *L.P.*, p. 306 : "The public evils which weigh upon us most heavily are so formless, so universally-penetrating that it seems hopeless to combat them. Luther had a definite foe. He believed that if he could overthrow the Papacy the world would be regenerated. Happy prophet! What can we do against omnipresent dishonesty, moral scepticism, and modern political methods?"

[55] *R.T.L.*, p. 125.

so fundamentally to alter the relations between politics and religion, and men and women, as the century progressed.

Through Major Maitland, Zachariah was gradually drawn into a revolutionary organization, "The Friends of the People," and through this connection met those emancipated revolutionists, Caillaud and his daughter Pauline. He liked them from the first, but he was troubled by the fact that, as a good Calvinist, he ought to convert them, or at least try to. But he "could not face the question":

> ... he ought to have ... looked straight into their eyes, and told them ... that they were in the bonds of iniquity, sold unto Satan, and in danger of hell-fire. But, alas! he was at least a century and a half too late. He struggled, wrestled, self against self, and failed, not through want of courage, but because he wanted a deeper conviction. The system was still the same ... but the application had become difficult.[56]

Zachariah continued his attendance at chapel and his daily reading of the Bible, but his love for these unregenerate people bred a fatal broadening of his religious tolerance—"The man rose up behind the Calvinist, and reached out arms to touch and embrace his friends."[57]

His apostasy, however, was by no means complete, and at least some of the habits instilled by the old religion came to his assistance in times of trouble. In a chapter entitled, "A Strain on the Cable," Hale White shows Zachariah's first passage through the Slough of Despond. After the murder of the traitorous Secretary of The Friends of the People, Zachariah, though innocent, had to flee to Manchester to avoid possible arrest, while Caillaud and Pauline fled to their native France. Without friends or external resources to sustain him, he called again upon a half-rejected faith and found it still vital:

> Then he fell into the old familiar controversy with himself, and it was curiously characteristic of him, that, as he paced those dismal Manchester pavements, all their gloom disappeared as he re-argued the universal problem of which his case was an example. He admitted the unquestionable right of the Almighty to damn three parts of creation to eternal hell if so He willed; why not, then, one sinner like Zachariah Coleman to a weary pilgrimage for thirty or forty years? He rebuked himself when he found that he had all his life assented so easily to the doctrine of God's absolute authority in the election and disposal of the creatures He had made, and yet that he revolted when God touched him, and awarded him a punishment which, in comparison with the eternal loss of His presence, was as nothing. At last—and here, through his religion, he came down to the only consolation possible for him—he said to himself, "Thus hath He decreed; it is foolish to struggle against His ordinances; we can but submit."[58]

But one cannot adopt such a gospel of resignation and be a revolutionist at the same time. Unless the testimony of one's suffering suggests that there is something askew in the world instead of reminding one of the eternal rightness of things, no political action can consistently

---

56 *Ibid.*, p. 60.
57 *Ibid.*, p. 62.
58 *Ibid.*, p. 84.

follow. But this was, in Zachariah's career, only a passing phase. In the months that followed, his Calvinism was put to more and more severe tests—by poverty, illness, unemployment, and finally the workhouse. But his despair was fed most seriously by reading a book by Ferguson on astronomy, wherein he learned that the world would one day end by falling into the sun, and that the pious author could not admit that the planets or stars "were created for the sake of man."[59]

Ferguson was a Christian, and the thought of the destruction of our present dwelling-place, with every particle of life on it, did not trouble him. He had his refuge in Revelation. Zachariah too was a Christian, but the muscles of his Christianity were—now at any rate, whatever they may once have been—not firm enough to strangle this new terror. His supernatural heaven had receded into shadow; he was giddy, and did not know where he was.

His compensation for these shocks was found in the revolutionary movement itself. As his religion became less dogmatic, his need for his Republican friends became greater. And when, after a separation of two years, Zachariah again meets the Major, Caillaud, and Pauline on the eve of the ill-fated march of the "Blanketeers," he felt "much nearer and dearer to them than he was before. He had unconsciously moved on a line rapidly sweeping round into parallelism with theirs."[60] Consequently, "From 1816 downwards it may be questioned whether he would not have felt himself more akin with any of his democratic friends, who were really in earnest over the great struggle, than with a sleek half Tory professor of the gospel, however orthodox he might have been."[61] The strengthening of these allegiances drew him by degrees away from the narrow world of the meetinghouse into a world of great issues. This change was, in a sense, Zachariah's "new birth," even though it involved no open break with his religious heritage and no open divorce from his uncongenial wife—whose opposition to these changes in her husband was bitter and violent. As with Hale White's own apostasy, there was both a negative and positive side to it, but the difference was that Zachariah had a more clear-cut surrogate for the faith he gradually discarded.

The relations between Zachariah and his wife belong properly to our study of the theme of incompatibility in the novels, but it is so intimately related to the whole spiritual metamorphosis of Zachariah that we must treat it here. Three months after his marriage, Zachariah realized that he did not love his wife. There had been no quarrel, no infidelity, but the old passion had evaporated and nothing had come to take its place.[62]

. . . he became at last aware of the sad truth—the saddest a man can know—that he had missed the great delight of existence. . . . Henceforth all that was said and sung about love and home would find no echo in him. He was paralysed, dead in half of his soul, and would have to exist with the other half as well [sic] he could.

59 *Ibid.*, p. 143.
60 *Ibid.*, p. 96.
61 *Ibid.*, p. 95.   62 *Ibid.*, p. 11.

Mrs. Coleman symbolized the dead world Zachariah was outgrowing. A polished tea caddy, observance of family prayers, chapel attendance, and strict respectability in social observances were as necessary to her as intellectual stimulation and "great causes" were to her husband. She lived in a world of forms, not ideas, and politics meant nothing to her.

But while her cold, prudish demeanor makes her an unsympathetic character beside the generous and enthusiastic Zachariah, nevertheless Hale White admits that he was a difficult man for a domestic precisian to live with. He was clumsy, untidy, and heavy both in thought and action. He would often take tea before washing the printer's ink off his hands and stain the sugar lumps with his dirty fingers. He was, in general, "weak in the absence of the innumerable little sympathies and worldlinesses which make life delightful, and but too apt to despise and tread upon those gentle flowers which are as really here as the sun and the stars, and are nearer to us."[63] He was more at home with "Isaiah, Milton, a storm, a great passion" than he was or ever could be in his own house.

A man of his temper naturally found in Pauline a more congenial companion. She, like him, was "by nature a poet," and in her company he found "no polished tea-caddy to stare at him and claim equal rights against him."[64] Mrs. Coleman, in turn, found in Major Maitland a gallantry which could bring "the faint flush on the cheek" and arouse, strangely enough, an "unusual little rippling overflow of kindness to her husband."[65] There is never the slightest hint of infidelity or separation, and it certainly cannot be said that Mrs. Coleman entertains a carnal affection for the Major nor Zachariah for Pauline, but the tension of these attractions underlies most of the action in the first half of the book. Mrs. Coleman makes it easier for Zachariah to leave the world of the meetinghouse, for she symbolizes to him all its loveless aspects. The breach between them widens by degrees, and Hale White depicts the severance with subtlety and skill. On one occasion when the three friends were taking tea with the Colemans, Caillaud had informed the gathering of Pauline's illegitimate origin. Thus does the scene close:

> As soon as they were in the street Pauline said, "Father, I abhor that woman. If she lives she will kill her husband."
> Mrs. Coleman, on the other hand, at the same moment said, "Zachariah, Pauline and Caillaud cannot come to this house again."
> "Why not?"
> "Why not, Zachariah? I am astonished at you! The child of a woman who lived in open sin!"
> He made no reply. Years ago not a doubt would have crossed his mind. That a member of Mr. Bradshaw's church should receive such people as Caillaud and Pauline would have seemed impossible. Nevertheless, neither Caillaud nor Pauline were now repugnant to him; nor did he feel that any soundless gulf separated them from him, although, so far as he knew, his opinions had undergone no change."[66]

63 *Ibid.*, p. 15.
64 *Ibid.*, p. 46.   65 *Ibid.*, p. 14.   66 *Ibid.*, p. 104.

As he was more and more drawn into their orbit, he more and more came to judge his wife by the standard set by Pauline. And Mrs. Coleman, with keen feminine instinct, suddenly awoke to this fact, and thereupon jealousy came to fill the space between herself and her husband. After the conversation recorded above, Mrs. Coleman retired to her bed, "The figure of the Major hovering before her eyes," when she suddenly "bethought herself that Pauline, if not handsome, was attractive."[67]

She started, and lay awake for an hour. When she rose in the morning the same thought again presented itself, to dwell with her henceforwards, and to gnaw her continually like vitriol.

With the corrosive acid of jealousy added to their differences of temperament, habit, and opinion, the last remaining pretense of affection between husband and wife vanished. Zachariah, slower than his wife to feel suspicion, gradually in his turn came to realize that perhaps his wife was in her heart untrue to him, for he noticed that she objected considerably more to Caillaud and Pauline than to the Major, although they were all of them reprobate. The domestic tempest resulting from the voicing of this jealousy has an authentic ring to it. Mrs. Coleman, in the course of the argument, exclaimed:

". . . I didn't say I didn't object to the Major. Besides, there is a difference between French infidels and English people, even if they are not church members. But I see how it is. You want to go there, and you will go. I am of no use to you. You care nothing for me. You can talk to such dreadful creatures as Caillaud and that woman who lives with him, and you never talk to me . . ."[68]

To this Zachariah replies with unaccustomed anger and vindictiveness:

"Whose fault is it that I do not talk to you? When did I ever get any help from you? What do you understand about what concerns me, and when have you ever tried to understand anything? Your home is no home to me. My life is blasted, and it might have been different. . . ."

Under adversity she showed all that was worst in her. We can perhaps pity her frustration, but Hale White at this point in the story is completely the partisan of Zachariah. When she failed to give Zachariah emotional support in his black Manchester experience, when his fortunes were at their lowest ebb, he saw her not only as a cold partner, but as a dangerous enemy, "a reptile with cruel fangs which at any moment might turn upon him when he was at his weakest and least able to defend himself."[69]

The final mark of their rupture appeared in the chapter entitled, "The End of the Beginning." Caillaud was in prison, condemned to death for the murder of a soldier who had killed the Major as he led the Manchester "Blanketeers" in their march on London. Zachariah, at con-

[67] This might also be said of George Eliot.
[68] *Ibid.*, p. 114.
[69] *Ibid.*, p. 87.

siderable risk, resolved to see Caillaud before he died. His wife could not see "what is the use of it" and reminded him that he would be likely to lose his job and possibly be jailed himself as a sympathizer.[70]

> Zachariah could not restrain himself.
> "Good God!" he cried, "you hear that one of my best friends is about to be hung, and you sit there like a statue—not a single word of sympathy or horror—you care no more than a stone. *Use* of going! I tell you I will go if I starve, or have to rot in jail all my lifetime."

There is as much spite as noble resolution expressed here, a fact which is of considerable interest when we remember the resemblances between Zachariah and Hale White and Mrs. Coleman and Hale White's mother. As a result of his temerity, Zachariah had to rot in jail only two years and during that period Hale White conveniently lets Mrs. Coleman die. In a brief note at the end of Part One, we learn that Pauline finally married Zachariah. The hero gets his revenge.

But he also finds a kind of deliverance. Though the "happy" ending strikes the reader as contrived, Zachariah is nonetheless saved, no less than Catharine, by his love. For it was this attraction which led him from those cramping and unhealthy quarters which his spirit had outgrown and where he could only have withered and died, into a life of action and service. We might even say that, as with Madge, his faith in love rather than marriage made him whole. His domestic disharmony was a symbol of the underlying disharmony between himself and a whole religious and cultural tradition which was beginning to end with men like him. The removal of his wife's dominance over him was in this book an artistic and psychological necessity, for she was the very embodiment of all that was rigid, cantankerous, and inhumane in that narrow chapel-world. Politically he found active expression for an inactive conviction; domestically he repudiated conventionality and formalism for life; religiously he exchanged a formula for a faith. Zachariah is not a success—not even a great man— but his was a growing life and thus, to Hale White, an essentially hopeful and righteous one. "The End of the Beginning" marks the closing of a period when faith was embedded in the very life of a religious community, and the beginning of that necessary preparation, in truly religious souls like Zachariah, to accept psychologically the burdens of faith.[71]

Not only, not mainly upon the Cross, is Paradise regained, but in those deserts of utter solitude where man puts forth the strength of his reason to resist the fiend.

[70] *Ibid.*, p. 149.
[71] Aldous Huxley, *Music at Night* (London, 1950), p. 38.

Chapter Eleven

THEMES IN THE NOVELS: INCOMPATIBILITY

Incompatibility is so pervasive a theme in all of Hale White's novels and stories that we have unavoidably touched on it before this. But it deserves special treatment not only because it illumines in particularly fruitful ways Hale White's personality and emotional problems, but because it leads us to consider some of Hale White's short stories, a few of which are entirely built around this theme. There is hardly any question that Hale White's fascinated preoccupation with the theme reflects his own experience of married life, but we can, unfortunately, know that experience only in general terms, for the only available historical record of it is the brief mention made by his sons in their *Notes*. In the *Early Life* the subject is conspicuously underemphasized. Hale White passes over this long and vitally important period of his life with the laconic statement: "Meanwhile I had married."[1] Such brevity is, to say the least, strange in a man whose creative work is overflowing with an interest and concern in the problems of the marriage relationship. Obviously, it was a subject he preferred to speak about from behind a mask, and this fact invites us to remove, so far as we can, the fictional disguise.

About five years after his marriage in 1856 to Harriet Arthur, his wife developed signs of a disease which, in the words of Hale White's grandson,[2] is more to be dreaded than cancer. It is a disease of the nervous system for which no cure is to this day known. It brings a gradual paralysis of the limbs and decay of the organs, and it can kill its victim in five years or extend its torture for thirty or more. This is the record given us by Sir William Hale-White, the eldest son of the author and one of England's leading physicians at the turn of the century and after:

He had one great sorrow, enough to overwhelm most men. It was this. Shortly after his happy marriage, my mother showed signs of disseminated sclerosis—an incurable disease of the nervous system—which had been completely unsuspected. Slowly she became paralysed in the legs, so that both indoors and out of doors she had to be taken about in a bath chair; next the paralysis spread to the arms so that she could not write and hardly feed herself. The disease, marching on, made her almost blind during her last few years, but it did not kill her until 1891. For thirty weary years she endured but never once complained. To all of us she was more than a saint for she awakened in us not only reverence but great love. Sometimes my father spoke to me as he wrote to my brother of what our mother's illness meant to him. Both he and she bore this thirty year long tragedy without wincing, devoted in their affection for one another. Although, after my mother became incapable of housekeeping, my father tried to do it for a while, he soon found this impossible, consequently lady housekeepers appeared. Thus, in addition to her suffering and his consequent unhappiness,

[1] *E.L.*, p. 88.
[2] A London physician, Dr. Reginald Hale-White. See *L.3F.*, p. 123.

the privacy of the home was destroyed. When he came home from his work, he and she together would have liked to be alone, but a stranger was always there. My father cannot be understood by those who are unaware of his wife's illness. The quality of my mother is also shown in the deep affection all my father's family had for her from the very first. In 1854 she began spending much of her time with his parents, and at the last, my grandfather [William White], having retired to Carshalton to live near his children took his daily morning walk with his dog to see his dear Harriet.[3]

Although there can be no doubt about Hale White's deep loyalty to his wife, there can be no doubt, too, that he often resented the heavy cross he had to carry and that her affliction intensified his self-pity and depression. Indeed, few men could bear such an ordeal with equanimity. But Hale White dealt with the problem almost as if it were something to be ashamed of. Miss Partridge told Mrs. D. V. White that he shut up the house and entertained few friends,[4] and John in his *Notes* seems to bear this out. John found the household of his Uncle John and Aunt Henrietta, neighbors in Carshalton, a happier place to be than his own home, and he consequently spent much time there. Their house was ". . . free from the cloud of illness which overcast ours, not ruled by such exacting standards, and generally more cheerful. . . ."[5] And his son frequently mentions the "restricted" life in his home, the rarity of "congenial acquaintances" and his father's "absorption in work and study." For these and other reasons, therefore, we suspect that the statement in the *Autobiography* referring to Mark Rutherford's relations with Mary Mardon is the expression of an attitude toward his own wife which he often could not overcome.[6]

. . . my pride suffered most. I could have endured, I believe, even discord at home, if only I could have had a woman whom I could present to my friends, and whom they would admire.

Hale White's wife was a lover of music and had studied under Sir Charles Hallé, yet—as Dr. R. Hale-White has pointed out[7]—there is no evidence that ever during their married life he took her to a concert or, in later years, tried to bring music into the home. Dr. Hale-White went on to say that, in his opinion, he was completely lacking in the equipment to cope with such an emotional burden: he could not rise above the depression

[3] *P.N.b.*, pp. 39–40.

[4] Conversations between Mrs. White and the author at Sherborne, October 16, 1949.

[5] *P.N.a.*, p. 3. John Arthur, the brother of Hale White's first wife, married Hale White's elder sister, Henrietta. (*P.N.a.*, p. 3.)

[6] *A.*, p. 67.

[7] This grandson is the son of Sir William Hale-White. In spite of his professions to the contrary, Hale White's love of music was not very deep. Both Mrs. D. V. White and Dr. R. Hale-White attest to this. In "Confessions of a Self-Tormentor," *M.P.*, pp. 114–15, he himself writes: "I had no real love of art and did not understand it. . . . Wanting an ear for music and an eye for pictorial merit, I believed, or affected to believe, that the raptures of people who possessed the ear and eye were a sham. It irritated me to hear my aunt play, although she . . . was a skillful performer. I know she would have liked to feel that she gave me some pleasure, and that her playing was admired, but I was so openly indifferent to it that at last she always shut the piano if I happened to come into the room while she was practising. I remember saying to her when she was talking to me about one of Mozart's quartets . . . that music was immoral. . . ."

it wrought in him, and instead of bringing cheer and relief to those around him who were suffering, he increased their misery by making his own so conspicuous and omnipresent. As with Miriam, the misery of others tended to increase his own self-sympathy.

Although Mrs. White was an accomplished musician and had other cultural interests,[8] her life was "one almost entirely of the affections," a fact suggesting that Hale White may not have found in her the intellectual companionship he craved in a woman—in, say, a George Eliot. Her relationship to her husband was, writes John, "one of devotion, almost of adoration; she was absorbed in him."[9] Now while such devotion was doubtless pleasing and necessary to Hale White, it could not have been stimulating. As we have seen before, he liked women possessing a "liveliness of temperament, and with an intellect which was on equal terms with that of a man."[10] And John confesses that his mother could not play that role:

I do not say that she influenced his intellectual conclusions or the contents of his books: that was not in her power: but there was nothing in her that ran counter to them. . . .[11]

Although this son seems generally clear-sighted and objective in his estimate of a father whom he loved, we are justified in taking slight issue with him here. For while Mrs. White may not have provided *ideas* for her husband's books, it is unquestionable that she involuntarily helped to create those moods and tensions which are so intimately recorded there. We may reasonably suspect, for example, that she was in his mind when he described the patient, long-suffering nature of the saintly Mrs. Butts:

Mrs. Butts never uttered one word of reproach to her husband . . . and she said to herself that as perhaps it was through her lack of sympathy with him that he had strayed, it was her duty more and more to draw him to herself. She had a divine disposition, not infrequent amongst women, to seek in herself the reason for any wrong which was done to her. That almost instinctive tendency in men, to excuse, to transfer blame to others, to be angry with somebody else when they suffer . . . in her did not exist.[12]

That "instinctive tendency" was in Hale White particularly strong, and there can be little doubt that his wife, innocently and unconsciously, often did much to provoke it. The very fact of her existence caused him suffering, and at times he could not keep from blaming her for it. In such circumstances, adoration and hate can lie side by side, the first a corrective to the second, replacing it, but never really mingling with it. The presence of a saint in his own house (and after her death Hale White spoke of her in almost those terms),[13] who might be worshiped but not loved, could breed its own revulsion.[14] In actual life it is doubtful that

----

[8] In the *P.N.a.*, p. 5, we learn that she read French and some Italian, loved simple lyrical poetry, and read her Bible regularly.

[9] *P.N.a.*, p. 5.   [10] *R.T.L.*, p. 51.   [11] *P.N.a.*, p. 6.

[12] *D.*, p. 60.   [13] See *L.3F.*, p. 50.

[14] We should remember that Hale White had small sympathy for the "saintly" qualities of Mazzini.

Hale White ever spoke a cross word to his wife, but it seems more than probable that she inspired those extremities of frustration which find repeated expression in his writing.

In *Miriam's Schooling*, for example, written just before his wife's death, we are shown a woman driven almost to madness by the burdens imposed upon her by a hostile world and a sick brother. With Miriam, "Sorrow took the form of revolt,"[15] and she raged against the evils which had come to her through no fault of her own. As her brother lay ill and helpless on his bed:

Miriam's hatred of his silent white face increased. She had too much self-control to express herself; but at times she was almost on the point of breaking out, of storming at him, and asking him whether he had no pity for her.[16]

Her brother, noting her tears, asked her what was the matter:

"Matter!" she cried. "I don't believe you understand or care any more than the bedstead on which you lie," and she rose and flung herself out of the house.[17]

In the saintly Mrs. Butts and the vengefully frustrated Miriam we are introduced not only to two people but to two moods: those extremes of adoration and hate which might very understandably have grown from Hale White's own domestic experience. The first was a mood which was socially acceptable, and in all his public utterances about his wife that mood dominates. But the second was one that he could not fully understand, and that provoked a deep sense of guilt and shame. How could one *blame* a helpless invalid? What excuse was there for hating a saint? Hale White's struggle with this duality in himself was of a piece with struggles we have seen before, but it was in many ways the most harrowing of his entire life. And, as usual, we find it delineated most clearly in his writing.

A Dream of Two Dimensions is at once one of the strangest and one of the most revealing of Hale White's stories. It was begun around 1873 and was first published for private circulation in 1884. In its first form it was entitled *Flatland*. We know very little about the composition of this story, but it is significant that Hale White spoke about it to his second wife immediately following some remarks about his "invalid wife" and the "perpetual nightmare" of his office work and journalism.[18] The association of this small book with his memories of those unhappy days seems clearly to indicate a close connection between them. And Mrs. D. V. White is today convinced that the story is a close reflection of his state of mind in those years.[19] She writes in *The Groombridge Diary*:

He mentioned to me a pamphlet, *Flatland*, which he began to write one Sunday, (he thinks) about 35 years ago [1873]. He cannot remember who printed it, and he burnt

15 *M.S.*, p. 111.
16 *Ibid.*, pp. 111–12.
17 *Ibid.*, p. 112.
18 See *G.D.*, p. 72.
19 Conversations with the author at Sherborne, October 16, 1949.

all the surplus copies in the rubbish heap some long time since, because he was ashamed of it and thought it wanted such a lot of correction. Now of course he is sorry and would like to get hold of a copy again ![20]

Why he was ashamed of it we can only conjecture, but a study of the story leads us to believe that he felt it to be an almost too-honest confession of his secret self. In later life, however, he found a copy[21] and revised it for publication in *Last Pages*. Though some of the printed copies may still be extant, this is the version we must consult.[22]

The tale opens on a Sunday afternoon in a suburban home very like Hale White's at Carshalton.[23]

One Sunday afternoon, a few years ago, I was very discontented. I had been bothered by attempting to teach my son his Euclid. I had been explaining the definitions to him, and I did not want to explain definitions to him but to go on with my own book, Sunday being the only day I had for reading. He ought to have done his lessons on Saturday, but he had boggled over them and would not comprehend the simplest truths. He obstinately stuck to it that a line had breadth, and was inclined to argue that point. Nothing irritates me more in children than idle debate when they ought to be learning what is set before them, and at last I told him to cease his silly chatter and commit to memory what I had uselessly tried to make intelligible to him. I bundled him off upstairs and proceeded to bewail to his mother, as I generally did on Sunday afternoons, my hard lot, my lack of leisure and society, &c, &c. Whenever I went into other houses everything seemed cheerful and bright: here there was nothing but gloom; life for me was a perpetual grind and nobody cared two pins about me. My poor little wife,[24] as her habit was, tried to console me, and observed that our greatest blessings were, perhaps, those of which we took the least notice because we were so used to them. I held my tongue. I had got into the habit of despising her counsels as feeble. She did not appreciate me, and I could never hope she would. What a thing it would be to have a wife with some intelligence, who could see that my sufferings were real and could soothe them! I answered her by turning my head on one side in my easy chair and obtrusively shutting my eyes, as if what she had said were not worth notice. It was my usual way of meeting her endeavours to help me. She looked at me quietly for a moment; there were tears in her eyes; she rose and left the room.

Following this episode, the narrator falls asleep and has a dream which symbolically reflects many of the conditions of his real life. He finds himself in a world of two dimensions, of shadows, where he was the only three-dimensional individual. Life in this strange society followed a very normal pattern, except that speech was carried on by lip reading and the food— though satisfying—was shadow food. No one, however, noticed his three-dimensionality. At first he was delighted with the simplicity and gaiety of the life, but by degrees he came to miss earthly disharmonies and grew

[20] *G.D.*, pp. 72–73.

[21] Hale White vaguely refers to "another *Flatland*" (*G.D.*, p. 73). This may have been the paper of "The Fourth Dimension" which was unearthed in September 1908 by Mary Theodora Hale-White and from which he prepared the final version for publication. Or it may refer to E. A. Abbott's *Flatland*, published in 1884.

[22] A photograph of the original published pamphlet appeared in Simon Nowell-Smith's *Bibliography* of the first editions of Hale White's books.

[23] *L.P.*, pp. 138–39.

[24] "My poor wife" was an expression he frequently used. See *L.3F.*, p. 50.

tired of what he regarded as their childish philosophizing about "the death of shadows" and such matters. His discontent brought on the disease of hypochondria, and he was advised by a physician "to give up work, to go into society, and . . . to get married." Dutifully, he found a wife—"a bright, charming damsel"—and took a house in the suburbs. The relationship was satisfactory in all respects but one: she, like all these shadow people, disappeared every evening at sunset and did not again appear until sunup the next morning. His frustration was acute: " 'What does it matter,' said I to myself, 'that she is with me all day if she is dead during the rest of the twenty-four hours?' "[25] She, noticing his depression, became in turn dejected and anxious. But her suffering only made things worse.[26]

In a measure I was touched by her suffering, but although I tried to calm her and put my arms round her, I wished all the time she were something different.

But his greatest frustration (perhaps a mere rationalization of his sexual frustration) was her ignorance of his third dimension, her insensibility to his "immense superiority to her." When he tried to enlighten her on the point, she thought he was raving. He tried to tell himself that this intellectual pride was stupid and unjust, but the matter continued to obsess him.

But what a creature is a man! My third dimension was always in my mind, and I came to the conclusion I would rather be without a wife who did not appreciate it. I am sorry to say I had not sufficient self-command and generosity to keep my ill temper to myself, and I rejected all her advances towards me. She, on the other hand, redoubled her efforts to conciliate and entertain me. She received me in the most exquisite colours when I came home, lovelier far than any we have here, and her ways were so aërial and so bewitching that, at times, if I had not obstinately held off from her, cruelly shutting up myself within myself, I should have fallen on her neck and endeavoured to return her self-sacrificing devotion.[27]

As his "hard-heartedness began to tell upon her," she became gradually ill and their life became almost unendurable. He became even more secretive and self-absorbed.

To a being ignorant of my third dimension it was not worth while to communicate my plans, and I actually felt a secret pleasure in stalking out of the house, informing her, in answer to her earnest inquiries, that I could not tell her when she might expect me.[28]

One day he discovered that his wife had been secretly consulting a physician and that a cure for her mental distress and bodily weakness was possible. If both of them simultaneously took a potion which the doctor would provide, they would be restored to "the same level of insight and affection," but if only one were to drink, that one would surely die. The husband allowed the medicine to be sent, but when the test came he refused

---

[25] *L.P.*, p. 144.
[26] *Ibid.*, p. 145. Compare Miriam's romantic wish fulfillment as she embraced her husband. (*M.S.*, p. 132.)
[27] *Ibid.*, p. 146.
[28] *Ibid.*, p. 147. Cf. above, p. 164.

to drink. The wife, however, unable to move him by words, resorted to the desperate expedient of drinking her potion, hoping by this demonstration of her love and trust to win his co-operation. He refused and she died. Immediately afterward, as we might expect, he was plunged into inconsolable remorse—accusing himself of being worse than a murderer and agonizing over the fact that there was no one to whom he could confess his guilt or reveal his anguish. At the height of his despair, however, his wife appeared as a kind of spectre before him and, hearing his confessions of love, produced a phial "filled with a liquor which was the colour of blood and glowed like fire." They both drank, and he was moving to embrace her when he woke up.

Where was I ? I was in my chair in 10 Albert Villas, the Euclid was on the floor, and my own earthly wife was sitting opposite to me. She had entered the room noiselessly, for I had slept long beyond my usual time.[29]

The very fact that Hale White was such a literal artist makes this fantasy of special significance. It is, we feel, too realistic in its details and too close to what we already know of Hale White's true experience to have been a mere imaginative flight. And doubtless he would have kept it hidden from the world had he suspected that a later generation would take something like a scientific interest in tracing men's secret lives through their dreams. But we do not need Freud to help us here and shall not attempt to see more than is obviously revealed in the story.

Hale White has here recorded an experience which is neither uncommon nor mysterious. A man suffering a great frustration wants to destroy the frustrating object, much as a child kicks at the table against which he has stubbed his toe. That the object is innocent does not matter if his hurt is serious and deep enough. Such feelings can breed murderous desires and, in people of small self-discipline or conscience, can breed murder itself. With Hale White, however, these aggressive impulses were locked up and seldom, one suspects, found expression even in a cruel word, and certainly never in an overt act beyond, perhaps "stalking out of the house" or turning his head on one side and "obtrusively shutting" his eyes. But the very fact of this self-control made the pressures of the aggressive devils haunting him almost unbearable. They must therefore be exorcised; the pressure must be released. In this story, Hale White shows us how, by a vicarious experience, this may be done.

In the dream his aggression was consummated in murder, thus releasing the pressure and making room for healthier feelings. Cleansed of his hate, purified by remorse, he is in the dream giving himself the luxury of a second chance. He has felt evil and now he feels good. As Karl Menninger describes this phenomenon, the "aggressions become softened by the admixture of positive feelings; the hate, as we say, turns with more or less completeness to love."[30] Here Hale White is delineating in sym-

---

[29] *Ibid.*, p. 152.   [30] Menninger, *Man Against Himself*, p. 27.

bolic fashion the method of deliverance we have seen before. The blood-red liquor in the magic phial was simply the knowledge—which Hale White gained on many levels of experience—that the insistence upon realizing an ideal completely in this world only brings misery and un-happiness; that the righteous path is to see the good inhering in the fa-miliar and the commonplace, and to learn to love and live with it. It was the lesson taught both Catharine and Miriam: that we must divest our-selves of the notion of singularity, we must lose that stupid affection for our own third dimension, before we can be saved. That was an affirmation which his wife helped him to form, for unwittingly she provided much of the suffering by which he was purified.

But it is wrong to think of this story as having a happy ending. He has described for us a psychological process, not a goal attained. But, as we have seen before, he clung with passionate earnestness to the formula for turning hate into love, which, in this story, we see in the process of dis-covery. It was for him a miraculous concession wrung from the stubborn, intractable stuff of which his own personality and the world of experience was made—and just about the only concession. It was realized in a do-mestic setting and not in a sanctuary, it was understood in secular and not sacred terms, but it was nonetheless a religious experience and could, by a change of language, receive conventional religious expression.

Though the ultimate issue of Hale White's life was into a positive love, and though that love was made possible to no small degree by the lessons he had learned in his first marriage, the record of his stories and novels is primarily one of disharmony and maladjustment. In *A Dream of Two Dimensions* we have the pattern of marital incompatibility which is repeated with little variation throughout his writing. In nearly every case the fault lies with an individual's loving to excess his third dimension and feeling resentful and abandoned because others do not recognize it. That was in part Zachariah's problem, and it was most certainly that of Mr. Cardew in *Catharine Furze*, whose wife to him was an exasperating "echo" of his own opinions. Thus does Hale White moralize on Cardew's fault:

Mr. Cardew was far more wrong than he was right. He did not take into account that what his wife said and what she felt might not be the same; that persons, who have no great command over language, are obliged to make one word do duty for a dozen, and that, if his wife was defective at one point, there were in her whole regions of un-explored excellence, of faculties never encouraged, and an affection to which he offered no response. He had not learned the art of being happy with her: he did not know that happiness is an art: he rather did everything he could do to make the relationship intolerable. He demanded payment in coin stamped from his own mint, and if bullion and jewels had been poured before him he would have taken no heed of them.[31]

This necessity to feel contempt for somebody or something, to feel superior, rises in some of his characters to almost Faustian dimensions. And these characters are always the ones who complain most loudly about

[31] *C.F.*, p. 83.

being misunderstood. They never really lose their pride, but they find a different and a wiser expression of it. Mr. Cardew, for example, learns humility, but there is always a certain snobbery in it. He remains superior in his wisdom, for it is *he* who has found the cure for his marital maladjustments.

In "The Sweetness of a Man's Friend" the pattern is repeated, altered only by the fact that the wife's shortcoming here was her failure to appreciate Shelley, while Mrs. Cardew had failed to appreciate Milton. The husband in this story takes his third dimension seriously indeed. His dream of marital happiness was to spend long evenings with his wife studying Shelley together, gaily discussing "the connexion of the story in *The Revolt of Islam.*"[32] He was, of course, disappointed. She could neither master this nor *Alastor*. But the reader feels that if Shelley had not come between them some other issue would. Shelley was simply the symbol of a deeper and more fundamental frustration—a projection of that bitter monasticism endured by their author. The reconciliation takes place when a friend points out to him virtues in his wife which he, in his self-pity, had been blinded to. This friend performed the same service that George Eliot did for Mark Rutherford in healing him of his "self-despisings."[33] "Of all the dreadful trials which human nature has the capacity to bear unshattered," writes Mark Rutherford, "the worst . . . is the fang of some monomaniacal idea which cannot be wrenched out."[34] The hero of this story, suddenly aware that his wife was admired by others and warmed by the discovery that she had secretly been reading *Alastor* to make herself worthy of him, was pulled out of his self-absorption and lost his shame for her. Now, presumably, he could ask his friends to the house. Like so many of Hale White's leading characters, he is something of an intellectual bully. When the need for bullying is past, when he is taken off the defensive by realizing the world is not all against him, he can relax his fraudulent concerns with Shelley in favor of the real love he had wanted all along.

Again and again in Hale White's writings we find statements such as these:

"O Margaret, I do wish I could find a little more sympathy in you. What a joy it would be for me if you cared for the things for which I care, those which really concern me."[35]

"You must know that ever since we have been married you have never cared for one single thing I have done or said: that is to say, you have never cared for me. It is *not* being married."[36]

In *Catharine Furze*, Mr. Cardew says much the same thing,[37] and we have already quoted Zachariah's rebuke to his wife.[38]

32 *L.P.*, p. 39.   33 See *A.*, p. 157.   34 *Ibid.*, pp. 115–16.
35 *L.P.*, p. 40.   36 *A.*, p. 78.   37 *C.F.*, p. 83.
38 See above, pp. 182–83.

With the exception, perhaps, of Zachariah, all these men really need and love their wives and yet are forced by an inner compulsion to hurt them. They suffer from a frustration which they must take out on something, and they select the most defenseless victim they can find. They are all "self-tormentors" who realize at last, as Hale White did, that self-torment means cruel torment of one's neighbors; that at the root of their self-righteous complainings was a suffocating egotism. In their several ways, they make Hale White's confession:

I am not regenerate, but who is ever regenerate? My insignificance and defects do not worry me as they did: I do not kick at them, and I am no longer covetous of other people's talents and virtues. I am grateful for affection, for kindness, and even for politeness. What a tremendous price do we have to pay for what we so slowly learn, and learn so late![39]

It should not pass our notice that Hale White wrote those words with George Eliot in mind. Earlier in the same essay ("Confessions of a Self-Tormentor"), he had been discussing a "Mrs. A." who had once asked him to see the French actress, Rachel, with her, and to whom he wrote in later years "asking if she could get work for a starving man." These facts, plus many other corroborating details, identify with almost complete certainty "Mrs. A." as the young assistant editor at Chapman's[40] to whom Hale White was so deeply attracted at the time he was courting his wife. It would be a mistake to make too much of this ambiguous relationship, but on the other hand it cannot be ignored. In late life he confessed that "my love for her after so long an absence . . . is unchanged,"[41] and he remembers not only her intellectual attainments but her "particularly beautiful" hair and the "curiously shifting light" of her gray eyes—eyes which were "generally soft and tender, but convertible into the keenest flash."[42] It was the *avant garde* George Eliot whom he found "most attractive," and he seriously criticized the impression of "respectability" given by G. W. Cross's *Life*.[43] And in both the "Confessions of a Self-Tormentor" and the *Early Life* he deplores that "Demon of Pure Malignity," that fatal shyness and sense of inferiority which led him to resist her overtures of kindness and friendship.[44]

Oh! when I look back now over my life and call to mind what I might have had simply

---

39 "Confessions of a Self-Tormentor," *M.P.*, p. 123.

40 In 1876 Hale White wrote to Mrs. Lewes asking her to help in securing work for his old friend, William Maccall, of whom Carlyle had said: "there was never a man who went about with any dignity on so little money." (David A. Wilson, *Carlyle at His Zenith* [London, 1927], p. 67.) Both George Eliot and Hale White had known him at Chapman's. For further references to Maccall see: *L.3F.*, pp. 40–41, *L.P.*, p. 134, and *P.N.a.*, p. 4.

Concerning the invitation to see Rachel, see *E.L.*, p. 84.

Compare the description of George Eliot in "George Eliot as I Knew Her" (*L.P.*, pp. 131–37) and "Mrs. A." (*M.P.*, 117–18).

41 *L.3F.*, p. 87.

42 *L.P.*, p. 132.

43 Letter to *The Athenaeum* (November 8, 1885), p. 702.

44 *M.P.*, pp. 119–20. See also *M.S.*, p. 103; *A.*, p. 156, and *E.L.*, pp. 83–85.

for taking and did not take, my heart is like to break. The curse for me has not been plucking forbidden fruit, but the refusal of divine fruit offered me by heavenly angels.

However we may explain this attraction and these regrets, we cannot explain them on the grounds of a mere literary enthusiasm. Very likely George Eliot was always for him rather more an ideal than a person, a wish fulfillment than a real object of desire. But it seems certain that this ideal in subtle ways infected his marital content from the first. She was a woman who would not be merely his "echo," but a strong and original being whom he could proudly present to his friends and who could understand and share the depths of his spiritual suffering. The supposition that she was to Hale White very much what Catharine was for Mr. Cardew and Pauline for Zachariah is inevitable. He could see the tragedy of his life springing from that fatal flaw, that negative "damping" tendency which kept him from seizing opportunities of love offered him. Had he not so failed, he reminds himself, he might have avoided a lifetime of physical and intellectual incompatibility. Hale White in his stories and novels is continually asking this question and making these conjectures:

"Why did I marry that woman? I do not know, excepting that I was seized and driven, as if by a wave breaking on the shore. The marriage was over before I knew where I was. How is the co-existence in the same person of such strange contradictions to be explained? I suppose it is weakness. It is weakness which causes a man to stumble this way and that way, and makes it impossible to understand him."[45]

And throughout his writing we are shown middle-aged men who in second marriages find the opportunity to rectify their earlier mistakes, to marry their George Eliots, and to find the ideal happiness their youthful inhibitions had lost for them. In "Mr. Whittaker's Retirement," which presents a slightly disguised picture of Hale White himself following his own retirement in 1892,[46] he reveals a desire to take a second wife. And Baruch Cohen in *Clara Hopgood* shared the same desire and same fear of making himself ridiculous:

He was now . . . at a time of life when a man has to make the unpleasant discovery that he is beginning to lose his right to expect what he still eagerly desires, and that he must beware of being ridiculous. It is indeed a very unpleasant discovery. If he has done anything well which was worth doing, or has made himself a name, he may be treated by women with respect or adulation, but any passable boy of twenty is really more interesting to them, and, unhappily, there is perhaps so much of the man left in him that he would rather see the eyes of a girl melt when she looked at him than be adored by all the drawing-rooms in London as the author of the greatest poem since *Paradise Lost*, or as the conqueror of half a continent.[47]

Clara Hopgood, we remember, was published in 1896, well after his wife's death. In this period he was becoming widely known as an author,

---

45 "The Love of Woman," *L.P.*, pp. 98–99.
46 He said it had "a web of truth and woof of fiction" (*L.3F.*, p. 181). See *M.P.*, pp. 93–95.
47 *C.H.*, p. 112. See also *M.P.*, pp. 93–95.

and his own drawing room then and until the end of his life was frequently the gathering place for a host of female admirers.[48] One interesting relationship belonging to a slightly later period was that between Miss Gladys Ellen Easedale (later Mrs. Killen) and Hale White. In her book, *Middle Age, an Autobiography, 1885–1932,* she has given us some glimpses of their association and included some of the many letters which passed between them. She visited him frequently during his residence at Groombridge.[49]

> During those years, on and off when staying near Groombridge, I would then arrange to spend the day with Mark Rutherford. We would stroll in Groombridge Park or sit beside his fireside and talk. Once we were deep in conversation and I was kneeling by the fire when he leant forward and kissed my lips. We were both deeply moved. It was an extraordinarily beautiful moment. It was the only time we kissed—our friendship is difficult to explain, it was spirit to spirit, with no veil of flesh between. I hardly like to bring it into the book at all, only it was one of the most precious experiences of my life. . . . He was old and ill, but the brilliance of his intellect and spiritual vision lit up his melancholy like the stars and planets light the darkness of the night.

Shortly after this episode she was married, and her husband, misunderstanding the nature of the relationship between the two, broke it off.[50] At the time of her engagement, Hale White had written, characteristically,

> All I meant was that I never could exult in a marriage. I never could assume as a matter of course that a woman should be congratulated on an engagement, as if her soul were saved thereby, that is to say by the bare fact of ceasing to be single.
>
> Love, of course, is apt to lead to identity with the person beloved. I don't want you to be sunk in anybody or assimilated to anybody. I don't want you to think *from* your lover or to love *from* him, but to think and love by the unchanged direction hitherto vouchsafed to you.[51]

Though this particular friendship is, perhaps, somewhat atypical, it

---

[48] Some of these ladies were Mabel Marsh, Sophia S. Partridge, Frances Low, and finally, Miss D. V. Smith, whom he married on April 8, 1911. They were nearly all initially attracted to him by his books or through some common intellectual interest. He became attracted to Miss Smith through her novel, *Miss Mona,* and wrote to Miss Partridge in August 1907 that he would like to meet the author (*L.3F.,* pp. 254–55). He met Miss Partridge before the death of his wife when they were neighbors in Ashtead, Surrey (*L.3F.,* p. 144) ; his letters to her betray a deep affection and a commonality of interest on many subjects. Other feminine admirers were Erica Storr, whose poetry filled many pages of his scrapbooks and which she sent to him for criticism and correction over many years ; Beryl de Zoete, introduced to him by Professor de Sélincourt (*L.3F.,* 32 n.) ; Rose Paul, living at Hartfield during his Groombridge years (*L.3F.,* p. 256) ; and Mrs. Cobden-Sickert, whose unpublished novel he read in manuscript (*L.3F.,* p. 257).

The remarks by Miss Frances Low in *The Birmingham Post* of March 22, 1913, indicate in some measure the power he had to charm such an admirer as she : "Those who had the privilege of knowing him, of watching that rather solidly carved face, irradiated at times with a smile inexpressibly sweet and translating the rugged Carlylean brow, the heavy eye-brows, the sensitive mouth, and half tender, half ironical eyes, into geniality, have no apologies to make for him, as is, alas ! too often the sad necessity for genius."

[49] (Gladys Ellen Easedale) *Middle Age, an Autobiography, 1885–1932* (London, 1935), pp. 183–84. Hale White moved to Groombridge on June 15, 1903, and died there March 14, 1913.

[50] *Ibid.,* pp. 216–17.   [51] *Ibid.,* pp. 193–94.

is the only one about which we have any detailed information. It is, however, doubtless a fair reflection of his needs and impulses following his wife's death. Like Baruch Cohen, he would rather see the "eyes of a girl melt" than be "adored by all the drawing-rooms in London."

In the short story, "Mrs. Fairfax," written around 1899, we are again shown a man whose wife, like Baruch's, died within two years of his marriage and who, in middle life, decides to take a new wife. His first marriage had been "the arbitrary selection of a weary will,"[52] but now he experiences an Indian summer miracle: the discovery of a love in which he is *sure*, for which, like Madge Hopgood, he has "a perfectly clear direction."[53] The same pattern appeared earlier in the *Deliverance* when Mark Rutherford returns to Ellen, his first love.[54] Though this book was written six years before his wife's death, we can detect the same thoughts about second marriage which possessed him when, after 1891, such a step could be realistically considered. The following words can be read as the vicarious consummation of a long-frustrated dream:

I begin to believe that a first love never dies. A boy falls in love at eighteen or nineteen. The attachment comes to nothing. It is broken off for a multitude of reasons, and he sees its absurdity. He marries afterwards some other woman whom he even adores, and he has children for whom he spends his life; yet in an obscure corner of his soul, he preserves everlastingly the cherished picture of the girl who was first dear to him. She, too, marries. In process of time she is fifty years old, and he is fifty-two. He has not seen her for thirty years or more, but he continually turns aside into the little oratory, to gaze upon the face as it last appeared to him when he left her at the gate and saw her no more.[55]

In these examples we can detect the impulses which prepared him for marriage long before he met that remarkable woman who became his second wife. Although, through the long years of his first wife's suffering, he had learned—if we may believe the "self-tormentor's" confession—to be content with less than an ideal consummation, the dream never ceased to haunt him. *The Groombridge Diary* is the record of how a man finally found the Celestial City after a long pilgrimage. Though their relations were not uniformly serene, Hale White was almost miraculously softened by her influence, and her love for him was that for a man and not for an idol.[56]

But before leaving this subject we must mention one other story and make one further observation. While these broken lives which are scattered throughout his pages are, in one way or another, reflections of his own domestic tragedy, they are not valuable simply for this reason. They stand also as records of an age—an age in which the marriage convention was particularly binding, an orthodoxy which stood firm even while other

---

[52] *P.J.*, pp. 266 ff.
[53] *Ibid.*, p. 267.
[54] It appears again in the second marriage of Miriam's father also.
[55] *D.*, pp. 97–98.
[56] For a thorough account of this relationship see *The Groombridge Diary*.

orthodoxies were falling. Hale White was peculiarly equipped to show us this aspect of the Victorian malaise—those tensions resulting from restiveness within the iron frame of social convention. Hale White's personal experience was an unusually taxing one, but he lived out his marriage according to the rules. And in doing so he dramatized for us that almost intolerable emotional dilemma known by thousands of sensitive Victorians. They had, on the one hand, been fed in their youth on romantic ideals of moral individualism and spiritual freedom; on the other, they had been disciplined by Puritanism and Victorian convention in the duties of law-abiding citizenship and moral sobriety. The full expression of both impulses was, in any active or realistic sense, impossible. The "good" citizen caught in an unhappy marriage was caught in a very real prison. If he cared for his status in society, he could find no justification for his discontent in smashing idols or homes or legal ordinances. And if he simply ran away from the unpleasant relationship, there was always his conscience to deal with.

In the short story, "Esther," Hale White gives us a study in these problems. By an exchange of letters between an unhappy wife and her mother, we witness the disintegration of a Victorian marriage which in many ways reminds us of that slow decay recorded by Meredith in *Modern Love*. Here was a union which, on Victorian premises, would appear almost perfect, but Hale White shows it to be eaten by a fatal cancer. The conventional, provident, hard-working, duty-conscious husband—by the very tyranny of his virtues—makes existence for his partner a death-in-life. In her youthful ignorance, being untutored in the needs of her own spirit, she had compared him favorably with other men "who were extravagant and who had vices." Knowing no other standards of merit by which to judge a man, she accepted him. But after marriage, the "deadly sameness" of his soul, "to which nothing is strange and wonderful and a woman's heart is not so interesting as an advertisement column in the newspaper,"[57] became a heavy frost to those emotional wants which appeared as she matured. She wrote to her mother:

If Charles drank I might cure or tolerate him; if he went after another woman I might win him back. I can lay hold of nothing.[58]

The passionless stagnation of the relationship finally drove her to separation. And the exchange of letters following it shows clearly the claims of two kinds of outraged Victorian sensibility: on the one hand, the claims of duty and law; on the other, those of love and spirit. He writes, legalistically:

You will please bear in mind that *you* have abandoned *me*; I have not abandoned you. You disappointed me: my house was not managed in accordance with my wishes, but I was prepared to accept the consequences of what I did deliberately and I desired to avoid open rupture.

[57] *M.P.*, pp. 45–46.
[58] *Ibid.*, p. 46.

. . . I shall require of you a document which my solicitor will prepare, completely exonerating me. This will be necessary for my protection. A Bank manager's reputation is extremely sensitive, and a notorious infringement of any article of the moral code would in many quarters cause his commercial honesty to be suspected.[59]

She replied in words that might have been coined by Madge Hopgood:

I shall not return. The reason for my refusal shall be given with perfect sincerity. I do not love you, and you do not love me. I ought not to have married you, and I can but plead the blindness of youth, which for you is a poor excuse. I shall be punished for the remainder of my days, and not the least part of the punishment will be that I have done you a grievous injury. Worse, however—ten thousand times worse— would it be for both of us if we were to continue chained together in apathy or hatred. I would die for you this moment to make good what you have lost through me, but to live with you as your wife would be a crime of which I dare not be guilty.[60]

The contrast here is between a reality and an ideal, the world and the spirit. Hale White was on both sides, and in this situation there is no resolution. "Legal freedom," writes Hale White, does not ". . . excite much enthusiasm in me."[61] He could not think of divorce as a solution

to Esther's problem, for he imposed upon her those same moral restrictions he had known in his own married life. She had no grounds just as he would have had no grounds for abandoning an invalid wife. Yet the satisfaction of her own spirit was a vital—and almost sacred—right.

How to satisfy both the claims of legal duty and the claims of spiritual aspiration was, throughout his studies of incompatibility, the fundamental problem. The two solutions he presents are rebellion and resignation. But neither one is ever complete. Rebellion must stop within the pale of the law; resignation must be learned again and again, for suburbs or provinces afford small outlet for the passions of one who would be a "sublime" man.

[59] *Ibid.*, pp. 58–59.
[60] *Ibid.*, pp. 57–58.
[61] *B.N.B.*, p. 60.

Chapter Twelve

STYLE

To come upon Hale White's prose after knowing the oratorical effects of Macaulay, Carlyle, and Meredith, or the elaborate refinements of Pater, Ruskin, and Swinburne, is to experience something like a cold shower after a milk bath. For in Hale White we find none of that phrasemaking, none of that impulse to decorate, burnish, and inlay which embellished the pages of Hale White's contemporaries until, as Oliver Elton has said, "you cannot see the page for the phrase."[1] Hale White's pages were few and visible, and his sentences lucid and even austere. He worked and did not play with language; words were to him as precious as men's souls and like men's souls must be purified by their intensity, simplicity, and honesty. "If the truth is of serious importance to us," he writes, "we dare not obstruct it by phrase-making: we are compelled to be as direct as our inherited feebleness will permit."[2]

This moral impulse made Hale White a conscious stylist and gave to his writing many of those same qualities which recommend him to us as a man. Much of his own life was dedicated to a search for absolutes, but the direction of his endeavor was always toward reducing complexity to the absolute of simplicity. With a scientific passion for precision and clarity he looked for the unity of life in particulars, for truth in the hard facts, and he disciplined his prose to be almost the perfect vehicle for such a search. "Painted glass is very beautiful, but plain glass is the most useful as it lets through the most light"[3] was a quotation used by his father, and it was a principle to which Hale White gave assent in nearly every line he wrote. We shall look far to discover another writer whose prose style was a more direct expression of his own personality. We have already looked through that clear glass to see the man behind it, and have discovered a remarkably clear and undistorted picture. The quality which he admired in Milton—"the power to keep in contact with the soul of man"[4]—was his supreme gift as well, and he seldom lost contact with himself or the concrete stuff of his own deeply felt experience. Hale White had, therefore, no theory or practice of art which was not part of his theory and practice of life, and the reader who is attracted to his style must inevitably have some sympathy with the nature of its creator, for they are the same. And if we discover unevenness in that style—an oratorical quality sometimes competing with a cold austerity—it is only because in his own personality the public and private man never completely came to terms.

A rewarding approach to this study is to examine Hale White's habits

---

[1] Oliver Elton, *A Survey of English Literature* (New York, 1923), IV, 371.
[2] *E.L.,* pp. 30–31. [3] *Ibid.,* p. 31. [4] *P.J.,* p. 124.

of composition and revision. The original manuscripts of his novels were all, unfortunately, destroyed by the author, and we are told little about the conditions surrounding their composition except that the first of them was done at "extraordinary high pressure"[5] and was often worked on at four o'clock in the morning.[6] But there is abundant evidence that his normal habit was to write slowly and painstakingly,[7] revising carefully before publication. When an article for *The Nation* was printed with a minor error in it, before he had been given a chance to see the proofs, he was extremely upset and "danced about the bed and swore."[8] W. Robertson Nicoll wrote to Mrs. D. V. White that Hale White always "made the alterations himself" in his articles and that "he was extremely careful and punctilious in all his work."[9] His advice to at least one of the young feminine authors who gathered about him in his advancing years was drawn from his own rule book. The manuscript under discussion was a manual of instruction for teachers of arithmetic being prepared by Mabel Marsh:

I speak from experience. My counsel remains the same. Do *not* begin to rewrite for a twelvemonth. Read every work on which you can lay your hands that bears on the subject . . . Ask nobody's opinion till your MS. is complete . . . Your facility in writing will be rather a hindrance than a help . . . You will have to curb your eager longing for results . . . You must *not* be anxious to see the thing done. Each page must be an end in itself.[10]

The systematic precision of method which he advocated for others was evident in all his own work, even in his letters. The original of the letter partially reproduced above, for example, gave signs of careful proofreading. The word "work" had been substituted for "book," and elsewhere on the page "should prepare and outline" had been changed to "were to prepare an outline" and "I thought it failed rather in completeness of plan" had been altered to read, "I thought you failed rather in plan." These are small matters, but they indicate a concern for point and accuracy which never left him. As his first son wrote, "He hated shoddy," and the manuscripts of his letters have the same careful interlineations that his manuscripts for publication bore.

A number of the articles appearing in his journals had previously appeared in periodicals, as an examination of the Bibliography will indicate. The alterations he made in those earlier printed versions show clearly the tendency as his style matured to substitute the small word for the big, the simple phrase for the complex, and to expunge from a long paragraph the illustrations which originally clothed the thought, leaving only the

---

[5] *G.D.*, p. 51.   [6] *P.N.a.*, p. 2.

[7] In deciding not to write on William Morris, whom he knew personally (*L.3F.*, p. 24) and whose work he knew well, he wrote: "The author is rather too large a subject for the pen of such a slow writer as myself." (*L.3F.*, p. 155.)

[8] *G.D.*, p. 328. The article was "Faith," printed April 2, 1910, and reprinted in *P.J.*, pp. 326–32.

[9] Unpublished letter dated September 1, 1914.

[10] Unpublished letter dated October 13, 1900.

distilled essence of the thought itself. These habits can be illustrated by three examples. Hale White's article, "Notes on Shelley's Birthplace," appeared both in *Macmillan's Magazine* for March 1879 and in *The Bookman* for June 1912. Mrs. D. V. White has counted twenty-seven revisions in the 1879 version and compared them with the 1912 product. A random selection from her list provides a convincing demonstration of the growth of his stylistic discipline over these years.

Macmillan's	*The Bookman*
picturesque	attractive
meditate on	admire
in memory of different members of the Shelley	in memory of the Shelley
compared with the superior grandeur of the relationship	compared with the relationship
to note, and perhaps to accept, the inevitable	to note the inevitable
It is of primary importance	It is important
For Shelley's most central characteristic is insurgency and in him the Revolution	For in him the Revolution
And it is a curious fact that many	And many
Of the best English scenery	Of England at its best

A second revision deserving study is found in an article which originally appeared in *The British Weekly* for March 17, 1898,[11] entitled, "An Ancestor of Emerson," and was revised for publication in *Last Pages* as "Peter Bulkley."[12] The wealth of illustration in which the main thought was imbedded has all been pared away, and we are left with hardly more than an elaborate aphorism.[13] This is a paragraph from the 1898 version:

Nowadays we should consider this as mere raving, and, indeed, it is not true; but BULKLEY'S *method* was not madness. All genuine thinking leads to noble results. The celestial system constructed by the transcendent genius of HIPPARCHUS is not ours; but he was more right than wrong, and if he had not been born the discoveries of KEPLER and NEWTON might have been impossible. What was it which drove HIPPARCHUS to spend his life over these problems of the Almagest? He could not rest so long as the movements of the heavenly bodies seemed to observe no order. They *must* move by some law of geometry at once human and divine. From this *must* all his discoveries proceeded. The Puritan theology started from a similar necessity. Whether it was so successful theologically as the Greek astronomy was

11 Pp. 421–22.
12 Pp. 194–208.
13 For a brief consideration of Hale White's position in literature as a writer of aphorisms, see J. E. T. Wright, *William Hale White* (thesis, University of Pittsburgh, 1932), p. 160.

scientifically may be doubted; but one thing is certain—that it is not to be considered obsolete as a foolish superstition.

This is the same material as it appears in the version revised for *Last Pages*:

This may be called mere raving, but Bulkley's *method* was not madness. Nowadays we have no antecedent *must*. We do not understand the position of men who can obstinately attribute Divine authority to principles which are not in accord with experience and who continue to adhere to them although facts may thunder contradiction. Yet it is true, no matter how often we may be mistaken in our interpretations, that unless we believe in principles and their supremacy we are lost.[14]

But the most fruitful and suggestive materials available for studying his habits of revision are the "Notes" appearing in *More Pages* and the originals for those notes in his *Black Notebook*. The contrasts between the original and corrected versions tell us important things not only about his writing habits, but about the bent of his mind as well.

Black Notebook	*More Pages*
What I have felt the want of more than anything in my life is wise counsel for particular occasions; of somebody who could *advise* me. Principles I could get by the bushel anywhere. My father was able to help me best. And yet the reason why people are so useless is not because they cannot be anything else, but because they will not take trouble. (p. 21)	What we want is wise counsel on particular occasions. Principles we can get by the bushel anywhere. The reason why our friends are so useless is that they will not take trouble. The selection and the application of the principle are difficult. (pp. 226–27)
I find myself talking some times as if I were responsible for the effect of what I say. I am responsible for nothing but saying it. For the effect God is responsible who has ordained all causes & effects and the magnitude of the effect which is to follow from each cause. (p. 27)	We should not talk as if we were responsible for the effect of what we say. We are responsible for saying it, and for nothing more. A higher power is responsible for the effect which is to follow from each cause. (p. 229)
The emotion I feel in the presence of sunlight is not that which is due to it. It is the average of previous emotion in hours indifferent, good and bad. It is the product of association. Oh for power to struggle against this tyranny of association. I pray for no miraculous gifts, but simply for the ability to see that green field as it would be if association and "the film of custom" did not enslave me. (p. 28)	I pray for a gift which perhaps would be miraculous: simply to be able to see that field of waving grass as I should see it if association and the "film of custom" did not obscure it. (p. 231)

14 Pp. 204–5.

I have no capitalized happiness; nothing on which to draw when temporary sources fail.

(p. 30)

We have no capitalised happiness, nothing on which to draw when temporary sources fail.

(p. 232)

I exaggerate so foolishly ingratitude to me. Am I to require that a man should be always confessing obligation to me? Yet really it seems at times as if nothing less would satisfy me. Indifference to me is hard to bear, it is almost worse than cruelty, yet why should I care? "Seek Him that maketh the Pleiades and Orion."

(p. 90)

We foolishly exaggerate ingratitude to us. Ought we to require of those whom we have served, that they should be always confessing their obligations to us? Why should we care about neglect? "Seek Him that maketh the Pleiades and Orion," etc.[15]

(p. 253)

In each of these revisions we can see the process of a particular experience, feeling, or thought being turned into a generalized principle.[16] In nearly every case the "I" is expunged in favor of the editorial "we"—transmuting what is true of him into a truth for the race. And this, as we have seen before, is no mere literary habit but part of that lifelong effort to "get beyond the notion of personality,"[17] to learn to live not in the "I" but in "truths."[18] Hale White desperately wanted his personal experience to be representative, and the hope that it would be was one of the strongest motives prompting him to publish. "An individuality which is *most* individual is so because it is universal,"[19] he wrote in his *Black Notebook*. Hale White wanted to be private but he also wanted to be public; he wanted to be solitary but he also wanted to be loved; he craved individuality but he also needed the security of identity with a cosmic scheme of values. In changing "I exaggerate so foolishly ingratitude to me" to "We foolishly exaggerate ingratitude to us" all these contending impulses are revealed. He casts off his own identity not only in order to join his personal experience with a general truth, but also to escape from being judged. He is not only universalizing his experience, he is in a sense *blaming* the world of men for his own faults. Hale White again and again talks about the

[15] In *M.P.*, the rest of this quotation from Amos (5:8) is given. But in the MSS quotation a reference is made to the preceding page where the quotation is given in full. So the two quotations as they stand here represent the true bulk of the two statements.

[16] Mrs. D. V. White has also noted this generalizing tendency. See *L.P.*, pp. v–vi.

[17] *M.P.*, p. 236. In his *Black Notebook* (p. 6) appears a most revealing statement. He writes: "There are three orders of production. In the first the workman has a material outside him which he manipulates. It is external to him and nothing of himself passes into what he does. In the second he expresses himself and his work is a confession. When he has exhausted himself he has nothing more to say. In the third he is beyond the limits of personality. He is an organ of the universal and his sphere is unlimited. Shakespeare could write the world with an intimacy in the case of each character equal to Rousseau's with himself."

This objective-subjective-universal dialectic can be observed both in the development of his own writing and in the growth of his personal philosophy. Though he himself remained primarily in the "order" of confession, he strove—as we have seen here—to rise above it.

[18] *Ibid.*, p. 232.   [19] *B.N.B.*, p. 22.

need for *principles*, as if principles *per se* were good quite apart from their ethical content. He was not, in reality, so undiscriminating as this, but it is nonetheless true that his need to escape from the lonely insecurity of solitude into the security of humankind's common fate made him an inveterate aphorist. But it was not because he wanted to coin phrases; it was because he wanted to be at home in the world.

Hale White's style, therefore, is intimately related to his moral impulses. The alterations in these paragraphs reveal not only changes in his writing habits, but the growth of a personality seeking deliverance from itself. His emphasis was continually toward greater precision, veracity, and simplicity—toward the discovery of the pure idea embedded in the crude ore. "What a mistake it is to be afraid of lucidity!"[20] he wrote to Miss Partridge, and in saying this he was rephrasing a piece of unforgettable advice he had once received from his father: "My boy, if you write anything you consider particularly fine, strike it out."[21] Hale White always tried to avoid—as he was tempted by—the fatal habit of Mr. Cardew, who

. . . saw himself in things, and not as they were. A sunset was just what it might happen to symbolise to him at the time, and his judgments upon events and persons were striking, but they were frequently judgments upon creations of his own imagination, and were not in the least apposite to what was actually before him. The happy, artistic, Shakesperian temper, mirroring the world like a lake, was altogether foreign to him.[22]

Capriciously to forge judgments out of one's own "singularity" bred imprecision and self-deception. But equally bad was casting one's thought in the verbal molds of the crowd, in that popular jargon which made the expression of personal insight impossible. M'Kay, for example, insisted that his children not merely

. . . speak the truth in the ordinary, vulgar sense of the term, but . . . speak it in a much higher sense, by rigidly compelling, point by point, a correspondence of the words with the fact external or internal. He never would tolerate in his . . . children a mere hackneyed, borrowed expression, but demanded exact portraiture; and nothing vexed him more than to hear one of them spoil and make worthless what he or she had seen, by reporting it in some stale phrase which had been used by everybody.[23]

Hale White never tired of criticizing the stale phrases and hypocritical verbiage which he was forced day after day to listen to in the House. The changed language of the House in the latter half of the century was to him an indication of its changed character and a symptom of the nation's moral decay. This was the language of the myrmidons, who had schooled themselves in the phrases of the popular newspaper instead of those of the Bible or an earlier political oratory. In *The Norfolk News* of August 1, 1874, he writes:

We have got members who speak the English of Mrs. Gamp, and now it appears we have one who speaks that of the cheapest penny-a-liner. I heard a gentleman speak

20 *L.3F.*, p. 290.   21 *E.L.*, p. 31.   22 *C.F.*, p. 122.   23 *D.*, p. 10.

this week—not reported with accuracy—who in a few minutes brought in the following choice and original expressions—"Were launched into eternity," "mutilated remains," "hecatomb of victims," "primeval sentence of our race," "scene of the catastrophe," and many others which I have forgotten. We were also introduced to the sword of Damocles, which in the next sentence "descended like an avalanche scattering ruin." Radical as I am, I must own to a touch of sorrow as I sat and listened. It is significant of a good deal—not, mind you, of the popularisation of the House (that we should not regret), but of its growing wealth. It is not the genuine working man who talks this rubbish, but the millionaire. Mr. Burt and Mr. Macdonald are loyal to our native Saxon; it is the cotton-spinner and colliery-owner who murder it.

And in an article submitted to *The Pilot* on July 20, 1901, he adds a footnote to this remark, criticizing those jargon phrases which were on everyone's lips and which had become stale from overuse.[24]

There are many words which have been married so long that it is time they were divorced. They have lost their proper quality by prolonged association, and in some cases an inseparable adjective has also in some cases an injurious effect in limiting the noun. For example, if "diametrical" always comes into my head when I speak of opposition, I shall most likely describe incorrectly a particular opposite, for those which are really "diametrical" are rare. I subjoin a preliminary list of words which it would be as well to disconnect, say for a hundred years, and perhaps some of your readers may be inclined to add to it. I exclude all mere penny-a-lining phrases, such as "progressing favourably" and "devouring element."

Inevitable consequence.	Rooted aversion.
Inclined to surmise.	Pet ditto.
Sweep from recollection.	Cardinal objection.
Arrived at his destination.	Profound sensation.
Hurled from power.	Hopeless muddle.
Apprehensive of danger.	Hopeless confusion.
Checquered career.	Inextricable ditto.
Fabulous sum.	Initial blunder.
Acme of absurdity.	Palmy days.
Depth of disgrace.	Element of uncertainty.
Irretrievable disaster.	Bone of contention.
Penetrated with the conviction.	Master of the situation.
Unavoidable necessity.	Vexed question.
Indispensably necessary.	Transports of enthusiasm.
Blood curdle.	Trying ordeal.
Sovereign contempt.	Diametrically opposite.
Supreme ditto.	
Ditto moment.	
Ditto excellence.	
("Supreme," in fact, almost always).	

Now we might suppose that such an artistic conscience brought to the writing of novels would produce prose of a level sameness, lacking in color and sparkle, and—while free of jargon—reducing things and people alike to the crystalline purity of abstraction. To some degree this is true, but we need to remember that Hale White always worked *through* fact and experience to his generalizations and that, while the moralizing habit

[24] "Misleading Unions," *The Pilot* (July 20, 1901), pp. 80–81 (letter).

was never abandoned, he often found himself stuck fast in the fact itself. He first tried to see the particular clearly and whole, whether it was a sunset, a flower, a person, or an event. He often could not construct a general hypothesis from such data, but he always took it as his duty to examine the data to the limit of his capacity. And through such methods he has given us line drawings which, though sparse, have nevertheless often a terrible intensity and a shocking beauty. His imagination was almost entirely visual; he seldom describes for us a smell, or touch, or sound, for the world of soundless, odorless, bodiless spirit embodied in the concrete was what most interested and lured him, and the eye and the brain afforded the most direct and trustworthy entrance to such a world.

But his writing is not, therefore, lacking in emphasis or contrast. He draws his characters with an eye on their insides more than their outsides, but occasionally he gives us a sensuous detail, a lighted eye or a lovely fold of hair—so unusual, so lightly and justly sketched in—that the picture shocks and excites us. It is the pleasure of seeing a lovely woman in the company of starched old maids reading their prayer books. The escape to a sensuous delight becomes so urgent for the reader that he flies to embrace it, and it is magnified by the restraint and discipline with which it is surrounded. With the masterly touch of a few brilliantly chosen details, Hale White says in this passage[25] all he has to say about the beginning of a passionate relationship:

He stooped down, picked up a leaf, smoothed it between his fingers, and then raised his eyes. They met hers at that instant, as she lifted them and looked in his face. They were near one another, and his hands strayed towards hers till they touched. She did not withdraw; he clasped the hand, she not resisting; in another moment his arms were round her, his face was on hers, and he was swept into self-forgetfulness.[26]

This reminds us almost of the close of *Paradise Lost*, the beginning of human love and the beginning of a long atonement, and the modulation shows something of the same repressed excitement as the great adventure begins. Such artistry is achieved not by conscious striving after effect, but by the determined omission of everything irrelevant or tangential to the *idea*, the moral idea at the center of Hale White's thought and art. "The long apprenticeship has ended . . ." he writes in *More Pages*. "How much I might have gained had I taken life as an art I cannot say."[27] In his terms, being truly serious about life and being "artistic" were two different things. This scene, therefore, is not given us for its own sake. It is simply a necessary adventure on a spiritual pilgrimage, and it must

25 *C.H.*, pp. 48–49.

26 To be swept into "self-forgetfulness" is, in Hale White's language, nearly always synonymous with being in love. In view of his own psychological problems, this choice of vocabulary is particularly revealing.

27 *M.P.*, p. 258. John writes (*P.N.a.*, p. 1): "I greatly doubt whether, with his passionate devotion to truth and liberty, and his acute puritanical conscience, it would ever have been possible for him to take life as an art."

be seen swiftly and precisely, for there is still much to learn and a long way to go.

Hale White was aware of a world "infinite both ways,"[28] the awesome immensity of the universe and the limitless mystery of *this* thing or *this* individual. We have seen this duality before. We have heard him advising us to "cease the trick of contrast," for in exercising it one provokes the comparison between what is and what might be, the reality and the ideal. To bring them into union was his lifelong ambition. But Hale White could never cease making such comparisons, and it is that fact more than any other which often makes him a brilliant satirist. Of all Hale White's critics, A. L. Morton has most perceptively detected this quality in his writing:

There is an evenness, a fusing of the plain and heroic, an apparent monotony, that deceives us into thinking it is dull until we turn a corner and a flash of irony or a quietly perfect phrase reveals to us that we have climbed a hill, that, inconsiderable in itself, gives us a wide view over a country that is certainly not romantic but nevertheless infinitely desirable. . . . Like the country, the style becomes rich by refusing to spend itself upon extravagances, and in this both style and country are at the very heart of the English Puritan tradition.[29]

The lives of his characters are for the greater part spent in suffering the passage of day after day "in unbroken, level succession"[30] and not in exciting adventures, and Hale White's style shares a tempo and mood appropriate to the matter he is presenting. But in those moments when we ascend from the plain, we are often given unforgettable views across the prospect of human life and society, and it is then that the heavens and the world of men seem at the same time to be most alien and most closely joined.

We might expect, therefore, that those characters whose lives never "touched the universal"—like the Snales, Broads, and Hextons—would provoke Hale White's richest contempt. He was a student of the ways the divine and human could meet in living men, and when they did so meet he could not be ironical, for the very contrasts out of which irony is made disappeared. And to him there were "very few . . . of God's creatures to whom the supernatural does not in some way present itself. . . ."[31] But when he had to deal with a character who was not so illumined

---

[28] *C.H.*, p. 70.   [29] Morton, *Language of Men*, pp. 54–55.
[30] *C.F.*, p. 14.
[31] *Ibid.*, p. 140. His acid satire on the Anglican Church would seem to indicate that he also included that institution among those things which never "touched the universal." He writes as follows in *The Norfolk News* of August 15, 1874: "To the innumerable clubs which have sprung up in London during the last ten or fifteen years, a 'Church Club' it appears is to be added. It is to be exclusively for clerical and lay members of the Church of England. . . . It is to be presumed that there will be no sweepstakes on races, and, one would suppose, no billiard-room. Perhaps some game in lieu of billiards might be devised without its secular and semi-profane associations. Nine-pins, for example, dressed like bishops, might be provided, and the clergy might bowl at them. . . . The conversation at the club will be entirely professional. . . . Of course, it will turn upon livings, exchanges, appointments, and so forth."

and who showed no signs of amendment, his capacities for subacid satire were freely exercised. Mr. Thomas Broad met these requirements perfectly. He was the son of the man we identified earlier as the Reverend Mr. Jukes, the Bedford preacher. One of the habits of Mr. Jukes's fictional prototype was that on the day following the Sabbath he normally professed to feeling a little "Mondayish." His son Thomas, who was also preparing for the ministry, proved himself an able apprentice by telling a young lady after his *first* attempt at preaching that he too felt "a little Mondayish."[32]

But a later episode in Thomas Broad's career provoked from Hale White a more telling criticism. The young man had in his repertoire one sermon, based on the text, "The carnal mind is at enmity with God," and furbished with ideas from his college lecture notes. Before he preached this sermon a second time, however, an unfortunate event occurred. He had tried to seduce a young lady (none other than the high-minded daughter of Pauline and Zachariah) and had had his wrist slashed with scissors for his pains. He appeared in the pulpit the following Sunday, however, and found the sermon on the carnal mind still appropriate.[33]

The accident was a little inconvenient on the following Sunday, when he had to preach at Hogsbridge Corner; but as he reproduced the sermon on the carnal mind, which he knew pretty well by heart, he was not nervous. He had made it much simpler, in accordance with the advice given on a former occasion. He had struck out the metaphysics and had put in a new head—"Neither indeed *can* be." "The apostle did not merely state a fact that the carnal mind was not subject to the law of God; he said, 'Neither indeed *can* be.' Mark, my brethren, the force of the *neither can*."

Sometimes, after striking such satirical blows, Hale White feels called upon to append an explanatory comment, but this is left where it should be, without footnotes, permitting the dramatic irony to speak for itself. Hale White seldom gains his effects by raising his voice, but as we mark the force of the "*neither can*" we are reminded that his calm manner is deceptive and that there is often a surprising power in his low tones.

A dualistic habit of mind is an inevitable breeder of comparisons and contrasts. It is rather strange, therefore, that Hale White is so sparing in his use of simile and metaphor. The explanation lies in the fact that the most fundamental dualism of his life was the conflict between monism and dualism itself—between his longing for unity and his keen awareness of multiplicity. His effort to resolve this dualism manifested itself in an attempt to see the person or thing in itself and not in terms of comparisons which in turn needed explanation:

By the third, which is neither ourselves nor the object, do we recognise it. The third is the celestial light.[34]

With few exceptions, when he employs metaphor at all, he finds his stand-

---

[32] *R.T.L.*, p. 192.
[33] *Ibid.*, p. 196. See *Romans* 8: 6–8. ". . . because the mind of the flesh is enmity against God; for it is not subject to the law of God, neither indeed can it be. . . ."
[34] *M.P.*, p. 227. Cf. note 17, above.

ards of comparison in the elemental forces of nature, and draws his illustration as closely to the central nerve of life as words and his own insight will permit him.

Catharine's new birth is thus described:

It was with her as we can imagine it to be with some bud long folded in darkness which, silently in the dewy May night, loosens its leaves, and, as the sun rises, bares itself to the depths of its cup to the blue sky and the light.[35]

And later in the same book, the beginning of Catharine's repentance is marked by a strange correspondence between her own ebbing sorrow and the behavior of nature:

The clouds had passed away to the south and east, but the lightning still fired the distant horizon far beyond Eastthorpe and towards Abchurch. The sky was clearing in the west, and suddenly in a rift Arcturus, about to set, broke through and looked at her, and in a moment was again eclipsed. What strange confusion! What inexplicable contrasts! Terror and divinest beauty; the calm of the infinite interstellar space and her own anguish. . . .[36]

Hale White's comparisons are usually of this kind, brought in when nothing else will do, when his consciousness of human separateness is most acute and the individual must double up in a relationship with forces beyond himself in order to be relieved of his own isolation. Here, if the powers of nature are not in actual sympathetic correspondence with Catharine's emotions, they at least awaken in her, and in the reader, the awareness that she is part of an elemental unity. Hale White spent more effort in seeing the thing as it is in itself than as it compares with something else, but when he does detect comparisons or identifications he draws them with just precision. Simile and metaphor did not, however, come easily to his pen. We have already seen how he saved and served up Pauline's likeness to a "wild seagull in a farm-yard of peaceful, clucking, brown-speckled fowls" on two occasions,[37] and we remember the passage because such comparisons are unusual in his work. In general, it may be said that he uses these devices when he is dealing with either the very high or the very low, when he is moved by the almost wordless wonder of a deep spiritual experience, or moved to almost speechless disgust at a temporal world which must be satirized. Thus with the preacher at Zoar "The Calvinistic creed was stuck in him as in a lump of fat";[38] but he can say of Mrs. Carter, "Her presence was like the south-west wind and sunlight after long north-easterly gloom and frost."[39]

While there is no radical change between his early and later books, a tendency to get away from the sermonizing essay style to a more dramatic and objective recording of experience is apparent. Hale White's first two books are, presumably, written by a Dissenting minister from

[35] *C.F.*, p. 74.
[36] *Ibid.*, pp. 118–19.
[37] See above, p. 141.   [38] *R.T.L.*, p. 159.   [39] *Ibid.*, p. 140.

whom a pulpit vocabulary and a didactic attitude might be expected. Here we find, indeed, "prose of the center"[40]—the colorless, sober, well-filed instrument for self-examination and spiritual surgery. While even the casual reader would not doubt that the later books were also written by Mark Rutherford, he would nevertheless see the preacher becoming increasingly emancipated from his old pulpit habits and prejudices. There is a growing tendency to let the lesson be acted out without sermonizing about it, without telling the reader quite so obvioulsy where to cast his attention. There is a noticeable movement from the pious vocabulary of an orthodox Calvinist in favor of less parochial language. And there is, above all, a tendency to let dialogue carry a larger share of the dramatic burden. In *Clara Hopgood*, for example, roughly seventy-two of its one hundred eighty-eight pages are dialogue and, though much of its talk is bookish and lacking in the vernacular flavor we find in the *Revolution* and *Catharine Furze*, it often has great dramatic effectiveness. When the child, Madge, and her roommate, Selina, discuss the problem of election at their boarding school, we can hear the words and phrases of their parents being parroted in quite realistic fashion. Selina speaks:

"I suppose your father is a foreigner?"

"No, he is an Englishman."

"But if he is an Englishman you must have been baptised, or sprinkled, or immersed, and your father and mother must belong to church or chapel. I know there are thousands of wicked people who belong to neither, but they are drunkards and liars and robbers, and even they have their children christened."

"Well, he is an Englishman," said Madge smiling.

"Perhaps," said Selina timidly, "he may be—he may be—Jewish. Mamma and papa pray for the Jews every morning. They are not like other unbelievers."

"No, he is certainly not a Jew."

"What is he, then?"

"He is my papa and a very honest, good man."

"Oh my dear Madge! honesty is a broken reed. I have heard mamma say that she is more hopeful of thieves than honest people who think they are saved by works, for the thief who was crucified went to heaven, and if he had been only an honest man he never would have found the Saviour and would have gone to hell. Your father must be something."

"I can only tell you again that he is honest and good."[41]

And following this exchange there is a paragraph of comment, but it is all part of Selina's stream-of-consciousness and not conspicuously the author's. In the *Autobiography* or *Deliverance*, however, Hale White would have surrounded this parable with editorial comment. In a sense, this objectifying of experience was simply another aspect of that tendency we detected in his revisions of his *Black Notebook*: an attempt to get away from the self by immersion in nonpersonal facts and action. We see the stage by degrees being substituted for the confessional.

[40] Matthew Arnold's phrase, quoted in E. H. Jeffs, *Great Christians* (London, 1933), p. 608.

[41] *C.H.*, pp. 8–9.

But in general it must be admitted that, while Hale White's prose was capable of both great organ tones and sharp incisiveness, its range was normally not wide and its character not, in the deepest sense, poetic. It was, rather, the conversational language of a fastidious, painstaking man. Even his "copperplate"[42] handwriting was a reflection of his cautious, businesslike intensity. While he could respond to "preachments in tones" he could seldom, in his own writing, rest until those preachments were re-uttered in plain prose. He had poetic impulses but could never be a poet, for he lacked the moral confidence to be content with suggestiveness. He could, like a poet, let his characters, events, and descriptive sketches suggest meanings beyond themselves, but then—afraid of ambiguity and pressed on by the urgency of his message—he would normally destroy the suggestiveness by a prosaic examination of it. The poetic qualities we have seen in his work are fragments and not characteristic of the whole—brief ripples on a level lake. On those few occasions when Hale White tried to write poetry,[43] the labored self-consciousness he brought to the task is obvious. He could not sing, but had to talk. Among the papers Mrs. D. V. White found after his death was this partially finished attempt. We reproduce it here with its corrections as a demonstration of his addiction to the prose-writing habit and as a self-evident confession that this man could be only a passing visitor on Parnassus.

I wandered idly on the waste sea shore
And saw with careless eyes a dull, green ~~stone~~ stain
Upon a stone I picked up with disdain
For I believed it worthless for my little store
Of minerals which glittering colours wore.
I broke it on the rock where it had lain
And when I turned it o'er I found no vein
~~Of~~ Rarer ~~worth~~ than that which lies in thousands more
Dragged down and then rejected by the waves
Rounded & smooth and in to sameness worn.
I look again—one fragment chides my scorn
With purest tint of sea in sunlit caves
Of that which underneath a dark cloud laves
A tempest cleansed sky in early morn.

"Tempest cleansed sky" and "sunlit caves" show something of a Wordsworthian perception of natural beauty, but such fragments find small service in the total conception.

André Gide has said, "The work of art is the exaggeration of an idea," and the symbol of that idea is "the thing around which a book is composed."[44] Whereas Hale White would doubtless have agreed with this

[42] See *A.,* p. 4. See sample of his handwriting in *L.3F.,* p. 109.
[43] We have the record of only four poems, besides the one quoted, from Hale White's pen. One was a *jeu d'esprit* called "How Madge Was Cocky Because of Her Learning and How Her Cockiness Went Away" found among his papers. Printed poems included the one prefacing the *Autobiography* (pp. xxxvii–xxxviii); "Belief" in *More Pages* (pp. 184–85); and a hymn for a book used in William Chignell's chapel in Exeter.
[44] *Journals,* I, 76–77.

pronouncement, he would have had to confess that he achieved such central unity in paragraphs rather than in whole books and that, as he has revealed in his poem, he was prone to become almost hypnotically fascinated with fragments of experience. He once wrote in his *Black Notebook*: "The deeper the emotion, the greater the need of symbolism as a means of expression. Religion: love are examples."[45] This was with him, however, a *principle* and not a statement of his artistic practice. The structure of his books is linear rather than nuclear. They are not plotless nor do they lack thematic unity, but they incline to what we might call the *spiritual picaresque*—the records of pilgrimages made up of many single events which are remembered, cherished, and preciously registered, as if for use at some future time when suffering modern man can find one and not many symbols for the meaning of life.

His meaning is seldom imparted as the single blow of a closed fist, where emotion and conviction become part of a single action and become clear through the action itself. The action is used rather to interpret a philosophy or an idea. While few Victorian writers were more aware of the psychological complexity of man's moral life, and while few avoided oversimplification more effectively than he, his characters nevertheless play their parts for the sake of something outside themselves. Hale White does not have D. H. Lawrence's ability to make this exterior force seem the same thing as the characters' bone and flesh; they all grow toward such union, but they never seem to *be* that union. They cannot just speak and say the truth, they must always consult some oracle. And even when that oracle is their own conscience, it does not seem completely native to what would ordinarily be considered their personality. Hale White invented the action of his characters to illustrate the power and working of this monitor, but there was always a dualism between the monitor and the character. And because the action served such a purpose, Hale White always remained essentially a descriptive and not a dramatic artist; he tended to use his characters as means toward ends rather than ends in themselves. The essayist in Hale White has not, therefore, been completely metamorphosed into the perfect novelist. The abstracted idea has the final say, and we know at last that Hale White loves God more than people and wants us to do the same. The dramatic fist never quite closes.

One's liking or disaffection for Hale White's style is largely a matter of taste. Some critics have been chiefly aware of its chilling quality, and one felt that it had the effect of "lowering [his] blood pressure," calling Mark Rutherford the "apostle of low spirits, of masculine vapours, of matured green sickness."[46] But most have warmed to its strength, vigor, and austere beauty.

. . . there will always be some who will be drawn to him by the silver-point of his style, and a genius, not very fertile or energetic, but steady, penetrating, fine, at rest,

---

[45] *B.N.B.*, p. 18.
[46] "Mark Rutherford and Henry James," *The Pioneer*, May 9, 1913.

in a world of which it found three-fourths unintelligible and the remainder only just tolerable, in a kind of Calvinistic Quietism of its own devising.[47]

But whatever one's reaction may be, Hale White's originality cannot be questioned. He belonged to no school and played the "sedulous ape" to no models, but spun these words, phrases, and paragraphs out of his own inner needs and compulsions. He was a greedy borrower of ideas but not of phrases.[48] He steeped himself in the great literature of his own day—Tennyson, Wordsworth, Carlyle, and Ruskin were his particular heroes—and knew intimately such earlier writers as Virgil, Montaigne, Milton, Bunyan, Bacon, and—most especially—the authors of the Bible. But he cannot be said to have modeled himself after any one of them exclusively. That peculiar combination of scientific accuracy with moral earnestness gives his style, at times, a striking similarity to Bacon's; but in its more passionate moods it captures qualities reminiscent of Milton. And his mind was so thoroughly saturated with the vocabulary and syntax of the Bible that there is no telling where its influence begins or leaves off. He shaped his own vehicle of expression out of what may be said to have been a double impulse: to capture something of the oratorical tone and manner of a past heroic age, and to achieve a scientific precision appropriate to his own. But in his age there was little of that certainty which supported the confident articulation of the past.

To be articulate is a duty, but if the thing itself does not admit complete articulation, we must not attempt it, but be satisfied with so much definiteness as the object yields.[49]

His prose is gray with this knowledge and this regret. Oratory demands assertion, and Hale White was aware that in his day honest writing must be disciplined on the side of understatement and reserve.

Though he belonged to no school, he was drawn—almost in spite of himself—into something of the attitude toward art and life which characterized the Pre-Raphaelites and their generation, of whom he was a profound admirer (particularly Turner, Ruskin, Rossetti, Swinburne, Holman Hunt, and Arthur Hughes). Humphrey House has written:

Because the Romantic tradition said that Nature was somehow the source of important spiritual experience and because the habit of mind of the following generation, with an empirical scientific philosophy, was to dwell so lovingly on factual detail, a suspicion came about that perhaps the cause of the experience lay in the detail.[50]

[47] "The Pilgrimage of a Victorian," *Times Literary Supplement* (July 25, 1936), p. 612.

[48] See *M.S.*, p. 68: "Great is the power of a thought, but greater still is the power of a phrase, and it may be questioned whether phrase is not more directly responsible than thought for our religion, our politics, our philosophy, our love, our hatred, our hopes and fears."

[49] *L.P.*, pp. 275–76.

[50] "Man and Nature: Some Artists' Views," in *Ideas and Beliefs of the Victorians* (London, 1950), p. 226.

This encouraged a tendency to impose "feeling as an afterthought upon literalness," and Hale White's practice was precisely in this direction.

In the final passage of the *Deliverance* we can see on the one hand a straining toward oratorical effects and the expression of high emotion, and on the other a loving attention to scientific accuracy and precise fact. The synthesis of these two tensions is a piece of Doric sublimity of rare quality and power. The emotion is not, however, so much "imposed" as worked in, brought to the color of autumn leaves by the precision of a naturalist and the passion of an artist. In passages such as these Hale White perfected his art. His success came in fragments, but such fragments are themselves symbolic of the life of this man—of the particulars in which he found his confidence.[51]

We were beyond the smoke, which rested like a low black cloud over the city in the north-east, reaching a third of the way up to the zenith. The beech had changed colour, and glowed with reddish-brown fire. We sat down on a floor made of the leaves of last year. At midday the stillness was profound, broken only by the softest of whispers descending from the great trees which spread over us their protecting arms. Every now and then it died down almost to nothing, and then slowly swelled and died again, as if the gods of the place were engaged in divine and harmonious talk. By moving a little towards the external edge of our canopy we beheld the plain all spread out before us, bounded by the heights of Sussex and Hampshire. It was veiled with the most tender blue, and above it was spread a sky which was white on the horizon and deepened by degrees into azure over our heads. The exhilaration of the air satisfied Marie, although she had no playmate, and there was nothing special with which she could amuse herself. She wandered about looking for flowers and ferns, and was content. We were all completely happy.

[51] *D.*, pp. 132–33.

BIBLIOGRAPHY OF W. HALE WHITE*

I. Original Works

An Argument for an Extension of the Franchise. London: F. Farrah, 1866.

A Letter Written on the Death of Mrs. Elizabeth Street. London: W. P. Griffith
& Son, 1877. Privately printed and circulated.

The Autobiography of Mark Rutherford, Dissenting Minister. Edited by His Friend,
Reuben Shapcott. London: Trübner & Co., 1881.

A Dream of Two Dimensions. Printed for private circulation, 1884.

Hymns, Psalms & Anthems. Compiled for George's Chapel, Exeter. Exeter: *Devon
Weekly Times* Office, 1884. Hymn 119.

Mark Rutherford's Deliverance, Being the Second Part of His Autobiography.
Edited by His Friend, Reuben Shapcott. London: Trübner & Co., 1885.

The Revolution in Tanner's Lane. By Mark Rutherford. Edited by His Friend,
Reuben Shapcott. London: Trübner & Co., 1887.

The Autobiography of Mark Rutherford and Mark Rutherford's Deliverance. Edited
by His Friend, Reuben Shapcott. 2d ed: Corrected and with Additions. London:
Trübner & Co., 1888.

Miriam's Schooling and Other Papers. By Mark Rutherford. Edited by His Friend,
Reuben Shapcott. London: Kegan Paul, Trench, Trübner & Co., Ltd., 1890.

Catharine Furze. By Mark Rutherford. Edited by His Friend, Reuben Shapcott.
2 vols. London: T. Fisher Unwin, 1893.

Clara Hopgood. By Mark Rutherford. Edited by His Friend, Reuben Shapcott.
London: T. Fisher Unwin, 1896.

An Examination of the Charge of Apostasy Against Wordsworth. London: Longmans, Green & Co., 1898.

Pages from a Journal With Other Papers. By Mark Rutherford. London: T. Fisher
Unwin, 1900.

John Bunyan. London: Hodder and Stoughton, 1904.

More Pages from a Journal With Other Papers. By Mark Rutherford. London:
Henry Frowde, Oxford University Press, 1910.

The Early Life of Mark Rutherford (W. Hale White). By Himself. London: Humphrey Milford, Oxford University Press, 1913.

Last Pages from a Journal With Other Papers. By Mark Rutherford. Edited by
His Wife. London: Humphrey Milford, Oxford University Press, 1915.

II. Works Edited and Translated by W. Hale White

*Ethic Demonstrated in Geometrical Order and Divided into Five Parts, which treat
I. Of God. II. Of the Nature and Origin of the Mind. III. Of the Origin and
Nature of the Affects. IV. Of Human Bondage, or of the Strength of the Affects.
V. Of the Power of the Intellect, or of Human Liberty. By Benedict De Spinoza.*
Translated from the Latin By William Hale White. London: Trübner & Co.,
1883.

*Tractatus de Intellectus Emendatione et de Via, Qua Optime in Veram Rerum Cog-
nitionem Dirigitur.* Translated from the Latin of Benedict De Spinoza By W.
Hale White. Translation revised by Amelia Hutchison Stirling, M.A. (Edin.).
London: T. Fisher Unwin, 1895.

* See *Mark Rutherford: A Short Bibliography of the First Editions,* by Simon
Nowell-Smith. Supplement to *The Bookman's Journal,* 1930.

The Inner Life of the House of Commons. By William White. Edited with a Preface by Justin McCarthy, M.P., and with an Introduction by the Author's Son. 2 vols. London : T. Fisher Unwin, 1897.

A Description of the Wordsworth & Coleridge Manuscripts in the Possession of Mr T. Norton Longman. Edited with Notes by W. Hale White. London : Longmans, Green & Co., 1897.

Coleridge's Poems, A Facsimile Reproduction of the Proofs and MSS. of Some of the Poems. Edited by the late James Dykes Campbell . . . With Preface and Notes by W. Hale White. Westminster : Archibald Constable and Co., 1899.

Selections from Dr. Johnson's "Rambler." Edited, with Preface and Notes by W. Hale White. Oxford : at the Clarendon Press, 1907.

The Life of John Sterling. By Thomas Carlyle, With an Introduction by W. Hale White. London : Henry Frowde, Oxford University Press, 1907.

III. LETTERS (Incomplete)

Letters to Three Friends. London : Humphrey Milford, Oxford University Press, 1924.

Correspondence with Thomas Hutchinson, typescript. With Notes by his Second Son, 1939. These letters are now in the Brotherton Library, Leeds.

Letters Written to his Second Son and his Second Son's Wife, typescript. Copied extracts of letters between 1882 and 1912.

52 letters to Mr. and Mrs. Horace Smith, Dorothy's parents, between January 1908 and February 1913. Unpublished. In possession of Mrs. D. V. White.

49 letters to Mabel Marsh between May 1897 and August 1910. Unpublished. In possession of Mrs. D. V. White. Seven letters from Mabel Marsh were included in *L.3F.,* but these are not among them.

About 30 letters to Lady Robert Cecil in her possession, written between 1907 and 1913. Unpublished. These I have not examined.

Letter to William Chignell dated October 22, 1875. From a copy in possession of Mrs. D. V. White.

3 letters to Ernest Coleridge, dated June 27, 1896 ; June 30, 1896 ; July 10, 1896. Unpublished.

1 letter to Rose Paul, February 18, 1900. In possession of Miss Mary Theodora Hale-White.

1 letter sent to "The Book of the Exhibition" on May 30, 1911. Copy in possession of Mrs. D. V. White. About his notions for building a house.

1 letter to William Dean Howells, dated February 25, 1886. In Howells' collection, Houghton Library, Harvard.

2 letters to Henry Arthur Jones. Published in Doris Arthur Jones, *The Life and Letters of Henry Arthur Jones.* London : Victor Gollanez, Ltd., 1930, pp. 76, 92–93, 111.

24 letters to his eldest son and eldest son's wife between March 2, 1874, and August 24, 1911. Copies or excerpts in *P.N.b.,* pp. 21–28.

1 letter to his second son, dated November 3, 1891. Copy in *P.N.b.,* p. 29.

2 letters from Hale White to his father dated May 3, 1853, and March 6, 1852. Copies in *P.N.b.,* pp. 29–31.

7 letters to George Jacob Holyoake. Copies or excerpts in *P.N.b.,* pp. 32–34. From July 10, 1865, to January 20, 1882.

1 letter to George Mayes, March 7, 1882. Copy in *S.B.a.*

IV. BOOKS CONTAINING LETTERS AND COMMENT

The Groombridge Diary. By Dorothy V. White. London : Humphrey Milford, Oxford University Press, 1924.

Middle Age, an Autobiography, 1885–1932. By Gladys Ellen Easedale. London : Constable & Co., Ltd., 1935.

V. Short Contributions by Hale White in Books

Selected English Short Stories (Nineteenth Century). 1st Series, with an Introduction by Hugh Walker. London: Humphrey Milford, Oxford University Press, 1916. Contains "Mr. Whittaker's Retirement," pp. 301–12, first printed in *M.P.*, pp. 87 ff.

Selected English Short Stories (XIX and XX Centuries). 2d Series. London: Humphrey Milford, Oxford University Press, 1921. Contains "Sweetness of a Man's Friend," pp. 169–75, first printed in *The Nation* (September 24, 1910) and reprinted in *L.P.*, p. 37 ff.; and "An Afternoon Walk in October," pp. 1–3, first printed in *The Nation* (May 18, 1912) and reprinted in *L.P.*, pp. 32 ff.

Selected Modern English Essays. Edited by Humphrey Milford. London: Humphrey Milford, Oxford University Press, 1925. Contains "The Break-Up of a Great Drought," pp. 1–3, first printed in *P.J.*, pp. 28 ff.; and "Judas Iscariot— What Can Be Said for Him?" pp. 3–9, first printed in *P.J.*, pp. 87 ff.

The Imperial Dictionary of Universal Biography. 6 vols. Edited by John Francis Waller. London: William Mackenzie, 1857–66. Contributions by Hale White are as follows: "Life of Benjamin Franklin," II, 478–80 (the principal contribution), and lives of P. S. M. Galba, S. S. Galba, S. S. Galba, A. Gallus, C. A. Gallus, C. S. Gallus, David Garrick, E. M. Garrick, T. Gaza, Saint Genevieve, M. A. A. Gordianus, M. A. P. F. Gordianus, Gorgias (III, 532, 544, 562–63; IV, 577, 585, 677–78, 681).

VI. Translations of Hale White's Books

Vlastni Zivotopis Marka Rutherforda. Vydal Jeho Pritel Ruben Shapcott. Autoris, Preklad Dle 12. Vydani Anglickeho Originalu. Praze: Nakladem J. Otty, 1905.

VII. Hale White's Regular Journalistic Contributions*

The Morning Star (London), "Below the Gangway," from February 13, 1865, to July 10, 1865 (every Monday).

The Aberdeen Herald, "Metropolitan Notes," from May 11, 1861, to January 27, 1872 (every Saturday).

The Birmingham Post & Journal,† "Sketches in Parliament," from February 3, 1866, to January 31, 1880.

The Rochdale Observer, "Letters by a Radical," from January 19, 1867, to March 30, 1872 (every Saturday).

The Nonconformist, "Sketches in Parliament" and "How it Strikes a Stranger," from February 14, 1872, to August 6, 1873 (occasional contributions).

The Norfolk News, "Our London Letter," from March 2, 1872, to March 17, 1883 (every Saturday).

VIII. Private Manuscripts by Hale White

The Dorothy Book. An occasional diary kept between 1907 and 1913, originally intended as a companion to *The Groombridge Diary*, in which Hale White kept Dorothy's letters and recorded thoughts pertaining to their relationship.

---

* *The Morning Star* was examined at the British Museum Newspaper Library at Colindale; *The Nonconformist* at Dr. William's Library, London. All the others were found in the files of the newspapers themselves. (*The Aberdeen Herald* is, however, also at Colindale.)

† This paper changed its name several times. It began as *The Birmingham Journal;* on Feb. 20, 1869, it amalgamated and became *The Birmingham Daily Post and Journal* for the Saturday issue, which was the one to which Hale White contributed; on Nov. 18, 1871, its name became *The Birmingham Daily Post*, which it still maintains. Sometimes his letters were called "Vacation Letters" (during recesses).

The Black Notebook. A small memoranda book in which, between 1894 and 1904, Hale White recorded his private thoughts and emotions and made comments on and quotations from his reading.

The White Notebook. The same continued until near his death. This has a white cover. Of the two it is the less complete and less valuable.

Scrapbooks. Two large folio-size books full of clippings from newspapers and magazines of things which particularly interested Hale White. Many of his own periodical writings are included.

The 1910 Manuscript. A statement by Hale White of the nature of his relationship with his second wife (5 pages destroyed by Mrs. White).

IX. Hale White's Unpublished Essays and Short Stories

"Courage." A short story written October 23, 1908, for Mrs. D. V. White's Bible class.

"Romney Marsh: Mozart." Written between 1907 and 1912. (Revised version in *M.P.*, pp. 154–55.)

"The End." Written between 1907 and 1912.

"A Waking Dream." Written about 1910.

"History." Written between 1907 and 1912.

An untitled short story about a serving man stealing victuals.

X. Hale White's Periodical Writings

Letter from R. H. Theobald, F. M. White, and W. H. White on the expulsion from New College, *The Nonconformist*, March 31, 1852. Reprinted in *To Think or Not to Think*, pp. 16 ff.

"Births, Deaths, and Marriages," *Chamber's Journal*, IX (March 6, 1858), 155–57.

"The Priesthood *versus* the Human Mind and Science," *The Exeter and Plymouth Gazette*, January 6, 1864. Letter.

"Modern Houses," *The Daily Telegraph*, October 16, 1865. Letter.

"Walks out of London. Caterham," *The Working Man*, No. 13 (n.s.) (September 29, 1866), pp. 152–53.

"Walks out of London. Carshalton," *The Working Man*, No. 14 (n.s.) (October 6, 1866), pp. 164–65.

"Walks out of London. Epsom to Leith Hill," *The Working Man*, No. 15 (n.s.) (October 13, 1866), pp. 176–77.

"Why Do We Differ About Governor Eyre?" *The Working Man*, No. 17 (n.s.) (October 27, 1866), p. 199.

Letter to the editor, "Why Do We Differ About Governor Eyre?" *The Working Man*, No. 22 (n.s.) (December 1, 1866), p. 262. Reply to letter to the editor by T. J. Dunning of 5 Racquet Court, Fleet Street, in *The Working Man*, No. 19 (n.s.) (November 10, 1866), p. 225.

"Isabella and the Pot of Basil," *The Aberdeen Herald*, May 2, 1868.

"House-Building," *The Spectator*, XLII (January 30, 1869), 137–38. Letter. Also reprinted in *The Birmingham Journal*, February 6, 1869.

"Banstead Downs," *The Times* (London), October 31, 1876. Letter.

"House-Building," *The Spectator*, L (January 27, 1877), 113. Letter. Reprinted in Ruskin's *Fors Clavigera*.

"Notes on Shelley's Birthplace," *Macmillan's Magazine*, XXXIX (March 1879), 461–65.

"A Proposal to the House of Commons," *The Spectator*, LIII (March 6, 1880), 301.

"The Genius of Walt Whitman," *The Secular Review** (March 20, 1880).

* I have been unable to locate this magazine in this year at any of the following libraries: British Museum, Bodleian (Oxford), London Library, Harvard, New York Public, Library of Congress. I read the articles originally in scrapbooks where volumes and pages were not indicated.

"Froude and the Bedford Modern School," *Notes & Queries*, 6th series (April 17, 1880), p. 313.

"Marcus Antoninus," *The Secular Review* (July 3, 1880), pp. 5–6.

"Ixion," *The Secular Review* (September 11, 1880).

"Heathen Ethics," *The Secular Review* (November 27, 1880).

"Byron, Goethe, and Mr. Matthew Arnold," *The Contemporary Review*, XL (August 1881), 179–85. Reprinted in *P.J.*, pp. 133 ff.

"A Mysterious Portrait," *The Birmingham Daily Post*, December 24, 1881. Reprinted in *D.*, pp. 173–83.

"The Late Mr. White," *The Bedfordshire Mercury*, March 18, 1882. Letter.

"Mr. John Francis," *The Athenaeum*,* No. 2842 (April 15, 1882), p. 476. Obituary.

"What Mr. Emerson Owed to Bedfordshire," *The Athenaeum*, No. 2846 (May 13, 1882), pp. 602–3.

Letter on the use of the term "affect" in his translation of Spinoza's *Ethic*, *The Athenaeum*, No. 2922 (October 27, 1883), p. 534.

Letter on the inaccuracies in Knight's edition of Wordsworth, *The Athenaeum*, No. 2995 (March 21, 1885), p. 378.

"Stray Dogs," *The Herald* (London), November 3, 1885. Letter, signed "X."

Letter on the subject of George Eliot's respectability, *The Athenaeum*, No. 3031 (November 28, 1885), p. 702.

"A Victory on the Downs," *The Pall Mall Gazette*, August 16, 1886.

Letter on the inaccuracies in Knight's edition of Wordsworth, *The Athenaeum*, No. 3187 (November 24, 1888), p. 700.

"War Office Reform," *The Times* (London), April 21, 1890. Letter.

Notes on Turner's painting, "The Téméraire," *The Athenaeum*, No. 3336 (October 3, 1891), p. 459. Letter.

"The Téméraire Tugged to her Last Berth," *The Athenaeum*, No. 3341 (November 7, 1891), p. 623. Letter.

"Our Debt to France," *The Bookman* (London), II (August 1892), 139–40.

"The Cheap Trippers," *The Spectator*, LXIX (November 5, 1892), 646. Letter.

"Two Martyrs," *The Bookman* (London), III (February 1893), 153–54.

"Dr. John Chapman," *The Athenaeum*, No. 3502 (December 8, 1894), pp. 790–91.

"The Wilsonian Theory of Sunspots," *The Journal of the British Astronomical Association*, V (February 23, 1895), 218.

"The Growth of a Legend," *The Athenaeum*, No. 3517 (March 23, 1895), pp. 378–79.

"A Good Edition of Wordsworth," *St. James's Gazette*, January 9, 1896. Review of Oxford Wordsworth, ed. Thomas Hutchinson.

"Admiralty Contracts," *The Times* (London), April 2, 1896. Letter.

Review of *The Poetical Works of William Wordsworth* (edited by William Knight, Vols. I and II, Macmillan & Co.), *The Athenaeum*, No. 3575 (May 2, 1896), pp. 575–76.

"Spinoza's Doctrine of the Relationship between Mind and Body," *The International Journal of Ethics*, VI (July 4, 1896), 515–18.

"Mark Rutherford," *The British Weekly*, XX (July 30, 1896), 232. Letter signed "Reuben Shapcott."

"Wordsworth's 'Convention of Cintra,'" *The Athenaeum*, No. 3591 (August 22, 1896), pp. 258–59.

"Mr. White's Parliamentary Sketches," *The Weekly Sun*, September 20, 1896. Letter.

Review of *The Poetical Works of William Wordsworth* (edited by William Knight, Vols. III–VII, Macmillan & Co.), *The Athenaeum*, No. 3609 (December 26, 1896), pp. 893–94.

"Coleridge on Spinoza," *The Athenaeum*, No. 3630 (May 22, 1897), pp. 680–81. Unpublished notes by Hale White.

* Volume numbers of this periodical are not given.

Review of *The Poetical Works of William Wordsworth* (edited by William Knight, Vol. VIII, Macmillan & Co.), *The Athenaeum*, No. 3648 (September 25, 1897), pp. 412–13.

Review of *Poems in Two Volumes* by William Wordsworth (reprinted from the Original Edition of 1807, edited by Thomas Hutchinson, M.A., Nutt.), *The Athenaeum*, No. 3655 (November 13, 1897), p. 672.

"An Ancestor of Emerson," *The British Weekly*, XXIII (March 17, 1898), 421–22. Reprinted as "Peter Bulkley" in *L.P.*, pp. 194 ff.

"William Gilbert," *The Athenaeum*, No. 3676 (April 9, 1898), pp. 468–69.

Review of *Lyrical Ballads by William Wordsworth and S. T. Coleridge, 1798* (edited, with Certain Poems of 1798 and an Introduction and Notes, by Thomas Hutchinson, Duckworth & Co.), *The Athenaeum*, No. 3690 (July 16, 1898), pp. 87–88.

"An Accomplished Scholar," *Sketch*, XXIII (September 7, 1898), 290.

"Unaccountable," supplement to *The Hastings and St. Leonard's Times*, December 3, 1898. Reprinted in *L.P.*, pp. 209 ff.

"A Forgotten Book," *The British Weekly*, XXV (December 8, 1898), 141–42. Reprinted in *L.P.*, pp. 153 ff.

"Carlyle and Bacon," *The Athenaeum*, No. 3732 (May 6, 1899), p. 565. Letter.

"War Office Reform," *The Times* (London), January 24, 1900.

"The Author of Mark Rutherford on National Affairs," *The Bedfordshire Times and Independent*, January 4, 1901. Letter.

"Godwin and Wordsworth," *The Pilot*, III (April 20, 1901), 491–92. Reprinted in *M.P.*, pp. 205 ff.

"A Note or Two for Readers of Wordsworth," *The Bookman* (London), XX (June 1901), 83–85. Reprinted in *L.P.*, pp. 164 ff.

"Misleading Unions," *The Pilot*, IV (July 20, 1901), 80–81. Letter.

"Tolstoi's Astronomy," *The Athenaeum*, No. 3870 (December 28, 1901), p. 879. Letter.

Review of Joachim's *Study of the Ethics of Spinoza, The Bookman* (London), XXI (January 1902), 135–37.

"Caleb Morris," *The British Weekly*, XXXI (March 6, 1902), 532. Reprinted in *L.P.*, pp. 244 ff.

"Edward Fitzgerald on Carlyle's and Tennyson's Astronomy," *The Athenaeum*, No. 3881 (March 15, 1902), p. 388. Letter.

"Coleridge's Astronomy," *The Manchester Guardian*, May 3, 1902. Letter.

"The Habits of the Tripper," *The Spectator*, LXXXIX (July 12, 1902), 52. Letter.

"Sightseers: Their Rights and Duties," *The Spectator*, LXXXIX (July 19, 1902), 78–79.

"George Eliot as I Knew Her," *The Bookman* (London), XXII (August 1902), 159–60. Reprinted in *L.P.*, pp. 131 ff.

" 'The Well-Attired Woodbine,' " *The Pilot*, VI (October 4, 1902), 351–52.

Unpublished Letters from Dorothy Wordsworth to Mrs. Clarkson together with An Unpublished Letter to Mrs. Clarkson from William Wordsworth, edited by William Hale White, in *The Athenaeum*, No, 3978 (January 23, 1904), pp. 112–13; No. 3979 (January 30, 1904), pp. 145–47; No. 3980 (February 6, 1904), pp. 176–77; No. 3981 (February 13, 1904), pp. 211–12; No. 3982 (February 20, 1904), p. 241; No. 3983 (February 27, 1904), pp. 270–71.

"How Can We Tell?" *The Speaker*, IX (February 20, 1904), 496–97. Review of J. J. Fahie's *Galileo: His Life and Work*.

"A Monument to Joan of Arc," *The Speaker*, X (January 28, 1905), 415–16. Reprinted in *L.P.*, pp. 214 ff.

"Trades-Unionism in the Civil Services," *The Speaker*, XII (July 15, 1905), 366–67. Letter.

"Carlyle on Parliamentary Reform," Supplement to *The British Weekly*, XXXIX (November 2, 1905), 113–14.

"Mr. W. S. Lilly and the *Times*," *The Speaker*, XIII (February 10, 1906), 457–58. Letter.

"The Golden Nail," *The Rochdale Observer*, February 17, 1906.

"American Advertising," *The Athenaeum*, No. 4102 (June 9, 1906), pp. 701–2.

"The Téméraire," *The Times* (London), December 11, 1906.

Review of *Spinoza: Éthique* (Traduction inédite du Comte Henri de Boulainvilliers, publiée avec une Introduction et des Notes par F. Colonna d'Istria, Professeur de Philosophie au Lycée Carnot, Paris, Armand Colin), *The Athenaeum*, No. 4171 (October 5, 1907), pp. 398–99.

"The Scottish Journal of Dorothy Wordsworth," *The Scottish Review*, XLIII (November 28, 1907), 512–13. Reprinted in *L.P.*, pp. 234 ff.

"A Study in 'Overlooking,'" *The Nation*, III (July 11, 1908), 519–20. Review of Mrs. D. V. White's novel, *Miss Mona*.

"The Maid," *The Nation*, V (April 24, 1909), 117–18.

"Frank Burnet," *The Nation*, V (July 10, 1909), 532–34. Review of Mrs. D. V. White's novel of this title.

"A Homemade Religion," *The Nation*, VI (January 1, 1910), 566–67. Reprinted in *P.J.*, pp. 320 ff.

"Faith," *The Nation*, VII (April 2, 1910), 13–14. Reprinted in *P.J.*, pp. 326 ff.

"The Sweetness of a Man's Friend," *The Nation*, VII (September 24, 1910), 906–7. Reprinted in *L.P.*, pp. 37 ff.

"Johnson," *The Nation*, VIII (October 22, 1910), 165–66. Reprinted in *L.P.*, pp. 72 ff.

"Captain James's 'Strange and Dangerous Voyage,'" *The Nation*, VIII (January 28, 1911), 715–17. Reprinted in *L.P.*, pp. 53 ff.

Letter on St. James's Park, *The Times* (London), April 4, 1911.

"An Omitted Passage in the 'Pilgrim's Progress,'" *The Nation*, IX (May 13, 1911), 250–51. Reprinted in *L.P.*, pp. 47 ff.

"James Bradley and the Stars," *The Nation*, IX (August 19, 1911), 738–40. Reprinted in *L.P.*, pp. 19 ff.

"The Text of Wordsworth," *The Nation*, X (October 28, 1911), 172–73.

"F-E-D," *The Nation*, X (January 27, 1912), p. 693. Reprinted in *L.P.*, pp. 67 ff.

"An Afternoon Walk in October," *The Nation*, XI (May 18, 1912), 247–48. Reprinted in *L.P.*, pp. 32 ff.

"Notes on Shelley's Birthplace," *The Bookman* (London), XLII (June 1912), 62–71. Reprinted in *L.P.*, pp. 219 ff.

"The Fire at Milldeep Manor," *The Nation*, XII (February 15, 1913), 815–16. Reprinted in *L.P.*, pp. 81 ff.

"The Love of Woman," *The Nation*, XIII (June 21, 1913), 453–55. Reprinted in *L.P.*, pp. 81 ff.

"Revolution," *The Nation*, XIII (August 9, 1913), 708–9. Reprinted in *L.P.*, pp. 88 ff.

XI. MISCELLANEOUS

Comments Made Upon Sir James Fitzjames Stephen's Book "Liberty, Equality, Fraternity." By William Hale White. Annotated by John Hale White. This is a study of Hale White's copious marginalia and comment upon them by Hale White's second son. Typescript.

CRITICAL BIBLIOGRAPHY

I. MAJOR CRITICAL WORKS

BUCHMANN, URSULA CLARE. *William Hale White (Mark Rutherford). The Problem of Self-Adjustment in a World of Changing Values.* University of Zürich thesis. Zürich: Juris-Verlag, 1950.

KLINKE, HANS. *William Hale White, Versuch einer Biographie.* Griefswald dissertation. Frankfurt, 1930.

MASSINGHAM, H. W. "Memorial Introduction" to *The Autobiography of Mark Rutherford.* London: T. Fisher Unwin, 1923.

NICOLL, WILLIAM ROBERTSON. *Introduction to the Novels of Mark Rutherford.* Pamphlet. London: T. Fisher Unwin, 1924.

NICOLL, WILLIAM ROBERTSON. *Memories of Mark Rutherford.* London: T. Fisher Unwin, 1924.

OKO, A. S. *William Hale White, 1831–1913 in Dissertatio ex Chronici Spinozani, Tomo Secundo, Separatim Edita.* Hagae Comitis, 1922. This author was connected with the Hebrew Union College, Cincinnati, Ohio.

SILLÉN, ERICK. *Rutherford and the Conflict of Ideas in England after 1860.* University of Uppsala dissertation. Uppsala, Sweden, 1947.

SMITH, HENRY ARTHUR. *The Life and Thought of William Hale White.* University of Birmingham thesis. Birmingham, 1938.

TAYLOR, A. E. "The Novels of Mark Rutherford," *Essays and Studies by Members of the English Association,* Vol. V. Oxford at the Clarendon Press, 1914.

WARNER, ALAN JOHN. *Mark Rutherford, A Victorian Pilgrim. A Study of the Mind and Writings of William Hale White (1831–1913).* University of the Witwatersrand thesis. Johannesburg, South Africa, April 1949.

SMITH, WALTER R. *The Novels of Mark Rutherford.* University of California thesis. Berkeley, California, 1952.

STONE, WILFRED H. *Religion and Art of William Hale White ("Mark Rutherford").* Harvard University thesis. Cambridge, Massachusetts, 1950.

WOLFF, RENATE CHRISTINE. *Currents in Naturalistic English Fiction, 1880–1900: With Special Emphasis on "Mark Rutherford."* Bryn Mawr thesis. Bryn Mawr, Pennsylvania, 1951.

WRIGHT, JOHN ERNEST THORINGTON. *William Hale White (Mark Rutherford).* University of Pittsburgh thesis. Pittsburgh, Pennsylvania, 1932.

Works in Progress

STEVENS, R. T. H. *Contemporary Criticism of Gissing and Mark Rutherford as Novelists, 1870–1900.* Christ's College thesis, Cambridge University. Cambridge, England.

STOCK, IRVIN. *A Critical Revaluation of the Works of Mark Rutherford.* Columbia University thesis. New York.

II. PRIVATE STUDIES

Notes about W. Hale White (Mark Rutherford), by his Eldest Son, W. Hale White, May 1932, typescript.

William Hale White "Mark Rutherford" 1831–1913. Notes by his Second Son. Geneva, 1931, typescript.

III. SELECTED LIST OF BOOKS REFERRING TO HALE WHITE

BAKER, ERNEST A. *The History of the English Novel.* London: H. F. & G. Witherby, Ltd., 1938. IX, Chap. 3, "Mark Rutherford and Others," 97–121.

BARINE, ARVÈDE. *Essais et Fantaisies.* Paris: Librairie Hachette et Cie., 1888. "Histoire d'un homme Médiocre," pp. 47–75.

BENNETT, ARNOLD. *The Journal of Arnold Bennett, 1911–1920, 1921–1928.* New York: The Viking Press, 1933. II, 100; III, 27–29.

BULLETT, GERALD. *George Eliot, Her Life and Books.* New Haven: Yale University Press, 1948. Pp. 66–68.

CAZAMIAN, MADELEINE L. *Le Roman et les Idées en Angleterre. L'Influence de la Science (1860–1890).* Doctoral thesis, University of Strasbourg. Strasbourg, 1923. "The Tragedy of Doubt: Mark Rutherford and Robert Elsmere." Pp. 263–74 and pp. 11 n., 52, 62, 288, 368, 370.

CRUSE, AMY. *The Englishman and his Books in the Early Nineteenth Century.* New York: Thomas Y. Cromwell Co., 1930. Pp. 55–56, 154, 161, 233.

CRUSE, AMY. *The Victorians and their Books.* London: George Allen & Unwin, Ltd., 1936. Pp. 74, 114, 129, 150, 175, 194, 200, 331, 419.

DARLOW, T. H. *William Robertson Nicoll, Life and Letters.* London: Hodder & Stoughton, 1924. Pp. 76, 332, 366, 418.

DAWSON, W. J. *The Makers of English Fiction.* London and Edinburgh: Fleming H. Revell Co., 1905. "The Religious Novel in England," pp. 283–89.

DAWSON, W. J. *Quest and Vision.* London: Hodder & Stoughton, 1892. "The New Realism," pp. 205–17.

DE VOOYS, SIJNA. *The Psychological Element in the English Sociological Novel of the 19th Century.* University of Donderdag thesis. Amsterdam: H. J. Paris, 1927. Pp. 117–29.

Dictionary of National Biography, 1912–1921. Oxford University Press, 1927. Pp. 573–74.

FARRAR, REV. C. F. *Old Bedford, The Town of Sir William Harper, John Bunyan and John Howard the Philanthropist.* Bedford: F. R. Hockliffe; London: Simpkin, Marshall & Co., Ltd., 1926. Pp. 260–62.

FINDLATER, JANE HELEN. *Stones from a Glass House.* London: James Nisbet & Co., Ltd., 1904. "On Religious Novels," pp. 33–64.

FORD, FORD MADOX. *The English Novel from the Earliest Days to the Death of Joseph Conrad.* Philadelphia and London: J. B. Lippincott Co., 1929. P. 109.

FORSTER, E. M. *Aspects of the Novel.* London: Edward Arnold & Co., 1927. P 184.

FOX, RALPH. *The Novel & the People.* New York: International Publishers, 1945. Pp. 93–94.

GIDE, ANDRÉ. *The Journals of André Gide.* Translated from the French and annotated by Justin O'Brien. 3 vols. New York: Knopf & Co., 1949. I, 306; II, 99–100, 101, 117, 120–21, 125, 132 n, 184; III, 337–38.

GIDE, ANDRÉ. *Voyage au Congo, Carnets de Route.* Paris: Librairie Gallemard, 1927. P. 213.

Great Christians, edited by R. S. Forman. London: Ivor Nicholson and Watson, 1933. "Hale White, 1831–1913" by Ernest H. Jeffs, pp. 607–15.

GUERARD, ALBERT, JR. *Joseph Conrad.* New York: New Directions, 1947. Pp. 37–38.

HALDANE, ELIZABETH S. *George Eliot and Her Times.* London: Hodder & Stoughton, 1927. Pp. 77–78, 306–7.

H.W.M. A Selection from the Writings of H. W. Massingham. With Preface and Notes by H. J. Massingham. London: Jonathan Cape, Ltd., 1924. Pp. 156, 165–71.

HOLYOAKE, GEORGE JACOB. *Bygones Worth Remembering.* 2 vols. New York: E. P. Dutton & Co., 1905. I, 24, 274.

JONES, DORIS ARTHUR. *The Life and Letters of Henry Arthur Jones.* London: Victor Gollancz Ltd., 1930. Pp. 76, 92–93, 111.

LAWRENCE, D. H. *The Letters of D. H. Lawrence.* Edited with an Introduction by Aldous Huxley, New York: The Viking Press, 1932. Pp. 82–83.

A Literary History of England. Edited by Albert C. Baugh. New York: Appleton-Century-Crofts, Inc., 1948. Pp. 1488–89.

MAUROIS, ANDRÉ. *Aspects of Biography.* Translated from the French by Sidney Castle Roberts. New York: D. Appleton & Co., 1929. P. 167.

McCABE, JOSEPH. *Life and Letters of George Jacob Holyoake,* 2 vols. London: Watts & Co., 1908. I, 355; II, 307.

MORTON, A. L. *Language of Men.* London: Cobbett Press, 1945. "The Last Puritan," pp. 49–57.

MURRY, JOHN MIDDLETON. *To the Unknown God, Essays towards a Religion.* London: Jonathan Cape, Ltd., 1924. "The Religion of Mark Rutherford," pp. 260–75.

PEEL, ALBERT. *The Congregational Two Hundred.* London: The Independent Press, 1948. Pp. 212–13.

ROTH, LEON. *Spinoza.* London: Ernest Benn Ltd., 1929. Pp. 26, 35, 163.

RUSKIN, JOHN. *The Works of John Ruskin.* Library edition, edited by E. T. Cook and Alexander Wedderburn. London: George Allen, 1907. XXIX, *Fors Clavigera,* 79–80. XXXIV, *On the Old Road,* 386 n. XXXV, *Praeterita*—I, 49 n. XXXV, *Dilecta,* 582 ff.

SECCOMBE, THOMAS. *An Introductory Survey* to *The House of Cobwebs* by George Gissing. New York: E. P. Dutton & Co., 1906. Pp. vii–viii.

SÉLINCOURT, ERNEST DE. *Wordsworthian and Other Studies.* Oxford, at the Clarendon Press, 1947. Pp. 184–85.

SPERRY, WILLARD L. *Wordsworth's Anti-Climax.* Harvard Studies in English, Vol. XIII. Cambridge, Massachusetts: Harvard University Press, 1935. Pp. 49, 70.

SPERRY, WILLARD L. *"Yes But——" The Bankruptcy of Apologetics.* New York and London: Harper & Bros., 1931. Pp. 4, 18.

WILLEY, BASIL. *The Eighteenth Century Background, Studies on the Idea of Nature in the Thought of the Period.* London: Chatto & Windus, 1946. Pp. 270–72, 290–91.

WILSON, DAVID ALEC. *Carlyle at His Zenith.* London: Kegan Paul, Trench, Trübner & Co., Ltd., 1927. P. 251.

WILSON, DAVID ALEC, AND MACARTHUR, DAVID WILSON. *Carlyle in Old Age (1865–1881).* New York: E. P. Dutton & Co., 1934. Pp. 156–58.

WILSON, DAVID ALEC. *Carlyle to Threescore-and-Ten (1853–1865).* London: Kegan Paul, Trench, Trübner & Co., Ltd., 1929. P. 586.

IV. SELECTED CRITICISM IN MAGAZINES

The Academy:

"Spinoza's Ethics," XXIV (September 15, 1883), 177. Review.

"Miriam's Schooling," XXXVIII (August 2, 1890), 88. Review.

NOBLE, JAMES ASHCROFT. "Catharine Furze," XLV (March 10, 1894), 206. Review.

BENN, ALFRED W. "Spinoza's Tractatus de Intellectus Emendatione," XLVII (June 22, 1895), 520–21. Review.

COTTERELL, GEORGE. "Clara Hopgood," L (August 15, 1896), 112. Review.

"The Inner Life of the House of Commons—1860–1870," LI (June 5, 1897), 587. Review.

Brief mention of *Description of Wordsworth and Coleridge MSS.*, LI (June 5, 1897), 591.

"Description of Wordsworth and Coleridge MSS.," LII (July 17, 1897), 43–44. Review.

C. "The Art of Mark Rutherford," LVI (February 4, 1899), 161–62.

"Spinoza's Ethic," LVII (July 1, 1899), 7–8. Review.

DAVIS, OSWALD H. "Mark Rutherford. I. Novels of Men, and Philosophy," LXXXIX (August 7, 1915), 86–87.
DAVIS, OSWALD H. "Mark Rutherford. II. Novels of Women, and Technique," LXXXIX (August 14, 1915), 102–3.

Accent:
STOCK, IRVIN. "André Gide, William Hale White, and the Protestant Tradition," XII (Autumn 1953), 205–15.

The Adelphi:
MURRY, JOHN MIDDLETON, "The Religion of Mark Rutherford," II (July 1924), 93–104.

Anglia Beiblatt:
CAZAMIAN, L. "Hans Klinke, William Hale White (Mark Rutherford)," XLIII (October 1932), 311–13. Review.

Anglica. Rivista di Studi Inglesi e Americani:
PRAZ, MARIO. "L'Autobiografia di Mark Rutherford," I (April–June, 1946), 49–65.

The Athenaeum:
"*The Autobiography of Mark Rutherford, Dissenting Minister,*" No. 2791 (April 23, 1881), p. 555. Review.
"*Spinoza's Ethic.* Translated by W. H. White," No. 2921 (October 20, 1883), p. 493. Review.
"*Mark Rutherford's Deliverance,* etc.," No. 2998 (April 11, 1885), p. 469. Review.
An erratum notice for the *Deliverance,* No. 3000 (April 25, 1885), p. 537.
"The Revolution in Tanner's Lane," No. 3103 (April 16, 1887), p. 510. Review.
"Miriam's Schooling and Other Papers," No. 3274 (July 26, 1890), p. 124. Review.
"Catharine Furze," No. 3460 (February 17, 1894), p. 209. Review.
HUTCHINSON, THOMAS. "The Eversley Wordsworth: Errata in Vol. II," No. 3576 (May 9, 1896), p. 620. Reply to review by Hale White in *The Athenaeum* of May 2, 1896.
"Clara Hopgood," No. 3590 (August 15, 1896), p. 220. Review.
"An Examination of the Charge of Apostasy against Wordsworth," No. 3678 (April 23, 1898), p. 528. Review.
"Our Library Table," No. 3819 (January 5, 1901), p. 15. Review of *L.P.*
"Literary Gossip," No. 3820 (Janary 12, 1901), p. 53. Errata in *P.J.* review.
Notice of the new popular edition, No. 3997 (June 4, 1904), p. 723.
"A New Popular Edition of the Works of Mark Rutherford," No. 4004 (July 23, 1904), pp. 101–2. Review.
"John Bunyan," No. 4039 (March 25, 1905), p. 368. Review.
"William Hale White," No. 4456 (March 22, 1913), p. 335.
"The Early Life of Mark Rutherford," No. 4472 (July 12, 1913), p. 40. Announcement.
"The Early Life of Mark Rutherford," No. 4479 (August 30, 1913), p. 200. Review.
Notice of the sale of Hale White's library, No. 4500 (January 24, 1914), p. 135.
"The Book Sales of 1914," No. 4549 (January 2, 1915), p. 10. Comment on sale of Hale White's library.
"Artist and Sage," No. 4580 (August 7, 1915), p. 87. Review of *L.P.*

The Bookman (London):
GARNETT, RICHARD. "Was Wordsworth an Apostate?" XIV (May 1898), 41–42. Review.
SCOTT, G. FORRESTER. "Pages from a Journal," XIX (March 1901), 191. Review.
"Mark Rutherford," XXVI (August 1904), 162–64.

MACLAREN, IAN. "Mark Rutherford's Bunyan," XXVII (December 1904), 114–16. Review.
Death notice, XLIV (April 1913), 2–3.
A. "Mark Rutherford," XLIV (September 1913), 263. Review of *E.L.*
ARMSTRONG, MARTIN. "Mark Rutherford," LXV (December 1923), 140–42.
CLAYTON, JOSEPH. "Mark Rutherford," LXVI (June 1924), 167–68. Review of *G.D.* and *L.3F.*
PEEL, DR. ALBERT. "A Hundred Years Ago. William Hale White (Mark Rutherford)," LXXXI (December 1931), 171–73.

The Bookman (New York):
Notice of Hale White's translation of Spinoza, I (February 1895), 4.
"Tractatus de Intellectus Emendatione," I (May 1895), 271–72. Review.
NICOLL, SIR WILLIAM ROBERTSON. "Mark Rutherford," III (July 1896), 438–40.
"Mark Rutherford," XXXVII (May 1913), 245.
Review of *L.3F.* and *G.D.*, LX (December 1924), 508.

The British Museum Quarterly:
BELL, H. I. "Autographs of Nathaniel Hawthorne and 'Mark Rutherford,'" XI (March 1937), 79–80.

The British Weekly:
NICOLL, W. R. "Dr. George Macdonald in the Pulpit" ("The Correspondence of Claudius Clear"), IV (August 3, 1888), 233.
MACKENNAL, ALEX. "Mark Rutherford," V (November 2, 1888), 6. Letter.
NICOLL, W. R. "Miriam's Schooling" ("The Correspondence of Claudius Clear"), VIII (June 20, 1890), 121. Review.
NICOLL, W. R. "Mark Rutherford," XX (July 9, 1896), 185.
SKEGG, FREDERICK. "Mark Rutherford," XX (July 16, 1896), 198. Letter.
NICOLL, W. R. "Notes on English Style in the Victorian Period—'Mark Rutherford,'" XXV (January 26, 1899), 290.
A MAN OF KENT. "The Works of Mark Rutherford," XXXVI (July 21, 1904), 365. Review.
BURGIN, GEORGE B. "Mark Rutherford," XXXVI (September 8, 1904), 507. Letter.
NICOLL, W. R. "Mark Rutherford and Dr. A. C. Simpson," XXXVI (September 8, 1904), 517.
"Mark Rutherford on John Bunyan," XXXVII (November 10, 1904), 108–9.
NICOLL, W. R. "The Spiritual History of Mark Rutherford," LIII (March 20, 1913), 713–14.
STIRLING, AMELIA HUTCHISON, AND BETHAM-EDWARDS, MISS. "Some Reminiscences of the Author of 'Mark Rutherford,'" LIII (March 20, 1913), 714.
NICOLL, W. R. "Memories of Mark Rutherford," LIII (March 20, 1913), 725.
A MAN OF KENT. "Mark Rutherford," LIII (March 27, 1913), 749.
LORNA. "'Exquisite Housewives,'" LIII (March 27, 1913), 745.
"Party and Non Party," LIII (March 27, 1913), 748.
GARDNER, ALFRED. "Mark Rutherford," LIII (March 27, 1913), 746. Letter.
JONES, REGINALD F. "Two Whites," LIV (April 3, 1913), 13. Letter.
A MAN OF KENT. "Mark Rutherford Among the Spiritualists," LIV (April 3, 1913), 13.
WHITMEE, S. J. "Mark Rutherford," LIV (April 3, 1913), 3.
"The Lust for Talk," LIV (April 10, 1913), 25–26.
THEOBALD, R. M. "Mark Rutherford and His Father," LIV (April 10, 1913), 27. Letter.
A MAN OF KENT. "Genius and Talent," LIV (April 24, 1913), 85.
A MAN OF KENT. "Mark Rutherford for Sevenpence," LIV (May 8, 1913), 141.

A MAN OF KENT. "Mark Rutherford on Sentimentalism," LIV (May 15, 1913), 173.
NICOLL, W. R. "The Early Life of Mark Rutherford," LIV (August 7, 1913), 469.
NICOLL, W. R. "Mark Rutherford as a Politician," LIV (August 14, 1913), 491.
NICOLL, W. R. "Mark Rutherford as a Critic," LIV (August 21, 1913), 511.
A MAN OF KENT. "Christina Rossetti and Mark Rutherford," LV (January 22, 1914),
509.
NICOLL, W. R. "Mark Rutherford," LVI (June 18, 1914), 314.
L. "A Mistake of Mark Rutherford," LVI (July 2, 1914), 369.
"Mark Rutherford's Successor," LVII (October 8, 1914), 27.
NICOLL, W. R. "Can Puritans Love Romantically?" LVIII (May 6, 1915), 121.
NICOLL, W. R. "The Last Pages of Mark Rutherford," LVIII (July 22, 1915), 347.
NICOLL, W. R. "The Trouble of Being Overestimated," LIX (February 24, 1916),
431.
"A Hymn of Mark Rutherford," LX (June 22, 1916), 231.
CRISP, ANTHONY. "Fresh Light on Mark Rutherford," LXXVI (June 5, 1924), 221.
STODDART, JANE T. "Mark Rutherford and Social Reform: His Message to Youth,"
LXXXVI (May 30, 1929), 195.
"Mark Rutherford in Germany," LXXXVII (October 3, 1929), 5.
STODDART, JANE T. "A German Life of Mark Rutherford," XC (April 23, 1931), 63.
STRONG, ROBERT. "Mark Rutherford (1831–1913)," XCI (December 31, 1931), 279.
CATFORD, E. ALICE. "Mark Rutherford: The Bedford Meeting," XCI (December
31, 1931), 277.
"New Competitions," XCL (March 3, 1932), 466.

Classical Philology:

WOODHEAD, W. D. "The Daimonion of Socrates," XXXV (October 1940), 425–26.

The Contemporary Review:

"Some Recent Books," LXXXVII (February 1905), 299–301. Review of *B.*
"Last Pages from a Journal," CVIII (October 1915), 543. Review.
KENT, MURIEL. "Mark Rutherford (1831–1913)," CXL (December 1931), 757–64.

The Critic:

"Clara Hopgood," XXVI (August 15, 1896), 103. Review.

Deutsche Literaturzeitung:

MEISSNER, P. "The Novels of 'Mark Rutherford,'" LIX (July 31, 1938), 1092–96.
Review of Oxford 1936 set.

The Dial (Chicago):

"Mark Rutherford on John Bunyan," XXXIX (September 1, 1905), 119. Review.

The Englishwoman:

TEMPEST, EWART V. "Women in Mark Rutherford," XX (February 1914), 167–79.

Everyman:

KENT, W. "Mark Rutherford," VI (December 24, 1931), 731.

The Fortnightly Review:

LOW, FRANCES H. "Mark Rutherford: An Appreciation," XC (September 1, 1908),
458–73.

Great Thoughts from Master Minds:

KNOWLSON, T. SHARPER. "Confessions of Enquiring Spirits. The Autobiography of
Mark Rutherford," XXXII (February 10, 1900), 319.

Low, FRANCES H. "Mark Rutherford of the Books: As I Knew Him," XCVI (December 1931), 122–24.

SMALL, ALEX. "Mark Rutherford, His Philosophy of Life," CVII (September 1937), 269–70.

Harper's Monthly Magazine:

HOWELLS, WILLIAM DEAN. "Editor's Study," LXXII (February 1886), 485–86. Review of *A. & D.*

HOWELLS, WILLIAM DEAN. "Editor's Study," LXXV (October 1887), 802. Review of *R.T.L.*

The Harvard Theological Review:

SPERRY, WILLARD L. "Life and Writings of Mark Rutherford," VII (April 14, 1914), 166–92.

The Hibbert Journal:

KENT, MURIEL. Review of *L.3F.*, XXIII (July 1925), 761–63.

The Holborn Review:

H. B. K. "Mark Rutherford as Revealed in 'Last Pages,' " XIII (n.s.) (April 1922), 114–18.

MANTRIPP, J. C. "Mark Rutherford," XIII (n.s.) (April 1922), 182–94.

Land and Liberty:

" 'Mark Rutherford' on 'Progress and Poverty,' " Nos. 454–55 (March–April, 1932), p. 35.

The Literary Guide:

"The 'Mark Rutherford' Series," No. 99 (September 1, 1904), pp. 140–41.

KENT, W. "Mark Rutherford," No. 312 (March 1932).

The Literary Review:

HEYNE, J. C. Review of *G.D.* and *L.3F.* (September 20, 1924), 12.

Living Age:

"Mid-Victorian Church and Chapel," CCLXIII (November 6, 1909), 369–71.

"Sweetness of a Man's Friend," CCLXVII (November 12, 1910), 424–27.

SECCOMBE, T. "The Literary Work of Mark Rutherford," CCLXXVII (May 24, 1913), 498–501.

The London Mercury:

HARWOOD, H. C. "Mark Rutherford," III (February 1921), 388–97.

"Memories of Mark Rutherford," IX (April 1924), 665–67. Review of Nicoll's *Memories.*

"Mark Rutherford," XXV (December 1931), 129. "Editorial Notes."

FREMANTLE, ANNE. "A Hero to His Valet," XXV (January 1932), 280–87.

"Mark Rutherford," XXV (March 1932), 481. Letter.

"Little Errors," XXV (April 1932), 583. Letter—rejoinder.

MEYERSTEIN, E. H. W. "William Hale White," XXXIV (September 1936), 463–64.

The London Quarterly and Holborn Review:

"Last Pages from a Journal and Other Papers," CXXIV (October 1915), 365. Review.

JACKSON, GEORGE. "Mark Rutherford's Scrapbooks," CXXXI (April 1919), 191–204.

HARRISON, A. W. "Mark Rutherford and J. A. Froude," CLXIV (January 1939), 40–44.

The Manchester Quarterly:

HEARN, A. "Mark Rutherford," LI (October-December, 1925), 205–14.

The Nation (London):

"Idols of Education," VII (September 24, 1910), 902–3.
MASSINGHAM, H. W. "The Art of 'Mark Rutherford,'" XII (March 22, 1913), 1017–18.
Notice of sale of Hale White's library, XIV (January 3, 1914), 613.
"The World of Books," XVI (December 19, 1914), 386. Comment on A. E. Taylor's article in *E.S.E.A.*
"The Wisdom of Mark Rutherford," XVIII (February 26, 1916), 758–59. Review of *L.P.*

The Nation (New York):

"The Autobiography of Mark Rutherford," XXXII (June 2, 1881), 392–93. Review.
"Mark Rutherford's Deliverance," XL (May 14, 1885), 405. Review.
"Clara Hopgood," LXIII (September 3, 1896), 180. Review.
"Description of Coleridge and Wordsworth MSS," LXV (September 9, 1897), 210. Review.
"John Bunyan," LXXX (January 26, 1905), 79. Review.
"Notes," C (April 1, 1915), 361. About A. E. Taylor's article.
"Last Pages from a Journal," CI (October 7, 1915), 440. Review.

The Nation and Athenaeum:

CECIL, LADY ROBERT. "Mark Rutherford," XXXIV (October 27, 1923), 151–52.
BIRRELL, AUGUSTINE. "One of the Last of the Historical Nonconformists," XXXIV (March 1, 1924), 767. Review of Nicoll's *Memories.*
ALDINGTON, RICHARD. "Mark Rutherford in Old Age," XXXV (June 14, 1924), 355. Review of *L.3F.* and *G.D.*
A.S. "Mark Rutherford," XXXV (June 21, 1924), 376. Letter.

The New Age:

POPE, T. MICHAEL. "Mark Rutherford," XVI (August 17, 1904), 516–17.
"Readers and Writers," XVII (n.s.) (July 1, 1915), 204–5. Romantic love in the novels.

The New Leader:

MASSINGHAM, H. W. "More of 'Mark Rutherford': A Revelation of Personality," VII (June 6, 1924), 10. Review of *L.3F.* and *G.D.*

The New Republic:

ALDINGTON, RICHARD. "Mark Rutherford in Old Age," XLI (December 24, 1924), 125–26.

The New Statesman and New Statesman and Nation:

Death notice, I (April 12, 1913), 20.
Review of *E.L.,* I (September 13, 1913), 733.
"Mark Rutherford," V (August 7, 1915), 429. Review of *L.P.*
RATCLIFFE, S. K. "The Novels of Mark Rutherford," Supplement, XXII (October 13, 1923), viii–x.
"Mark Rutherford in Old Age," XXIII (September 13, 1924), 654. Review of *L.3F.* and *G.D.*
GARNETT, DAVID. "Books in General," XII (August 8, 1936), 193. Review of Oxford set.
GARNETT, DAVID. "Books in General," XIII (January 2, 1937), 17.

The New Witness:
SECCOMBE, THOMAS. "Mark Rutherford," I (March 27, 1913), 658–59.

New York Times Book Review:
" 'Mark Rutherford's' Indian Summer Romance" (August 24, 1924), 15.

The Nineteenth Century:
ELLIS, S. M. "Three Centenaries," CX (December 1931), 753–57.

Nineteenth Century Fiction:
MERTON, E. S. "The Autobiographical Novels of Mark Rutherford [William Hale White]," V (December 1950), 189–207.
MERTON, E. S. "The Personality of Mark Rutherford," VI (June 1951), 1–20.

The North American Review:
WILLIAMS, STANLEY T. "Biographies of Mystics," CCXX (December 1924), 352–58. Review of *L.3F.* and *G.D.*

Notes and Queries:
"White's *Examination of the Charge of Apostasy Against Wordsworth*," 9th series, I (March 26, 1898), 260.
" 'Mark Rutherford' and 'George Eliot,' " 9th series, X (September 13, 1902), 204–5.
FAHIE, J. J. " 'Mark Rutherford' as a Practical Astronomer," 11th series, VIII (September 27, 1913), 246.
CHIGNELL, A. K. "Mark Rutherford," 12th series, VIII (March 19, 1921), 231.
R. A. H. "Mark Rutherford," 12th series, VIII (April 2, 1921), 278.
CLINTON, W. WILLS. "Mark Rutherford," 12th series, IX (August 13, 1921), 137–38.

The Nottingham Library Bulletin:
"Mark Rutherford," No. 10 (n.s.) (November 1904), pp. 81–82.

The Oxford Magazine:
"Mark Rutherford and Oxford," LVI (November 18, 1937), 184–85.

Papers of the Manchester Literary Club:
HARTLEY, L. CONRAD. "Mark Rutherford," LV (1929), 116–42.

The Prospective Review:
THEOBALD, ROBERT M. "Heresies About Inspiration. Statement of Facts Connected with the Expulsion of Three Students from New College, London," VIII (August 1852), 340–46.

The Queen, The Lady's Newspaper:
"Books of the Week," CXVI (July 30, 1904), 186. Notice of Unwin reprint.
"Notes on the Magazines," CXXXV (February 28, 1914), 390. Criticism of Tempest's essay in *Englishwoman*.

Queen's Quarterly (Kingston, Ontario):
TAYLOR, W. D. "Mark Rutherford," XXV (October–December, 1917), 153–71.

The Review of English Studies:
STONE, WILFRED H. "Browning and 'Mark Rutherford,' " IV (n.s.) (July 1953), 249–59.

Revue des Deux Mondes:

CHEVRILLON, ANDRÉ. "Ruskin et la Vie," XLVI (August 1, 1908), 564–90. See especially pp. 573–79.

The Saturday Review:

Review of *A.*, CXXXVI (October 13, 1923), 407.

The Speaker:

"An Artist in Grey," II (August 30, 1890), 248. Review of *M.S.*
GARNETT, EDWARD. "Mark Rutherford and Others," X (July 16, 1904), 361–63. Criticism and review of *R.T.L.*

The Spectator:

Review of *C.F.*, LXXII (June 16, 1894), 830.
"Mark Rutherford," CX (April 12, 1913), 608–9.
S. B. "Mark Rutherford," CX (April 19, 1913), 654. Letter.
"Some Books of the Week," CXI (August 9, 1913), 218. Review of *E.L.*
"Mark Rutherford," CXV (September 11, 1915), 341. Review of *L.P.*
FAUSSET, HUGH I'A. "'Mark Rutherford' from Within," CXXXIII (August 2, 1924), 164.
MASSINGHAM, H. W. "The Other Side. The Necessity of a Labour Party," CXXXI (July 7, 1923), 6.
JONES, OSWALD. "Mr. Massingham and 'Mark Rutherford,'" CXXXI (July 28, 1923), 119. Letter.

Spectator Literary Supplement:

FAUSSET, HUGH I'A. "Mark Rutherford," CXXXI (November 3, 1923), 643–44.

The Sphere:

"A Literary Letter," XVIII (July 23, 1904), 90. Occasioned by Unwin reprint.
"A Literary Letter," LII (March 29, 1913), 346. Death notice.
"A Literary Letter," LIX (December 19, 1914), 294. Criticism of A. E. Taylor's article in *E.S.E.A.*

Times Literary Supplement:

"Mark Rutherford's Youth" (August 7, 1913), p. 330. Review of *E.L.*
"Last Pages from a Journal" (July 1, 1915), p. 223. Announcement.
"Last Words from Mark Rutherford" (July 15, 1915), p. 236. Review of *L.P.*
"The Defects of English Prose" (January 15, 1920), p. 25.
"John Bunyan" (February 15, 1923), p. 111. Announcement.
"Mark Rutherford" (October 4, 1923), p. 649. Review of the novels of Mark Rutherford, edited by Fisher Unwin.
"Memorials of Mark Rutherford" (May 15, 1924), p. 299. Review of *G.D.* and *L.3F.*
"The Pilgrimage of a Victorian. Hale White in Literature and Life" (July 25, 1936), p. 612.
"William Hale White (Mark Rutherford)" (July 2, 1931), p. 528. Review of Klinke's dissertation.

T.P.'s Weekly:

"Mark Rutherford's Early Books," IV (August 12, 1904), 199.
SWAN, F. R. "Mark Rutherford's Social Message," XX (August 16, 1912), 199.
"At Number 1 Grub Street," XXI (March 21, 1913), 359.
"Notes and News," XXI (May 23, 1913), 658. The will of Mark Rutherford.
"Notes and News," XXII (July 18, 1913), 82. Announcement of *E.L.*

"Mark Rutherford," XXII (August 8, 1913), 170. Review of *E.L.*

"Opinions and Expressions of Sir William Robertson Nicoll," XXII (November 21, 1913), 662.

O'LONDON, JOHN. "Readings and Misreadings," XXII (November 21, 1913), 661.

O'CONNOR, T. P. "Mark Rutherford," XLIV (July 26, 1924), 456.

University of Toronto Quarterly:

STONE, WILFRED H. "The Confessional Fiction of Mark Rutherford," XXIII (October 1953), 35–57.

The Westminster Review:

"Contemporary Literature," LXIV (July 1883), 208–9. Review of *Ethic.*

TEMPEST, E. V. "Optimism in 'Mark Rutherford,' " CLXXX (August 1913), 174–84.

The Yale Review:

"Pages from a Journal," III (October 1913), 189–94. Review.

INDEX

Abbott, E. A., 188 n.
Aberdeen Herald, The, 26, 40, 40 n., 60–61, 64, 133, 133 n., 158
"Activist ethic," 85, 86, 87, 96
Adeney, Gladys, *see* Easedale, Gladys Ellen
Admiralty, 4, 5, 89–90, 90 n., 126, 132
Affirmation, theme of, in novels, 43, 95–100 168, 175, 191
After Office Hours, 163
"Afternoon Walk in October, An," 70
Aids to Reflection (Coleridge), 65
Alastor (Shelley), 192
"Ancestor of Emerson, An," 201
Ancient Mariner, The (Coleridge), 66
Anderson, Rev. Charles, 137 n.
Anglicans and Anglicanism, 17–18, 26, 33, 53, 207 n. *See also* Church of England
Apologia pro Vita Sua (Newman, J. H.), 43
"Apology, An," 178
Argument for an Extension of the Franchise, An, 176 n.
Arminianism, 21–23, 32 n.
Arnold, Matthew, 12, 16, 61 n., 88, 102, 137 n., 210 n.
Arnold, Dr. Thomas, 25, 37 n.
Arthur, Harriet, *see* White, Mrs. William Hale
Arthur, Henrietta, 185, 185 n.
Arthur, John, 185, 185 n.
Ashtead, 29 n., 154 n., 195
Athenaeum, The, 129, 161, 172
"Atonement," 113–14, 119
Autobiography of Mark Rutherford, Dissenting Minister, The, 3, 4, 7, 9, 13, 14, 19, 24 n., 36, 37, 42, 43, 46, 50, 60, 69, 74, 77, 78, 82, 88, 89, 91, 98, 106, 108, 122, 123, 125, 127, 128–31, 142, 146, 159, 167, 172, 185, 210
Ayres, Miss Alice, 114

Bacon, Sir Francis, 64, 97, 213
Banstead Downs, 176 n.
Baptists, 18, 48
Beaconsfield, Lord, *see* Disraeli
Bedford, 4, 10, 11–31, 41, 45, 128, 130, 144, 151, 154–57
Bedford Charity Not Sectarian, The (White, William), 28

Bedfordshire Union of Christians, 25
Beethoven, Ludwig van, 60
Bell's Weekly Messenger, 13
Bennett, Arnold, 123
Béranger, Pierre-Jean de, 178 n.
Bergson, Henri, 109 n.
Betham-Edwards, Miss, 157 n.
Bible, 25, 33–38, 47, 49, 51–62, 79, 115, 204, 213
Biblical criticism, 34–38, 158
Biblical Review, The, 37 n.
Biographia Literaria (Coleridge), 160
Birmingham Daily Post, The, 27, 137, 217 n.
Birmingham Post, The, 13, 134, 139, 217 n.
Birmingham Post and Journal, The, 133, 217 n.
Black Notebook, The, 77, 95, 118, 163, 202, 203, 203 n., 210, 212
Blake, William, 112
"Blanketeers," 180, 183
Bolingbroke, Viscount, 177
Bookman, The, 97, 201
Boxel, Hugo, 116
Bradlaugh, Charles, 49, 139, 140
Bray, Charles, 34 n.
Bright, John, 30, 41 n.
British Astronomical Association, 117
British Standard, The, 40
British Weekly, The, 41, 101 n., 171, 172, 201
Broad Church Movement, 20, 25, 158, 159
Brooke, Stopford A., 137 n.
Brown, Rev. John, 20–21, 21 n., 24, 25, 29
Browning, Robert, 158 n., 161, 161 n.
Bruno, Giordano, 102 n.
Bunyan, John, 8, 12, 13, 18, 19, 42, 55, 57, 115, 213
Bunyan Meeting, 4, 13, 18, 19, 20
Burne-Jones, Sir E. C., 157 n.
Burns, Robert, 29
Butler, Samuel, 18
Byron, George Gordon, Lord, 14, 15, 29, 37, 64, 65, 78, 146
"Byron, Goethe, and Mr. Matthew Arnold," 65 n., 78

"Caleb Morris," 41 n., 52 n., 157, 159 n.

Call Me Carpenter (Sinclair), 136
Calvinism and Calvinists, 4–9, 11–33, 48, 74, 75, 85, 87, 88, 100, 130, 136, 141, 146, 151, 165, 177, 178–83, 209. *See also* Moderate Calvinism
Campbell, J. Dykes, 158 n., 160
Carlyle, Thomas, 10, 15, 29, 30, 42, 43, 57, 58, 64, 65, 65 n., 66, 66 n., 67, 71, 78, 88, 94, 105, 108 n., 158, 193 n., 199, 213
Carshalton, 4, 137 n., 154 n., 185, 188
Cartwright, Major John, 29, 144, 146
Catharine Furze, 9, 14, 16, 76, 122, 149, 149 n., 154–57, 173–76, 191, 192, 210
Cecil, Lord David, 126
Chamber's Journal and *Miscellany,* 14
Chapman, John, 41, 41 n., 44, 46 n., 50, 51, 52, 57, 101 n., 129, 131, 156–57, 172
Chapman's Publishing House, 50–52, 57–58, 193, 193 n.
Characters, fictional:
  George Allen, 28, 69, 73, 146, 158 n.
  Isaac Allen, 146
  Mr. Bradshaw, 23, 30, 144
  John Broad, 21, 23, 24, 27, 144, 207
  Priscilla Broad, 146
  Thomas Broad, 24, 24 n., 38 n., 208
  Mr. Butts, 140–41
  Ellen Butts, 73, 129, 131, 132, 141, 186, 187, 196
  Caillaud, 71, 179, 180, 181, 182, 183
  Rev. Mr. Cardew, 127, 157, 174, 175, 191, 192, 194, 204
  Mrs. Cardew, 192
  Baruch Cohen, 116, 127, 131 n., 161–64, 170, 171, 194, 196
  Pauline Coleman, 30, 71, 127, 130, 141, 179, 180, 181, 182, 194, 208, 209
  Zachariah Coleman, 28, 29, 65, 73, 127, 141, 144, 146, 178–83, 191, 192, 193, 194, 208
  Didymus Farrow, 151, 168
  Mrs. Furze, 16, 17, 26, 141
  Catharine Furze, 26, 76, 79, 127, 154–57, 173–76, 177, 183, 191, 194, 209
  Harden, 21
  Clara Hopgood, 87, 127, 157–64, 170–71, 173, 177
  Madge Hopgood, 87, 127, 157–64, 169–73, 176, 183, 196, 198, 210
  Mrs. Joll, 68, 69, 151
  Miss Leroy, 140–41, 172
  Major Maitland, 179, 180, 181, 182, 183
  Mardon, 46–47, 55–56
  Mary Mardon, 78, 92, 129, 130, 131, 132
  M'Kay, 79, 134, 136, 137, 176, 204
  George Montgomery, 166
  Frank Palmer, 158, 159, 160, 169, 170
  Reuben Shapcott, 7–8
  Deacon Snale, 14–15, 24, 47, 128, 144, 207
  Miriam Tacchi, 127, 147–51, 165–69, 173, 175, 177, 186, 187, 189 n., 191
  Theresa, 60, 129, 130, 131
  Michael Trevanion, 151–54
  Robert Trevanion, 151, 152–54
  Dr. Turnbull, 156, 174, 175
  Wollaston, 129
Cheshunt College, 11, 32, 36, 40 n., 63, 64
Chignell, Mary Anne, *see* White, Mrs. William
Chignell, T. William, 40 n., 45, 50 n., 53, 64, 211 n.
Christabel (Coleridge), 66
Christian World Pulpit, The, 61
Christianity, 5, 6, 11, 25, 47, 49, 51–59, 91, 115, 135
Church of England, 53, 61 n., 139, 153
Clara Hopgood, 9, 116, 122, 145, 157–64, 169–73, 194, 210
Clark, Henry W., 23, 34
Clough, Arthur Hugh, 12
Cobbett, William, 29
Cobden-Sickert, Mrs. 195
Colchester, 140
Colenso, Bishop J. W., 40, 53
Colenutt, Richard and Sarah, 40 n., 41 n., 50 n., 148
Coleridge, Samuel Taylor, 10, 14, 15, 24, 36 n., 37 n., 64, 65, 66, 66 n., 69, 71, 78, 102, 160, 161
"Coleridge on Spinoza," 101 n.
Collingwood, Julia, 157 n.
Commune, 135
Confessions of an Inquiring Spirit (Coleridge), 34 n., 66
"Confessions of a Self-Tormentor," 185 n., 193
Confessions of a Young Man (Moore), 114–15
Corn Law, 30 n.
Cornwall, 152–53
Course of Time, The, 14
Cowfold, 13, 15, 21, 24, 149, 165, 167–68, 177
Cowper, William, 14
Creed of Christendom, The (Greg), 34 n.
Critique of Pure Reason (Kant), 71–72
Cromwell, Oliver, 8, 13, 27, 28
Cross, George W., 50, 193

Dale, R. W., 22
Dannreuther, Mrs., 157 n.

Darwin, Charles, 80
Davidson, Joshua, 135–36
Dawson, George, 45 n.–46 n.
De Imitatione Christi (Kempis), 73, 140
Deliverance, theme of, in novels, 6, 8–9, 165–83, 190–91
Development of English Theology in the Nineteenth Century (Storr), 22, 34
Dickinson, Emily, 91
Disinterestedness, 104, 105
Disraeli (Lord Beaconsfield), 133 n., 135, 136
Dissent and Dissenters, 11–31, 34, 40, 128. *See also* Puritanism *and* Independents
Ditchling, 45, 46, 47, 48, 68
Doll's House, The (Ibsen), 176
Donne, John, 9
Dorcas Meeting, 14–15
Doughty, C. M., 81
Dream of Two Dimensions, A, 187–91
Drury Lane, 136–39, 144, 176
Dundas, Sir David, 28

Early Life of Mark Rutherford (by Himself), The, 17, 30, 32, 50, 140–41, 143, 146, 150, 156, 157, 184, 193
Easedale, Gladys Ellen (Mrs. Killen), 164 n., 195
Eastthorpe, 14, 16, 173, 174, 178, 209
Egmont (Beethoven-Goethe), 64, 158
Election, doctrine of, 22, 179
Eliot, George, 34, 50, 51, 54, 60, 100, 101 n., 102, 108, 126, 129, 130, 131, 186, 192, 193–94, 193 n.
Ellaby, Rev. James, 36
Elsmere, Robert, 136
Elton, Oliver, 199
Elwes, R. H. M., 101 n.
Emerson, Ralph Waldo, 15, 51, 57 n., 64, 65
Emmaus, road to, 42
Empedocles, 98
Ende, Clara Van den, 161 n.
" Epoch, An," 109
Essays and Reviews, 61–62
"Esther," 197
Ethic (Spinoza), 10, 101, 102, 103, 104, 105, 106 n., 107, 110, 111, 116, 161
Evangelical Voluntary Church Association, 25
Evangelicalism, 20, 24–27, 34
Evans, Marian, *see* Eliot, George
Evis, Mrs., 129
Exeter and Plymouth Gazette, The, 53

"Faith," 97, 200 n.

Faucit, Helen, 51
Faust (Goethe), 64
Fenmarket, 157, 158
Feuerbach, Ludwig, 34 n., 140 n.
Fichte, J. G., 72
Fidelio (Beethoven), 158
Fitchew, Bill, 149–50
Flatland (Abbott), 188 n.
Flatland (Hale White), 187
Fors Clavigera (Ruskin), 137 n.
Fortnightly Review, The, 103
Fox, George, 15, 75
Fox, Ralph, 176
Foxton, Frederick, 27, 50 n., 52, 56, 57–58
Frederick the Great (Carlyle), 66
Freud, Sigmund, 165
Friar St. Chapel, Ipswich, 45
"Friends of the People, The," 146, 179
Fripp, Jean (Lady William Hale-White), 153 n.
Froude, James Anthony, 12, 34 n., 50 n., 51, 102, 172–73

Galileo, 53, 103
"George Eliot as I Knew Her," 60 n., 193
George Eliot's Life (Cross), 50, 193
Gibbon, Edward, 54 n.
Gide, André, 9, 154, 176, 211
Gil Blas (Le Sage), 27
Gissing, George, 166
Godwin, William, 63
Goethe, Johann Wolfgang von, 15, 40 n., 43, 64, 65, 73 n., 88, 102, 103, 104, 105, 158
Gosse, Edmund, 18
Grace Abounding (Bunyan), 13
Greatheed, Rev. Samuel, 25
Greenhill, Dr., 157 n.
Greg, William Rathbone, 34 n., 50 n., 51 n.
Groombridge, 109, 195
Groombridge Diary, The, 10, 66, 80, 84, 90, 122, 130, 133, 159, 187, 196

Hale and Hale-White, *see also* White
Hale, William (author's great uncle), 157
Hale-White, Ernest (author's third son), 26, 153 n.
Hale-White, John (author's second son), 26, 77, 89 n., 93, 93 n., 117–18, 124 n., 129, 145, 152–53, 160, 178 n., 184, 185, 186, 206
Hale-White, Mrs. John, *see* Hughes, Agnes
Hale-White, Mary Theodora (author's daughter), 26, 124 n., 129, 153 n.
Hale - White, Dr. Reginald (author's

grandson), 38 n., 89 n., 92, 120, 184 n., 185, 185 n.

Hale-White, Sir William (author's first son), 26, 50 n., 53, 123, 129, 132, 153 n., 184, 185, 200

Hale-White, Lady William, see Fripp, Jean

Halle, Sir Charles, 185

Hardy, Thomas, 149, 176

Harper's Monthly Magazine, 124

Harpur Charity, 28

Harris, Rev. John, 33–38, 46, 59

Harrison, A. W., 172

Hastings, 29, 117, 154 n., 155, 157, 158 n.

Hawthorne, Nathaniel, 154

Hazlitt, William, 77

Hegel, G. W. F., 47 n., 71–74, 88, 103

Helmholtz, Hermann von, 97

Hemans, Mrs. Felicia Dorothea, 166

Hennell, C. C., 34, 50 n.

Herbert, George, 140

Herder, Johann Gottfried von, 103

Heroes and Hero Worship (Carlyle), 29, 58 n., 66

Hillyard, Rev. Samuel, 20, 22, 25

Hipparchus, 201

History of the Bedfordshire Union of Christions, The (Brown, John), 25, 25 n.

History of the English Congregationalism (Dale), 22

History of the Hebrew Monarchy (Newman, F.), 58

Holyoake, George Jacob, 30, 41 n., 43, 135, 157 n.

Homerton College, 40 n.

Horace, 115

House, Humphrey, 213

House of Commons, 19, 28, 78, 140, 204

Howells, William Dean, 9, 123–25

Hughes, Agnes (Mrs. John Hale-White), 153

Hughes, Arthur, 153, 158 n., 213

Hunt, Holman, 213

Huntington, Selina, Countess of, 32 n.

Hutchinson, Thomas, 158 n., 160

Huxley, Aldous, 89 n., 183

Huxley, Thomas Henry, 58 n.–59 n.

Ibsen, Henrik, 169, 176

Ignatius, Father, 139

Iliad, 49

Image, Selwyn, 129 n., 137 n.

Imitation of Christ, The, see De Imitatione Christi

In Memoriam (Tennyson), 43

Incarnation, 72–73, 88–89

Incompatibility, theme of, in novels, 124, 131, 146, 152, 180–83, 184–98

Independents, 11, 34, 47–48, 128. *See also* Dissent and Dissenters, *and* Puritanism

Inquiry Concerning the Origin of Christianity (Hennell), 34

Inspiration, theory of, 34–37, 61–62

"Inspiration of Scripture, The" (Harris), 33–36

International Journal of Ethics, The, 101

Introduction to the Novels of Mark Rutherford, An (Nicoll), 54 n.

Ipswich, 45

Isaiah, 181

"Ixion," 47 n., 61

Jefferies, Richard, 70

Jenyns, Soame, 177

Jesus Christ, 37, 42, 46–67, 51–59, 72–74, 88–89, 91

Joan of Arc, 75

Job, 98, 113

Job, Book of, 84

John Bunyan, 10, 13, 71

Johnson, Dr. Samuel, 10

Jones, Henry Arthur, 153

Jowett, Benjamin, 60–62

Joyce, James, 9

Jude, the Obscure (Hardy), 176

Jukes, Rev. John, 19, 20, 21, 22, 23, 24, 26, 29, 144, 208

Lamb, Charles and Mary, 14

Lambert, Rev. Brooke, 137 n.

Land, J. P. N., 101 n.

Langborough, 14

"Laodamia" (Wordsworth), 161

Last Pages from a Journal, 44, 96, 102, 113, 116, 119, 157, 188, 201, 202

Latitudinarianism, 159

Latter Day Pamphlets (Carlyle), 66

Lawrence, D. H., 9, 109 n., 212

Leben Jesu, Das (Strauss), 51, 54, 55, 158

Le Sage, René, 27

Lessing, Gotthold Ephraim, 102, 103

Letter on the Death of Mrs. Elizabeth Street, 41 n.

Letters to Three Friends, 10, 61, 161

Leviticus, 55

Lewes, George Henry, 51, 102, 103

Liberty, Equality, Fraternity (Stephen, J. F.), 178 n.

Life and Thought of William Hale White (Smith, H. A.), 19, 20, 21, 29, 36, 40 n., 65, 152, 153 n.

Life of Christ, The, see Leben Jesu, Das
Life of Sterling (Carlyle), 66, 158
Linton, Eliza Lynn, 134–36
Lockwood, Rev. Isaac E., 28
London, 4, 82–84, 128, 144, 149, 151, 157, 166, 167, 176, 178
London Quarterly and Holborn Review, The, 172
"Love of Woman, The," 194 n.
Lovell, Samuel, 150, 156
Low, Frances, 157 n., 195 n.
Luther, Martin, 8, 178 n.
Lyrical Ballads (Wordsworth, Coleridge), 63, 65, 68, 83

Macaulay, Thomas Babington, 199
Maccall, William, 50 n., 51, 193 n.
Mackay, R. W., 34, 35, 51 n.
Macmillan's Magazine, 201
Maitland, Miss, 157 n.
Mammon, or Covetousness the Sin of the Christian Church (Harris), 36
Manchester, 144, 179, 182
"Marcus Antoninus," 61 n.
Mark Rutherford: A Short Bibliography of the First Editions (Nowell-Smith), 188 n., 215 n.
Mark Rutherford's Deliverance, 3, 5, 9, 14, 17, 43, 49, 73, 86, 89, 107, 108, 122, 123, 128, 131–42, 143, 146, 172, 196, 210, 214
Marsh, Mabel, 117, 158 n., 164 n., 195 n., 200
Martineau, Harriet, 51
Martineau, James, 40, 46 n., 51, 51 n.
Marx, Karl, 136
Marxist critics, 176
Massingham, H. W., 9, 127, 144
Matheson, William, 159
Maurice, Frederick Denison, 25 n., 34 n., 39, 41, 60–61, 158, 159, 159 n.
Mazzini, Giuseppe, 160, 170, 171, 177, 178
Memories of Mark Rutherford (Nicoll), 29, 46
Mendelssohn, Moses, 103
Menninger, Karl, 93, 190
Meredith, George, 197, 199
Miall, Edward, 39 n., 134 n.
"Michael Trevanion," 77, 97, 151–54, 163
Middle Age, An Autobiography 1885–1932 (Easedale), 195
Mill, John Stuart, 30, 43 n.
Milton, John, 14, 27, 28, 181, 192, 199, 213
Miriam's Schooling, 9, 14, 48, 54, 68, 122, 146–51, 165–68, 171, 187
Misérables, Les (Hugo), 143

"Misleading Unions," 205
Miss Mona (Smith, D. V. H.), 195
Moderate Calvinism, 19, 21–27, 34
Modern Love (Meredith), 197
Moir, Macrae, 40 n.
Montaigne, Michel E. de, 213
Moore, George, 114, 115
"Morality of Byron's Poetry, The," 78
More, Hannah, 22
More Pages from a Journal, 109, 163, 202, 206
Morning Chronicle, The, 13
Morning Star, The, 133
Morris, Caleb, 41 n., 46, 52, 55, 64 n., 157, 159, 164 n.
Morris, William, 157 n., 158 n., 200 n.
Morton, A. L., 176, 207
Mozart, Wolfgang A., 185 n.
"Mr. Whittaker's Retirement," 154 n., 194
"Mrs. Fairfax," 14, 196
Murray, Rev. A. Victor, 36
Myrmidons, 178, 204

Nation, The, 200
Natural-Supernaturalism, 69–70
Negation, theme of, 165–67. *See also* White, William Hale
Nemesis of Faith, The (Froude), 34 n., 51, 51 n., 172–73
New birth, 43, 44, 167. *See also* White, William Hale
New College, London, 11, 21 n., 33, 40, 50
Newman, Francis, 12, 35, 51, 51 n., 52, 56–59
Newman, John Henry, 43, 77
Newton, Sir Isaac, 201
Nicoll, Sir W. Robertson, 9, 21, 29, 45, 46, 54 n., 171, 200
Nonconformist, The, 39 n., 41, 133, 134
Nonconformity, *see* Dissent and Dissenters
Norfolk News, The, 27, 51, 71, 96 n., 133, 134, 135, 136, 138, 139, 151, 204, 207
"Notes" (in *More Papers from a Journal*), 202
Notes About W. Hale White (Hale-White, Sir William), 129, 184
"Notes on Shelley's Birthplace," 143 n., 201
Novalis, Frederick, 57 n., 103
Nowell-Smith, Simon, 188 n., 215 n.

"Ode on the Intimations of Immortality" (Wordsworth), 160–61

"Oenone" (Tennyson), 159
Oko, A. S., 101 n.
"On the Interpretation of Scripture" (Jowett), 61
On the Origin of Species (Darwin), 59 n., 80
Original Sin, doctrine of, 22
"Our Debt to France," 143
"Ourselves," 16 n.
Oxford Movement, 20
Oxford University, 26, 26 n.

Pages from a Journal, 70, 97, 101 n., 171
Paine, Thomas, 29
Palmerston, Viscount, 133 n.
Papacy, 178 n.
Paradise Lost (Milton), 206
Parker, Theodore, 51 n.
Partridge, Sophia S., 33, 61, 149, 158n., 160, 161, 164 n., 185, 195 n., 204
Pater, Walter, 199
Patmore, Coventry, 157 n.
Paul, Rose, 157 n., 195 n.
Pengelly, Mr., 53
"Peter Buckley," 201
Phases of Faith (Newman, F.), 58
Philosophy of Necessity, The (Bray), 34 n.
Pilgrim's Progress (Bunyan), 12
Pilot, The, 205
Plato, 27, 61
Pollock, Sir Frederick, 101 n., 102, 105, 106, 118
Pollok, David, 14
Popular Christianity: Its Transition State and Probable Development (Foxton), 57
Portrait of the Artist as a Young Man (Joyce), 9
Portsmouth, 39, 41, 45
Predestination, doctrine of, 23
Preface to Spinoza's *Ethic* (1883), 101–2, 101–2 n.
Preface to Spinoza's *Ethic* (1894), 101–2, 101–2 n., 104, 107, 112
Prelude, The (Wordsworth), 63
Pre-Raphaelites, 213
Priesthood and the People, The (Foxton), 27, 57
"Principles," 96 n.
Progress of the Intellect (Mackay), 34, 35, 51 n.
Prometheus Bound (Shelley), 49
Puritanism, 4–9, 11, 12, 43, 44, 74, 75, 76, 78, 80, 86, 90, 105, 111, 197, 201–2, 207. *See also* Dissent and Dissenters

Rabelais, 115
Rachel (Eliza Felix), 193
Rationalism, 35
Reed, Jane, 129, 155
Reform Bill (1832), 28
Reform Bill (1867), 176 n.
Religion of "human nature," 35, 46, 58, 73, 74, 88–89
Religions of the World, The (Maurice), 34 n.
Religious Freedom Society, 25
Renan, Ernest, 56 n., 61 n., 97
Renunciation, theme of, 43, 82–94, 169, 170–71, 175
Revolt of Islam, The (Shelley), 192
"Revolution," 101–2, 105–6, 116
Revolution in Tanner's Lane, The, 9, 13–14, 19, 21, 23, 28, 29, 30, 65, 69, 71, 122, 123, 141, 143–46, 172, 177, 178–83, 210
Richter, Jean Paul, 112
Rochdale Observer, The, 133
Roman Catholicism, 27, 77
Romans, Epistle to the, 208 n.
Romanticism, 44, 76, 78, 80
Rossetti, Dante Gabriel, 157 n., 213
Rousseau, Jean-Jacques, 29, 42, 203 n.
"Ruined Cottage, The" (Wordsworth), 81, 161
Ruskin, John, 94, 137 n., 158 n., 199, 213
Russell, Charles J. F., 28
Russell, Lord John, 25, 26

St. John, Gospel of, 55
St. Paul, 37, 63, 167
Santayana, George, 108
Sartor Resartus (Carlyle), 29, 66, 108 n.
Sartre, Jean Paul, 109 n.
Scarlet Letter, The (Hawthorne), 154
Schelling, F. W. J. von, 72, 103
Schleiermacher, F. E., 34 n, 37 n, 74, 103
Schweitzer, Albert, 56 n., 85, 86, 96
Scott, Sir Walter, 14, 29
Secret of Hegel, The (Stirling, J. H.), 71
Secular Review, The, 47 n., 61
Secularists, 49
Sélincourt, Professor de, 195
Shadows of the Clouds (Froude), 34 n.
Shakespeare, William, 203 n., 204
Shelley, Percy Bysshe, 15, 49, 65, 102, 161, 192
Sinclair, Upton, 136
Singularity, 174, 191
Smith, Dorothy Vernon Horace, *see* White, Mrs. Dorothy Vernon
Smith, Henry A., 19, 20, 21, 29, 36, 40 n., 65, 152, 153 n.

Soul, Its Sorrows and Aspirations, The (Newman, F.), 35, 58
Specialization, in modern world, 96, 96 n.
Spencer, Herbert, 51
Sperry, Willard L., 43, 43 n., 172 n.
"Spinoza," 101 n., 110, 115
Spinoza, Benedict de, 10, 43, 73 n., 95, 101–21, 161–63, 174
Spinoza, His Life and Philosophy (Pollock), 101 n.
"Spinoza's Doctrine of the Relationship Between Mind and Body," 101, 111
Stallknecht, Newton, P., 69
Stamm, Dr. A., 50 n.
Standard, The, 134
Stanley, Arthur P., 61
Stephen, Sir James Fitzjames, 178 n.
Stephen, Sir Leslie, 12
Sterling, John, 158
Stirling, Amelia Hutchison, 101 n., 158 n.
Stirling, James Hutchison, 71, 71 n.
Stoke Newington, 42, 50 n., 127, 166
Stonehenge, 147–49, 167
Storr, Erica, 195 n.
Storr, V. F., 22, 34
Strauss, D. F., 34, 34 n., 47 n., 51–57, 54 n., 97
Street, Mrs. Elizabeth, 15 n., 41 n., 75, 76, 85, 131 n.
"Supplementary Note on the Devil," 115
Swan, Rev. Edward, 28
"Sweetness of a Man's Friend, The," 192
Swinburne, Algernon Charles, 158 n., 199, 213
Symphonie Pastorale (Gide), 154

Tales of Ulysses (Lamb), 14
Temple, Cowper, 137
Tennyson, Alfred, Lord, 43, 65, 83, 148, 159, 161, 213
Test Acts, 26
Text-Book to Kant (Stirling, J. H.), 71
Thelwall, Algernon Sydney, 36
Theobald, Robert M., 34, 45, 65
Thirlwall, Bishop Connop, 53
Thirty-nine Articles, 33
To Think or Not to Think (White, William), 36, 36 n.–37 n., 38–39, 66
Tractarian Movement, 20, 22
Tractatus de Intellectus Emendatione et de Via (Spinoza), 10, 101
Tractatus Theologico-Politicus (Spinoza), 102 n., 103
Trelawney, Sir John, 30
True History of Joshua Davidson, The (Linton), 134–36

Turner, J. M. W., 213
"Two Martyrs," 97, 167
Tyrrell, Father George, 75

Unitarians and Unitarianism, 20, 45, 46, 47–49, 128, 167

Vicar of Wakefield, The (Goldsmith), 14
Victorian convention, 197
"Victory on the Downs, A.," 176 n.
Villiers, C. P., 134
Virgil, 213

Water Lane, 14
Watts, Isaac, 14
Webb, Philip, 154 n.
Weimar, 64, 158
Wesley, John, 22, 75
Wesleyans, 18, 48
Westbrook, Harriet (Mrs. Percy B. Shelley), 161
Westminster Review, The, 41, 50, 51, 52, 103, 132, 157. *See also* Chapman, John, *and* Eliot, George
White, *see also* Hale-White
White, Mrs. Dorothy Vernon (author's second wife), 10, 17 n., 26, 65, 80, 90, 98, 114, 118, 122, 125, 127, 130, 147, 159, 164 n., 185, 187, 195 n., 196, 200, 201, 203 n., 211
White, Frederic Meriton, 34, 34 n., 50 n.
White, Thomas, 39 n.
White, William (author's father), 18, 27–31, 36–39, 41, 43, 59, 65, 146, 185, 199, 204
White, Mrs. William (author's mother), 17, 45, 131, 140–42, 146, 183
WHITE, WILLIAM HALE
Events in his life: life in Bedford, 11–31; early reading, 13–15, 43, 50–62, 64–66; escape from drowning, 97, 152, 162–63; conversion, 32–33, 63; Cheshunt College, 32–33; arrival in London, 151; New College, London, 33–42, 159; expulsion, 11, 32–42; first preaching experience, 37; relations with John Harris, 36–37; influence of Caleb Morris, 41 n., 52, 55, 157, 159; influence of T. William Chignell, 40 n., 45, 53, 64; unemployment, 50 n.; work with John Chapman, 50–60; lay preaching, 45–46; visits to Germany, 64, 158, 158 n.; other employment, 132; the Admiralty, 89–90, 132; promotion, 132; political activity, 176 n.; work in London slums,

89–90, 136–39; journalism, 126, 133–37; various residences, 154 n., 156, 194; first marriage, 184–87, 191; tensions in first marriage, 129–32, 188–91; first wife's illness, 184–85; death of first wife, 146, 184, 187; desire for second marriage, 165 n.; second marriage, 194–96; marriages of sons, 92, 147, 152–54; retirement, 132, 146, 154 n., 194; literary and scholarly activity after retirement, 157–58; circle of feminine admirers, 195–96; death, 195 n.

Influence of and relations with parents: mother, 4, 16–17, 17 n., 140–42, 146, 183; father, 4, 29–31, 38–39, 41, 65, 146, 185, 199, 204

Thought and personality: dualism and dualistic conflicts, 3–11, 44, 69, 86, 87, 105, 108, 111, 114–16, 120, 125, 130, 169–71, 173–76, 186, 207–9, 212; return to Calvinism, 4–5, 87; monomania, self-absorption, and the desire to overcome them, 4, 6, 7–8, 9, 12, 13, 31, 98–99, 107, 114, 120, 121, 125, 204, 206 n.; love of veracity 4, 12, 23, 24, 33, 204; fear of moral infection, 5–6, 138, 139, 155, 177; scientific bent, 5, 9, 53, 117–19, 149, 149 n., 180; idealism and search for absolutes, 6, 8, 60, 67, 80, 198, 199, 203 n., 203–4; love of precision and nice distinctions, 6, 16, 23–24, 33, 204, 213; dislike of saints, 6, 160, 186, 186 n., 187, 188; sense of inferiority, 7, 155, 156; hero worship, 8–9, 29–31, 178; taste for "tremendous problems," 11; hypochondria and the role of suffering in his life and thought, 11–13, 43, 63, 87–94, 112–14, 186, 189, 193–94; melancholia and spiritual despair, 12, 13, 41–42, 48, 60, 91, 93–94, 114, 120–21, 147; spiritual pride, 12, 37, 40, 46, 86, 91, 99; craving for self-expression and recognition, 12, 38, 48, 125–26, 164; political and social attitudes, 16, 17, 24–31, 68, 143–44, 169, 173, 176–78, 178 n.; search for a "perfect friend," 28, 125; self-pity, 31, 91; desire for martyrdom, 31, 171; the "horrors," 42, 50 n., 127, 166; stages in religious development: (negation) 43–62, (new birth) 63–81, (renunciation) 82–94, (affirmation) 95–100; agnosticism, 44, 95; love of Bible, 45, 51–62; faith in emotion, 48, 57, 77–81, 118–19; anti-

theological bent, 57, 59, 98–99; nature worship and its decay, 57–58, 68, 69, 82–85; interest in music, 60, 185, 185 n.; philosophical bent, 71, 74; moral individualism and the habit of "inner reference," 74–77, 127, 169, 173–76; problem of immortality, 83–84, 106–10; interest in evolution, 84 n., 95, 96, 110; belief in "principles," 87, 204; habit of "damping" enthusiasm, 90, 185, 185 n., 194; possessive love of sons, 92, 153, 162–63; the "trick of contrast," 108–9, 110, 120, 207; tendency to alienate people, 162

Art and writing: anonymity as author, 4, 7–8, 124 n., 124–26; motives for writing, 7–8, 42, 122–26, 153, 165; style and stylistic principles, 9, 97–98, 98 n., 123, 145, 209–10; love of simplicity, 9, 204; handwriting, 16, 211; writing habits, 118–19, 133, 199–214; poetic impulses and poetry, 119, 211–12; difficulty in making plots, 123, 123 n.; characterization, 127, 206; literalness, 127–64, 190, 206; defense of *Clara Hopgood*, 171–72; aphorisms, 200, 200 n., 204; love of lucidity, 204; hatred of jargon, 204–5; art vs. seriousness, 206, 206 n.; satire and irony, 207; simile and metaphor, 209; oratorical quality, 213–14

White, Mrs. William Hale (author's first wife), 4, 93, 124, 125, 129, 130, 131, 132, 146, 184, 186

White, Mrs. William Hale (author's second wife), *see* White, Mrs. Dorothy Vernon

Whitefield, George, 22

Whiteing, Richard, 166

Whitmee, S. T., 41 n.

Wilhelm Meister (Goethe), 64

William Hale White (Wright), 201 n.

William Hale White "Mark Rutherford," 1831–1913 (Hale-White, John), 129, 184, 185

"Wilsonian Theory of Sunspots, The," 117

Wordsworth, William, 10, 18, 43, 60, 63, 64, 65, 67, 68, 69, 70, 71, 75, 76, 81, 82, 84, 85, 151, 160, 161, 211, 213

Worthing, 40 n.

Wright, J. E. T., 201 n.

Zoete, Beryl de, 195 n.

Zola, Emile, 166